ESSENTIAL GCSE
BUSINESS STUDIES

Renée Huggett

Collins Educational
An Imprint of HarperCollinsPublishers

Also in the HarperCollins Essential Series

Essential Accountancy and Finance, Bijon Kar

Essential Business Studies, Stephen Barnes

Essential Government and Politics, Jim Cordell

Essential Marketing, Tony Proctor

Essential Mechanics, Owen Elbourn

Essential Practical Psychology, Keith Maglennon

Essential Psychology, G.C. Davenport

Essential Information Technology, Tony Berk

Essential Business Law, Paul Hilder

Published in 1995 by Collins Educational
An imprint of HarperCollins *Publishers*
77-85 Fulham Palace Road
Hammersmith
London W6 8JB

Reprinted 1996

ISBN 0–00–322301–9

British Library Cataloguing-in-publication data
A catalogue record for this book is available from the British Library

Cover design by Ridgeway Associates
Typeset by Harper Phototypesetters, Northampton, England
Printed in Great Britain by Scotprint, Musselburgh

Contents

Foreword

Every book in the Essential Series is designed carefully to put you in control of your own learning.

When using this book, you will not only cover the key elements of your course but you will also benefit from the author's use of modern learning techniques, with the result that you will make the best possible use of your time.

This book includes the following features.

- An introductory section at the beginning of each chapter, focusing your attention on its contents and telling you exactly what you should have learned by the end of the chapter. These are your 'learning objectives'.

- A list of key terms at the beginning of the chapter, alerting you to the important words in the vocabulary of the subject. You should know what each means by the end of the chapter.

- End of chapter reviews, giving you a synopsis of the most important points you should have learned.

- Notes in the margin of the text, where the author takes the role of a tutor: picking out key ideas and highlighting important concepts.

- Activities that allow you to learn by applying the ideas in the text, and that give you practice in analysing information and in carrying out research.

- Suggestions for making and organizing your notes.

- Short-answer questions, which reinforce your knowledge of the subject, and also provide useful practice for some examinations.

Learning is not easy; nobody learns without effort. However, if you use this book effectively, you will not only succeed in your course and assessment, but you will also enjoy the experience of learning.

Preface and acknowledgements

This book is suitable for students using the revised syllabuses of GCSE Business Studies for first examination in 1996 and for other Key Stage 4 business courses.

I should like to acknowledge the great help I have received from Susan Squires in interpreting the new syllabuses, though the way this is done in the book is my responsibility alone.

The case histories and stimulus material included in this book are all based on imaginary organizations, firms, persons, and situations, unless stated otherwise.

The author and publishers would like to thank the following for permission to reproduce photographs:

The Body Shop International plc (p. 50);
British Petroleum (p. 12);
Broadway Squash and Fitness Centre and David Perris (p. 19);
Ford Motor Company Ltd (p. 138);
Hulton Deutsch/Steve Eason (p. 269);
Hulton Deutsch (p. 307);
London Transport (p. 183);
The Lutterworth Partnership/Magna Park Distribution Centre (p. 167);
Outward Bound (p. 291);
Science Photo Library/Peter Ryan (p. 68);
Susie Hilsdon (p. 110);
United Biscuits (pp. 156, 191, 317);

and for permission to reproduce text or information in the form of charts, diagrams, graphs and tables:

CCN Group Ltd for market research questionnaire (p. 126);
Central Office of Information for HMSO crown copyright material from *Britain 1993: An Official Handbook* (pp. 168, 177);
Central Statistical Office for material adapted from *Social Trends*, 23, 1993 (p. 6); for National Income figures from *Digest of Statistics*, May 1993 (p. 28); for trade and balance of payments figures from *Annual Abstract of Statistics*, 1993 (p. 94);
Department of Trade and Industry for British Gas share advertisement (p. 33);
Department of Trade and Industry and Department of Employment for map showing assisted areas and enterprise zones (p. 203);
Financial Times for water companies share information (p. 247);
Ian Allen Publishing for material from *Modern Railways*, April 1993 (p. 36);
ICI for extract from Annual Review and Summary Financial Statement, 1993 (p. 251);
The Independent for wine sales forecast, 17 May 93 (p. 69);
Midland Bank plc for cash flow forecast form (p. 226);
Municipal Journal for material from the Modern Railways report, April 1993 (pp. 35–6);
Realeat Survey Office/Haldane Foods Group (p. 129);
School Curriculum and Assessment Authority for material from *GCSE Examinations Criteria: Business Studies and Economics*, SEAC, January 1993, p. 323).

Study skills

Chapter objectives

After working through this chapter, you will have the knowledge to:

■ understand and use the principles of active learning;

■ locate topics and key terms in the book;

■ appreciate the benefits of research;

■ understand and use the following key terms: report, memorandum, media, tabloid newspapers.

ACTIVE LEARNING

This book has been specially designed to make it easy for you to learn about business studies and to succeed in your examination, but it must be used in the right way. The book is based on active learning. This means that you shouldn't just sit back and read page after page of the book and copy out line after line of notes. Throughout the book, you will find signs in the text suggesting some activity that will make it much easier for you to remember and to use the information you have just acquired.

Activities

The four activity signs are:

This sign indicates that it would be useful for you to make notes at this point. This doesn't mean that you should copy out whole sentences of the text word for word. Sometimes, the amount of detail required is suggested. You may be asked to make 'brief notes', which would mean that only a general outline of the topic is required. Or you might be asked to make 'full notes', which suggests that much more detail is required. Occasionally, you are asked to add some examples of your own to the notes, either from your own knowledge or from research in your library.

It is up to you what kind of notes you make. Occasionally, you may only need a few words or a small diagram. A few words would be sufficient if you thought – really thought! – that you knew the topic well and that these words would bring the details flooding back into your mind. However, it is just as useless to make notes that are too short as it is to make notes that are too long. Only *you* can judge how long they need to be.

► Note-making.

► You can easily check if your notes are full enough. Go back to the notes after a week or so, and see if they are detailed enough for you to remember the whole topic.

There is one thing you should always do. Give the notes a heading. It might also be a good idea to include a reference to the page number in the book if you feel that you might need to look at the topic again.

 This sign indicates a set of questions on the text you have just read. They are mainly short-answer questions designed to consolidate, or strengthen, your knowledge of the subject. They also provide useful practice for some examinations.

► Activity inside your classroom, home or library.

► A **case study** is a description of a business situation or problem which involves readers by asking them questions about the problems and encouraging them to suggest possible solutions.

 This sign suggests an inside activity. It might be an exercise based on the text, or on research that you carry out yourself, or it might be a case study with questions for you to answer at the end. Most of the inside activities produce a written answer, illustrating a principle, applying knowledge, or giving you a chance to select and use information. Some of the questions are open-ended; you are asked to analyse information and draw your own conclusions. These questions will also provide useful practice for some examination papers at the end of the course. You should give your answers a heading and file them with your notes.

► Activity in the outside world.

ACT OUT These activities are done in the business world outside the classroom and the library. They will help you to develop social, interviewing and observational skills and to select the information most appropriate to your needs. In addition, they also provide a useful introduction to any coursework you may be doing during your course.

► See **Coursework assignments** in Chapter 24.

Occasionally, an outside activity is combined with note-making. You are asked to do some outside research which will then be incorporated in your notes.

Reports and memoranda

In a few of the activities, you will be asked to write a **report**. This is a very common business document. Reports are written by an individual or by a committee, and can deal with any topic, such as cutting costs in a firm. The report has a standard format. It is:

- Title
- History
- Recent changes
- Present situation
- Conclusions
- Recommendations

► The **format** is the order in which the sections of the report are arranged.

Not all of these headings need to be included in your exercises. Only use those that are appropriate.

A **memorandum** is another standard business document. It is a message between members of the same firm which is usually written or typed on a standard printed form.

FINDING YOUR WAY AROUND THE BOOK

If you wished, you could start at Chapter 1 and read right through to the end. There is nothing wrong with that, because the chapters are arranged in a logical order. However, syllabuses of different examining boards deal with topics in a different order. Therefore, to make it easy for you to follow your own syllabus, the book has deliberately been made extremely flexible.

At the beginning of the book, there is a list of contents which tells you the main topic in each chapter. As you can see, this chapter, like all the other chapters, is divided into sections by various types of headings. This makes it easier for you to find any section that you require.

At the end of the book, you will find a comprehensive index giving page references for all the major and minor topics. The main page reference in the index is in **bold** type. Key terms are also included in the index. They are printed in bold type in the text where they are defined.

Margins

The margins give you explanations, examples and definitions and contain cross-references to the same, or a related, topic.

Objectives and summaries

At the beginning of each chapter, there is a list of objectives which shows you what knowledge you should have acquired by the end of the chapter. There is also a summary at the end of each chapter. Both the objectives and the summary will help you to check that you really do know the subject. If you are doubtful about any aspect, go back to the relevant section and read it again.

RESEARCH

You will see that in some inside activities it is suggested that you use 'your library' or 'your main library'. You will find most of the reference books you need in your local or college library. However, they may not always have the suggested book. If you can't find the book you want, ask the librarian to help you. If you live in a big city, the main library will usually have a large business section or a separate business library. You will almost certainly find any book you want in the main library. Your local reference librarian will usually know if it is there.

You can increase your knowledge of business by using the media. There are specialist magazines, such as *The Economist*, and newspapers, such as the *Financial Times*, which deal mainly with business. However, all national newspapers, including the tabloid newspapers, contain some reports and articles about business. If you want to do well in your examination, you should try to read

▶ The **media** are the means by which news, information and entertainment are communicated to the public. Newspapers, television and radio are obvious examples.

▶ Tabloid newspapers, such as *The Sun*, are small in size, but have a big circulation.

these business reports every day. (It would be even better to keep a file of important newspaper and magazine cuttings.)

Television and radio also have some business programmes. Currently, the Money Programme on BBC2 deals with general business topics, Watchdog on BBC1 deals with business from a consumer's point of view, while Panorama, also on BBC1, sometimes has reports on business topics. The Financial World Tonight on Radio 4 deals with business mainly from the investor's point of view.

REVISION

You may think it's a little early to be thinking of revision, but the sooner you start revising, the greater your knowledge will be. Don't leave all the revision to the end of your course. It is much easier if you check your knowledge as you go through the course by looking back at your notes from time to time and revising anything you are not sure of.

▶ See Chapter 24.

The last chapter in the book deals with revisions and examinations. You don't need to read it now, but don't leave it too long before you do. It will help you to direct your learning towards the objective you have set yourself.

SUMMARY

- Notes can be of any length so long as they are full enough to make you remember the whole topic.
- The results of all your activities should be given a heading and filed.
- Use the index at the end of the book to find page references to topics and key terms. The main reference in the index is printed in bold type.
- General research in the media will increase your knowledge of business.

② Business activity

NEEDS AND WANTS

Needs

There are four basic human **needs**. They are:

- water;
- food;
- warmth;
- shelter.

Water, or drink of some kind, is the most important need. Without it, people could live for only a few days. Food is the second essential need. Without food, you could survive for only a couple of months or so. Warmth is more essential in northern countries than in southern countries favoured by the sun; but there are few places where people could live all the year round without the warmth provided by clothes and some kind of heating. Shelter, whether it is a traveller's caravan or a luxury house, provides essential protection against the extremes of cold and heat and also some form of security.

 Look at the shopping list over the page. Say which items are based on needs and which are based on wants.

▶ Words or phrases in **bold** type, such as **needs**, are key terms that are explained in the text.

▶ You will see this sign where I have suggested an inside activity for you to carry out in your college, library or home. Sometimes, it will be a short piece of written work, or a numerical calculation, or a case study with questions.

Mineral water (large bottle)
135 mm film
Barbecue charcoal
Small white loaf
Sunglasses
Jeans (Levis)

Wants

In the richer countries of the world, including Britain, most people's four basic needs are satisfied, and they are now more concerned with satisfying their **wants**. In the shopping list above, only the loaf and the jeans (if they were bought to replace a worn-out pair) could be classed as needs. The other items are not absolutely essential and can therefore be classed as wants. (For example, the shopper could have drunk tap-water instead of mineral water.) However, most people in the western world are not content to drink only tap-water and eat simple food just to keep alive. People living on low incomes, such as senior citizens receiving nothing but the State pension, may not, in the strictest sense, *need* a higher standard of living in order to survive, but most *want* it, and many would argue that they are entitled to it.

Shoppers are used to finding supermarket shelves filled with thousands of kinds of food and drink. In a similar way, most people don't buy clothes just to keep warm, but are usually more concerned with their appearance. A flat or a house meets the need for basic shelter, but most people want much more than shelter from their home. They want it to be warm, comfortable, beautiful and, in some cases, better than their neighbours' homes. This has led to the growth of many new industries, such as those connected with DIY, double glazing and garden supplies.

Unlike needs, which are small in number, wants are unlimited, as numerous as someone's desires and dreams. People want to travel to foreign countries, to have well-equipped sports centres, to have rapid treatment for any illness, and to eat out in restaurants instead of cooking every meal at home. Furthermore, the wants of one generation may become the needs of the next. For example, we could live without televisions, telephones and washing machines, but most British homes now have them. They have become an essential part of modern life, regarded as a need and no longer a want.

The world wasn't always like this. A hundred years ago, working people's lives were restricted to basic needs – water from a well; plain, simple food; working clothes and 'Sunday best' if they were lucky; and a small house that was often damp and sparsely fur-

▶ As a whole, Sainsbury's stores sell 250 types of cheese, including fourteen kinds of goats' cheese.

▶ There is a television in 99 per cent of homes, a telephone in 89 per cent, and a washing machine in 88 per cent.

nished. In times of war, life can still be reduced to a basic level, as it was for many people in Britain during the Second World War. Since then, economic growth and modern business have totally changed our way of life by providing thousands of kinds of **goods** for people to buy. The modern world of overflowing shops and all kinds of **services** was created by business.

Draw up a table with four columns headed *Drinks*, *Food*, *Clothes*, *Homes*. In each column, give four examples of the names of firms that satisfy these needs.

FACTORS OF PRODUCTION

Wants may be unlimited but, unfortunately, the **resources** that provide the goods to satisfy these wants are limited, so people cannot have everything they want. An economist would say that these resources are 'scarce'. One of the main ways of making sure that scarce resources are not used up too quickly is by increasing the price of a **product**. For example, roads in large cities have become so crowded that the government is considering ways of charging drivers for using them.

► Most foods were rationed during the Second World War and many, such as bananas and oranges, were virtually unobtainable. In 1945, the basic rations per person per week were: 2 pints of milk, ½ lb. of meat, 4 oz. of bacon, 4 oz. of sausages, 2 oz. of tea, 4 oz. of sugar, 2 oz. of butter, 2 oz. of lard, 4 oz. of margarine and 3 oz. of cheese. Sweets and tinned foods were also strictly rationed.

► A **product** is what a business produces and offers for sale. It can be a physical good that you can see and touch, such as a car or an ice cream, or it can be a non-physical service, such as advice from a bank manager or a solicitor.

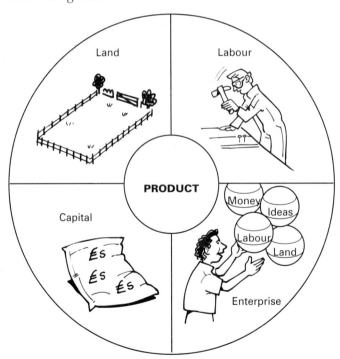

The four factors of production

There are four resources that are involved in the production of every product. These are known as the **factors of production**:

1 **Land** (which in this context includes the sea and the sea-bed) is necessary for all products, not just farming, as businesses must be sited, or located, somewhere.
2 **Labour** is the physical and mental efforts of workers.
3 **Capital** is the plant and machinery that allows workers to

do their jobs efficiently.

4 **Enterprise** refers to the skills of **entrepreneurs**, who can see business opportunities and who are willing to take the risk of trying to exploit, or use, them.

All these are scarce resources; there is not an unlimited supply of them.

 Make brief notes on the four factors of production.

Is there a real shortage of resources?

At first, it may seem strange to speak of a shortage of resources when in the real world there seems to be far more land, labour, capital and enterprise than we actually need. For example, European farmers can grow such an abundance of crops on their land that the European Union (EU) is paying them a yearly fee to set some land aside and grow no crops on it at all. There also seems to be a surplus of labour, as there are many millions of unemployed people in the EU. Capital, too, appears to be in good supply. In every EU country, factories, mines and businesses are being closed and the plant or machinery is being scrapped or sold off very cheaply. There are also many entrepreneurs, to judge from the large numbers of businesses that are set up, although many of them do not survive.

1 What is the difference between needs and wants?
2 Why is there a shortage of resources?
3 How can prices influence the use of resources?
4 What does EU stand for?

Reasons for shortage

There is a simple answer to these apparent contradictions. The factors of production may be in the wrong place or of the wrong kind. For example, there may be a great surplus of land that no one particularly wants in some parts of the country, such as the Scottish islands, but a great scarcity of land in other places, for example around the terminus of the Channel Tunnel on the south coast of England. There is a surplus of land on the Scottish isles, because the land is not suitable for growing crops and the islands are too far from main centres of population to be attractive to businesspeople. Land around Folkestone is in short supply because it is already densely populated and even more land is needed for business activities associated with the Channel Tunnel, such as warehousing and transport.

Land is geographically fixed; it cannot be moved from place to place or be increased in size. Labour, however, is mobile because people can go and work in different parts of Britain or in foreign countries where workers are wanted. It might seem that there shouldn't be a shortage of labour. However, people often do not want to leave the area in which they live, or they may have problems finding a house to go with their new job. Very often, the labour that is available may be of the wrong kind: unskilled, for

---

▶ You will see this sign where I have indicated that it would be useful for you to make notes. Always give your notes a heading. In this case, you could use the heading *The four factors of production*.

▶ See **Increase in self-employment** in Chapter 5.

▶ This sign indicates a set of questions on the text you have just read. They are mainly short-answer questions designed to strengthen your basic knowledge of the subject and provide useful practice for the shorter examination questions.

▶ Some raw materials are also scarce. For example, cobalt, the metal that is an essential ingredient in the steel alloys used in aero engines and aeroframes (the metal framework of an aircraft), is comparatively rare. It is found in mineable quantity in only five countries: Canada, Finland, Japan, Zaire and Zambia.

▶ Some low-lying land can be reclaimed from the sea, as in parts of East Anglia. The Dutch were pioneers in gaining land from the sea by using canals to drain it. They have also considered the possibilities of building artificial cities off their coasts.

example, when only highly skilled labour is needed, or skilled but in the wrong kinds of skill.

Capital is even more mobile than labour, because money can be moved about and invested in firms all over the world twenty-four hours of the day through share-dealing computer networks. However, many investors only want to invest in firms where their money is likely to be safe and which can provide a good return in high dividends and share prices. Firms in poorer, unstable countries that have a great need of capital may find it difficult to attract sufficient investment.

▶ For more on dividends and share prices, see **Distribution of profits** and **Measuring business success** in Chapter 6.

Enterprise is needed in all business activity, but successful entrepreneurs, who have the imagination to see or create business opportunities and the energy, skills and knowledge to set up successful firms to exploit these opportunities, are always scarce.

In the figure on page 7, the four factors of production are shown as fixed segments of the circle. In real life, the relative importance of each factor changes all the time. For example, as more machines and robots are installed in factories, the amount of capital needed will rise and the amount of labour used will fall. In a similar way, as farmers become more efficient at growing food, the amount of land needed for their produce will diminish. At the same time, the amount of capital (or machinery and plant) will increase, and the amount of labour (or numbers of farm workers) will fall. Resources are scarce because there are never enough of the four factors of production in the right proportion and the right place at the right time.

 Make notes on the reasons for the shortage of resources.

 Select a small business in your locality that, in your view, displays enterprise. Try to interview the owner to obtain his or her views about enterprise. Select one entrepreneur, such as Richard Branson of Virgin, and research his or her career and achievements in your library. (You could display some enterprise yourself by writing to the entrepreneur's firm to obtain information!) In your view, what are entrepreneurs' main characteristics? Illustrate your answer with examples from your research.

▶ You will see this sign where I have suggested a task for you to do in the outside world.

OPPORTUNITY COST

Because their resources are limited, businesses are faced with endless decisions about how they should spend their money. Should they have their shop front redecorated or buy new carpets? Should they spend more on advertising their chocolate bars or on increasing the weight of the products so that they are better value for money? Should a small firm replace its three company cars or keep the money in the bank for another year? Should a company reduce its manufacturing labour force and take on new sales staff, or vice versa?

When money is spent on one thing, something else must be sacrificed or given up. For example, if shopkeepers decide to have

▶ **Consumers** are people who buy goods or services for their personal use or for the use of their family or household.

their shop front redecorated, they will not be able to buy new carpets for the shop. The **opportunity cost** of the choice was the next best alternative, i.e. buying carpets. In a similar way, the opportunity cost of spending more on advertising was increasing the weight of the bars. The opportunity cost of buying new cars was the interest the firm would have gained if it had left the money in the bank. If the money had been left in the bank instead, the opportunity cost of that choice would have been buying new company cars.

We are all consumers; we are all faced with similar choices in our daily lives. The opportunity cost of buying new jeans may be buying a CD – the next best alternative. The opportunity cost of a weekend break could be a new leather jacket.

Opportunity cost also influences decisions made by the government, which spends about 40 per cent of the wealth that is produced in Britain every year. New roads or hospitals? More retraining or new RAF fighter-bombers?

▶ Opportunity cost is one of the most important principles in business. You should always bear it in mind when you are doing any case study.

> ### Opportunity cost
> There are never enough resources to go around. With every choice, there is always an opportunity cost – the best alternative that must be sacrificed, or given up.

1　What are opportunity costs?
2　What is meant by best alternative?
3　If you can afford to buy either a book or a CD and you buy a book, what is the opportunity cost?
4　Give two examples of your own of opportunity cost in any kind of business.

Interdependence

Each choice made by a business, by consumers or by the government has an impact. They are **interdependent**. Take a simple example. Alice decides to buy a new washing machine. She buys it from a chain store and pays the deposit with a credit card provided by her bank. Part of the purchase price is VAT, currently 17½ per cent of the basic price, which goes to the government to help finance public spending. The washing machine is not delivered by the store but by a separate firm of distributors who have collected the machine from a wholesaler, who obtained it from the manufacturer. The initial purchase has involved a whole network of people and businesses.

Describe, or draw a diagram to illustrate, a similar sequence of events and network of people when someone buys a flat or a house. Include as many different kinds of businesses as possible.

Chain of production

Firms are firmly linked to each other by the production of goods and services. For example, foresters sell their timber to furniture manufacturers, who sell their products to furniture shops. Each firm in this **chain of production** is a customer of another firm. The forester is the customer of a tree nursery; the furniture manufacturer is a customer of the forester; and the furniture shop is a customer of the furniture manufacturer. The furniture shop's final customer is a consumer or a firm or organization that wants to buy furniture.

Others are also involved: it is not only businesses that depend on each other but also consumers and the government. Manufacturers rely on other manufacturing firms – suppliers – to provide them with parts and machinery to produce their goods. They also rely on other firms to supply them with services, such as transport. All of these firms rely on banks to provide them with capital to finance their business. All the businesses and the banks rely on consumers to buy their goods or services. The consumers rely on firms to pay them wages and salaries and on banks to provide them with credit. The government relies on taxes and rates from both businesses and consumers to provide it with the money that it spends on goods and services for the benefits of consumers and businesses. Business activity forms an endless circle.

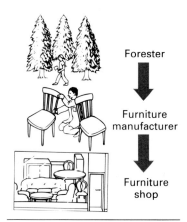

Forester

Furniture manufacturer

Furniture shop

A chain of production

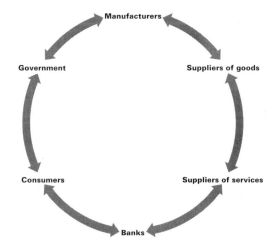

The endless circle

Division of labour

Centuries ago, when most people still lived in the countryside, each village tried to provide for most of its simple needs. There were some specialist workers, such as blacksmiths and thatchers, who worked for others, but many people, such as small farmers who owned their land, tried to provide most of the food, fuel and drink that their families needed.

It is very different in the modern business world. There is a great deal of specialization, which means that workers perform just one small part of the production process, which is made up of a whole series of specialized tasks. In most businesses, this **division of labour** is increasing all the time, as it is found to be a more effective use of the scarce resource of labour. In addition, there is specialization *between* firms. For example, many firms no longer distribute

▶ Division of labour: see also the box on **Internal economies of scale** in Chapter 7, page 73.

their own goods. It is cheaper and more efficient to hand the job over to a specialist firm of distributors who does nothing else.

The same principle applies at an international level, with parts of cars, such as the engine and the body, being made in different countries and assembled, or put together, in a third country.

 Make notes on the division of labour.

PRODUCTION

The production of goods and services can be divided into three main sectors:

- **Primary** – meaning first – refers to the raw materials needed to make something.
- **Secondary** – meaning second – refers to what is manufactured from the raw materials.
- **Tertiary** – meaning third – usually refers to industries that provide services for the other two sectors and for the government and consumers.

► Services are non-physical products ranging from dental care to insurance, and from advertising to education.

Primary sector of production

The **primary sector of production** can be split into four groups: mining and quarrying, farming, forestry and fishing. Mining and quarrying involve the extraction of raw materials from the land and the sea-bed, including metals such as cobalt and copper; fuels such as oil, coal and gas; precious stones, such as diamonds, from mines; and building stone from quarries. Farming provides food as well as some industrial crops, such as linseed, the seeds of the flax plant, whose oil is used in making linoleum, paint and printing ink. Forestry provides the raw materials for furniture and paper, both of which are in increasing demand throughout the world. The demand

► **Primary sector**
- Mining and quarrying
- Farming
- Forestry
- Fishing

BP oil exploration in Columbia – primary sector of production

for fish is also very great. As a result, the European Union has had to restrict fishing in European waters to conserve stock.

All countries have their own primary industry, but its importance is decreasing in developed countries all the time. Poorer, developing countries in the Third World, on the other hand, rely heavily on primary production, such as growing coffee beans to sell to more prosperous countries.

Secondary sector of production

The **secondary sector of production** can be divided into three main groups: manufacturing; building and construction; and public utilities such as water, gas and electricity companies which supply products used by the public. Manufacturing transforms the raw materials provided by primary producers into semi-finished and finished goods. A simple example is where the skills of the potter transform clay and minerals into a coloured, stoneware vase. Building and construction and public utilities are of vital importance in all countries.

During the 1980s, the British government tended to play down the importance of manufacturing. That policy is now being reversed. The government has realized that manufacturing is one of the main wealth creators. Nevertheless, manufacturing industry in Britain has become much smaller, partly because of fierce competition from Japan and developing countries in the East such as Hong Kong, Korea, China and Taiwan.

▶ **Secondary sector**
- Manufacturing
- Building and construction
- Public utilities

Tertiary sector of production

Throughout the western world, the **tertiary sector of production** is growing the most quickly. As production becomes more specialized and personal wealth increases, there is a growing demand for services – non-physical products – of all kinds. In addition, the new industrial revolution, based on the development of electronics and the need for information, has increased the demand for computer services for storing, retrieving, sorting and transmitting information.

The tertiary sector can be divided into three main groups. Personal services include the professional services of teachers, doctors, dentists and lawyers, as well as hairdressers, driving instructors and caterers; transport services are provided by road, rail and air; and publicly provided services include the fire service and town planning. Commercial services are provided for the other two sectors of production. They include insurance, transport, distribution, advertising and administration. Financial services are provided to both the personal and commercial groups by banks, building societies, financial advisors and the Stock Exchange.

▶ **Tertiary sector**
- Personal services
- Commercial services
- Financial services

1 What is the meaning of interdependence?
2 What is the chain of production for a packet of fish fingers?
3 What is tertiary production?

4 In which sectors of production would you find the following: lorry driver, computer operator in an insurance office, nurse, builder, fisherman, shop-keeper?

5 What is meant by specialization?

6 How has new technology affected employment in factories?

Sectors of production

- **Primary**: extracting raw materials from the land and sea, farming and fishing.
- **Secondary**: manufacturing, building and public utilities.
- **Tertiary**: services for the other two sectors, the public and the government.

Notes

1 Remember that public utilities are in the secondary sector.
2 The main activity of a firm determines which sector it is in. A firm that is building a house is in the secondary sector. Another firm that puts up the scaffolding is in the tertiary sector as it is providing a service to the builder.

 Make full notes distinguishing the three main sectors of production, and give examples from each sector.

 Now that you have worked your way through the chapter, look back at the objectives listed at the beginning. Can you do all the things that the objectives suggest? Look at each one in turn. If you feel uncertain about any of them, read the relevant part of the chapter again. Then, if you are still uncertain, ask for help and advice.

SUMMARY

- Business aims to satisfy people's basic needs and, increasingly, their wants.
- Wants are unlimited, but resources are restricted, which means that not all wants can be satisfied.
- Business is faced with endless choices because of the scarcity of resources.
- Choices always involve opportunity cost – the next best alternative that must be given up.
- Individual choices, whether they are made by business, consumers or the government, always affect each other because of interdependence.
- Division of labour is increasing because it is more efficient.
- Production is divided into three main sectors: primary, secondary, tertiary.

(3) Markets

Chapter objectives

After working through this chapter, you will have the knowledge to:

▌ select appropriate characteristics of consumers in market niches;

▌ distinguish between single-use consumer goods and consumer durables;

▌ describe the main influences on consumer markets;

▌ evaluate differences in regional spending patterns;

▌ analyse statistics and apply them to a sales situation;

▌ show how banks influence economic activity;

▌ identify the characteristics of industrial and commodity markets;

▌ explain geographical markets;

▌ understand and use the following key terms: market, consumer, recession, boom, market-orientated, market research, single-use consumer good, consumer durable, white good, consumer service, medium of exchange, financial market, interest rate, industrial market, industrial good, industrial service, product-orientated, commodity market, geographical market, tariff, core business.

WHAT IS A MARKET?

Originally, **markets** were places where sellers and buyers met face-to-face to sell and buy goods. They are still held in streets and market halls in towns and cities throughout Britain. In recent years, they have been supplemented by car-boot sales.

Markets of that kind satisfy general needs and wants. In modern business, the word 'market' has a different meaning. A market deals in one kind of good or service. Furthermore, buyers and sellers do not necessarily have to meet face-to-face. For example, you can buy a jacket from a mail-order catalogue by post. Or you can obtain a service over the phone, such as finding out the times of trains.

> **Markets**
>
> A market is a means whereby sellers of a particular good or service can contact potential buyers.

There are now as many markets as there are wants. A quick glance through a Yellow Pages directory will give you some idea of the number and the variety. There are markets for cleaning carpets and cars, for surveying houses and mending shoes. These markets are often split up into even smaller segments called niches or corners of a market.

▶ See **Market niches** in Chapter 9, pp. 109–10.

 Draw up a table with one column headed *Footwear* and a wider column headed *Buyers*. Copy one item at a time from the examples below into the first column and then describe the most likely buyers in the second column, including their sex and age range. The first item has been done for you:

Footwear
Orthopaedic shoes

Buyers
People of both sexes and all ages who have problems with their feet

- orthopaedic
- wide-fitting
- safety boots

- trainers
- washable
- street fashion

- hand-made
- western-style
- walking boots

Types of market

Before people start a business, it is essential for them to decide what the main market will be. This will help to focus all their business activity on a single objective and it will make their efforts far more effective.

Markets can be divided into four main types:

- consumer;
- financial;
- industrial;
- commodity.

CONSUMER MARKETS

Consumers are people who buy goods and services for their own use or for the use of their household or family. The consumer market is the most important in the whole economy as it accounts for nearly two-thirds of all the money spent in Britain each year.

Consumers' wealth and their financial fears or hopes decide how much they will spend. If people are in debt or frightened that they may lose their jobs, they reduce their spending and save a bigger proportion of their income. As a result, producers can sell fewer of their goods and services. If the reduction in consumer spending is

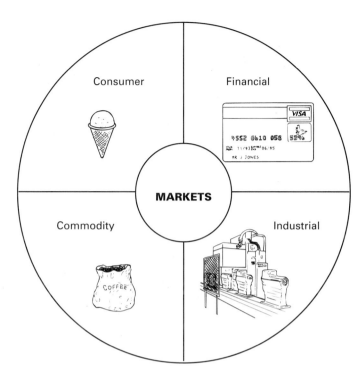

Four types of market

prolonged, as it was in the early 1990s, it can lead to a **recession**, or a decline in business activity. On the other hand, if consumers feel that they have plenty of money, they will spend freely. This happened in the 1980s when wages and salaries were rising at a fast rate and the value of houses was increasing even faster, so that homeowners were becoming richer every year. This is called a **boom**.

The consumer market is the most **market-orientated** of all markets. Consumers, and their wants, are at the centre of much business activity. Nothing is produced until **market research** has revealed the consumers' wants. A product is then designed to satisfy them and is marketed in a way that will appeal to them.

► See Chapter 10, p. 124.

The consumer market is divided into three main types:

1 **Single-use consumer goods** last for only a limited period. Some of these goods, such as ice-cream or hamburgers, can be used only once. Others, like tights or soap, can be used more than once, but are still classified as single-use because they do not last very long with repeated use.
2 **Consumer durables** last for a much longer time, usually giving many years of frequent use. They include cars, caravans, cameras, and household goods such as videos, televisions, radios and telephones. Some large consumer durables – those used in kitchens and utility rooms such as refrigerators, cookers and washing machines – are classified separately as **white goods**, because their casing is usually white.
3 **Consumer services** last as long as the want exists. These range from holidays to haircuts, and from MOTs to maternity services.

> ### Review: Consumer markets
> Consumers are people who buy goods and services for their own use. The consumer market is the most important because it accounts for nearly two-thirds of national expenditure.
> The consumer market is divided into three main types:
> - single-use consumer goods which are quickly used;
> - consumer durables which last for years;
> - consumer services which last as long as the need or want.
>
> Many factors influence consumer markets. The most important include:
> - total size of the population;
> - structure of the population, e.g. the number of young and old people;
> - consumers' income and wealth, and their feelings about the future;
> - regional differences;
> - fashions;
> - seasons of the year;
> - changes in taste.

 Look around a big department store and note down six items each of single-use consumer goods and consumer durables. Find out what consumer services the store offers and make a note of them.

 Make notes on the three main kinds of consumer markets and the distinctions between them, adding examples of your own.

Influence of fashions and seasons

The consumer market is the most volatile, or changeable, of all markets because it is based mainly on people's wants, which are always altering. Producers are constantly trying to discover consumers' new wants and to produce goods – or services – that will make them open their purses or wallets. Fashion, seasons and moods are big influences.

 This project involves visiting four different kinds of retailers and returning to them again after an interval of three months. Choose a travel agency, a cookware shop, a sports shop and a fashion shop for men or women. Make detailed notes about the goods or services displayed in the window, how they are displayed, special offers available, any seasonal influences and any new goods or services you have never seen before. Return to the same retailers three months later and make notes about the window displays again, paying particular attention to the changes. From this information, write a report describing what part the seasons and fashions play in each of these retailer's activities. Make recommendations on how their window displays could be improved.

Long-term influences

There are many other longer-term influences on consumer markets that are equally important. For example, long-term changes in people's tastes and ideas have a big effect. The decline in the consumption of red meat, and other factors such as competition from supermarkets, has led to there being fewer butcher's shops. Our greater interest in keeping fit has increased the number of sports shops, and led to the opening of more fitness centres and golf courses.

Sports and leisure centres sprang up with the fitness boom

This interest in fitness, however, is by no means universal. There are many people of all ages who take little exercise and drink and eat too much – especially fatty foods. People are not only growing taller, but they are also becoming fatter, with almost 50 per cent of men and 40 per cent of women being overweight. Business has to take account of these changes. Manufacturers are making longer beds. One firm has used the increase in people's size and weight to its own advantage by meeting the needs of a niche market with its High and Mighty fashion stores for larger men.

Size and structure of the market

The total size and structure of the population are closely related to consumer markets. The bigger the population, the greater the total demand; the smaller the population, the lower the total demand. The proportion of people in different age groups is also an important factor. For example, the growing number of people who are 65 years of age and over increases the demand for hospital services, wheelchairs and warmer clothes. The balance between the number of men and women in the population is another factor. There are now more women than men, so their wants, which are different from men's, have to be considered even more.

1 What is a recession?
2 What is a single-use consumer good?

3 Explain the difference between a single-use good and a consumer durable.

Regional differences

There are big regional differences in consumer markets because of different incomes and tastes. For example, consumers in East Anglia spend almost twice as much on leisure goods and services as consumers in the north, while consumers in the north-west spend more than any other region on alcohol and tobacco.

Information of this kind, which is obtained through market research, is of vital importance to all businesses. It enables them to choose and target their markets.

 Visit your main library and find a government publication dealing with consumer spending in different regions of the country. Select regions where consumers spend the highest and the lowest amounts on each of the following: housing, fuel and power, household goods and services, and transport. From your own knowledge, or research, try to explain the differences in the regions' spending on these items. (The reference librarian will help you to find a suitable publication.)

 Read the following case study and answer the questions at the end.

A chain store keeps a careful record of the value of the goods it sells per square foot of floor space. This is one way of measuring business efficiency. In one of its stores, sales for three classes of goods last year were as follows:

Value of sales per square foot, High Street branch

Type of good	1st quarter (£)	2nd quarter (£)	3rd quarter (£)	4th quarter (£)
Sun goods	37	89	221	40
Food and drink	121	107	99	106
Gifts	55	87	102	219

Managers are allowed to decide the layout of goods within the store. We know that the prime, or most eye-catching, counter is the first one on the right where customers enter the store. It has been calculated that putting goods on that counter can increase sales by up to 8 per cent.

1 What were the annual sales per square foot for each of the three classes of goods? (Add up the quarterly figures, e.g. for sun goods £37 + £89 + £221 + £40 = £387.)
2 What were the average sales for the three classes of goods? (Add the total annual sales and divide by three.)
3 If you were the manager, which goods would you select for the prime counter in the third quarter of the year and the fourth quarter? Why would you select these goods?

Financial markets

Money is the essential **medium of exchange** between sellers and buyers which allows them to measure the value of goods and services. For example, a hand-made sweater priced at £70 has thirty-five times the value of a pair of socks that costs £2. Money is the essential lubricant, or oil, which allows the complex system of specialization and division of labour to run smoothly. For example, a woman who makes hand-made sweaters for a living knows that each sweater she sells would buy her thirty-five pairs of socks (if she wanted that many!) or a radio costing £70, or a table for her sitting-room. A woman who works on an assembly line and earns £140 a week can divide her wages up and work out what she can buy with them after she has paid for essentials.

Financial markets deal in money and other essential services for both consumers and business. The willingness of banks to lend money, and the interest rates they charge, have an enormous impact on the whole economy. If interest rates are low, consumers and businesses are more likely to borrow money. As a result, business activity will flourish as consumers are spending more and firms can invest more in their business. If interest rates are high, there is likely to be less business activity.

Lending to consumers has become increasingly market-orientated with some people being tempted to spend more than they can really afford. The television advert's 'flexible friend' appeals to consumers' desire to buy goods and services instantly on their credit card.

 Write notes explaining how banks can influence economic activity.

INDUSTRIAL AND COMMODITY MARKETS

Industrial markets

There are two main kinds of industrial market:

1 **Industrial goods** are needed by business to produce its goods or services. These include capital goods, such as machine tools, which are used in the actual production process, and other industrial goods that enable business to function efficiently. Some goods in the second category, such as cars and computers, are also sold in the consumer market.
2 **Industrial services** are provided by one firm to enable another firm to function efficiently. An example would be security services.

Industrial markets tend to be more **product-orientated** than consumer and financial markets. The **market-orientated** firm tends to look outwards at the consumers that make up its market; the product-orientated firm tends to look inwards at the goods it produces.

However, producers of industrial goods and services are also

▶ See Chapter 18.

▶ **Interest rates** are the price a person or a firm pays for borrowing money. If you borrowed £100 for a year at a rate of 20 per cent, you would have to pay back the loan of £100 plus £20 in interest charges by the end of the year.

▶ **Industrial markets** serve not only firms in the private sector but also public sector organizations, such as local authorities, public corporations and the government. (The American term 'organizational markets' is more precise.)

A product-orientated approach

A market-orientated approach

▶ Modern firms with quality management systems now treat everyone as customers, both externally and internally. They are the customers of firms that supply them with parts; and the industrial firms who buy their goods are their customers. Internally, departments in the firm are seen as both suppliers and customers of other departments. The aim is to create an unbroken chain of quality. See Chapter 8.

▶ The pureness of gold is measured in carats: 24-carat gold is pure; 18-carat gold contains 25 per cent of other metals.

now becoming far more market-orientated. Manufacturers of industrial goods often ask potential customers about the kind of machine they want before they start production. They sometimes ask customers to test the first, or prototype, machine before they go into full production.

There is even more market-orientation in industrial services. Services such as company conferences, publicity and the recruitment of top managers are marketed in almost the same way as consumer goods.

 Look in the Yellow Pages directory and find examples of goods and services that are provided only for industry, and others that are provided for both industry and consumers. Use these as examples in making notes on industrial markets.

Commodity markets

Commodity markets deal in raw materials like metals, and foodstuffs like wheat. These markets are almost entirely product-orientated. The quality of the goods is more important than anything else. Foodstuffs, and some precious metals such as gold, are graded by quality. Industrial metals must be pure. For example, zinc traded on the London Metal Exchange is 99.995 per cent pure.

1 How do interest rates affect consumer spending?
2 What is a credit card?
3 Give three examples of capital goods.
4 What is a commodity market?
5 Explain the difference between a market-orientated and a product-orientated firm.

Geographical markets

Markets can also be classified geographically. The different **geographical markets** are:

- local markets, where products are bought and sold in a limited area, e.g. some kinds of farmhouse cheese;
- national markets, where goods or services can be bought all over the country, for example the *Radio Times*;
- multinational or single markets, such as the European Union, where barriers to trade between member-nations are abolished and **tariffs**, or taxes, are imposed on imports from other countries;
- international or global markets, where there is a demand in practically all countries for one kind of good, such as canned non-alcoholic drinks like Coca-Cola.

Choice of market

Business people are faced with a bewildering choice of markets, but it is usually better for them to choose only one, particularly when they are starting out. If they succeed, it will provide their **core business**, the central business activity that they know best and that produces a reasonable profit.

Take a young person who is thinking of setting up a business that has 'something to do with food'. Before any action is taken, all the varied markets relating to food must be considered.

Is the person thinking of growing food, or processing, importing, retailing or cooking it? If the plan is to cook food, will it be for consumer or industrial markets? If it is for consumers, will it be a roadside snack bar, a mobile fish and chip van, a sandwich bar, a café, a restaurant, a fast-food restaurant, or a home delivery service of home-made pies, fast food, or party meals? If it is for the industrial market, will it be a canteen or a hot drinks service? This is just a small selection of possible markets.

1 What is a tariff?
2 What is meant by the term 'core business'?
3 State the different kinds of geographical markets and give one example of your own for each kind of market.

A young man who started playing video games and then progressed to other uses of computers would like to set up a small computer business after he has had some training. Advise him on the most suitable kinds of business he could set up in your area. What would be the benefits and drawbacks of each?

► Look for possible markets in your Yellow Pages directory – an invaluable reference book for business.

SUMMARY

- A market is a means by which sellers and buyers can contact each other.
- There are as many markets as there are needs and wants.
- Consumer markets, which are the biggest in financial terms, are based upon research into the wants of consumers, or buyers.
- Finance is an essential ingredient in virtually all business transactions. Financial markets provide vital services for both consumers and industry.
- Industrial markets provide goods and services for other businesses and organizations. They concentrate more on the technical quality of the goods than on the fashions that greatly influence consumer markets, though they now consider their customers' wants more than they did in the past.
- Commodity markets deal in raw materials such as metals and foodstuffs. In these markets, the quality of the product is the most important factor.
- Markets can also be classified geographically into local, national, multinational and global markets.

4 Private and public sectors

ECONOMIC SYSTEMS

There are three main ways of running a country's economic affairs:

1 a **market economy** (also called a free economy);
2 a **command economy** (also called a planned economy);
3 a **mixed economy**, in which some business activity is free and some is planned.

The main difference between them is the amount of government control.

 Where would you place Britain's economic system on the scale on the opposite page – in the low, middle or high range of government control? Why have you placed it at that point?

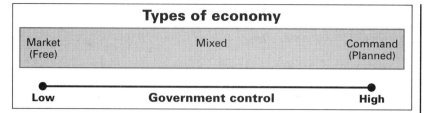

Types of economy

| Market (Free) | Mixed | Command (Planned) |

Low   **Government control**   High

MARKET ECONOMIES

Market economies in theory

In a pure market economy, there would be no government interference of any kind. Market forces of **supply** and **demand** would decide what is produced, where it is produced and who produces it. There would be no planning and no regulation.

There would be unrestricted competition between firms. Firms that failed to make a profit would go out of business. This fierce competition would lead to greater efficiency and lower prices for the consumer.

There would be total freedom for individuals. They would be free to spend their money how and where they liked, to move where they wished and to buy any goods or services.

Think what a totally free market would be like, in which anything could be bought or sold and people could set up any kind of business they liked. Describe what changes this would make to the business world. Do you think there are any kinds of goods and services that should never be freely traded and, if so, for what reasons?

Market economies in practice

That is the theory. In practice, no economy has this total freedom. Probably, the United States has most. Even there, however, as in the rest of the western world, there is some government control: planning regulations, laws against monopolies, control over what can be sold. Nevertheless, freedom from unnecessary government control, competition and enterprise are all greatly prized and supported.

Give three examples of government control over road transport in Britain, including vehicles and drivers. Explain what effects, if any, your chosen controls have on business.

COMMAND ECONOMIES

In a command economy, the State plans and controls all economic activity. The government decides what is produced, how it is produced and where. There are no privately owned businesses or

► **Supply and demand**. In economic theory, price is determined by supply and demand. A market price is established when supply and demand are equal. If the price rose, there would be excess supply. Stocks would start to increase, shopkeepers would reduce their orders and manufacturers would cut production, forcing the price down. If the price fell, demand would exceed supply, leading to a shortage. Shops would run out of goods, manufacturers would increase their output, and prices would start to rise. Supply and demand tend to bring the price back into balance again. In general terms, there is some truth in the theory. The market price, or **equilibrium price**, maintains a balance between scarce resources and consumers' wants. However, for market forces to work effectively, there must be perfect competition. The product must always be the same and everyone must know the market price. In practice, there are a number of versions of a product with different prices; and customers do not know every price that is being charged. Moreover, supply and demand are affected by many outside factors, such as shortage of labour or changes in people's tastes.

houses. Workers can be told to move to any part of the country. The State decides what work they should do and what they should be paid. In theory:

- central planning creates greater efficiency by cutting out unnecessary competition;
- resources are fully used so that there is no unemployment;
- production satisfies the needs of all, not the wants of the wealthy.

In practice, the command economies established in the Soviet Union after the First World War, and in other Eastern European countries and in China after the Second World War, were almost total disasters. Apart from achievements in a few spheres, such as space travel, sport and some branches of medicine, these Communist countries provided people with a poor, restricted life lacking practically all freedom and choice.

The economy was dominated by State monopolies, in which one organization completely controlled production and pricing in any sector of the economy, such as steel-making. These monopolies were run by remote officials whose printed forms and rigid rules were far more important to them than economic reality. They told farmers on huge collective farms hundreds of miles away which crops to grow and when to plant them. They set up production quotas for each factory with little quality control. As a result, the goods produced were often faulty or shoddy.

Communist countries, like many other countries, were riddled with dishonesty and corruption. There was poverty for many, and luxury for just a few. The countries' real wealth declined year after year. It was no wonder that their currencies were almost worthless outside their national borders.

At the end of the 1980s, the people rose up in the Soviet Union and other Eastern European countries and swept away the Communist parties and their creaking economic systems. At the time of writing, these countries are trying to introduce greater economic freedom by privatizing State factories and allowing entrepreneurs to set up their own private businesses. In China, agriculture has been freed from most State control and foreign manufacturers have been encouraged to invest in the coastal provinces north of Hong Kong.

 Make notes on market and command economies to illustrate the differences between them.

MIXED ECONOMIES

Like other countries in the western world, Britain has a mixed economy which contains both a private sector and a public sector.

The **private sector** is composed of individual businesses that make their own decisions about what they produce and where they produce it. The government imposes some controls, but these are kept to a minimum in the interests of freedom and competition. In

▶ The Soviet Union also established a global monopoly in one of the most expensive luxury foods – caviar, the roes of the sturgeon fish. Most sturgeon live in the rivers and lakes around the Caspian Sea, so caviar is exported from the countries bordering the Caspian Sea, mainly Russia, Kazakhstan and Iran. In 1927, the Soviet Union persuaded Iran to sign an agreement to control world prices. The top grades of caviar currently retail at about £1,500 per lb.

▶ Western businesspeople sometimes got round the problem by **barter**, the practice of exchanging one good or service for another without using money. For example, telephones were exchanged for tobacco.

▶ **The private sector**
Ownership: private individuals
Funding: owners' money or borrowed money
Main objective: profit

very simple terms, firms in the private sector are owned by individuals, or by shareholders who have become part-owners of a company by buying its shares. The business is financed by the owners' money or by borrowed money. The main objective of businesses in the private sector is profit.

In the **public sector**, the government or other public authorities, such as local councils, make the main decisions about policy and finance. In very simple terms again, public enterprises are owned by the government or some other public authority. They are financed mainly by taxes on consumers and businesses in the private sector; and their main objective is to provide a public service.

In recent years, the government has greatly reduced the size of the public sector by privatizing many public corporations such as British Airways, and by forcing local councils to transfer some of their services to the private sector.

The government has tried to encourage charities in the **voluntary sector** to provide more services for the public. Unlike the public sector, which usually provides a general service, charities provide a targeted service for specific sections of the community that need help. For example, Shelter is a charity that exists mainly to help the homeless and other people who have housing problems.

Although charities rely heavily on volunteers who work for nothing, managers and specialists in large charities are paid professionals who have often held top jobs in the private sector. There are now about 200,000 charities in Britain; but most of them are very small. Their estimated income in 1990 was over £16 billion. Fund-raising is one of the most important activities for charities. In some big charities, most of their money now comes from business. The general public and public authorities also provide financial support.

> ► **The public sector**
> **Ownership:** the State or public authorities
> **Funding:** government or local authority money
> **Main objective:** public service

> ► **The voluntary sector**
> **Ownership:** charities
> **Funding:** business, individuals, public authority grants
> **Main objective:** targeted services

1 What is a mixed economy?
2 State two ways in which the government can influence market economies.
3 How is a private company financed?
4 What are the sources of finance for a publicly owned enterprise?
5 What was the total income of charities in 1990?

The balance between the public and private sectors

One of the most difficult problems in a mixed economy is getting the right balance between the public and the private sectors. From 1945 (when the Second World War ended) until 1979, the pendulum swung heavily towards the public sector; critics would say that it swung too far. Since 1979 (when the Conservatives came into power), the pendulum has swung heavily back towards the private sector; now, critics would say that it has gone too far. The rest of this chapter will examine the changes in balance between the private and the public sectors in more detail.

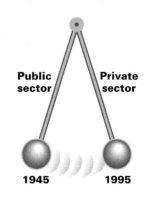

Public sector   Private sector

1945   1995

Swings of the pendulum

The table below shows Britain's national income which measures the value of all business activity in a year.

Wages and salaries (£m)	Company profits (£m)	Public corporation surplus (£m)	Government enterprise surplus (£m)	Rent and self-employment (£m)	Total (£m)
342,925	63,570	2,808	272	107,615	517,190

Adapted from Central Statistical Office Digest of Statistics, May 1993

► Formula for calculating percentage (%):

$x = \dfrac{\text{value or quantity of one item} \times 100}{\text{total value or quantity}}$

e.g. $(342{,}925 \div 517{,}190) \times 100 = 66.3\%$

1 Calculate the percentage of the national income that goes to (a) workers, (b) companies, (c) public corporations, (d) government enterprises and (e) self-employment and rent.
2 If the total national income remained the same, but the public corporation surplus increased to £10,000 million, which other section or sections of the national income would be likely to fall in value?
3 What political and/or economic event might cause such a change in the public corporation surplus?

THE PRIVATE SECTOR

During the last fifty years, businesses in the private sector have created enormous wealth for the majority of British people. Most people have more money to spend, and own more goods, than they ever did before. How has this been achieved?

Business objectives

► See also **Measuring business success** in Chapter 6.

As the marginal note on page 26 shows, profit is the main objective of private sector business. In general terms, profit is the surplus, or amount that is left, after the costs of running a business have been deducted from its sales. Take a simple example. A corner shop has sales of £100,000 in a year. The total costs of buying the goods and running the business come to £75,000. Therefore, the gross profit for the year (before allowing for tax and other charges) is £25,000.

► For more on gross profit, see **Trading accounts** in Chapter 19.

It is essential for a business to make a profit. If it did not, it could not survive for long as it would start to spend more money than it receives. It would fall into debt and would eventually have to close. Profit is needed for various reasons:

• It enables the business to pay its taxes and interest on any debt.
• It compensates owners for the risk in investing their money and time in the business, or can be used to pay a dividend to shareholders who have taken the risk of investing in the firm.
• It improves the efficiency of the business or increases its size.

Profit has further benefits. It stimulates firms to seek new opportunities. For example, oil companies spend millions of pounds every year searching the land and sea to find profitable new oil fields to provide the fuel that both other businesses and all consumers need.

The annual gross profit of the corner shop mentioned above was £25,000 (£100,000 sales – £75,000 costs). If costs were reduced to £70,000:

1 What would be the new annual profit?
2 What would be the percentage rise in profit?
3 How do you think costs might have been reduced?

Other objectives

Although businesses in the private sector need to make a profit to survive, not all of them want to make the highest possible profit. For example, some craft workers, such as wood carvers or bookbinders, may gain so much job satisfaction, or pleasure from their work, that they are content with a minimal profit that will allow them to pay their taxes and interest on their debts.

In contrast, other owners of small businesses may be far more interested in **profit maximization**, or making the largest possible profit, so that they can obtain the status symbols of success – a Mercedes, a bigger house and a second home here or abroad.

Another objective might be to increase the **turnover**, or total sales, of a business, and so increase its size. Some businesses, particularly large companies, set themselves another objective: to increase their **market share** or their percentage of total sales in a national or international market for a particular product, such as instant coffee.

▶ For more on turnover, size of business, and market share, see Chapter 6.

In this increasingly competitive world, all businesses have to keep costs low so that they can match or beat their rivals' prices. Therefore, all businesses must try to increase their cost-effectiveness. This is achieved by making sure that the costs of running the business are kept as low as possible in relation to the financial returns.

▶ For more on cost-effectiveness, see Chapter 6.

Read the following case study and answer the questions at the end.

During the slump in the property market at the beginning of the 1990s, Sue lost her job as a negotiator with a firm of estate agents. A few weeks later, she bought a repossessed flat for the bargain price of £27,000, giving her own house as security for the bank loan. Sue soon found a tenant for the flat at a rent of £80 a week which more than covered the interest on the loan. Encouraged by this, she bought another cheap flat which had been repossessed because its owners, a young couple with three children, had both lost their jobs and were unable to keep up their mortgage repayments. Eventually, she bought four flats of a similar kind. Her total bank loan for the four properties was £128,000.

Sue did not plan to keep the flats for long. As soon as the housing market picked up again, she planned to have them redecorated and to sell them. It would be no problem getting rid of the tenants as they were on one-year leases. She estimated that the flats would sell for £41,000, £40,500, £48,000 and £51,000 respectively.

1 What would be the total selling price of the flats?
2 How much profit would Sue make before allowing for tax and other expenses and charges when she sold all four properties?
3 What kinds of risk was Sue taking in buying the flats?
4 Comment on the ethics, or morality, of Sue's business activities.

Disadvantages of profit maximization

The case study also shows some of the downside, or disadvantages, of the private sector when profit maximization is the main objective.

Excessive profits

Sue was only interested in short-term profit, not long-term growth. Her activities added very little of real value to the properties apart from a few coats of paint. If she had refurbished the flats to a high standard and then let or sold them for a reasonable profit, there would have been long-term growth as the value of the country's housing stock would have increased.

Unemployment

The young couple in the first flat had both lost their jobs. In its drive for ever greater efficiency and profit, business cuts its costs by making more and more workers redundant without taking much consideration of the social costs. The government is left to solve the problems and the taxpayer to pick up the social security bill for the unemployed.

Gap between rich and poor

A lack of public sector housing forces many people to buy homes they cannot really afford. As a result, hundreds of thousands of houses are repossessed every year because the owners lose their jobs or cannot afford to repay the mortgage. During the last decade, some middle-class home-buyers fell into the same trap. They bought their houses when interest rates were fairly low and the monthly mortgage repayments were within their means, but the repayments became unmanageable when interest rates rose.

Since 1979, the share of the richest 10 per cent of the population in national wealth (income and capital) has increased significantly, while the share of the poorest 10 per cent has fallen.

THE PUBLIC SECTOR

In 1979, when the Conservative Party came to power under Margaret Thatcher, there was a very large public sector. It consisted of five main groups:

1 nationalized industries;
2 company shareholdings;
3 central government services;
4 quangos;
5 local council services.

Nationalized industries

After the Second World War, the Labour government bought many industries, such as coal mines and the railways, from their private owners and **nationalized** them, or placed them under public control. They were run by **public corporations** such as British Coal (formerly the National Coal Board) and British Rail. In a nationalized industry, the managers are responsible for the day-to-day running of the industry, but the government owns the public corporation and retains final control through the Board of Governors, which it appoints.

▶ The Post Office, founded in 1657, was the first 'nationalized industry'. The telecommunications section was privatized from 1983 and eventually became BT.

Company shareholdings

Governments can gain control of a firm by buying all, or a majority, of a private company's shares. This was done with the oil company British Petroleum (BP) in 1914, just before the First World War, in order to secure supplies of fuel for the Royal Navy. In the 1970s, the Labour Government bought shares in sunrise industries.

▶ **Sunrise industries** are new, fast-growing industries in electronics and communications that have superseded the old, declining heavy industries like coal mining and steel making.

Central government services

Services are provided by the State to members of the public either free or for a fee that is below the market price. For example, the National Health Service provides a mainly free service, although most people have to pay for prescriptions and dental treatment. Other central government services include main roads and defence.

Quangos

Quangos are boards and committees that are financed by the government, but have considerable independence in the way they are run, for example the British Council, which exists mainly to publicize British culture abroad. There has been an enormous growth in the number and power of quangos in the last fifteen years. They have come under increasing attack as a means of providing jobs for members of the majority political party.

▶ The word quango comes from **qu**asi-**a**utonomous **n**on-**g**overnmental **o**rganization.

Local council services

Councils provide a wide range of services such as libraries, planning, police and fire services.

1 What is a nationalized industry and how is it run?
2 Give two examples of services provided by local councils.
3 What is a quango?
4 Name two public services provided by the government.

The public sector revolution

► See **The public sector** in Chapter 18.

Since 1979, when the Conservatives came to power, there has been a revolution in the public sector. Many of the public sector firms and organizations have been **privatized**, or sold off to the private sector. Those that remain have had to face increasing competition from private firms. The Conservatives set out on an ambitious and controversial programme of privatization, which is still continuing at the time of writing.

> **Privatization**
> * It means replacing public corporations with private companies and selling off the shares to private investors and financial institutions.
> * The government can sell its own shares in companies such as BP.
> * It permits private firms to provide public services.
> * It forces local councils to introduce compulsory competitive tendering (CCT) (see page 34), which allows private firms to compete with the council's own labour force.

 Make brief notes on the different kinds of privatization.

Main privatizations

From 1979, many of the major public corporations and government shares in major companies were sold off to financial institutions, such as insurance companies and pension funds, and to private investors, both British and foreign. The main privatizations are shown below.

► The dates indicate when the first batch of shares was sold. Often, the shares were sold in stages. BT, for example, was sold in three lots, the last in 1993.

1979	British Petroleum	1987	British Airports Authority
1981	Cable and Wireless	1987	Rolls Royce
1983	British Telecommunications	1988	British Steel*
1986	British Gas	1989	Water authorities
1986	National Bus Company	1990	Electricity suppliers
1987	British Airways	1991	Non-nuclear electricity generation (CEGB)

*British Steel was privatized in 1953 and renationalized in 1967.

British Gas share advertisement, 1986

Since 1979, Conservative administrations have privatized nearly fifty major businesses. This has produced a net income for the government (after expenses have been paid) of over £55 billion. Critics claim that these national assets were sold off too cheaply.

British Rail was privatized in 1995. A government organization, Railtrack, is responsible for the track, signalling and stations. Railtrack grants franchises to private firms to run their own train services. British Coal's sixteen remaining mines were privatized in 1994 with most of them being sold to one mining company. One group of miners bought their own colliery which they now run profitably. In 1994 the Conservative government decided not to privatize the Post Office as the result of backbench pressure! The only other major businesses re-maining in the public sector are London Transport and Nuclear Electric.

 Select any of the businesses in the list on page 32 that you think should have remained in the public sector. Use your own knowledge or research to explain your choice.

Privatizing public services

In recent years, the government has given private firms the chance to provide public services. Britain's share of the Channel Tunnel was financed by a private firm, not the government. The government also plans to let private companies build motorways and pay the companies tolls, or fees. A private firm now manages the Aldermaston atomic weapons establishment; a private security firm runs a prison; and the BBC, a public corporation, is forced by the government to offer 20 per cent of television programme time to independent producers.

National Health Service trusts have been set up to sell hospital services to their local health authority and to GPs (family doctors) who control their own budgets as fund-holders. The self-governing trusts manage the hospitals and control their own finances. In 1993, the government opened the way for private firms to run some services in trust hospitals, such as day surgery centres.

► By 1994, nearly 600 hospitals or other health service units, such as ambulance services, had either become self-governing trusts or had applied to do so. This represents the vast majority of big hospitals.

The Civil Service faces increasing challenges. Since 1988, the government has set up **executive agencies** to do all or part of the work that was formerly done by government departments. Although the executive agencies remain part of the civil service, they have greater independence. However, they now have to meet demanding financial targets set by the government. There are about 100 executive agencies, including the Royal Mint, which makes notes and coins.

In addition, **internal markets** have been set up in many public sector organizations, such as the BBC. Under this quality management system, departments are treated as each other's customers. Like all customers everywhere, they have to pay for the services they receive. In this case, they have to pay other departments for their services. It is claimed that this system creates much greater efficiency because each department has to break even, or make a 'profit', if it is to survive.

▶ See the box on **Quality management systems** in Chapter 8, page 95.

 Make notes on how the provision of public services has changed in recent years.

1 What is the importance of profit?
2 Name two industries that were privatized in the 1980s.
3 What is an executive agency?
4 Explain what is meant by the phrase 'internal market'.

Council services

The government has applied similar principles to local council services. In the past, many manual services were provided by a council's own labour force, or **direct service organization** (DSO). This work was usually in the tertiary sector. It was usually labour-intensive, or based more on the use of labour than on machines, as in refuse collection. It was also monopolistic: private firms were not allowed to do the work, only council employees. In 1988, the government introduced **compulsory competitive tendering** (CCT). This allowed private firms to put in an estimate to do the work in competition with an estimate from the council's own DSO. As the table below shows, private firms now do almost a third of the work.

Local authority contracts won by DSOs

	June 1992 (%)	June 1993 (%)
Building cleaning	57.8	51.5
Refuse collection	70.5	71.9
Other cleaning	73	70.3
Vehicle maintenance	77.7	78.2
School catering	97.5	90.6
Grounds maintenance	66	67
Sports and leisure	76.6	84

Source: *Municipal Journal* 18–24 June 1993

▶ Formula for calculating average, or arithmetic mean:

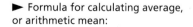

$$\text{average} = \frac{\text{total quantities}}{\text{number of items}}$$

e.g. (57.8 + 70.5 + 73 + 77.7 + 97.5 + 66 + 76.6) ÷ 7 = 519.1 ÷ 7 = 74.16

1 What was average percentage of contracts won by DSOs in June 1992 and June 1993?
2 What was the average percentage of contracts won by private firms at these times?

3 Look at the figures for each of the seven kinds of work. In which kinds of work did private firms' share of the contracts (a) increase and (b) decrease between June 1992 and June 1993?
4 Select one of the seven kinds of work that has been taken over by a private firm in your area. State whether you think the service has improved or become worse.

The government is now extending CCT to clerical and professional work in local authorities. Private firms will be allowed to tender for a proportion of the work carried out by local authority departments, such as finance, legal and personnel.

Local authority education committees (LEAs) once ran all primary and secondary schools in their area. From 1994, all these schools managed their own financial affairs – a total budget of £11.6 billion a year.

 Make notes on the changes that have been made in local councils.

ADVANTAGES AND DISADVANTAGES OF THE PUBLIC SECTOR

There are arguments for and against the public sector. The main arguments in favour of the public sector are:

- No dividends have to be paid to shareholders, therefore any surplus can be used for improving the service.
- There is no wasteful duplication, particularly where it might be inefficient and wasteful to have more than one supplier operating in the same area, for example with water.
- Services are provided for all on the basis of need and not on the ability to pay.

The main arguments against the public service – and in favour of privatization – are:

- The absence of the profit motive makes the public sector rely too much on government subsidies.
- Many public sector industries had a monopoly, which made them less efficient as they had no competitors.
- Market forces would force the public sector to be more efficient by introducing better management systems.

 Draw up a table with two columns, one headed *For the public sector* and the other headed *For privatization*. Make notes of each of the opposed arguments in the lists above, putting them in order of importance.

 Read the following case study about the London Underground and answer the questions at the end.

As a result of underinvestment over many years, London

▶ Unlike the other case studies, this one deals with a real-life situation. The information is taken from the Modern Railways report, April 1993. (For how the public sector is financed, see Public sector finance in Chapter 18.)

Underground has become run down. It plans to spend a total of £8.5 billion over ten years on modernizing the system. Some of the items are:

Trains	£1.4 billion to replace much of the existing rolling stock.
Stations	£1.5 billion to modernize stations.
Track	£1.5 billion to improve track that is in an appalling state.
Lifts	£200 million to replace virtually all the lifts.
Communications	£600 million to improve public address system and train control.
Pumps	£260 million to upgrade the 635 pumps in the drainage system to prevent tunnel flooding and smelly stations.
Train depots	£460 million to upgrade depots which produce quality work in spite of the poor working conditions.

In addition, new lines are needed to reduce present congestion and to serve new areas. Proposed new lines are: the Jubilee line extension to Docklands; the Crossrail link; East London line extensions; and a Chelsea–Hackney line. The total cost is estimated at £6.5 billion.

Some of the money will come from internal savings including reducing the number of staff and employing the rest more efficiently. London Underground has already saved nearly £150 million in 1992–3 and hopes to increase this to £570 million by 1996–7. Revenue will be increased by raising fares in line with wage levels. However, most of the money, in the first years at least, will come from the government. Because the government needs to cut its own spending, it has reduced the **subsidy**, or grant, to London Underground from £724 million to £508 million for 1993–4.

1 What is the total cost of the ten-year plan for modernizing the Underground and building new lines?
2 By what percentage has the government subsidy been cut?
3 As a result of the reduction in subsidy, some of the new lines and improvements to the Underground may have to be delayed. If the budget had to be cut by half, select the items you would postpone. State your reasons for selecting them.
4 Most other European governments give bigger subsidies to their railways than the British government does. In your view, what are the advantages and disadvantages of the smaller British subsidies?

The Post Office

Public sector efficiency and productivity could probably have been improved without privatization if better management and stricter cost controls had been applied.

The Post Office illustrates the point. From being a record loss-maker, with poor service and a demoralized staff, it has transformed itself into the star business of the public sector. Since 1976, it has made a profit every year without any subsidy from the government. In 1993, its pre-tax profit rose 15 per cent to £283 million. The percentage of first-class post delivered the next day has increased from 74 per cent in 1989 to 92 per cent in 1993. Improved management and increasing competition from private courier firms spurred on the Post Office to make the necessary changes.

The changes were brought about by using modern management techniques, such as:

- improving quality control, training and communication;
- reducing centralization by drastically cutting the size of Head Office staff;
- giving managers performance-related bonuses.

► See **Centralization and decentralization** in Chapter 8.

► See **Performance-related pay** in Chapter 20.

If these modern management techniques had been introduced into all nationalized industries, what effects would this have had on the industries themselves and on the economy as a whole?

Changes in other public sector businesses

Some other public sector businesses also became more efficient when the government set clear financial and performance targets for them to achieve. However, the big nationalized industries, such as electricity, water and gas, were always a much bigger problem. They had little incentive to change because they had a virtual monopoly. As a result, they did not have to face any competition from the private sector. If they had not been privatized, it seems unlikely that they would have been able to improve their performance as much as they have. Other European countries, which were opposed to privatization, have come round to that view. Many of them, particularly France, are now introducing huge programmes of privatization.

GOVERNMENT IMPACT ON BUSINESS

Although the government has given up some of its power by privatizing much of the public sector, it still remains a very big force in the economy. Apart from consumers, the government is by far the biggest spender in the country. If the government decided that it wanted to cut the rate of taxation, which provides a large part of its income, it might decide to cut its own spending, for example on defence. This would have a big impact on consumers and business. If taxation was cut, consumers would have more to spend, which would help some kinds of businesses. However, other businesses in the defence sector would suffer because they would have fewer orders.

► See **Value added tax** and **Customs and excise duties** in Chapter 12.

The government also has a great impact on business in general through its control over taxes, such as VAT on a wide range of goods and services, and duties on such goods as alcohol and tobacco. An increase in these taxes would tend to slow down business activity, while a decrease would be likely to increase business activity.

Interest rates

The government also has a major influence on the whole of business through its control of **interest rates**, or the price paid for borrowing money. The government controls the **bank rate**, or the basic rate at which money can be borrowed, through the Bank of England. If the government wants to increase demand in the economy, it can reduce the interest rate. This is likely to make consumers and businesses spend more, which will increase business activity. However, it may also have other effects. If the interest rate is reduced, foreigners might withdraw some of the money they have invested here because the return on their investment would fall. This might lead to a change in the exchange rate, with the pound falling in value against other currencies. In addition, the increased business activity at home might cause an increase in the rate of inflation.

► See **Exchange rates** in Chapter 12.

► For more on inflation, see **Economic policy** in Chapter 12.

The government might reduce interest rates in an attempt to stimulate business activity because unemployment is high. It might also try to put the unemployed back to work by starting a nationwide programme of training and retraining.

► See **Government training schemes** in Chapter 21.

The government also has a major impact on business through the laws it passes.

 Make notes on government controls and influences on business activity.

THE EUROPEAN UNION

► The **European Union** (EU), formerly known as the European Community (EC), was set up by the Treaty of Rome in 1957. The twelve member-countries are: Belgium, Britain, Denmark, France, Germany, Greece, Holland, Ireland, Italy, Luxembourg, Portugal and Spain. In 1994, Austria, Finland and Sweden decided to join the EU, but the people of Norway chose in a referendum to remain outside. Britain did not become a member until 1973. The British government has usually taken a less enthusiastic view of the EU than the other big countries like Germany and France. It favours a much freer and decentralized association of countries with a greater number of

The European Union (EU) has an increasing impact on business activity in Britain. The EU sets the prices paid for most farm products and the **quotas**, or amounts, that can be grown by British farmers. The **Single Market**, which came into effect in 1993, means that all member-countries can compete in selling goods and services in each other's countries without restrictions. They can also **tender**, or make a bid to do the work, for public service contracts such as building roads.

Many of the laws that control business activities are made in Brussels (the main headquarters of the EU) and not in London. For example, the Health and Safety Regulations, which came into force in 1993, are based on EU directives (or laws). The EU has the power to fine British businesses millions of pounds if they break EU laws.

At the time of writing, the government is fighting an EU directive that would restrict working hours to a maximum of 48 hours per week. The government wants a higher limit – or no limit at all – because British firms rely heavily on employees working long hours of overtime. The government is also opposed to EU plans to introduce decision-making works councils in large firms.

1 What is a National Health Service trust?
2 What does 'labour-intensive' mean?
3 What is the function of a DSO?
4 What is meant by quality control?
5 What does VAT stand for?
6 What would be the likely effect of lower interest rates on:
   (a) the consumer?
   (b) a bank investor?
   (c) a borrower?
   (d) foreign investment in this country?
7 State the ways in which the European Union can affect British business.
8 Give two examples of government control on businesses.

members. Particularly problematic was the **exchange rate mechanism** (ERM), which tries to keep the exchange rates of the members' currencies in harmony. Britain did not join the ERM until 1990 and left two years later when pressure from international speculators forced it to do so. There was also much political debate surrounding the Maastricht Treaty of 1991, which was designed to lead to full **economic and monetary union** (EMU) by 1999. Britain opted out of the EMU and also out of the Social Chapter, designed to give workers greater protection and power.

SUMMARY

- In theory, a market economy would be completely free of regulation and control and have unrestricted competition. Market forces would automatically control the whole economy, including prices, without any government intervention.
- In a command, or planned, economy, the State controls all economic activity. In theory, resources are used mainly for the benefit of the whole population, not a wealthy minority.
- Most countries in the western world have mixed economies, which contain both a private and a public sector.
- The private sector is run and financed by individuals and companies and has profit as its main objective.
- The public sector is owned by the government or local councils and run by managers and officials they appoint. It is financed mainly by taxes. Its main objective is to provide a public service.
- Since 1979, when the Conservative party came to power, there has been a huge programme of privatization with nationalized industries being sold to the private sector. The private sector also competes for some of the work done by the Civil Service and local councils.
- The government still remains a powerful force in the economy through its control of taxes, interest rates, inflation and exchange rates, and its right to pass laws.
- The European Union has an increasing share of control over British business activities through its control of some sectors of the economy, such as agriculture, and its right to pass laws which Britain and other member-countries have to adopt.

5 *Self-employment*

Chapter objectives

After working through this chapter, you will have the knowledge to:

▌ understand the reasons for the increase in self-employment;

▌ select the personal qualities needed by sole traders;

▌ identify the benefits and drawbacks of a partnership compared with a sole trader;

▌ describe how a worker cooperative is organized;

▌ calculate the financial benefits for both sides in a franchise operation;

▌ state the objectives, control, sources of finance and distribution of profits of different business structures;

▌ select the most suitable kinds of insurance for self-employed people;

▌ understand and use the following key terms: self-employed, working population, sole trader, unlimited liability, partnership, deed of partnership, worker cooperatives, franchising, franchiser, franchisee, royalty, working capital, business format franchising, risk, insurance.

BUSINESS STRUCTURES

There are five main ways in which businesses are owned and controlled:

* sole traders;
* partnerships;
* worker cooperatives;
* franchises;
* limited companies.

Limited companies, which are owned by shareholders and run by managers, are dealt with in Chapter 6. This chapter deals with the other four kinds of business which are run by the self-employed.

The **self-employed** are people who run their own business, either alone, like the sole trader, or in cooperation with other people.

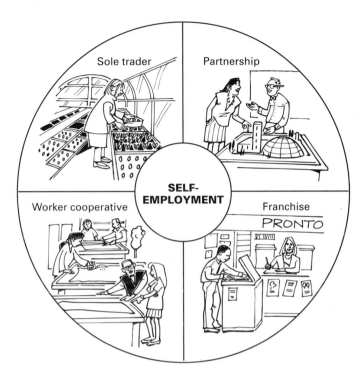

Increase in self-employment

During the 1980s, there was a great increase in self-employment. The percentage of self-employed people in the working population increased from 7.9 per cent to 11 per cent, and that figure is still rising, though at a slower rate. There are now well over 3 million self-employed people, a third of whom are women.

There are three main reasons for the increase:

1   The government supports the self-employed and gives them financial help, because it believes that small businesses can create new jobs more easily than bigger companies.
2   Some employees who have lost their jobs in big companies use their redundancy money to set up a small business.
3   The new spirit of enterprise has encouraged some employees to resign and start their own business.

Many self-employed people have set up successful businesses, but a great number have failed. About one-quarter of all new businesses fail in the first two years; and, at the end of ten years, only one-third are still trading.

 Describe the main factors that have caused an increase in self-employment.

▶ The **working population** is the total number of people in a country who are working or available for work. It is composed of employees, self-employed people, the armed forces, people on government training programmes and the unemployed.

▶ **Enterprise** is having the ability to see new market opportunities and the initiative to exploit them.

SOLE TRADERS

In law, the **sole trader** is a type of business organization in which one person is the owner. Some sole traders, such as house painters and decorators, often work by themselves without any employees; other sole traders, such as garage owners, usually employ a number of people. Sole traders are found in all sectors of production, but 60 per cent are in the tertiary sector.

► To refresh your memory on the sectors of production, see **Production** in Chapter 2.

 Give three examples of sole traders in each of the three sectors of production: primary, secondary and tertiary. In your view, why are the majority of sole traders in the tertiary sector?

Sole traders must have certain personal qualities if they are to succeed. They need to be: self-sufficient, persistent, thick-skinned, hard-working, adaptable and dedicated.

 Copy out this list of characteristics, adding other personal qualities that you think should be included. Put all the qualities in order of importance, and explain why you believe that the first three in your list are particularly important.

Main features of the sole trader

Here are some of the features that distinguish the sole trader:

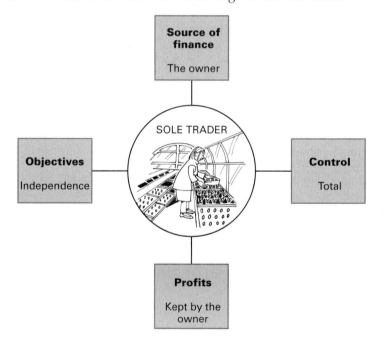

Objectives
Although these vary from one sole trader to another, independence and job satisfaction are usually very high on the list.

Control
Sole traders can exercise total control because they are in direct touch with their customers or clients, suppliers, banks, advisors and any employees.

Sources of finance

Finance is usually provided by the owner, though the government, banks and friends may also help. It is often difficult to obtain more capital for expansion.

Distribution of profits

Owners keep all of the profits (if there are any!).

Being a sole trader has certain advantages and disadvantages.

Advantages

- **Ease of starting up:** There is very little regulation, or red tape, involved in setting up as a sole trader. The Inland Revenue and the Department of Social Security must be told, and you must register with the Customs and Excise authorities for VAT if your **turnover**, or annual sales, is likely to be over a certain figure. (This is £45,000 at the time of writing.) You may also need to obtain planning permission from the local council if you use your home for certain trades.
- **Flexibility:** The owner can make quick decisions and change the nature of the business rapidly in response to market forces.

Disadvantages

- **Unlimited liability:** Sole traders have unlimited liability. This means that they are personally responsible for all the debts of the business, so all their possessions, including their home, could be at risk if the business failed.
- **Lack of continuity:** It may be difficult for the business to continue if the owner is ill; and it may be impossible to sell it after the owner's death.

 Draw up a table with two columns headed *Pros* and *Cons*. List concisely all the advantages and disadvantages of being a sole trader.

1 What percentage of businesses fail within ten years?
2 Which sector of production has the largest number of sole traders?
3 What is job satisfaction?
4 Give three sources of finance for a sole trader.
5 What is meant by unlimited liability?

 Contact a sole trader and find out about his or her working life. Using the comments you get and the information contained in this section, write a short summary of the sole trader's working life, suggesting the kind of person who might be most successful.

PARTNERSHIPS

 Read the following case study and answer the questions at the end.

James had always wanted to make jewellery. On leaving school, he took a course at his local college and then obtained a job with a goldsmith. He got on so well that he soon started work with a famous London firm.

When he was 24, he decided to set up his own business. He managed to sell his jewellery to one or two shops, but he had very few private customers. Although he still liked making jewellery, he disliked the administration – forms, accounts, letters – and he found it almost impossible to publicize himself. The business wasn't going very well at all and he was thinking of trying to find a job again.

Then he had a lucky break. He met an older man, Brian, who had many years experience of marketing and publicity. They became partners, with Brian looking after the management side of the business, while James concentrated on making jewellery.

From that moment, the business took off. Sales to shops increased almost straight away and, within months, articles about James – and his skills – started to appear in newspapers and magazines.

The partnership began to attract more up-market customers. James was commissioned to make more elaborate and expensive jewellery. There was a small feature about his jewellery, with photographs of it, in one of the Sunday newspaper colour supplements. This brought in more new customers.

At Brian's insistence, James met one or two of the new customers for lunch in expensive restaurants in the West End of London; but James was always glad to get back to his work-bench again. He was pleased that he could just make jewellery without bothering about management, publicity and finance.

Then, one evening, his world fell apart. A letter arrived by special messenger addressed to the partners. Thinking that it must be urgent, James opened it. He couldn't believe what he read. It was a letter from the bank demanding instant payment – for the final time – of the partnership's debts of £37,000.

James had a tremendous row with Brian. They almost came to blows. As Brian stormed out of the room, he shouted that he was dissolving their partnership. He delivered a formal letter of confirmation to James's flat that night.

The following day, James went to see a solicitor. He found that the situation was even worse than he had imagined. When he left the solicitor's office, and went into the nearest pub for a drink, he could still hear the grim words of the solicitor echoing in his ears.

Partnerships – what the solicitor said

'You should have come to see me right at the start. . . '

'Under the Partnership Act of 1890, he's quite entitled to end the partnership immediately by giving notice to the other partners.'

'All partners are jointly liable for all debts and obligations.'

'Every partner's liability is unlimited, which means that your flat could be at risk.'

'If you'd come to see me at the beginning, I'd have drawn up a deed of partnership and this would never have happened.'

1 Why did James want a partner?
2 How did Brian increase the volume of business?
3 Who is legally responsible for the debts of a partnership?
4 Which Act of Parliament governs partnerships?
5 What are the main lessons you have learnt about sole traders and partnerships from the case study?

LEGAL REQUIREMENTS

Legally, a **partnership** can have up to twenty partners, though some professionals, such as solicitors, are allowed to have more. Solicitors, accountants, doctors and architects are most likely to form partnerships. However, any two or more persons carrying on a business for profit together are legally partners even if no documents have been signed. Their partnership is governed by the Partnership Act of 1890.

This law does not provide a solution to the many disputes and problems that can arise in partnerships. Therefore, it is essential to have a solicitor draw up a legal **deed of partnership**. This should deal with such topics as the partners' duties; voting rights; arrangements for retirement, death or change of partners; insurance; share of profits; partnership expenses; and annual audit of accounts.

Main features of partnerships

Here are some of the features that distinguish a partnership:

```
                    ┌──────────────┐
                    │  Source of   │
                    │   finance    │
                    │              │
                    │ The partners │
                    └──────────────┘

┌──────────────┐      PARTNERSHIP      ┌──────────────┐
│  Objectives  │                       │   Control    │
│              │                       │              │
│    Shared    │                       │    Equal     │
│responsibility│                       │              │
└──────────────┘                       └──────────────┘

                    ┌──────────────┐
                    │   Profits    │
                    │              │
                    │  Shared by   │
                    │   partners   │
                    └──────────────┘
```

Objectives

Partners want to do their own work without having total responsibility for running the whole business.

Control

Control is usually shared with other partners on an equal basis, though there are sometimes senior and junior partners with the former having more control.

Sources of finance

The partners usually provide the initial capital. A partnership can borrow money more easily than a sole trader.

Distribution of profits

Under the Partnership Act (1890), profits – and losses – are distributed equally among the partners, but this can be varied by a deed of partnership. Partners who have contributed more capital can then receive a proportionately bigger share of the profits.

ACT IN What are the benefits of a partnership compared with a sole trader? Are there any drawbacks?

WORKER COOPERATIVES

You are probably familiar with the Co-op shops and stores; they were originally set up by the Co-operative Society. Did you also know that there are about 1,500 **worker cooperatives** run on similar lines? They are most common in catering, engineering, farming, printing and dressmaking. Worker cooperatives are sometimes set

▶ Co-operative Retail Societies have 4,700 shops and stores (including about eighty superstores); a combined turnover, or annual sales, of well over £7 billion; and over 8 million members. The shops and stores are owned by members of the society who elect the management committees.

up when a big manufacturing company closes one of its factories. A group of former employees may then use their redundancy money to set up their own business. They can sometimes buy machinery and equipment cheaply from their former employer. Small groups of unemployed people also set up worker cooperatives, sometimes with grants from local councils or other public authorities. The size of worker cooperatives varies, but most are small.

Main features of worker cooperatives

Here are some of the features that distinguish a worker cooperative:

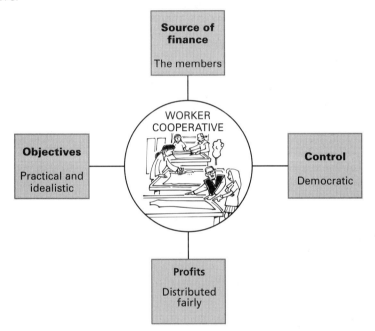

Objectives
The objectives of worker cooperatives range from the practical – working instead of being unemployed – to the idealistic – believing that worker cooperatives will lead to a better and fairer business world. In all cooperatives, however, there are usually some idealistic members who have a vision of a more equitable future.

Control
Cooperatives are run by all the members who hold regular meetings to make decisions. They are run as a democracy, with each member having one vote, whatever their job.

Sources of finance
Members provide the finance, though they sometimes get financial help from sympathetic local authorities. Borrowing money is sometimes difficult because banks are often suspicious of this kind of business organization.

▶ See Chapter 6.

Distribution of profits

Profits are distributed to members in a 'fair' way, not necessarily in proportion to the amount of money invested.

Worker cooperatives – for and against

Advantages

- One of the main advantages is that worker cooperatives are usually registered as limited companies. This means that a member's financial liability is restricted to the amount of money he or she has put into the cooperative.
- There is a great sense of involvement as the business belongs to the workforce, not outside shareholders.

The main disadvantages are:

- It is often difficult to reach decisions as each member has a vote regardless of whether he or she has any knowledge or experience of the problem involved. Practical and idealistic views often clash.
- Financial control is often weak, unless an accountant is employed. Many cooperatives have failed because members did not acknowledge that profit is an essential objective in all businesses.
- Public interest in worker cooperatives, and support for them, is often low. Worker cooperatives are more common, and successful, on the Continent.

 Make notes on worker cooperatives, emphasizing the differences between them and partnerships.

1 How are profits usually shared in a partnership?
2 How many worker cooperatives are there in this country?
3 What is the usual size of a worker cooperative?
4 Can you think of two possible effects if cooperative principles were applied throughout British industry?

FRANCHISING

 Read the following case study and answer the questions at the end.

A personnel recruitment agency, Better Staff, already has four branches in Liverpool and the surrounding area. It wants to expand by opening six new branches in another region of the country. It has drawn up a full business plan with projected financial results, but banks and other financial institutions haven't shown much interest.

As the company does not have enough capital to set up the new branches, it has decided to use **franchising** instead. As the **franchiser**, it will allow other people to set up their own recruitment business under the trade name of Better Staff in a particular area of the country. These **franchisees** will pay the company a royalty for using the trade name and for the training and support they receive in running their branch.

The company's financial director is working out the figures to see if the scheme is viable, or likely to work, before a pilot scheme is set up.

► A **royalty** is a percentage of the sales paid to the owner of a trade name, a patented invention or a work of art in return for using his or her property.

- The start-up fee will be £25,000 to cover equipment, and fitting out and furnishing the office.
- The franchisee will also need another £10,000 for working capital, and £5,000 to pay the company for providing publicity, full training and support.
- The franchisee will pay the company a royalty of 10 per cent on the franchise's turnover. The royalty includes a 2 per cent levy on turnover that the company spends on advertising and promotion.
- There will be a five-year contract, which is renewable if turnover, or annual sales, has reached £250,000. Otherwise, the franchisee can sell the business; but the buyer must be approved by the franchiser.

► **Working capital** is the money needed to cover the day-to-day cash requirements of a business. See also Working capital in Chapter 17.

The finance director has calculated the following figures based on the financial results of their main office and four branches:

	Projected turnover (£)	Projected profit* (£)
Year 1	80,000	12,000
Year 2	130,000	19,500
Year 3	180,000	27,000

*after all expenses and franchisee's own drawings have been met.

1 What is the total amount the franchisee will need to start the business?
2 Why do you think the company insists that any buyer of the business must be approved by them?
3 How long will it take the franchisee to recover the initial expenditure out of the annual profit? Show how you have arrived at your answer.
4 What was the percentage profit in relation to turnover in years 1, 2 and 3?
5 If the turnover was £215,000 in year 4 and £260,000 in year 5, how much would the franchiser make over the five-year period?
6 Assuming that the percentage of profit in relation to turnover remained unchanged, how much gross profit would the franchisee make over five years?
7 If you were the financial director, how would you explain the scheme to the other company directors?

Business format franchising

Business format franchising, or running a firm under the trade name of a bigger company, has increased greatly in recent years. There are now over 500 franchisers and nearly 30,000 franchisees in many different kinds of business, from mortgage services to marquees and from pet food suppliers to pawnbrokers. Some of the most popular franchises are services to business, fast-food restaurants, leisure products and services, clothing and fashion, and home improvements and maintenance. Some of the top franchising names are Wimpy, The Body Shop, Prontaprint and Fast Frame.

The Body Shop, Oxford Street, London

▶ Franchisers and franchisee's contributions to franchising

Franchiser	Franchisee
Trade name	Finance
Product	Effort
Equipment	Time
Training	Learning
Support	Experience
Advice	Motivation

Joint benefits

This unique business arrangement, which originated in the United States, can be of great benefit to both parties. The franchiser is providing a total way of doing business. For example, Better Staff not only lends its trade name to franchisees, but also its distinctive blue and yellow livery, or uniform, and its own company-designed computer software. Because the franchisee has paid a large fee to set up the business, he or she is usually more highly motivated and ambitious to succeed than an employee might be.

Advantages for franchisees
There are also special advantages for the franchisee. The main ones are:

- The franchisee retains some independence. For example, he or she can usually choose the legal structure of the business, by setting up as a sole trader, a partnership if a spouse or friend is also involved, or as a limited liability company.
- It is usually relatively easy to obtain a bank loan for part of the initial costs, particularly if the franchiser has a well-established product and a good reputation.

Disadvantages for franchisees
There are also disadvantages:

- Franchisees are not nearly as free as sole traders or partners. They have to do as the franchiser says and their work is supervised.
- They have to make continuing royalty payments to franchisers.

Advantages for franchisers

The main advantages for franchisers are:

- They can expand their business without investing large amounts of capital.
- Royalty payments will increase as the franchised businesses succeed.

Disadvantages for franchiser

The main disadvantages are:

- The company's trade name – and reputation – can be damaged if franchisees do not maintain standards.
- The profits might have been greater if the company had set up its own branches.

 Who gains more from franchising – the franchiser or the franchisee? Write four sentences, numbered in order of importance, to support your view.

Main features of franchised businesses

Here are some of the features that distinguish a franchise:

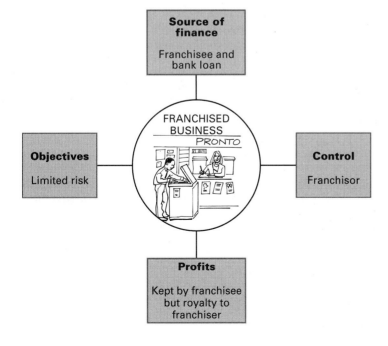

Objectives

Franchisees want to run their own business without facing all the risks of the small trader.

Control

The franchisee's control is limited as the franchiser governs many aspects of the business, including the name, site and advertising.

Sources of finance

Franchisees provide some of the initial capital, but banks are more willing to lend money to franchisees associated with a well-established company as they know that the applicant will have already been checked and approved by the firm. Banks also know how well the company's other franchisees have done.

Distribution of profits

Franchisees keep all the profit after they have paid a royalty, usually of around 10 per cent, to the franchiser.

 Draw up a table with four columns headed *Objectives*, *Control*, *Sources of finance* and *Distribution of profits*. Write Sole traders, Partnerships, Worker cooperatives and Franchising on separate lines in the left-hand margin of the table. Fill in the table.

RISKS OF SELF-EMPLOYMENT

Sole traders

There are varying degrees of **risk** (of financial loss or failure) in all forms of self-employment. They are usually higher than they are for employees.

The risks are probably greatest for sole traders who set up their own business. The failure rate is highest among those who have no previous training: for example, builders who have had no greater experience of their trade than carrying out DIY projects in their own home.

There are fewer failures among people who inherit their family's small business, such as a market stall or a petrol filling station.

The lowest rate of failure is among former employees who have gained specialized knowledge of a particular industry or profession which they believe they can put to better use than their former employer: for example, an art gallery employee who sets up a new gallery, or an Inland Revenue employee who becomes an independent tax consultant.

Buying a business from an established sole trader reduces the risk, as the business already has its own customers. You need to have expert advice, however, when you check the accounts! Even advertisements can sometimes be misleading. Look at the following advertisement:

WEST COUNTRY High-class tea rooms for sale. Own detached four-bedroom property in ½ acre grounds. Turnover £100,000 which could be increased. Annual profit £65,000. Must be viewed. Offers over £170,000.

The annual profit of £65,000 is almost certainly the gross profit and not the profit the owner actually receives after all expenses and running costs have been deducted, which would be considerably less.

► For more on gross profit, see **Trading accounts** in Chapter 19.

Other forms of self-employment

Worker cooperatives are probably the next highest risk group as they are a relatively new and little-tried form of business structure.

Partnerships, particularly long-established businesses with a large number of professional partners, are a lower risk. There is, however, always the risk that a new partner may not get on with the others. With only two or three partners, the risk of the partnership failing is probably about as high as it is in marriage!

Franchises with reputable firms may be the least risky, but care needs to be taken with some newer, smaller franchise operations.

Suggest what form of business organization you would recommend for the following people and explain why you have chosen them:

1   A 35-year-old man who cooks in a café in Hull and has just inherited £150,000 from an uncle in the United States. He wants to go on working, but doesn't want to take too many risks.
2   A woman of 23 who has been a New Age traveller and now wants to lead a more settled life. She has very little money, but is an expert dressmaker. She likes working with people in a small group where everyone is equal.
3   A woman architect from a wealthy family who has a large monthly income from a trust fund. She has very strong views about architecture and is ambitious to make a name for herself as quickly as she can. She likes working with others so long as they do what she says.

INSURANCE

Like all business people, the self-employed have to accept risks; but they try to reduce them as much as possible by taking out **insurance**. They take out a contract with an insurance company, which covers them or their business against stated risks, in return for a **premium**, or fixed amount of money paid to the company each year. If the business suffers loss or damage, the insurance company will pay financial compensation.

Compulsory insurance

There are two kinds of insurance that businesses must have by law:

- **Motor vehicle:** All motor vehicles must have third party insurance covering the owner against the death or injury of other people in an accident.
- **Employers' liability**: If you employ people, this insurance covers you for the death, injury or illness of an employee that occurs while he or she is working for you.

Other kinds of insurance

There are many other kinds of insurance, some more important than others. There are two factors that you need to consider when taking out insurance:

- the loss or damage you might suffer;
- the degree of risk.

It would be stupid to over-insure by taking out insurance against loss to goods in transit if you rarely send goods by road or if the actual value of the goods is small. Equally, it would be stupid to under-insure by not taking out public liability insurance which provides cover against death or injury to members of the public as a result of your business activities.

The following are some of the other types of insurance:

- **Property:** Business premises, plant and equipment, and stock should all be insured against fire, at least, and possibly other perils, or risks.
- **Product:** Cover is provided against defects in products you make, sell or repair that cause injury or damage to customers.
- **Theft:** This insurance is of growing importance because of the increase in break-ins and burglary.
- **Fidelity guarantee:** This insures against theft or fraud by employees.
- **Money:** Cover is provided against loss of cash, cheques, postage stamps and other documents of value on an all-risks basis, not only theft.
- **Bad debts:** Businesses are covered against the risk of debtors becoming insolvent and being unable to pay the money that they owe.
- **Computers:** Computer equipment is insured against theft, fire and other perils.
- **Frozen food:** This provides cover against loss of food in deep-freeze units if equipment or power fails.
- **Plate glass:** Expensive plate glass is insured against accidental damage and vandalism.
- **Business interruption:** This provides covers against loss of income or extra expenses caused by damage to property, such as a fire.

- **Professional indemnity:** This protects professional people, such as solicitors, against errors in their advice or actions.
- **Personal accident and sickness:** A self-employed person receives a weekly benefit if unable to work through accident or illness.
- **Permanent health:** A self-employed person receives a regular income if unable to work through long-term illness.
- **Life insurance:** If a self-employed person dies, the dependants receive a sum of money.

Businesses can obtain insurance through an insurance broker or from an insurance company. They usually offer packaged deals for particular kinds of businesses.

 Suggest which types of insurance the following businesspersons should take out and explain why you have chosen them.

1 A dealer in gold jewellery who is 55 years old and who has had a serious heart attack.
2 An antiques dealer who sells many antiques in Australia and the United States.
3 A butcher whose shop is situated on a run-down council estate.

1 Who usually runs the greatest risk of failure – a sole trader with no previous experience or a franchisee?
2 How does buying an established business reduce risk?
3 What kinds of insurance are compulsory for businesses?
4 Who would take out a professional indemnity insurance?
5 What is a fidelity guarantee insurance?

SUMMARY

- The number of self-employed people has risen sharply from the beginning of the 1980s because of government encouragement, the rise in unemployment in big companies, and a new spirit of enterprise.
- It is very easy to set up as a sole trader, but much more difficult to make the business work. Those who do best are people who inherit a family business or former employees who have a better knowledge of the market or a greater spirit of enterprise than their former employer.
- Partnerships of professionals, such as doctors and solicitors, often work well; but smaller partnerships of non-professionals have a greater tendency to split up.
- Worker cooperatives are a relatively new and not very common form of business structure in Britain. Some have failed through poor management and unrealistic objectives.

- Franchising is another fairly new form of business structure which originated in the United States. It can work very well if the franchiser is a reputable, well-managed and honest company.
- Risks are inherent in all business activities. They are probably greatest in new businesses set up by inexperienced small traders, and smallest in franchising, particularly where a well-established company is the franchiser.
- All businesses guard against excessive risk by taking out insurance. There are two kinds of insurance that are compulsory: motor vehicle and employers' liability. Other insurance policies provide cover for a large range of eventualities, or events that may occur. Unfortunately, this does not cover the failure of the business, as this is an uninsurable risk!

6 Limited companies

Chapter objectives

After working through this chapter, you will have the knowledge to:

▮ state the differences between limited companies and other kinds of businesses;

▮ describe the differences between a private and a public limited company – and their similarities;

▮ evaluate the significance of limited liability;

▮ calculate the tax advantages and disadvantages of forming a limited company;

▮ apply the principles of leadership to a declining business;

▮ identify possible conflicts over company profits;

▮ write a simple business plan;

▮ calculate percentage rise in profits;

▮ select methods of measuring business success;

▮ understand and use the following key terms: limited company, private limited company, public limited company, limited liability, unlimited liability, memorandum of association, articles of association, certificate of incorporation, board of directors, chief executive, autocratic leader, democratic leader, charismatic leader, retained profit, distributed profit, dividend, ordinary share, preference shares, business plan, turnover, size of business, profitability, market share, cost-effectiveness.

WHAT IS A LIMITED COMPANY?

A **limited company** has a totally different structure from any other kind of business. You will remember that the owners of the businesses described in Chapter 5 were all actively involved. They were sole traders, working alone; partners working with other partners; members of a worker cooperative working with the other members; and franchisees working under contract for a franchiser. Ownership and labour were combined.

In a limited company, ownership and labour are separated. The business is owned by its shareholders, who have bought a number of ordinary shares in the company. In most cases, the shareholders do not work in the firm; and many shareholders have never even seen the firm's premises.

The limited company is the most important type of business organization, producing the great majority of the wealth that is created in Britain and providing employment for the majority of the nation's workforce.

Private and public limited companies

There are two main types of limited company: the private limited company and the public limited company. There are essential differences between them.

Shares in the private limited company cannot be bought by members of the public, but only by a small circle of people who are personally known to the people who started the firm or to members of their family. That is why they are called private limited companies. Usually, shareholders who want to dispose of their shares can sell them only to the other shareholders. Companies of this kind have the word 'Limited', usually abbreviated to 'Ltd', after the name of the firm or its founder, such as John Smith Ltd.

In contrast, anyone can buy and sell shares in a public limited company through a share shop or a stockbroker. That is why they are called public limited companies. The company must have a minimum **share capital** of £50,000 – money that the shareholders have invested in the business. Companies of this type have 'plc', standing for 'public limited company', after their name, such as Sunrise plc.

 Draw up a table with two columns headed *Private limited company* and *Public limited company* and note the main differences between them. When you have read the following section, add notes on their similarities.

Limited liability

A company is a legal entity: the law and the courts recognize that the company has a legal existence separate from its owners. Like people, a company can own property, make legal contracts with other companies or individuals, and sue them in the courts if there is any dispute.

As a consequence of the company's separate existence, the owners of the company, the shareholders, are not responsible for the debts of the company. Their liability is limited to the amount of money they have invested in the company. If a company stopped trading with debts of £500,000, each shareholder would lose only the money that he or she had invested individually, which might be just a few hundred pounds.

If investors were responsible for all the debts of a firm, many of them would refuse to invest. The risks would be much too high. This limited liability is the foundation of most modern business activity.

▶ An **entity** is something that has a real existence in itself.

▶ This means that the people and firms who were owed money by the company – or the creditors – would receive only part of the money they were owed if the firm was sold.

> **Limited liability**
> A form of legal protection for shareholders of a company who are liable only for the money they have already invested in the company and not for its debts if the company stops trading.

Retrieve your two-column table with the headings *Private limited company* and *Public limited company* and add notes on their similarities.

Unlimited liability

The devastating effects of **unlimited liability** were revealed in Lloyd's insurance market at the beginning of the 1990s. The wealthy investors – called 'names' – who helped to underwrite, or guarantee, insurance risks, had unlimited liability. When Lloyd's suffered huge losses, expected to total £4 billion for 1990–1, the names started to receive huge bills. Some were forced to sell their homes, their paintings and their jewellery, while others formed action groups to obtain legal advice about their situation. Lloyd's has now allowed limited liability companies to join its insurance market for the first time in its 300-year history.

Lloyd's was always exceptional. In the rest of business, it would be very difficult to raise the billions of pounds of capital needed every year to finance the development of existing firms and to create new companies if there were no limited liability.

You may be thinking that if limited companies have such great advantages, why don't all self-employed people form companies instead? Some of them do. Best-selling authors and top sports stars often form limited companies so that they can pay less tax. For the less wealthy self-employed, however, the financial costs would usually be greater than the gains.

1   Who owns a limited company?
2   What are the two main types of limited company?
3   Where would you buy shares in a public limited company?
4   What is meant by the phrase 'a company is a legal entity'?
5   Describe the risks of unlimited liability.
6   What other kinds of business also have unlimited liability?

 What would happen to British business if limited liability were abolished?

Disadvantages of limited companies

The main disadvantages of limited companies are:

- that they are complex to set up;
- that they must be publicly accountable;
- that they pay higher tax rates.

Complex procedures

It is more complicated, and expensive, to set up a limited company than it is to start a business as a sole trader. Under EU law, one

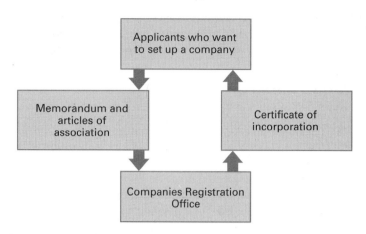

Setting up a limited company

person can form a company. You have to register the company with the Companies Registration Office. This involves sending a **memorandum of association**, giving the following information: the name of the company; the address of the company's registered office; the kind of business, for example making cakes; and the share capital. You would also have to send another document, the **articles of association**. This contains details of the internal management of the company, for example the powers of the directors and when shareholders' meetings will be held. If the Companies Registration Office is satisfied that everything is in order, it will issue a **certificate of incorporation** as a limited company. This all costs money.

Accountability

All company accounts have to be sent to the Companies Registration Office annually. Members of the public have the right to inspect them. An accountant must audit, or check, the company accounts, whereas the small trader can make out his or her own accounts. Companies can be fined if they are late in sending in their accounts.

Tax

Self-employed people with small profits would be worse off if they formed a limited company. At the time of writing, they pay tax at a rate of 20 per cent on the first £3,000 of their income (after expenses). They then pay 25 per cent on the rest, up to a maximum income of £23,700, when the tax rate changes to 40 per cent.

A company pays corporation tax at 25 per cent if its profits are £300,000 or less. Above that level, corporation tax rises to 33 per cent. A sole trader who became a limited company would therefore lose the benefits of the 20 per cent tax rate.

 A sole trader who drew up her own accounts had a profit of £16,000 in a year. What would be the total tax bill? If she had formed a limited company, and the fees for auditing the accounts were £850, how much would she now pay in tax and fees on a profit of £16,000?

Refer to the section on partnership in Chapter 5, and then make notes contrasting the respective benefits and drawbacks of a partnership and a private limited company.

> **A limited company**
> A limited company is a registered company with a separate legal existence whose shareholders are financially liable only for the money they have put into the company.

CONTROL OF PRIVATE LIMITED COMPANIES

Private limited companies and public limited companies are run in different ways. The diagram in the margin shows the system of control in a private company. The shareholders, who own the firm, have the ultimate power, or final say. They appoint the **board of directors** who decide the company's objectives and its policy. The managing director, who is appointed by the board, is responsible for carrying out the policy, along with other directors and managers.

However, in family firms and other small companies, these functions are combined. The directors are often the only shareholders. The chair of the board of directors is often also the managing director. The other directors are in charge of different departments. The structure is more like that of a partnership, with the important added advantage of limited liability.

Control can become more difficult if family friends or business associates have been allowed to buy a significant number of shares. They might have different ideas about how the firm should be run. Different opinions can be voiced at shareholders' meetings.

Control of a private limited company

CONTROL IN PUBLIC LIMITED COMPANIES

 Read the following case study and answer the questions at the end.

Daneside Hotels plc is a small chain of six hotels with a total of 300 rooms, in the West Country. All the hotels have a three-star rating.

The chairman of the board of directors was an autocratic, or high-handed, man who liked to make all the decisions himself. Coming from a wealthy family, he wanted to keep up the standards of the past. Men were requested to wear a jacket and tie in the restaurant, and women were asked not to wear trousers. There were flowers in all the bedrooms, and specially manufactured soap and shampoos in the bathrooms. Daily newspapers and early morning tea were provided free for guests. The hotels had large staffs with many full-time workers. The gardens and grounds of the hotels were always kept in immaculate order.

The hotels continued to attract a number of regular clients, many of whom were wealthy, elderly women who had been customers for many years. They were never grateful for the attention they received from the staff; in fact, their constant complaints about the service, and almost everything else, annoyed many of the younger guests.

Like many other hotels, the chain had a tough time in the recession at the beginning of the 1990s because individuals, businesspeople and companies had not been spending so freely. The room occupancy rate in the previous year was only 40 per cent on average, meaning that 60 per cent of the rooms were unlet. In the current year, room occupancy had dropped to 30 per cent, much lower than its local competitors, who had a room occupancy rate of 50 per cent. At the same time, sales of food and drink had also decreased from £2 million to £1.46 million a year.

The advertised rate of £75 for a single room was much more than the hotels actually received. With discounts and special offers, the real room rate, including both singles and doubles, was £50 a night.

The company was heavily in debt to its bankers. During the boom years of the 1980s, it had borrowed millions of pounds to refurbish and extend the hotels. It still owed the bank £5 million, which was more than the hotels were worth on the current market. It was obvious that the situation could not go on for ever; but the chairman refused to listen to other members of the board of directors.

The chief executive

The young chief executive of the group wanted to introduce new policies that would restore the profitability of the group and enable it to start paying off its debts. He wanted to target new kinds of customers. He wanted to attract more local organizations to hold dinner-dances and other events at the hotels. Nationally, he wanted to concentrate far more on business visitors and conferences during the week and on young families and couples at the weekends. One of the six hotels would be changed into an up-market family hotel with crèches and other facilities for children.

At the same time, he would cut costs by replacing any full-time workers who left their jobs with part-time workers and by cutting out the free newspapers and other frills. Breakfast, for example, would be made into a buffet meal, which would cut the number of waitresses needed by two-thirds. Hotel managers would be put on performance-related pay which, in this case, would mean that they would get pay rises and bonuses only if the profits of their hotels increased.

These measures, and others, would increase profits by 25 per cent in the short term.

However, the chairman, who dominated the rest of the board, just brushed the chief executive's plans aside. The

▶ See **Performance-related pay** in Chapter 20.

group's turnover continued to fall. Matters came to a head when the bank called in the chairman. The bank told him that unless the group increased its profits, it would demand immediate repayment of the £5 million debt.

1 How many rooms on average were let per day during the current year?
2 How much did the company make from letting rooms per day?
3 What was the total income from letting rooms per year?
4 What was the turnover, or total sales of the group in the current year, i.e. from letting rooms and selling food and drink?
5 If total costs were £3.25 million per year, what profit or loss would the company make?
6 What factors were responsible for the company's problems? Put them in order of importance and explain them.

Powers of shareholders

As the case study has shown, control in public limited companies can often be more complicated than in private companies. It is often more difficult to run a large organization than a small one.

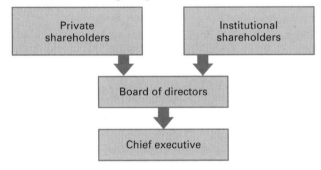

Control of a public limited company

As the figure above shows, large public limited companies, which attract millions of pounds of investment, usually have two kinds of holders of ordinary shares. At shareholders' meetings, investors have one vote for each ordinary share they hold. The vote of a private investor with a few thousand shares usually has little influence on company policy. If the company is doing well, most private investors never go to shareholders' meetings. It is only if the company is in trouble that a few private shareholders might attend the Annual General Meeting. Institutional investors, like pension funds and insurance companies, who hold hundreds of thousands of shares, have a much greater influence over company affairs. They can, for example, make demands for changes in policy, or for the chairperson of the board or the chief executive to be replaced. Like the bank in the case study, they have enormous power.

Powers of the chairperson and chief executive

In theory, the board of directors is responsible for deciding company objectives, but in practice the policy is frequently made by the

► The senior manager, who was in overall control of day-to-day running of a plc, was formerly known as the managing director. Now, he or she is frequently known as the chief executive. Occasionally, plcs have both a chief executive and a managing director.

chairperson of the board of directors. The chief executive is responsible for the day-to-day running of the company. If the chairperson and the chief executive (or managing director) agree on policy and get on well together, the company is likely to prosper. If there is conflict between them, the company usually suffers, as it did in the case study. Not only were there differences over policy, but there was also a clash of personalities, with a strong chairman and a weak, less experienced managing director.

1 What is underwriting?
2 Give three possible disadvantages for a small trader who forms a limited company.
3 Who is responsible for the day-to-day running of a private company?
4 What is a plc?
5 How much capital is required to start a public limited company?
6 Explain the difference between a private investor and an institutional investor.

Types of leader

There are three main types of leaders in companies, and they can be found at all levels of the organization from top managers to supervisors.

• **Autocratic leaders** want to have total control, make all the decisions, and be the boss all the time, like the chairman in the hotel case study above. The heads of many top companies are autocratic leaders.
• **Democratic leaders** like everyone to have a say and want to encourage people to work on their own and to delegate responsibility to other people. Leaders of this type are becoming more common in companies with quality management systems.
• **Charismatic leaders** have personalities that appeal to employees and inspire them to work hard. There are only a handful of charismatic leaders in Britain's top 100 companies. Charismatic leaders are born, not made.

Take either a democratic or a charismatic leader and explain what differences he or she might have made to the problems of the hotel chain in the case study above.

Make notes on the differences in control between public and private limited companies.

DISTRIBUTION OF PROFITS

The company directors decide what to do with the profit that remains after tax has been paid. They will keep some as **retained**

profit to expand the business by buying new assets, such as machinery and equipment, or use it to pay off debts.

The rest – the **distributed profit** – will be used to pay shareholders a **dividend**. This is the amount of money that shareholders receive as their share of the profits. It is paid once, or sometimes twice, a year – or not at all if a company cannot afford it. The dividend is expressed as a percentage. For example, if the dividend were 6 per cent, the owners of an **ordinary share**, which had a value of £1 when it was issued, would receive a 6p dividend for every share they hold. With ordinary shares, the size of the dividend varies according to how well or badly the business is doing and how much profit is retained. Dividends on preference shares are usually fixed. They have priority over ordinary shares in the payment of dividends and if the company is liquidated or closed down.

1 What are the three main kinds of business leader?
2 Who decides how profit is distributed in a plc?
3 Why is it necessary for a business to retain some of its profits?
4 What is a dividend?

Conflicts over profits

Conflicts over profit

In large companies, there is often a conflict of interests over profits. Shareholders want companies to pay high dividends. The directors, however, may want to pay as small a dividend as possible, so that they can keep a bigger share as retained profit. The company's employees, who usually have no voice in how profits are distributed, want higher wages and salaries for themselves rather than bigger profits for shareholders. Managers, too, may want higher salaries and for their salaries to rise faster than those of other employees. Directors may also be more interested in keeping money in the business so that they can increase its prestige, or status, by renting luxurious headquarters and providing themselves with personal jets. (Many chairpersons also want personal jets and yachts for their own use, but they are not always so keen for top managers and other directors to have them.)

Indirectly, many other groups are also interested in what happens to company profits. Consumers don't want companies to make higher profits if that means that they have to pay higher prices in the shops, or receive higher telephone, gas and electricity bills. Trade unions want higher wages for their members, rather than higher dividends for the shareholders or higher salaries for management. The government wants companies to make higher profits as this creates more wealth and boosts the nation's prosperity, and also increases the amount of corporation tax the government receives.

 Write notes to explain what conflicts there could be in a company over the distribution of profits and why they occur.

BUSINESS PLANS

Why business plans are necessary

Companies – and all other kinds of business – need to make a **business plan** if they are to succeed. Without a plan, the business will lack any sense of direction and will always be at the mercy of any change in outside conditions. Some sole traders keep their business plans in their mind, remember all the details and have total control. However, even they need to have a written business plan if they want to obtain a loan from a financial institution. In larger businesses, a written plan is essential, not only to raise money, but also to let the other people involved in the business – partners, franchisers, managers, etc. – know what is happening and likely to happen.

► For more on sole traders obtaining finance, see Chapter 18, page 235.

Essential elements in a plan

Although business plans may cover many sheets of paper, there are certain elements that all business plans should contain. They are essential if the plan is being used to raise money from a bank or other financial institution.

A business plan
- **Summary:** Highlight the best points about the existing, or proposed, business. Give forecasts of how the plan will increase sales and profits. State how much money is needed and what it will be used for.
- **Background:** If the firm is established, state when the business was started and what it has achieved so far. If it is

a new firm, the previous business records of its founders should be given.

- **Management:** Describe the methods of management and the quality of managers. Explain how the business plan will be put into effect.

  ► See Chapter 8.

- **Marketing:** Describe the size of the market and the firm's targeted segment or niche. Give details of any competitors and the strategy for competing with them.

  ► See Chapter 9.

- **Product(s):** Give a brief description of the firm's product or products. Show how they are differentiated from similar products. State future development plans.

  ► See Chapter 11.

- **Production:** Describe how production facilities will be changed and give details of any new equipment that will be needed. State details of any suppliers and sub-contractors. Note labour requirements and explain how they will be fulfilled. Describe the business location and any plans for change.

  ► See Chapters 15–16.

- **Financial:** Say what finances are required, for how long, and for what purpose. Give information about costs, breakeven (the point at which the business goes into profit), cash flow forecasts, the profit and loss account and the balance sheet.

  ► See Chapters 17–19.

- **Objectives:** State where the business is now and where it is hoped it will be next year, the following year and the year after that. Describe objectives in detail in relation to profitability, market share, products and production.

ACT IN Refer back to the hotel case study on pages 61–3 and use the information to write a brief business plan for the group.

MEASURING BUSINESS SUCCESS

Rate of growth

How do businesses judge if their plans are succeeding? The main indicator of success for all private businesses is profit. Without it, no business can survive for long. This indicator of success can be expressed in more positive terms as a planned rate of growth over a number of years. For example, a firm with a current net profit before tax of £200,000 might set itself the following targets for the next three years:

► These methods of measuring business success apply to all kinds of businesses, not just companies.

► See **Business objectives** in Chapter 4.

Year 1	Year 2	Year 3
£240,000	£288,000	£345,600

It is a great advantage to express indicators in numbers, as it allows the rate of success to be measured accurately. It is easy to calculate that the planned percentage increase in profit in Year 1 was 20 per cent.

ACT IN What was the planned percentage rise in profit in Years 2 and 3?

► The percentage rise can be calculated by using the formula:

$$\text{percentage rise} = \left(\frac{\text{new profit}}{\text{old profit}} - 1 \right) \times 100$$

e.g. $[(240\ 000 \div 200\ 000) - 1] \times 100$
$= (1.2 - 1) \times 100 = 20\ \%$

If the actual figures for the three years were:

Year 1	Year 2	Year 3
£230,000	£287,500	£373,750

what was the actual percentage increase in each year?

Other ways of measuring growth

► See also Chapter 7.

There are other ways of measuring the growth of a business or its total size. **Turnover**, or total sales, could be used. Turnover can be expressed either in money terms or in terms of volume. For example, a housebuilder might set a target for the year of £4.5 million in money or fifty houses in volume.

Another way of measuring company size is by the number of employees. A final method is by the assets or the capital employed.

Size of business

The size of a company can be measured officially using: (1) turnover, (2) the number of employees and (3) the assets, or what a company owns.

	Small companies	Medium-sized companies
Turnover	£2 million or less	£8 million or less
Employees	50 or fewer	250 or fewer
Assets	£975,000 or less	£2.8 million or less

It is sufficient to satisfy any two of the three criteria to be classified as a small or medium-sized company.

There is no official definition of a big company. The biggest companies are usually public limited companies, whose shares are quoted on the Stock Exchange. Of these, 100 companies are unofficially accepted as the biggest and the best. The *Financial Times* uses the share prices of these companies to compile one of its indexes of average share prices on the Stock Exchange. This index, called the

► There are about 1 million private limited companies in Britain, and 11,500 public limited companies.

Equity dealing room of stockbrokers Capel-Cure Myers in the City of London

FT SE 100 index and commonly known as 'Footsie', is updated by the minute to provide investors with the latest share prices.

 Look in the *Financial Times* or another quality newspaper over five days and make a note of the Footsie index each day. Read the financial pages and news pages to find out why the index has changed or remained more or less the same. Write a brief report accounting for what has happened.

MEASURING EFFICIENCY

It is important to remember that turnover, the number of employees, assets and even profit are a measure of size only. They do not measure efficiency.

Turnover shows how big a company is, but it does not measure efficiency. Total sales might increase, but net profit could have fallen if the firm has been forced to cut its prices because of low demand.

The number of employees is no measure of efficiency either. In fact, it can be argued that a large number of employees is an indication of inefficiency. Some privatized firms still have huge labour forces inherited from their years as nationalized industries. For example, British Telecommunications had 244,400 employees in 1989. This was reduced to 170,700 by 1993; and at the time of writing British Telecommunications is cutting another 30,000 jobs.

How a company's assets are employed is far more important than its size.

Profit is some guide to efficiency, but a better measure is **profitability**. This can be calculated by relating profit to the capital (or assets) used in a business.

▶ See also **Return on capital employed** in Chapter 19.

MARKET SHARE

A more reliable guide to efficiency is a firm's **market share**, or its percentage of total sales in a particular market. Competition for market share of mass consumption goods and services is always particularly fierce in such industries as cars, groceries and telecommunications.

Market share can be measured in two ways – by volume and by price. For example, the British market for wine is:

	Volume	Price
1992	744 million litres	£3.6 billion
1997 (forecast)	803 million litres	£5 billion

Therefore, a firm that wanted to gain a 5 per cent share of the market by volume in 1997 would have to sell 40.15 million litres.

▶ (803,000,000 ÷ 100) × 5 = 40,150,000

 If a supermarket had a 12 per cent share of the British wine market in 1992, how many litres would it have sold? If it wanted to increase its market share to 15 per cent by 1997, what would be its target volume sales?

Firms compete fiercely to gain the biggest market share of the British market whether it is for wine, instant coffee or cars. For the biggest companies, the world is their limit! They compete to gain the biggest global market share of, for example, computers or soft drinks.

One way of increasing efficiency is to keep prices low, because this will tend to maintain sales. Prices can be kept low by making the business more cost-effective. This is achieved by making sure that the costs of running the business are kept as low as possible in relation to the financial returns.

The ultimate test of long-term business success and efficiency is always customer satisfaction. Unless a firm's customers are satisfied with its products and the price they are asked to pay, the firm's market share will, sooner or later, start to decline.

1 What is another word for turnover?
2 What are assets?
3 How does profit differ from profitability?
4 State two ways of measuring market share.
5 How would you measure the size of medium and small companies?
6 What is the 'Footsie index'?

A plc's annual accounts contained the following information about this year's results compared with those of the previous year:

Turnover up 15 per cent
Profits down 2 per cent
Number of employees down 8 per cent
Market share up 1 per cent
Assets up 5 per cent

Select the most significant indicators of business success and explain what has been happening in general to the company during the past year.

SUMMARY

- There are two main types of company: private limited companies (Ltd), whose shares are only available to a small number of people; and public limited companies (plc), whose shares are listed on the Stock Exchange and can be bought and sold by members of the public.
- The great advantage of a limited company is that shareholders' liability is restricted to the amount of money they have invested. However, companies are expensive to set up, and their affairs are less private as their accounts are available for public inspection.
- There can be conflicts over control in private limited

companies if a large number of shares have been sold to other businesspeople or organizations.

- There are likely to be more conflicts over control and the distribution of profits in public limited companies.
- Institutional shareholders who hold a large number of shares may not agree with the policies of the board of directors. There can be conflicts between the chairperson and the chief executive. There can also be conflicts over how much profit should be retained for buying new assets and expansion, and how much should be distributed to shareholders.
- All businesses need to have a business plan to provide clear objectives, to enable them to measure success, and to help them to obtain loans.
- Business success can be measured in several ways – by net profit, turnover, number of employees and the value of assets. Efficiency is measured by profitability, market share and cost-effectiveness.
- The biggest measure of business success is always customer satisfaction.

Company growth and contraction

MOTIVES FOR COMPANY GROWTH

The owners of companies – the shareholders – and the directors and top managers usually have one common aim. They want their company to be big and powerful.

Shareholders want their company to grow because bigger companies have greater financial resources and are, therefore, less likely to go out of business. Also, dividends are likely to be higher.

Directors and managers want their company to grow because they will have much greater power and influence in the business world. Their views are more likely to be listened to and treated with respect by other business leaders and the government. They can spend more on developing new ideas and products. The company's prestige, or high reputation, attracts the brightest and most talented staff.

There are other reasons, too, why it is useful to be big. As a firm grows in size, its costs will fall owing to internal economies of scale. The most important internal economies, or savings, are:

Internal economies of scale

- **Technical economies:** Bigger firms getting more orders can afford to buy better machines. These produce more goods at lower costs. Although better machines cost more to buy, they provide greater savings in the end.
- **Buying economies:** Big firms can buy raw materials or goods in bulk, or large quantities, and can therefore get a discount – a lower price – from the supplier.
- **Marketing economies:** The cost of advertising products is spread over a larger number of units sold. Advertising is therefore cheaper than it is for smaller firms.
- **Financial economies:** It is easier for a big firm to borrow money because of its greater financial security. It can also borrow money more cheaply, as its size gives it the power to bargain with the lenders. The sources of finance are wider, too, including issues of new shares and rights issues for plcs.
- **Administrative economies:** As production and sales increase, the costs of management, particularly computer costs, do not go up at the same rate, creating a saving in administration costs.
- **Distribution economies:** Bigger firms can use their transport more efficiently by carrying larger loads.
- **Risk-bearing economies:** Big companies are exposed to fewer risks than smaller firms because they usually sell in more overseas markets and have a wider range of products. If one country is in recession, another country's economy may be booming; and if one product is not selling well, another product may be in great demand.

► For more on sources of finance for large companies, see Chapter 18, pp. 240–1.

ACT IN Visit the supermarket that you or your family use most frequently and ask a supervisor if you can have a brief talk with a manager. Ask him or her how the relevant economies of scale (listed in the box above) save money in the running of the business. Write a brief report giving details of how each applies to the store. If you cannot obtain an interview, ask someone you know who works in a supermarket to answer your questions – or maybe you can answer the questions yourself if you work, or have worked, in a supermarket. Alternatively, visit a supermarket and observe as many economies of scale as possible.

METHODS OF GROWTH

There are three main ways in which a business can grow. It can grow through:

- internal expansion;
- mergers;
- takeovers.

Internal expansion

Natural growth

If a business is being run efficiently, the sales of its products will rise. This will increase its profits. The owners may take some of this extra profit for themselves, but much of it will usually be ploughed back into the business. This new investment will make the business grow even more. There is, therefore, a natural tendency for efficient businesses to grow.

Planned growth

▶ See **Market share** in Chapter 6.

All successful firms plan to grow by increasing their share of the market. They can increase their market share by improving their products and making them more competitive in price. A manufacturer of disposable razors could use better steel to improve blade performance, and could sell a six-razor pack for the price of five. A sports shop could increase its range of goods to cover more sports and offer discounts to customers who spend more than £100.

 Look around your local high street and find three different examples of new products or competitive prices in (a) mortgages and (b) chemists' goods. State what effects you think they would have on sales.

Geographical expansion

A firm can also expand by entering new markets at home or overseas. For example, a supermarket with stores in the north of England might decide to open stores in the south. This might be a risky venture as there are many successful supermarkets already operating there. One strategy for success might be to sell discounted, or lower-priced, goods.

▶ Exporting is very important for Britain as we do not produce all the goods we want. Therefore, British business has to export a large amount of goods each year to pay for the goods we import.

Exporting goods to foreign countries is another way of making a business grow. There are many difficulties:

- The markets, the people and often the languages are different.
- Foreign countries often make it difficult for exporters by imposing **tariffs**, or taxes, on imported goods and by setting **quotas** that limit the number they can sell.
- Changes in exchange rates can have a great effect on the income generated from the sale of goods.

▶ See **Exchange Rates** in Chapter 12 and marginal note on p. 75.

- Buyers in some foreign countries may not pay for the goods they have received. (The government's Export Credits Guarantee Department provides insurance against this risk for a premium, or payment, by the exporter.)
- It is administratively complex, because many documents and forms have to be filled in

Many of these barriers to trade have been swept away by the European Union (EU). The member-countries form a single market without tariffs or quotas, where goods that are legally sold in one country can be sold in all. Although these changes have made it easier to sell in other member-countries, it is often more difficult to sell goods in the rest of Europe than it is at home.

1 State five economies of scale.
2 In what three main ways can a business grow?
3 Describe four difficulties firms may face in exporting.
4 What is the main advantage of the single market to British business?

Diversification

Diversification is another way in which a business can expand. A firm can diversify in various ways:

- It can develop new products for its present market. A small firm selling taped cassettes of live concert recordings in street markets could start producing cassettes of studio recordings. This is a fairly low-risk diversification as the market is already well known and it would be possible to make a firm estimate of likely sales.
- It can produce new products for a different market. The same firm could start producing CDs to sell in music stores. This is obviously a very high-risk diversification, as both the product and the market are new. To jump straight from a street market to a high-street market full of powerful competitors is never easy and may be the quickest way to commit business suicide!

Yet, some form of diversification is important for all businesses, except the most famous and specialized, such as Rolls-Royce cars. Diversification gives firms an opportunity to expand and reduces risks by spreading them over different products or different markets.

The **single-product firm** runs even greater risks because the market for its goods may collapse. Sub-contractors who work entirely for a bigger firm are at greatest risk. For example, when a coal mine is closed, many smaller engineering firms who have been making equipment for the mine are also affected.

1 What is diversification?
2 Give one example of (a) low-risk diversification and (b) high-risk diversification.
3 What advantage would a single-product firm gain by diversifying?
4 How might a shop selling early-learning toys increase its market share?

Make brief notes on the four methods of internal expansion, bringing out the differences between them.

▶ **Exchange rates**
- If the exchange rate stood at £1 = $1.40, a product costing £1,000 would sell in the United States for $1,400.
- If the pound strengthened to £1 = $1.50, the price in the United States would rise to $1,500.
- If the pound weakened to £1 = $1.30, the price would fall to $1,300.
- A weak pound makes exporting easier; a strong pound makes exporting more difficult.

▶ **Diversification** is making a new kind of product or going into a new market.

Mergers

Companies can also expand by merging with another company so that they become one firm. It is much quicker to grow through a **merger** than through internal expansion. A merger is also a very useful way of gaining a foothold in a foreign country. After the merger, the two companies are usually reorganized. Some employees are often made redundant to increase profitability and productivity.

There are four main kinds of mergers:

- horizontal;
- lateral;
- vertical forwards;
- vertical backwards.

Horizontal and lateral mergers

A **horizontal merger** occurs when a firm merges with another firm that has the same product. The main advantages are:

- economies of scale;
- greater market share;
- opportunities for more specialization.

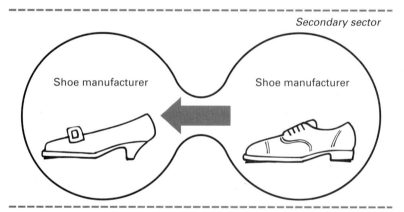

Secondary sector

Shoe manufacturer   Shoe manufacturer

Horizontal merger

A **lateral merger** is the joining together of two firms with similar products. The main advantages are:

- diversification;
- easy entry to a new market.

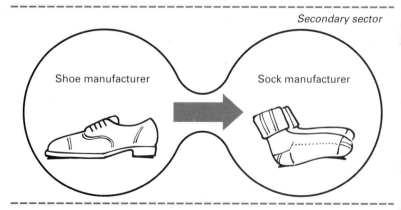

Secondary sector

Shoe manufacturer   Sock manufacturer

Lateral merger

Vertical mergers

A **vertical forwards merger** occurs when a firm in the same industry joins with another firm at a later stage of production. For example, a shoe manufacturer, which is in the secondary sector, might merge with a chain of shoe shops, which is in the tertiary sector. The main advantage for the shoe manufacturer is obtaining a guaranteed outlet for its products. The main advantage for the shoe shops is obtaining guaranteed supplies and having more control over them.

▶ To refresh your memory, see **Primary**, **Secondary** and **Tertiary sectors of production** in Chapter 2.

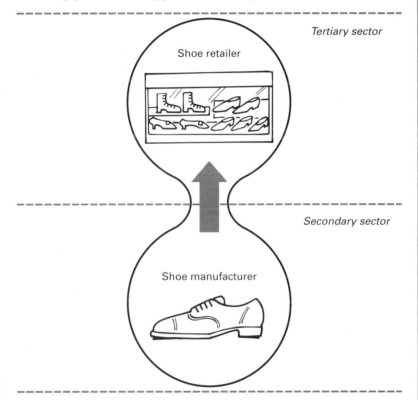

Tertiary sector

Shoe retailer

Secondary sector

Shoe manufacturer

Vertical forwards merger

A **vertical backwards merger** is when a firm combines with a firm in the same industry at an earlier stage in production. For example, the shoe manufacturer could merge with a hide merchant that supplies leather for shoes, which is in the primary sector. The main advantage for the shoe manufacturer is safeguarding supplies. The main advantage for the hide merchant is having assured sales.

▶ Hide, or animal skin, is made into leather by soaking it in tannic acid or treating it with mineral salts.

1 What is a merger?
2 State the four main types of merger.
3 With what kind of firm would a potter combine in a horizontal merger?
4 State the main advantage for a manufacturer who merges with a retail group. What is the full name of this kind of merger?
5 Draw a chart showing the mergers an oil company might make in its own sector of production and in the other two sectors.

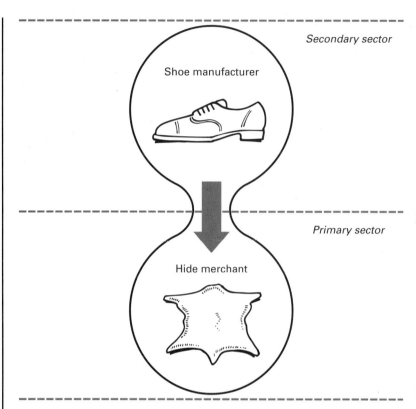

Vertical backwards merger

The following diagram combines all the different forms of merger.

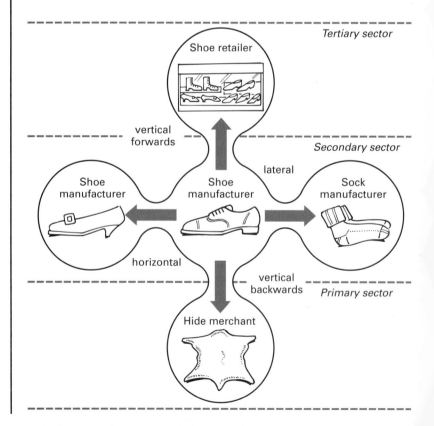

Different kinds of merger

A company is planning a merger. Determine the most suitable form of merger for the company if its primary objective is:

(a) to increase its market share;
(b) to enter a new market in Britain;
(c) to expand sales of its consumer goods in a foreign country;
(d) to safeguard its supplies; or
(e) to provide more work for its sales representatives, who currently cover the whole of Britain.

 Make notes on the different types of mergers. Include a diagram showing the four kinds of mergers for a music cassette manufacturer.

Takeovers

 Read the following case study and answer the questions at the end.

Now that Truckhire plc is coming out of recession, it is thinking of expanding again. It is considering making a takeover bid for a much smaller firm, Carhire plc.

Truckhire sells and rents out trucks and trailers. During the recession, it sold very few trucks. The recession also greatly reduced its long-term contract hire business, which involves hiring out trucks to firms and maintaining them for a fixed rental fee. However, it managed to survive by cutting staff and increasing its short-term truck rentals for which a higher daily or weekly rate is charged. It never failed to make a profit in any year, although its turnover declined. Now, both its turnover and its profits are shooting up again.

Carhire did not cope nearly as well during the recession. Its car-hire business for both business and personal use dropped dramatically. Its fixed costs, such as insurance, computer systems and car maintenance, remained as high as ever; but it failed to cut staff or to sell off surplus vehicles. As a result, it started to make a loss. Carhire's key results are shown in the following table.

	Turnover (£ million)	Pre-tax profit (£ million)	Dividend (£ million)
1989	9	1.9	2.5
1990	8	0.4	1.5
1991	7.5	−0.2	0.5
1992	6.9	−0.6	0.5
1993	7.2	−0.1	nil

The chairman of Truckhire is very keen to buy Carhire. He says that it had a good record before the recession and it should be easy to turn it round again. The finance director is opposed, as she thinks that it is risky to merge two firms that were affected in the same way during a recession. She would rather diversify into a different kind of business. The marketing director also has some doubts because Carhire was in a different section of the market. His staff are used to dealing with business users, but he is not so sure how they would cope with personal users. A great deal of training might be required. The Technical Director, however, supports the chairman. He thinks that the takeover would produce economies of scale in vehicle maintenance.

1 How did Truckhire survive the recession?
2 Why did Carhire make a loss during the recession?
3 Who would have been affected when Carhire failed to pay a dividend?
4 If the takeover succeeds, what kind of merger will it be?
5 Draw up a table with two columns headed *For the takeover* and *Against the takeover*. Fill in the table.
6 If you were on Truckhire's board of directors, would you be in favour of the proposed takeover or against it? Give your reasons.

Takeover bids

A **takeover bid** is a means of gaining control of another company by trying to buy over 50 per cent of its voting shares. For example, Company A wants to acquire Company B. It hopes to acquire shares in Company B by offering shareholders a better price for their shares than the current price on the Stock Exchange. The offer may be in cash, or in Company A shares, or a mixture of both.

> ▶ All owners of ordinary shares are entitled to vote at company meetings, although some companies have a smaller number of ordinary shares with limited or no voting rights, which are known as 'A' shares. Some preference shares have voting rights; others do not.

Most takeover bids are friendly and involve a plc taking over a private limited company when its founder wants to take his or her profit and retire. A few are unfriendly, for example when one plc wants to take over another plc to split it up and sell off property or unwanted subsidiary companies to make a quick profit. These bids are usually strongly resisted by the target company. The battle can become even fiercer if another plc makes a rival bid for the target company.

Conglomerates

Conglomerates are usually formed by a series of takeover bids. A conglomerate is a number of merged firms operating in different product and market areas. For example, a big brewer might fear that the Monopolies and Mergers Commission (see page 81) would stop it taking over any more breweries or public houses as it would have too big a market share. Instead, the brewer might expand by taking over companies involved in gas distribution, commercial property and packaging.

A conglomerate has the great advantage that risks are spread over a wide range of markets. If one market is lifeless, another may be very active.

 In your public library, find Volume 1 of the reference book *Who Owns Whom*, which is published by Dun & Bradstreet International. Turn to page xv at the beginning of the book, where you will find a list of Standard Industrial Classification (SIC) Codes, each composed of four digits. As you look through the index, you will see that the first digit from 0 to 9 indicates a broad group of industries.

Now turn to the main section, UK parents, which shows the main British companies and the **subsidiary companies** that they control. On the right of each entry, there are a number of SIC codes showing the broad group of industries in which the parent company and its subsidiaries operate. Choose a company with several SIC codes beginning with a different digit, e.g. 1311, 3281, 5088 and 7527. This indicates that the company is a conglomerate because it operates in different industries. Look up the codes in the index to find the industries.

Draw a chart showing the parent company and its name and address, and the industries in which its subsidiaries operate. Include the number of subsidiary companies at the bottom of the chart. (If you run into difficulties ask the reference librarian to help you.)

CONTROLS ON BUSINESS EXPANSION

Monopolies

A **monopoly** exists when one firm has total control over the production of a good or service. The firm is therefore able to charge what price it likes, which would be against the public interest. There are only a few monopolies, such as British Rail before privatization, but there are far more areas in which a near-monopoly situation might develop. The government and the EU try to make sure that fair competition exists so that consumers get low prices and a wide choice of goods and services.

The **Monopolies and Mergers Commission** (MMC) was set up by an Act of Parliament in 1948 to investigate mergers that would be against the public interest. It may start an investigation if the takeover firm already has a 25 per cent share of the market, or if the assets of the target firm exceed £30 million. When the investigation is complete, the MMC makes recommendations to the President of the Board of Trade, but only the President can stop the merger or allow it to go ahead.

The MMC can also investigate other anti-competitive practices such as:

- **price-fixing**, where two or more firms agree to keep prices at a high level;
- **cartels**, where two or more firms agree to restrict output to keep up prices.

The EU can also investigate mergers in Britain (and other member countries). Normally, it would investigate mergers that might prevent, restrict or distort competition in the Single Market. It has powers to stop mergers, or even to rule that the companies must be demerged, or split up, if they are in breach of EU competition rules. The EU has the power to fine companies millions of pounds if they break EU rules.

Make notes on the work the Monopolies and Mergers Commission and the powers of the European Union over British mergers.

Other controls

There are other business practices that might also be considered anti-competitive or unfair:

- **exclusive purchasing contracts**, where a firm has to agree to buy from a single supplier;
- **selective distributive systems**, where a supplier will deal only with distributors who keep a certain level of stock or provide specified before- and after-sales services;
- **tie-ins**, where a supplier of a product insists that customers must buy all, or part of, another product as well;
- restricting supplies of parts to dealers.

These practices can be investigated by the Director General of the Office of Fair Trading under the Competition Act of 1980. These practices are not necessarily anti-competitive in themselves. It is the effects that are important. If the Director General decides that the effects are anti-competitive, he or she can ask the firm to stop the practice. If the firm refuses, the matter can be referred to the MMC for further investigation.

The Fair Trading Act of 1973 set up the Office of Fair Trading with a Director General of Fair Trading. The Director General also has powers to protect consumer interests.

The Restrictive Trade Practices Act of 1976 prevents firms from fixing prices or dividing up the market between them, unless permission is obtained from the Restrictive Practices Court.

 Explain the work of the Director General of Fair Trading in relation to anti-competitive business practices.

DISECONOMIES OF SCALE

Takeovers and mergers are not a certain path to business success. The takeover company may have little knowledge of the new market, or it may be difficult to create an effective team out of the merged managements. As a result the new company becomes difficult to control and increasingly inefficient. This causes costs to rise, which produces diseconomies of scale. Here are some of the main causes:

▶ **Diseconomies of scale** are the result of the difficulties of controlling a very large organization. They can lead to inefficiency, inflexibility and increased costs.

- **Too many managers:** As the company grows in size, new layers of managers are installed. This not only increases costs, but also stops quick decisions being made.
- **Lack of vision:** Because the company seems so big and powerful, managers begin to think it is the centre of the universe. They start to lose touch with the real world outside the company walls.
- **Inflexibility:** The managers become too inflexible, or fixed,

in their attitudes. They do not respond to challenges from smaller competitors until it is too late.

- **Poor communications:** In a big firm, it is easy for top managers to lose touch with their subordinates, or managers of a lower rank, and for messages to become distorted or lost as they travel along the long lines of communication. This problem is even worse for multinationals with companies in many countries.
- **Lack of motivation:** Employees often feel that they are just a company number, not an individual, and lose their motivation to work hard and succeed.

Draw up a table with two columns headed *Economies of scale* and *Diseconomies of scale*. Use the information at the beginning of the chapter and the information above to make brief notes of the main points in the appropriate column.

1 What is the purpose of a takeover bid?
2 Why might a monopoly be against the public interest?
3 Give three examples of anti-competitive business practices.
4 State two reasons why a takeover may fail.

CONTRACTION OF COMPANIES

More than half of all takeovers fail, with great losses for the parent company. Sometimes, the subsidiary company has to be sold off cheaply or closed down. Occasionally, it drags the parent company into so much debt that both are forced out of business.

It is better for the parent company to take preventative action at an earlier stage by reducing its size, or **downsizing**. It can then concentrate more on its **core business** – its main business in the market that it knows best, which provides its biggest profits.

Demergers

One way of reducing company size is by demerging part of the group and making it into a separate company. There are various reasons for a demerger. It may be a defence to a threatened takeover of the whole group. Or it may give a successful part of the group greater independence and freedom to grow.

▶ In 1993, the ICI group demerged its medical drugs, agrochemicals and speciality chemicals business into a new company called Zeneca. ICI shareholders were given one Zeneca share for each ICI share they held.

Management buy-outs and buy-ins

Another way of downsizing is through a **management buy-out**. When a big company wants to get rid of a division or a subsidiary company, it will often offer it to the existing managers – for a price. The managers have to draw up a financial and business plan to see if venture capitalists, banks or other financial institutions will finance them. They also have to put some money into the business by buying shares.

▶ In the ten years between 1982 and 1992, there were 3,755 management buy-outs in Britain. There were also 823 management buy-ins.

Most management buy-outs succeed. The managers often know their business and their markets better than the group managers do. They are also highly motivated as their shares will soar in value if the company prospers. Sometimes the managers buy out the whole company to prevent it from being closed.

An alternative method of saving a company when it is in financial trouble because of bad management is a **management buy-in**. Financial institutions, which have lent money to the company, may threaten to close the company, unless new managers are brought in to buy and run the business.

 Find a story about a merger or a management buy-out or buy-in in the financial pages of the *Financial Times* or any other quality newspaper, or a specialist magazine such as *The Economist* or the *Investors Chronicle*. Make a brief summary of the event and explain why it happened.

SUMMARY

- Shareholders, directors and managers are usually all united in wanting to see their company grow in size because there are great advantages, or economies of scale, in being big.
- There are three main methods of growth: internal expansion, mergers and takeovers.
- Internal expansion can occur through natural or planned growth, geographical expansion, and diversification.
- A quicker way of growing is by merging, or joining together, with one or more other companies, by agreement. Takeover bids are another method of growth. One company tries to gain control of another by buying a majority of its voting shares. Most takeover bids are friendly, but some are resisted by the target company.
- Takeover bids are often used to form conglomerates. These are companies that own a large number of subsidiary companies operating in different product and market areas.
- The government and the European Union impose controls on company growth and anti-competitive behaviour. The Director General of Fair Trading has powers to investigate anti-competitive practices and to protect consumer interest.
- Companies sometimes become so big that they are difficult to control. Management failures and inefficiency cause diseconomies of scale that may result in increased costs. The company may have to slim down its size to regain control and profitability.
- It can demerge part of the group and make it into a separate company; or it can offer to sell part of the group to the existing managers in a management buy-out. Sometimes, new managers are brought in to buy and run the business in a management buy-in.

8 Management structures

SOLE TRADER'S ORGANIZATION

Read the following and do the exercise at the end.

A sole trader's day: Blooming Health

Samantha owns a small health shop, called Blooming Health. As well as serving in the shop with her assistant, Zoë, she has a number of responsibilities and tasks to carry out. One day's activities are shown in the following table.

9 a.m.	Checks stocks of herbs and spices.
10 a.m.	Delivers vegetarian meals to hotels in her van.
11 a.m.	Interviews applicant for a post as Saturday assistant.
12 noon	Herbs and spice salesman makes monthly visit. She places an order.
1 p.m.	Asks regular shop assistant if she would like to do window display.
2 p.m.	Visits bank manager to discuss business plan for a loan.
3 p.m.	Decides to reduce the price of organic potatoes by 25 per cent.
4 p.m.	Answers letters from suppliers and customers.
5 p.m.	Sketches out draft advertisement for local newspaper.

Describe Samantha's activities in each hour of the day in one business word, for example '10 a.m. Delivers vegetarian meals to hotels in her van' would be **distribution**.

The sole trader, like Samantha, is in constant, direct touch with the real business world: her customers, her employees, her suppliers and her sources of finance. She has to perform all the functions, or specialized activities, that would normally be carried out by a large number of people in a big firm. For example, during the day described in the table above, her functions were stock-taking, distribution, recruitment, buying, delegation, borrowing, pricing, administration and advertising. On different days, she will be carrying out other business functions, such as planning, marketing and packaging, all of which you will read about later in the book. Samantha carries out these tasks unaided, although as a sensible and ambitious businesswoman, she does obtain advice when needed from her bank manager, her accountant, her solicitor and the local Training and Enterprise Council (TEC).

Delegation

When Samantha's business started to grow, she opened another shop in a different part of the city. She could have tried to run both shops; but they were so far apart that she decided to employ a manager to run the new shop. This decision involved one of the most vital and basic principles in management: **delegation**.

► The government set up eighty-two Training and Enterprise Councils (TECs) to cover the whole country in 1989. The councils are led by local business leaders. They help small firms by providing them with information, advice, counselling and training services.

Delegation

Delegation occurs when a superior gives a subordinate, or an employee of lower rank, the authority to carry out a specific duty or number of duties.

Samantha had already delegated one task, arranging the window display, to Zoë. Now, she has entrusted a large number of duties to the manager of the second shop, although she will retain some duties, such as controlling finance and buying stock.

Delegation makes the work of employees more interesting and rewarding as they can make their own decisions. It also makes the business more flexible and responsive to customers' needs. Many decisions can be made on the spot without having to refer the matter to a superior.

For the superior, delegation saves time, as some of his or

her functions are being carried out by another person. The superior, however, is still responsible for the subordinate's actions and must therefore have some means of checking that the work is being carried out satisfactorily. It is easy for Samantha to do this, as she can visit the other shop and is in constant touch with the manager.

 Ask as many people as possible – your family, friends, acquaintances, college lecturers – about delegation in their jobs. Find out if they have authority to delegate, and what duties are delegated to them and by whom. Ask them about the benefits and problems of delegation. (Use your own work experiences as well.) Then draw up a table with two columns headed *Benefits of delegation* and *Problems of delegation* and make notes based on your own research and the text above.

 Imagine you are the chief executive of a large leisure centre with departments for different sports, such as squash and swimming, a bar and a restaurant. State what powers you would delegate to departmental heads and give your reasons.

PRIVATE LIMITED COMPANY'S ORGANIZATION

The second shop succeeds. Samantha decides to open another shop in a nearby town. Within four years, she has seven shops. She has already formed a private limited company, Blooming Health Ltd, of which she is both the chairperson and the managing director. The business is now so big that she no longer manages a shop so that she can concentrate on her vision of expanding the business. She has had to delegate many of her functions to others. The company's **organization chart** looks like this:

This stage in the company's development illustrates another fundamental, or basic, principle of business: **division of labour**.

Division of labour
Division of labour occurs when work is split up into separate specialized tasks that are performed by individuals.

Division of labour increases efficiency, because workers who specialize in particular tasks can perform them better and faster than workers who have to do many kinds of tasks. In general, specialist workers usually have some freedom to work in their own way, which

▶ An **organization chart** is a diagram showing the formal relationships in an organization and its structure. (This example shows only the top layer of management or the most senior managers in the company. There would be more layers if all managers and supervisors were included.)

The structure of a private limited company

is important for job satisfaction. However, if work is split up into very small fragments, such as keyboarding credit card transactions into a computer all day long, it can become monotonous and lead to inefficiency. This still happens in some workplaces, but good managers now try to make repetitive work more varied and interesting.

In Blooming Health Ltd, separate managers now perform the tasks that Samantha once did herself: selling, buying and administration.

▶ See **Job improvement** in Chapter 20.

1 What is a private limited company?
2 Explain what the following involve:
   (a) delegation;
   (b) division of labour;
   (c) being subordinate;
   (d) being responsive to customers' needs.

Ask as many people as possible about any repetitive jobs that they have to do at work. Find out what effects these jobs have on them. Do they become bored, careless, angry or ill? Or do they adopt a more relaxed attitude, and become indifferent as long as they get their wages regularly? Find out if any of the duties they had that were once repetitive have been changed to give greater job satisfaction. (Use your own work experiences as well.) Then use the information above and your own research to make notes about division of labour.

THE STRUCTURE OF A PLC

Samantha's vision finally comes true. She has built up a large chain of health food shops which covers the whole of England, apart from the north-west. She has diversified by taking over a small chain of cosmetics shops, and is franchising new branches. A central purchasing department buys goods for all the shops, which allows them to keep prices low. The marketing director organizes many more in-store promotions than rival shops. There is also a finance director and a personnel director.

The company has been floated on the Stock Exchange and become a public limited company, Blooming Health plc, with Samantha as its chairperson. She is in overall control of the company. Samantha has appointed a 42-year-old man as her chief executive, and he is responsible for the day-to-day running of the business. Although Samantha has to spend much of her time in her new headquarters, just outside Birmingham, she tries to keep in touch with her employees by visiting all the shops as frequently as possible. She is a charismatic leader who is inspired by talking to her employees just as much as they are by talking to her.

What are the main benefits to the company of (a) franchising and (b) Samantha's charismatic personality? (Refer back to your notes on franchising and leadership if necessary!)

Using the information above, draw an organization chart,

similar to the one on page 87, showing all the senior personnel in Samantha's new company.

RETAIL ORGANIZATIONS

Functional departments

The traditional way of running a company is to have separate **departments** to carry out different functions. For example, the top layers of the organization chart of a big retailer might look like this:

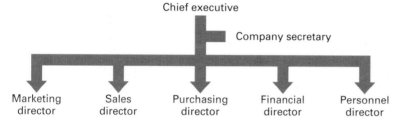

Chief executive

Company secretary

Marketing director   Sales director   Purchasing director   Financial director   Personnel director

Main departments in a big retailer

The senior managers, who are heads of departments, are also directors or members of the board. The main functions of each of the departments (which will be examined in much greater detail later in the book) are as follows:

- **Marketing:** This department identifies the needs and wants of customers both in the present and the future and providing goods (or services) that will satisfy them. It is in charge of market research, product planning, packaging, advertising, etc.
- **Sales:** This department makes sure that the shops provide an efficient service for customers by ensuring that quality is maintained and complaints are dealt with speedily and fairly. It is often in charge of distribution too, unless it is contracted out to a specialist firm.
- **Purchasing:** This department buys all the goods for sale and other goods that the company needs, such as office supplies of the highest quality and at the most economical price.
- **Financial:** This department is responsible for obtaining, controlling, analysing and recording company finance and making sure that it is used to the best advantage. It is in charge of the payment of wages, salaries and expenses, keeping accounts, making financial forecasts and borrowing money.
- **Personnel:** This department looks after the employees (or human resources) of the company and deals with recruitment, training, pay and conflicts.

1 What is the work of the purchasing department?
2 Explain what is meant by 'the company has been floated on the Stock Exchange'.
3 What is franchising?
4 Describe a charismatic leader.

► The chain of command would be much longer in a chart showing all the levels in the organization. There could be as many as seven levels.

5 State the main tasks of the marketing department and the financial department.

Hierarchies

There are several other important points you should note about the organization chart on page 89. The management structure is based on a **hierarchy**; people of the same degree of authority are on the same line of the chart, people with greater authority are above them and people with less authority are below. In the chart on page 89, the chief executive has authority over the five departmental directors. This creates a clear **chain of command**, showing the line along which orders and decisions are passed down to employees lower down the hierarchy.

Span of control

Each person has a number of other people who report direct to him or her. For example, the chief executive officer (CEO) has five people. His or her **span of control**, or the number of subordinates controlled, is five. The ideal span of control is generally considered to be four to six; but in practice it depends very much upon the abilities and personalities of the people involved. Some managers might find it difficult to cope with four subordinates while others could cheerfully deal with a dozen. It depends on how good all of them are at their jobs and whether the superiors are happy to delegate power to those below them in the hierarchy.

The span of control is also affected by the nature of the work being done. Simple work needs less supervision, so the span of control can be large. Complicated work may produce more problems. This may reduce the span of control, as more time will be needed to solve them.

Another factor is communications. Subordinates who are far away from their superiors may be more difficult to control, so a smaller span of control may be needed.

 Draw suitable organization charts for the following business situations, using the letter A for the head of the department and the letter B for his or her subordinates:

(a) a department where the head has very competent subordinates and is happy to delegate power;
(b) a financial department where several cases of fraud have been uncovered in the last few months;
(c) a department that is engaged in mainly routine work;
(d) a key department in a firm that has just been taken over by a bigger firm.

Line and staff

The CEO and the five departmental heads are all **line** managers, who command, or give orders, to subordinates. They are all directly involved in the production of the company's goods or services.

You can see that the company secretary is not on the same level as the five directors, but has a separate position at the side. The company secretary is responsible for the general administration of the company and its legal affairs. Duties include keeping the register of shares, paying dividends and keeping records of company meetings. The company secretary is not a line manager, but **staff**. Staff are not directly involved in the production process, and only give advice to the line managers. (Company secretaries, of course, have authority over their subordinates in their own department, and in this role are also line managers.)

With modern management systems, there is much less distinction between line and staff. All managers, and workers, participate actively in the firm's affairs, as you will see later in the chapter. Nevertheless, you should remember the distinction between line and staff.

 Draw diagrams, with brief descriptions or captions, to illustrate the key points relating to departments, hierarchies, span of control, line of command and line and staff.

1   What is the difference between line and staff.
2   Define (a) span of control; (b) hierarchy and supervision; (c) administration.

MANUFACTURING COMPANIES

The main departments in a large manufacturing company are similar to those in a big retailer. The main difference is that the purchasing department is replaced by a production department. This department is concerned with turning raw materials into finished goods and checking their quality. It is also heavily involved in purchasing, as manufacturers now spend more money on buying in parts and goods from other firms than they do on producing their own. These features are shown in the following organizational chart.

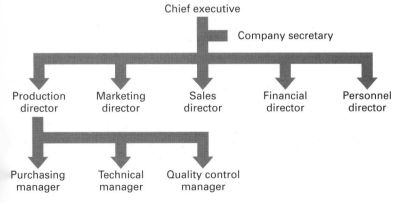

Main departments in a big manufacturing company

The chart emphasizes several points that have already been made about the hierarchical structure. Like the CEO, the departmental heads are all members of the board of directors. However, those in the second level of the hierarchy are usually only senior managers with no seat on the board of directors.

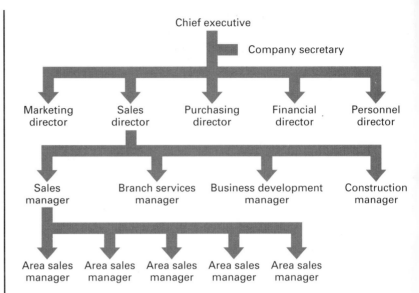

The sales department in a big retailer

It also becomes clearer that the chain of command extends right down the organization with the production director having a span of control of three, that is three subordinates who report directly to him or her. These senior managers, in their turn, will have their own subordinates. This point is illustrated in the chart above, which returns to a retailing business again.

A fuller organization chart for the company might look something like the one below. Of course it could be extended to show how the chain of command goes on down through middle managers, junior managers, supervisors and workers.

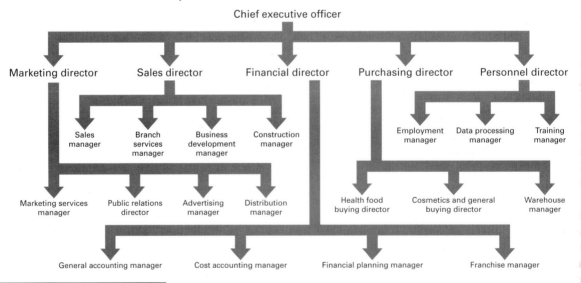

An organization chart of a big retailer

Copy this organization chart. Show it to people you know who work in large organizations and ask them how their company is organized. Draw an organization chart based on each person's information. Make notes analysing the differences between these charts and the one above.

Advantages of hierarchies

Hierarchies have advantages for both employers and employees. The advantages for employers are as follows:

- There are economies of scale as specialist staff can do work more efficiently.
- Each person has only one immediate superior so that there is unity of command.
- It is easier to check that work has been carried out because there are managers or supervisors at all levels of the hierarchy.
- Communications are better because the chain of command means there is a clear line for messages from the top of the hierarchy to the bottom.
- Cooperation between departments is easier because the manager can speak for all the employees that he or she controls.

The advantages for employees are as follows:

- They receive orders only from their own manager or supervisor so it is clear what their duties are.
- It is easier to get help because they can ask experienced colleagues in their own department or section, and take more difficult problems to their immediate superior.
- Being in a section or a department gives them a greater sense of unity and purpose.
- It makes it easier to carry out joint projects as employees already know their colleagues.

 Draw up a table called 'Hierarchies' with two columns headed *Advantages for employers* and *Advantages for employees* and fill it in with brief notes of your own.

Disadvantages of hierarchies

Some of the advantages of hierarchies are theoretical and do not always occur in real working life. For example, a woman secretary may still be asked to run personal errands for her boss or another manager, even though it is not her duty to do it for either manager. Experienced colleagues are not always helpful to junior employees. If the head of a department is incompetent, there may be chaos instead of unity in the department.

There can also be problems and conflict at higher levels of the hierarchy, particularly between marketing and sales. For example, a marketing manager might decide to promote a product with extensive advertising and point-of-sale material when the sales manager knows instinctively that it will not sell. The finance department is often accused of failing to see the long-term benefits of a development that it has refused to support. Departments can also keep information and knowledge to themselves and refuse to give help to other departments. Sometimes, two departments become such great rivals that they spend more time fighting each other than working for the interests of the firm.

However, the departmental system, with its hierarchy and chain of command, has even more basic disadvantages which have only become clear in the last few years.

Basic drawbacks of hierarchical system

Here are some of the main disadvantages of the hierarchical system of management:

1 The hierarchical system is rigid and inflexible, based on an army system of line officers who command, and staff officers who advise. It relies entirely on authority.
2 Status comes from your rank in the hierarchy. There are formal divisions between ranks; for example, senior managers often have their own car-parking spaces and dining rooms.
3 Too much work is specialized. Superiors often deal with any problems and then give orders about how they should be solved.
4 There are too many layers of management, and this creates a long chain of command. Decisions take a long time to reach employees at the bottom of the hierarchy.
5 Managers are too easily satisfied with what they have achieved and often judge success by growth rather than in terms of satisfying customers.

 Select the two most important advantages of hierarchies for employers and for employees and the two biggest disadvantages of the system. State why you have chosen them.

The effects of failure

The hierarchical system, based on a military model, made firms rigid and slow to respond to change. In the 1960s and 1970s, industrial disputes were common as a result of managers clashing with shop stewards in strong trade unions. British industry became inefficient and uncompetitive. It could not match the goods produced by Germany, the United States and Japan on either price or quality. As a result, Britain started to buy more goods from abroad, while foreign countries reduced their orders for British goods. British imports started to exceed exports.

QUALITY SYSTEMS

Basic principles

To cope with these internal and external challenges, British business has had to make many changes. Other countries had better management systems that helped to increase their productivity. In 1983, the government launched a campaign to persuade firms to use these new **quality management systems**. Many of Britain's biggest and most successful companies have already done so. These systems have a number of important features.

▶ Britain's **visible trade**, in raw materials, parts of goods, and complete, manufactured goods fell into deficit, or loss. In 1983, the deficit was £1,537 million pounds. By 1991, it had reached £10,290 million. This deficit used to be made up by a surplus on **invisibles**, the trade in services (which cannot be seen) such as banking, insurance, tourism and transport. This failed to happen in 1987, when there was a deficit on the current balance of £4,482 million. The current balance, or the balance of payments, is the difference between the total amount a country receives from foreign countries and the amount it pays to them. If a country is in deficit, it means that it is in debt to the rest of the world. Britain's balance of payments has been in deficit since 1987. In 1991, the deficit was £6,321 million.

Quality management systems

- Customers must be put first and their needs and wants discovered. The firm's suppliers are important too, and there should be an unbroken quality chain linking suppliers, firm and customers.
- Working relationships should be much more flexible, with emphasis on participation, or sharing, not authority. Relationships should be more people-centred.
- Status should come from performance – how well a person does his or her job – not from rank. Organizations should be as single-status as possible, for example by having one canteen for everyone.
- There should be less emphasis on departments, and more on the internal customer–supplier relationship between individuals and teams in the firm.
- The organization of the firm should be flat, with only four or five levels of managers instead of seven or more. This improves communications and saves costs as fewer middle managers are needed.
- There should be greater emphasis on training, not only for employees, but also for suppliers' employees. There should be as great an emphasis on personal flexibility as on specialized skills.
- The firm (and its employees) should be involved in a continual search for progress and improvement and should concentrate on its core business.

▶ The emphasis on the customer is reflected in a television advertising slogan for Ford cars: 'Everything we do is driven by you.'

▶ There are now single-status eating places in 86 per cent of companies.

▶ If someone in the personnel office is checking your pay for you to see that it is correct, that is his or her service as a supplier to you, the customer. If you are repairing a window in the personnel office, that is your service as a supplier to the personnel office, which is your customer.

ACT IN If these methods were applied in a big company what would be the likely effects on (a) departmental managers, (b) relations between departments and (c) employees' morale, or spirit?

Matrix organization charts

The old hierarchical system was based on people at the top telling people lower down the hierarchy what to do. The new quality management systems are based on sideways relationships in which people have greater equality. Some firms with a matrix structure combine both vertical and horizontal authority.

▶ The differences are reflected in the shape of the organization charts. The chart for a hierarchical system is pyramid-shaped with power at the top; the chart for a quality management system is box-shaped with power distributed sideways.

Managing director

Production director — Technical manager — Marketing director — Finance director — Personnel manager

Project A manager

Managers and workers from specialized departments who form part of the Project A team

A matrix organization chart

The matrix organization chart on p. 95 shows the management structure for a medium-sized manufacturing company. The top layer of the chart is vertical, with the managing director having a span of control of five. These five senior managers all have their normal line responsibilities for subordinates at a lower level. (These subordinates are not shown in the chart to make it clearer.)

In addition, however, the production director is responsible for the manager of Project A who reports directly to him. Project A involves producing prototypes, or original models, of a desk and chair for use in the offices of a large company. If the firm wins the contract it could be worth over £500,000.

The Project A manager is responsible for the team of people who are drawn from different departments in the firm. When they are in the team, they work closely together, listening to each other, and treating each other as equals, whether they are managers or clerical or shop-floor workers. They like working in this way because it is far more friendly and productive. A real team spirit has developed and they all feel confident that they will win the order. However, it is sometimes difficult for line managers to start giving orders again when they resume their normal duties. They also have to work harder in order to catch up. The shop-floor workers feel isolated when they go back to their normal duties and have to take orders again.

At the same time, the firm is producing two special orders. There are two other teams at work on Project B and Project C. The firm has been using this system for a number of years, long before most managers had heard of a matrix structure.

 State the effects of a matrix structure on (a) managers and (b) shop-floor workers.

   1 Identify three problems that may occur within a hierarchical structure.
2 Why may a hierarchical structure, based on an army system of authority, be difficult to operate in a business environment?
3 What have been the effects of the hierarchical system?

PROBLEMS OF MULTINATIONALS

It is much more difficult for a conglomerate or a multinational, which operates in a number of countries, to find a suitable organizational structure. The main problems are maintaining communications and dividing authority between the parent and subsidiary companies. The two main structures that multinationals generally adopt are the divisional structure and the geographical structure.

Divisional structure

In a divisional structure, separate **divisions** are created for different products, such as chemicals, medical drugs, paints, explosives, fibres and fabrics. The divisional heads are in control of the sub-sidiary companies. Each division has its own profit target so it is easy for the parent company to see if it is doing well. The divisional heads report directly to the main board of the parent company.

Smaller companies with closely related products also often divide their activities into divisions. A book publisher, for example, might have general and educational divisions.

Geographical structure

Large firms adopting a geographical structure could divide Britain into a number of geographical regions. The main board would tell each region what powers it had.

Multinationals usually use a mixture of both structures and try to combine them into a whole. The main problem is how much cen-tralization or decentralization there should be.

Centralization and decentralization

Centralization is when the parent company keeps most authority. This produces economies of scale, for example in buying. However, the long lines of communication can slow down decision making.

    Decentralization is when authority is delegated to subordinate companies. It speeds decision making and makes it easier to respond quickly to market forces. However, it can cause duplica-tion of work and might weaken the power of the parent company.

    In practice, the parent companies in most multinationals usually retain control of general policy, finance and the appointment of senior managers.

► See the box on **Internal economies of scale** in Chapter 7, page 73.

 Make brief notes on divisional and geographical structures and on centralization and decentralization.

 Write to the company secretary of any large multinational or plc and ask for a copy of its annual report and accounts. From the information it contains, draw an organization chart or write brief notes on the company's structure.

REAL-LIFE ORGANIZATIONS

Organization charts are useful for giving a general picture of the kind of management structure a firm's wants. However, they often describe the firm's intentions rather than what actually happens in practice.

    As you already know, the relative strengths and leadership styles of the chairperson and the chief executive can have a great impact on how a company is run. Conflicts can occur at any level of the business. Furthermore, the charts only show formal relation-ships. Informal relationships are just as important.

► To refresh your memory, see the box on **Types of leader** in Chapter 6, page 64.

Informal groups

Informal groups exist in all businesses – from the boardroom to the shop floor. They are loose associations of people sharing common views, interests or attitudes.

There may be only a few people in the group. For example, several members of a company's board of directors may feel that the chairperson is doing a poor job. They may join together to try to get rid of him or her by seeking the help of institutional investors.

Sometimes a large number of people are involved. For example, Greenwood Ltd is taken over by Bluebird plc. One of the first acts of the new management is to bring in new contracts of employment that will reduce the wages of shop-floor workers. Their official protests through their union representatives have no effect, so there is growing resentment among the shop-floor workers. Some of them, fearful of losing their jobs, go on working normally. However, a large informal group start to work at a slower rate, make deliberate mistakes, and take days off by phoning in sick.

Effects of leaders and management

The style of leadership and management decide to a large degree whether the informal groups will be beneficial or harmful to the firm. On the whole, autocratic leaders, who cause much fear and resentment, will create many harmful informal groups. Democratic leaders will produce some beneficial groups and charismatic leaders often produce even more. However, it also depends on many other factors, including how well the firm is doing and how widely the financial benefits are shared.

The new quality management structures are designed to use informal groups for the firm's benefit. Two of the methods used are:

- **quality circles**, which are voluntary meetings of supervisors and workers to suggest new methods of shop-floor working that will improve productivity and the quality of products;
- **joint consultation**, which gives elected committees a chance to bring up problems and grievances that have not gone through formal channels.

 Make notes on informal groups, showing how they can be affected by different types of leaders and organizational structures.

1 What is the difference between a divisional structure and a geographical structure?
2 What are the advantages and disadvantages of decentralization?
3 Why do organization charts fail to show the whole picture of how a firm is run?
4 What is a quality circle?
5 In what ways can informal relationships affect the performance of a company?

SUMMARY

- Sole traders have to perform a great range of management functions that would be done by separate individuals in bigger firms.
- Small firms have simple management structures with a limited amount of division of labour.
- Bigger firms have larger functional departments with much more specialization.
- Traditional management structures are based on a hierarchy of authority, with a chain of command of line managers that stretches down through the organization. Managers are responsible for a number of subordinates, and this number is their span of control. Staff advise the line managers.
- The hierarchical system has many disadvantages, including failure to put the customer first, rigidity, emphasis on status, and too many levels of management.
- The weaknesses of this system made it difficult for Britain to compete in world markets.
- New quality management systems have been introduced. These place greater emphasis on the customer–supplier chain, quality, teamwork, performance, flat organizations, training and continuous improvement.
- Matrix structures combine the old and new systems.
- Bigger firms with a large product range sometimes divide their firm into separate divisions, while multinationals often use a mixture of divisional and geographical structures. The main issue in these more complicated structures is whether the organization should be centralized or decentralized.
- Organization charts tend to show how a firm's intended management structure rather than it's real structure. Informal groups play a large part in what actually occurs in the day-to-day running of a business.

9 *Marketing*

Chapter objectives

After working through this chapter, you will have the knowledge to:

▌ evaluate the importance of marketing;

▌ make and apply a SWOT analysis;

▌ select the characteristics of consumers in a market segment;

▌ distinguish between a market segment and a market niche;

▌ apply the four Ps and the marketing mix to a selected business;

▌ describe how small firms can use marketing to their advantage;

▌ understand the similarities in industrial and consumer marketing;

▌ select the most important legal restraints on marketing;

▌ appreciate the effects of ethical restraints on marketing;

▌ understand and use the following key terms: marketing, SWOT analysis, strengths, weaknesses, opportunities, threats, benchmarking, down-market, mid-market, up-market, market segment, social grade, purchasing power, market niche, four Ps, cost-plus pricing, marketing mix, branding, decision-making unit (DMU), joint buyer, consumer protection, ethics, voluntary codes, pressure group.

WHAT IS MARKETING?

The Institute of Marketing defines marketing in the following way:

> ### Marketing
> Marketing is the management process responsible for identifying, anticipating and satisfying customer requirements profitably.

► See Chapter 10.

This means that market research is used to identify, or discover, what people require or want. The research may also reveal people's hopes or ambitions. Firms can then provide goods or services that satisfy people's wants, and they can anticipate, or satisfy in advance, people's hidden hopes. By doing this, firms will make a profit.

Note that the term 'customer' is used in the Institute's definition. At one time, marketing was used mainly in consumer markets, but increasingly it is used in all sectors of production, as you will see later in the chapter. Marketing is now at the centre of practically all business activity. The marketing plan provides the essential link between the needs of customers and the aims of company policy.

 Write a definition of marketing in your own words and file it with your notes. When you have finished reading the chapter go back to your definition and see if you need to change it. If you do, revise the definition and file it again.

SWOT ANALYSIS

Before the marketing department creates a marketing plan, it carries out a **SWOT analysis**. A SWOT analysis shows the firm's **Strengths** and **Weaknesses** compared with its business competitors, and the **Opportunities** and **Threats** in the general business environment, hence the word SWOT. The first part of the analysis – SW – looks inwards at the present achievements and problems of the firm and compares them with those of its closest rivals. The second part of the analysis – OT – looks at what is happening in the outside world and analyses how it will affect that firm in particular.

Internal analysis

The firm already knows a great deal about itself: its profit and profitability, its cost-effectiveness and its market share. These results can then be compared with what has happened in previous years to see how the firm is performing. For example, if the firm's profits increase each year, it would seem to be performing well. However, there is an even better test. The firm's performance can be compared with that of similar firms. So if the firm's profits are lower than those of its main competitors, its performance would not be so great after all.

Everything a firm does can be measured against the performance of other firms. These comparisons will show the firm's relative strengths and weaknesses. Take customers' orders. A major chain store selling electrical goods might order a camera for a customer and obtain it in a week. A specialist camera shop might be able to get it in four days. The specialist shop obtains the camera more quickly, so its order time is a strength; the chain store takes longer, so it is a weakness.

A British toy manufacturer takes eight months to bring a new product to the market. A Hong Kong manufacturer does it in six. That is a weakness for the British firm and a strength for the Hong Kong business. A manufacturer of refrigerators could compare its products with those of rival firms for price, reliability, design and other aspects. These comparisons would show the firm's strengths

► See **Measuring business success** in Chapter 6.

▶ Surveyors cut benchmarks, or fixed points, in rock when they are checking a line of levels. They look like this: ^.

in some aspects and weaknesses in others. This process of comparison is called **benchmarking**. Many big firms now use it regularly to compare their own performance with that of their rivals.

External analysis

The second part of the analysis is concerned with the general business environment. Just turn back to the review box, 'Consumer markets', in Chapter 3, page 18. You will see that consumer markets are affected by many external factors, including consumers' income, fashions, seasons of the year, changes in taste, the size and structure of population, and regional differences. To these may be added many more, such as foreign competition, new laws, changes in rates of VAT and Customs duties.

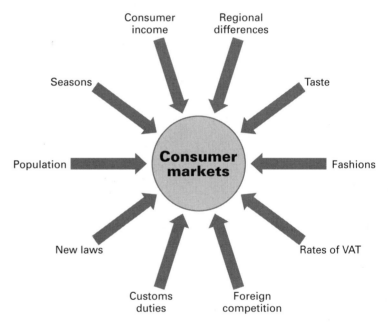

External influences on consumer markets

This diagram shows some of the factors in the business environment in which all firms have to operate. Firms can do very little – or nothing – to change these external factors. They have to learn to live with them. Some of the factors can be seen as opportunities and others as threats. For example, if consumer income is rising, it will be an opportunity because consumers are likely to increase their spending. However, if their income is falling, it will be a threat because consumers will probably spend less. On the other hand, an increase of 2½ per cent in the rate of VAT would be a threat because the price of goods and services would rise and people would buy less. A reduction in the rate of VAT by 2½ per cent would be an opportunity because it would reduce the price of goods and services and people would buy more.

Changes like these have a similar impact on all firms producing goods or services for the consumer market. Some changes, however, affect different firms in different ways. Say, for example, that it had been a cold, wet summer in Britain. It is easy to predict the possible effects on different kinds of firms. A cold, wet summer would be a threat for manufacturers of ice cream, sun glasses, summer clothes, etc., and for the British tourism industry. It would, however, be an opportunity for travel firms providing holidays abroad.

 State what kinds of firms would view the external changes below as (a) a threat and (b) an opportunity in each of the three cases:

1 a 2½ per cent increase in VAT on new cars costing over £15,000;
2 a law stopping British fishing boats spending more than three days a week at sea to conserve fish stocks;
3 an increase in the number of people over 65: life expectancy is four years longer then it was ten years ago.

 1 What does SWOT stand for?
2 How does a customer differ from a consumer?
3 What is marketing?
4 How might businesses be affected if there were an increase in the rate of VAT?
5 Complete the following sentences by selecting a word or phrase from the list that follows:
   (a) The . . . suffers if there is an increase in inflation.
   (b) A hot summer will benefit . . .
   (c) A rise in unemployment is likely to reduce the profits of . . .
   (d) Restrictions on tree felling in the rain forests may reduce the profits of . . .
   (e) High interest rates will adversely affect the . . . and benefit the . . .
   (f) A shortage of rubber on the world market may result in . . . prices.
   (g) A series of ferry disasters could increase the number of . . . customers.

**borrower   car manufacturers increasing their
investor   consumer   retailers   Channel Tunnel
swim-suit manufacturers   furniture retailers**

Purposes of SWOT analysis

The marketing director uses all this information – the strengths, weaknesses, opportunities and threats – to make the SWOT analysis. The first part of the analysis – SW, strengths and weaknesses – shows where a firm is now and how it compares with its rivals. The second part – OT, opportunities and threats – shows the direction a firm might take and the dangers that it might meet on the way. This information helps the marketing director to choose suitable market segments for the firm's products.

► In some ways, the marketing director is like the manager of a football team. The team has a known objective – to win the match that will take them to the top of the league. They have a mean opponent who will stop at nothing to win. It has been raining heavily and the team never plays well on a rain-soaked pitch. So that is a threat to their chances. On the other hand, their striker has scored five goals in the last two games. So that gives them an opportunity to win. Firms are engaged in 'needle' matches of this kind all the time. The main difference is that business is a 'game' that is being played by millions of people somewhere in the world every second of the day.

	Number	Reasons
Strengths		
Weaknesses		
Opportunities		
Threats		

The marketing director of a large supermarket chain is doing a SWOT analysis. Some of the items he is considering are given in the list below. Draw up a table like the one in the margin, leaving two or three lines between each of the headings at the left-hand side. Put the number of each of the items in the list beside the correct heading and, on the same line, state briefly why you have put it there.

1 A United States firm is opening more no-frills warehouse clubs in Britain selling 4,000 lines from tea to television sets in bulk at a price 20 per cent lower than supermarket prices.
2 A rights issue of shares to pay for new stores to be built was oversubscribed three times.
3 The trade union representing the majority of union members in the supermarket chain is threatening to strike over pay.
4 A market research survey shows that consumers are willing to spend more on luxury food items.
5 Prices of tea and coffee drop 20 per cent on the commodity markets.
6 Sales of wines and spirits have slumped in London and the south-east as people are buying in bulk on day trips to France.
7 A customer found strands of glass in a bottle of lemonade caused by a defect in the own-brand bottling plant.
8 Openings of new stores increased the chain's market share by 2 per cent last year.

MARKET SEGMENTS

Read the following case study and answer the questions at the end.

The Royal York Pottery has a long and famous history. It was founded in 1778 in York. The pottery quickly gained a high reputation among aristocrats and other landed gentry in the north of England. Within a few years, it started to receive orders from members of the Royal Family. The pottery became famous for its delicate porcelain dinner services, bearing the buyer's coat of arms, and decorated with lavish displays of flowers of various colours, usually pink. These early pieces are now collectors' items worth thousands of pounds.

During the nineteenth century, Royal York started to make cheaper bone china, which meant that it could widen its market. Its dinner services, bowls and vases, rimmed with gold and decorated with hand-painted flowers, birds and country scenes, also became popular among the middle classes throughout Britain and on the Continent. The continued prosperity of the firm seemed secure.

This prosperity lasted until the Second World War. After the war, the firm resumed full production, but it never regained its pre-war market position. The new generation was less keen to buy expensive china, especially large dinner services. Royal York started to produce less expensive items that could be bought separately to form sets. Demand increased. However, the total home sales were no longer high enough to balance the books. Overseas sales helped to do that – but only just.

A new managing director has decided that changes have to be made. He thinks that the firm has little chance of surviving without a firm domestic base. Market research shows that there is a continuing trend against formal meals, on which the firm's whole prosperity has been based. It shows that most people no longer have the time or money or the desire to have formal dinner parties. Some senior managers still entertain other business people in their own homes, but this is also becoming less common. Even members of the same family increasingly eat their meals alone. The main reasons are that more women work in paid part-time or full-time employment rather than as full-time housewives; there is more eating out and snacking throughout the day; working hours have changed; young people tend to live more independent lives, away from their parents; many people have social commitments independent of their spouse or partner; and there has been a general trend towards more casual attitudes towards the family meal.

Formal meals have increasingly been replaced by convenience food, TV dinners and informal dinner parties. Firms now produce new kinds of casual dinnerware to match these changes. The new dinnerware has various prices:

- **down-market:** £20 or so for a twenty-piece earthenware set of everyday crockery for regular use, sold by supermarkets and mail-order firms;
- **mid-market:** £40 to £80 for a twenty-piece china or porcelain set for frequent use, sold in high street independents and chain stores;
- **up-market:** up to £20 for a single fine china dinner plate for special occasions, sold in department stores and specialist shops.

Whatever the price, most casual dinnerware has one common feature. It is decorated in bright, bold patterns of colourful leaf, fish, fruit, flower or abstract design.

The marketing manager of Royal York wants to bring out a new range of casual dinnerware, called the Van Gogh collection, which would be sold at a lower price than their normal products.

The managing director is opposed to this idea. He thinks

► Vincent Van Gogh (1853–1890), the Dutch painter who is famous for his bright, vibrant colours.

that these bright colourful designs are a fashion that will not last. They do not match the traditional elegance of Royal York design and could harm the company's image. He favours using a more traditional design, with a rich pink rim, edged with 24-carat gold on a white porcelain body. The rim would be the exact shade of pink used in Royal York's original eighteenth-century pottery. He plans to provide display units and a well-designed customer leaflet for use in shops and stores. The leaflets would draw attention to the original colour and include a new slogan – 'priceless as Royal York'. The new range would be less expensive than their other lines, but it would not be as cheap as the dinnerware the marketing manager proposed.

1 Who were the first customers of Royal York pottery?
2 How were sales affected by manufacturing cheaper bone china?
3 Why did Royal York Pottery change its products after the Second World War?
4 For what reasons have formal meals become less popular in recent times?
5 In your view, what kind of customers would you expect to find in each of the following types of retail outlet: (a) down-market, (b) mid-market and (c) up-market?
6 Who has the better marketing idea: the marketing manager or the managing director? State the reasons for your choice.

FINDING THE RIGHT MARKET SEGMENT

The case study of the Royal York Pottery shows how the firm has responded to its own strengths and weaknesses, and the opportunities and threats in the business environment. Throughout its history, the firm has constantly had to adapt its products to make them appeal to different customers, or market segments. When the firm started, it was easy to identify a market segment, as only royalty, aristocrats and landed gentry had enough money to buy the kind of porcelain that the firm produced. During the nineteenth century, its market segment expanded as the growing numbers of wealthy middle-class families started to buy the same kind of bone china as aristocrats. During the present century, which has been called the era of the common man and woman, the total market has expanded greatly as more people are able to buy the porcelain and china of their choice. At the same time, the market has become more segmented, or split into a number of sections. The firm has had to adapt more quickly than it ever did in the past to changes in the market in an effort to find new segments for its products. Like all other markets, the market for china can now be divided into down-market, mid-market and up-market segments. These segments are mainly dependent on social grade and income, but other factors are also involved.

▶ A market segment is a group of consumers within a market who have characteristics in common, such as age, sex and income.

▶ For example, the total market for beer in Britain is worth about £13 billion a year. There is a wide range of products: lager, bitter, brown, draught, bottled and many more. People who drink each kind of beer have some characteristics in common that create a market segment. It may be that they are of a similar age, or the same social grade or live in the same part of the country.

1 What is a market segment?
2 Identify the market segment, by age, sex and income, of purchasers of the following goods:
   (a) cut-price households goods;
   (b) expensive sports cars;
   (c) mass produced ski-pants and leggings;
   (d) second-hand, semi-precious jewellery;
   (e) children's books;
   (f) classical music CDs.
3 What are the risks involved for an established firm in adapting and changing its product to fit in with current fashions?

Social grade

Social grades

Grade	Description	Example
A	Higher managerial, administrative and professional	Chief executive officer, judge, top civil servant
B	Intermediate managerial, administrative and professional	Lecturer, bank manager, solicitor
C1	Supervisory or clerical and junior managerial	Bank clerk, salesperson, shop-floor supervisor
C2	Skilled manual workers	Carpenter, electrician
D	Semi-skilled and unskilled manual	Refuse collector, assembly line worker, packer, porter
E	Casual labourers, state pensioners, unemployed	Senior citizens without private pensions, unemployed single parents

Social grade is one important factor in a market segment. The population can be divided into six social grades, A, B, C1, C2, D and E, which are based on the occupation of the head of the household. In broad terms, these social grades relate to income and purchasing power, or the ability to buy, and hence to lifestyle. For example, a judge (social grade A) has much more purchasing power than, say, a female single parent with three young children who has no time or opportunity to take on paid employment (social grade E). However, income is not linked exactly to each social grade. For example, a man's occupation may put him in the C1 social grade, while his working wife may be in social grade A. There are also many self-employed people who, though their work places them in a low social grade, have high incomes. For that reason, market researchers now often group the grades into broader categories – such as AB or ABC1 – instead of concentrating on the six separate social grades.

► The husband or male partner is generally considered to be the 'head' of the household, even though the wife or female may be working and earning more than her partner.

There are several other schemes for classifying market segments. In one scheme, the population is classified according to the newspapers they read and the TV channels they watch. There are seven categories in this scheme, ranging from M1 to M7. Other market researchers base their classifications on people's psychological needs and ambitions, which produce similar lifestyles and spending patterns.

► 'M' stands for media.

Age

Age is one of the most important features in a market segment.

Young and old people have very different tastes (which is one of the main causes of friction at home). Age also has an effect on income. In general, young people, particularly students, have low incomes. People achieve their top income in their forties. When they retire, their incomes fall. However, there are many exceptions. Young, single people with a well-paid job who are still living with their parents probably have more money to spend on things like clothes, holidays, entertainment and eating out than any other age group. Retired people of social grade A who have a large pension and have been given a 'golden handshake' – a large sum of money when they retire – are sometimes better off than they were when they were working.

Gender

Gender is also an important factor. Men and women still have very different spending patterns but sex-roles are not as rigid as they used to be. In some relationships, for example, the female does the DIY while the male does the cooking.

Geography

People's spending is influenced by where they live. People in different parts of the country often share similar tastes. For example, there are proportionately more cigarette smokers in the north of England than there are in the south (with the exception of London). Some of the differences occur through necessity. Because of limited rail and bus services, it is very difficult for people living in rural areas to travel far if they do not own a car. In London, and other major cities, it is relatively easy to get around without one. Owning a car is therefore more important in the country than it is in cities.

The size of the potential market for British goods has increased considerably now that the Single Market has abolished most of the barriers to trade between member-countries in the European Union (EU). However, differences in income, spending patterns, attitudes, tastes and family life are so great in the EU that it is difficult to identify market segments for the whole of Europe. The search for a typical Euro-consumer goes on!

Other factors in market segments

Education, religion, friends, occupation and other factors also have a big influence on market segments. The size and the shape of the segments are altering all the time as society is in a state of constant change. Marketing people have to do continual research to keep up with these changes.

 Find your answers to Question 5 (a), (b) and (c) in the case study about the Royal York Pottery. In view of what you have now learned about market segments, how would you alter them? Write new answers.

Look at the following list of characteristics and interests of hotel guests:

> social grade AB   raves till 4 a.m.   whisky drinkers
> retired people   swimming   lager drinkers
> 25–35 years old   buffet dinners   cinema-going
> six-course meals   dances   playing snooker
> social grade B C1   sightseeing   health and fitness

How many market segments can you find? Give the characteristics and interests of each segment. Are there any interests or characteristics that the segments share?

MARKET NICHES

A **market niche** is part, or a small corner, of a market segment. It consists of a smaller group of consumers whose needs or wants can be more accurately defined. Niche marketing has developed because:

- There has been an increase in the number of groups of people with specific needs. They might have unusual lifestyles, hobbies or special interests, or play minority sports. One example would be people who like playing computer games.
- Computers make it possible to target customers and to find suppliers of goods or services more easily.
- Advances in production methods make it easier to produce different versions of the same manufactured good to appeal to minority tastes.

► Just turn back to Chapter 3, page 16, and find the marginal note 'See market niches in Chapter 9'. You will see that you have already met the idea of market niches.

► See Chapter 23.

► See **Batch production** and **Computer-aided manufacturing** in Chapter 15.

Entrepreneurs are always searching to find a gap in the market that they can fill. It is not easy to find a gap, but it can be very profitable if they do.

 Write notes on market segments and market niches, bringing out the differences between them.

 In which social grade would you put the following people:

> (a) a 40-year-old director of a private company?
> (b) a young, unemployed builder?
> (c) a student at a local college?
> (d) an elderly woman living on inherited investments?
> (e) a 30-year-old bank clerk?

 Read the following case study and answer the questions at the end.

Mike worked in the sales department of a shoe manufacturing company. He wanted to move on, but jobs were scarce in the footwear industry. Then he had an idea. Mike, who was 39, was a keen walker. He noticed that many young, well-paid managers and professionals were taking

Shoemaking in a small workshop

up walking to relieve their daily stress at work. He wondered if he had found the classic gap in the market.

After making some careful enquiries among his friends in the footwear trade, he decided to go ahead with his idea. He worked out a business plan. His bank manager liked the idea and agreed to finance it, though Mike had to give his house as security for the loan.

His basic idea was to produce an up-market range of hand-stitched walking boots of the finest quality. Each style of boot was named after a walker who had written a best-selling regional guide. Mike paid them a small royalty on each pair of boots. The boots sold at £150 to £175 a pair and were only available in ten selected stores or by mail order.

Five years later, his business was doing well. A small London factory, owned and staffed by Spaniards, manufactured his total annual output of 8,000 pairs of boots. Mike had just returned from a sales trip to a few high-class retailers on the Continent. Half of them were very interested in his boots. He had already obtained one firm order.

1 Why did Mike start his own business?
2 Why is it a niche market?
3 If the average price of the boots was £165, what was Mike's annual turnover?
4 Why was Mike's business succeeding better than Royal York Pottery?

THE MARKETING MIX

The four Ps

Once a market segment or niche has been found, the product must be marketed in such a way that it will appeal to the chosen customers. Many factors are involved in the marketing of a product. For convenience, these are usually known as the **four Ps**: **product**,

price, **place** and **promotion**. (You will study these in detail in Chapters 11 to 14.) The case study shows how Mike had taken all these factors into account in marketing his walking boots:

- **Product**, or what versions of the basic product consumers will be offered. Mike offered up-market, quality walking boots in slightly different versions named after famous walkers.
- **Price**, or what consumers will have to pay. Mike's price was calculated on a cost-plus basis. About half of the production costs went on materials and the other half on paying the Spanish factory, or labour. Mike added on his overheads and then his percentage mark-up.
- **Place**, or where consumers will find the product. Mike had deliberately chosen to restrict the distribution to a few top-quality stores and mail order to maintain an up-market image. This also reduced his distribution costs.
- **Promotion**, or how consumers will hear about the product. Mike relied on word-of-mouth recommendations and a few small display advertisements in quality magazines.

Review: The four Ps

It is essential that products have the greatest possible appeal to the chosen market segment or niche. This is done by blending the four Ps – product, price, place and promotion – in the right proportions.

- **Product:** What kind of product will be offered to customers? Different versions of the same basic product vary greatly in quality, style, packaging and many other ways.
- **Price:** What will the customer have to pay for the product? This will vary according to the version of the basic product chosen. The simplest way of determining price is **cost-plus pricing**. The firm calculates the cost of producing the product, and adds on a percentage mark-up which gives the selling price. There are many other pricing strategies.
- **Place:** Where will the customer find the product? There are many channels of distribution ranging from corner shops to superstores. The choice is determined by the nature of the product and the kind of customer.
- **Promotion:** How will the customer hear about the product? Word-of-mouth recommendations are the cheapest and the best form of promotion; but there are many other methods. These range from advertisements in quality magazines for tens of thousands of readers to television commercials at peak time for millions of viewers.

For convenience, the four Ps are studied separately so that they are easier to analyse, but it should always be remembered that they form a whole. The essence of marketing is getting the right proportions of each kind of ingredient to produce the perfect marketing mix.

Finding the right mix

It is very important to mix the four Ps in exactly the right proportions for the target consumers. Mike had done this with his niche market. Bigger firms, dealing with a market segment and facing

► The new car market is particularly competitive, especially in the peak sales month of August. The average advertising cost per car was estimated at over £300 in 1993.

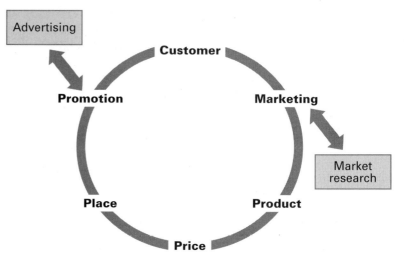

The marketing mix

▶ At any one time, the marketing director will be at a different stage in a number of different plans. These include the company plan, the marketing plans and the launch plan for a new product, as well as the day-to-day problems and difficulties that arise when the plans are put into practice. As every company has a different organizational structure and way of doing things, there cannot be a universal marketing plan.

stiffer competition, have a harder task. They still use the same techniques, but they expend much more time, money and effort on the four Ps. They hope that finding just the right mixture of the four Ps, or **marketing mix**, will give them a competitive edge, or advantage, over their rivals.

A marketing plan has to be drawn up for each of the firm's products. In every case, the customer is at the top of the marketing plan. Marketing is in close touch with customers' wants and needs. It uses specialist firms such as market research agencies to define its customers' needs more clearly. Promotion also uses specialist outside advertising firms. The circular process helps to maintain the quality flow between customers and internal and external suppliers.

 Choose a business you would like to start. How would you apply the four Ps and the marketing mix to your chosen business?

Marketing for the self-employed

As the case study above has shown, the four Ps and the marketing mix are just as important for small firms as they are for big firms. One of the reasons many sole traders go out of business quickly is their failure to make a marketing plan. This applies particularly to small shopkeepers.

The self-employed all need to do a SWOT analysis before the business is launched and at regular intervals after that. It need not be as detailed as a big firm's analysis, but must be as thorough.

The analysis may help the self-employed to find a market niche to exploit. For example, many big firms now employ their own full-time lawyer. However, these corporate, or company, lawyers cannot deal with all the work themselves. Therefore, they buy in services from other solicitors. Some legal partnerships have found a profitable niche market by specializing in some aspect of corporate law, such as employment law or copyright.

The self-employed can often compete successfully with big firms in terms of the four Ps because they are more flexible.

- **Product:** Small manufacturers will often make a special object to suit the customer's exact requirements. Small shops can stock specialist goods that larger stores do not sell. Although small grocery shops cannot compete with supermarkets on the price of standard or branded lines, they can provide a better neighbourhood service by staying open late.
- **Price:** Small firms can also be flexible on price, whereas branches of big firms usually need permission from their central office to cut prices. In many markets, for example photocopying and furniture removals, the self-employed can offer lower prices than larger firms as their overheads are smaller.
- **Place:** Big firms usually contract out delivery of their goods to a specialist firm and can only give a general indication of when the delivery will be made. Small firms can deliver goods at a time to suit the customer. Some sole traders, such as newsagents, fishmongers and greengrocers, provide a regular doorstep delivery service.
- **Promotion:** The best form of promotion for small businesses in a local market is word-of-mouth recommendation, particularly as it's free! It is easy for small firms to promote themselves by providing news stories and features for local newspapers. Advertising in local newspapers is also quite cheap.

ACT OUT Find a shop that is enlarging its premises or moving to a more expensive location. Try to interview the shopkeeper about how he or she applies the four Ps to the business. If you cannot obtain an interview, find the answers by personal observation.

▶ **Branding** is giving a product a name or trademark to persuade consumers that it is different from similar products made by other firms. See also Differentiation in Chapter 11.

INDUSTRIAL MARKETS

There are many similarities in the marketing of industrial and consumer goods or services. Firms providing products to other firms or organizations have to choose a suitable market. Within that market, they need to find their own market segment or niche. For example, a manufacturer of computer software might find a market segment in small businesses, large companies or local government. Within those segments, he might identify a profitable market niche. In local government, different software packages are needed for the council tax, social services, housing, etc.

The four Ps also play their part in industrial markets. For example, a computer manufacturer might apply the four Ps in the following way in its industrial market:

- **product:** producing a range of computers with different features, such as monochrome or colour in the visual display unit screen;
- **price:** discounts for large orders;

▶ **Software** is a program fed into a computer that allows it to perform a particular task. See Chapter 23.

- **place:** direct sales to customers to keep the price low;
- **promotion:** advertising in selected trade magazines.

Although the industrial market is much bigger and more profitable, computer manufacturers also sell their products to home users. The four Ps would still be used; but the emphasis would be different because it is a different market segment.

 Suggest how the computer manufacturer might apply the four Ps for personal customers.

Joint buying

In industrial markets, decisions about what to buy are made by a single buyer, for example a departmental buyer of china in a large store. For expensive purchases of items for factories or offices, a group of people, or a **decision-making unit** (DMU), usually makes the decision. There are often different views within the group. For example, when considering the purchase of an expensive new machine, the production manager may want a machine that is reliable; the works manager may want one that is easy to use; the finance director may want a machine that is a good investment, and so on. The firm that is marketing the machine must try to appeal to as many of the **joint buyers** as possible.

This kind of joint buying also happens in consumer markets. The food that parents buy is often influenced by the wishes of their young children. Joint decisions are even more important in purchasing expensive goods, such as cars and homes. Private buyers may be less knowledgeable than industrial buyers, but there can be a similar conflict of views. In buying a new house, the male partner may want a large sitting room; the female partner may want a south-facing garden; and the children may want rooms of their own.

 Make notes on the similarities between industrial and consumer buying.

1 What are the four Ps?
2 What is the marketing mix?
3 Why is a marketing plan important?
4 How can the self-employed compete with big firms?
5 What is an industrial market?
6 Where would you find a DMU?
7 Which of the four Ps might have most influence in the following cases:
    (a) a young married couple buying a second-hand car?
    (b) a woman with no car buying a refrigerator from a department store?
    (c) a small firm of accountants buying a computer?
    (d) a manufacturer buying technical equipment that will need regular servicing?

LEGAL AND ETHICAL RESTRAINTS

Legal restraints

There are hundreds of laws affecting business. Some of them apply particularly to marketing and **consumer protection**. The following ones are the most important.

Consumer protection laws

Some of these British laws have now been superseded, or replaced by EU laws.

Food and Drugs Act 1955

It is illegal to sell food that is not fit for human consumption. Goods must conform to their description. For example, raspberry jam must contain a certain minimum percentage of raspberries. The percentage of raspberries contained must be stated on the label. Packaged foods must give a list of ingredients. (This law has now been superseded by EU legislation.)

Trade Descriptions Act 1968 and 1972

Businesses are not allowed to give false or misleading descriptions of goods or services. For example, free-range eggs must come from chickens that have a certain area of open field at their disposal.

Consumer Credit Act 1974

It is compulsory for businesses to state the true annual rate of interest, or APR, when giving credit. Customers must have a cooling off period to change their mind about a hire-purchase contract signed at home. The Act also regulates advertisements relating to credit.

Consumer Protection Act 1978

It is a criminal offence to sell any unsafe goods that might cause death, injury or damage to property. This also applies to the way in which they are marketed, and any instructions. (Under EU law, manufacturers are liable, whether or not they are negligent or careless.)

Supply of Goods and Services Act 1982

Goods must be:
(a) 'of satisfactory quality';
(b) 'as described' on labels or in advertisements;
(c) 'fit for their purpose', or capable of fulfilling their normal function: for example, shoes must not let in water.

If goods do not meet these standards, customers can get their money back – even on sale goods. Similar standards apply to services.

Other consumer protection

In addition to these laws, there are many official and unofficial

► The Office of Fair Trading was set up by the Fair Trading Act of 1973. The Director-General is also responsible for investigating anti-competitive practices in business. See Chapter 7, page 82.

watchdogs protecting consumers. The Office of Fair Trading is the official watchdog on consumer protection. Its Director-General has wide powers to investigate and ban any business practices that are against consumers' interests.

The Consumers' Association investigates the marketing of goods and services, and many other consumer issues, in its *Which?* series of magazines. It is one of the oldest and strongest defenders of consumer rights. There are many other newspaper and magazine columns and radio and television programmes dealing with consumer rights: for example, Watchdog on BBC1. Citizens' Advice Bureaux (CABs) and local Consumer Advice Centres provide general help and advice for consumers on all topics, including the application of consumer protection laws.

Voluntary codes

An increasing number of industries and associations now have **voluntary codes**, which set a standard of business practice that all members are expected to follow. They include the Stock Exchange and the Association of British Travel Agents (ABTA).

One of the most successful has been the British Code of Advertising Practice which governs all print and cinema advertising. It has succeeded because it is run by an independent body, the Advertising Standards Authority, which was set up in 1962. The Authority has great influence and power. If it bans an advertisement practically no newspaper or magazine will publish it.

Under the code, all advertisements must be 'legal, decent, honest and truthful'. The code is regularly reviewed to keep it in step with changing public views. For example, what might have been considered shocking only ten years ago would be considered quite decent today. The Association investigates any complaints from the public about Press advertisements. It deals with hundreds of cases each year and bans quite a large number of advertisements.

 Select the three most important legal or voluntary restraints on the marketing of consumer goods and state why you have chosen them.

Ethical restraints

► **Ethics** is concerned with how we should behave in society.

► **Pressure groups** are groups of people who band together to try to bring about a change of policy by a firm or a public body.

Business is no longer able to ignore the **ethical aspects** of its activities. New laws and campaigns by pressure groups have forced businesses to change their products and to rethink the ways in which they market them. Consider cigarette smoking. The government has banned cigarette advertisements on television, and has forced manufacturers to put health warnings on cigarette packets, such as SMOKING CAUSES FATAL DISEASES. The pressure group ASH (Action on Smoking and Health) has carried out a relentless campaign against smoking. Partly as a result of these laws and campaigns, cigarette smoking fell from 42 per cent of the population over 16 years of age in 1972 to 29 per cent in 1990.

Other areas in which ethical considerations have affected marketing include:

- **Packaging:** Public opinion has become critical of excessive packaging and is generally opposed to litter. Manufacturers have been forced to recycle packaging material and to ask consumers to put cans in litter bins.
- **Animal testing:** Animal rights groups have carried out many campaigns against the use of animals for testing medical drugs and cosmetics. Many retailers advertise that their goods have not been tested on animals.
- **Green issues:** Public concern about environmental issues has made firms respond by recycling some of their products and making others ecologically safer.

► See **Packaging** in Chapter 11.

 Make brief notes on the ethical restraints on marketing, showing how they have affected different kinds of businesses.

 Retrieve from your folder or file the definition of marketing that you made at the beginning of the chapter. See if it needs revising. If it does, rewrite it and file it again.

SUMMARY

- Marketing is 'identifying, anticipating and satisfying customer requirements profitably'.
- The marketing department is the main link between a company and its customers.
- The marketing department carries out a SWOT analysis to see where the firm stands and where it might go. It measures its strengths and weaknesses by comparing itself with other firms, and examines the opportunities and threats in the business environment.
- This analysis helps the firm to identify suitable market segments or niches for its products.
- A market segment is a group of people who share certain characteristics, such as age, social grade and lifestyle. A market niche is part of a market segment in which the characteristics of consumers are even more clearly defined.
- The product is marketed by mixing the four Ps – product, price, place, promotion – in the right proportions so that this marketing mix will appeal to the chosen market segment or niche.
- The four Ps and the marketing mix are as important for small businesses as they are for big ones.
- Although small businesses face severe competition from

bigger firms, they do have certain advantages. They are more flexible in product, price and place. They are in much closer contact with their market segment or niche so they need less expensive and elaborate promotion.

- The marketing of products in consumer and industrial markets is similar. However, industrial buyers are usually more knowledgeable and there is more joint buying by decision-making units.

- Marketing is regulated by a number of laws and there are many official and unofficial watchdogs to keep an eye on its activities. Voluntary codes govern marketing in a number of industries.

- Businesses have to take account of campaigns by pressure groups and changes in public views, particularly about the environment.

(10) *Market research*

Chapter objectives

After working through this chapter, you will have the knowledge to:

▮ state the purposes of market research;

▮ use desk research and apply it to a business situation;

▮ evaluate the different methods of field research;

▮ explain how random and quota samples are selected in consumer surveys;

▮ compose appropriate questions for a consumer survey questionnaire;

▮ select information from the results of a market research survey and apply it to advertising;

▮ describe industrial market research;

▮ understand and use the following key terms: market research, desk research, field research, quantitative data, qualitative data, hall test, consumer survey, random sample, quota sample, sampling point, questionnaire, closed question, dichotomous question, scalar question, multi-response question, open-ended question.

THE PURPOSES OF MARKET RESEARCH

```
1  Do you use gas for
     central heating?                              ☐
     room heating?                                 ☐
     central heating and room heating?             ☐
     heating water?                                ☐
     cooking?                                      ☐
2  Is the gas you use
     mains gas?                                    ☐
     bottled gas?                                  ☐
```

Market research has become a feature of modern life. At some time, most people will be asked to take part in a consumer survey like the one above. You might be asked in the street. An interviewer might telephone you at home, or there might be a printed questionnaire inside a magazine you buy.

Market research is one of marketing people's main tools. It helps them to make many of their decisions. Market research has five main purposes:

> **Purposes of market research**
> 1 to obtain detailed information about the firm's chosen market;
> 2 to compare the firm's performance with that of its rivals;
> 3 to find out what customers want, why they prefer one product to another, and what makes them buy;
> 4 to help solve specific, or clearly stated, problems such as the reasons for a decline in sales;
> 5 to plan an advertising campaign and to assess its results.

▶ See the box on **Market research in advertising** in Chapter 14, page 178.

 Make a list of the kind of detailed information a daily newspaper would expect to obtain if it commissioned a market research firm to carry out a survey for the five purposes stated above.

METHODS OF MARKET RESEARCH

There are two main methods of market research.

- **Desk research** uses data that is already available in printed form or on a computer floppy disk.
- **Field research** obtains data from customers and other people.

▶ The word **data** is the plural of 'datum', from the Latin for 'given'. However it is now generally used as a singular noun. There are two kinds of data: **quantitative data**, which is facts, or anything that can be measured, and **qualitative data**, which includes views, attitudes and motivations. When data is analysed and put into order, it becomes information.

Desk research

Desk research is the best way to start a market research enquiry. It is much cheaper than field research. It can be done by one researcher, whereas field research needs many interviewers. It is also quicker. Sometimes, too, it may provide all the data required and field research is unnecessary.

The main disadvantage is that the pace of change is now so great that the information may be out of date by the time it is published. Field research gives up-to-date information.

Desk research is particularly useful for obtaining information about markets, including market share, size, trends and competitors. It also provides some basic data about consumers.

Sources of desk information

There is a mass of printed matter relating to business. Most big cities have a large commercial library filled with books, reports, trade magazines and other documents, which it would take you years to read. You need to know your way around a library so that you can find the material you really want. The following are some of the most important sources.

▶ See **Research** in Chapter 1.

Official business information

The European Union, governments, local councils and many other official bodies, such as the Monopolies and Mergers Commission, provide data and information on all kinds of topics. Some government publications are particularly useful:

- The *Annual Abstract of Statistics* covers a wide range of economic and business topics, including trade, balance of payments, national income and expenditure, household expenditure, and mergers of companies;
- *Social Trends* deals with many aspects of British society and ways of life. It provides data in tables and charts and analyses it.
- Different volumes of the *Census Returns, 1991* deal with the whole of Britain and separate counties. They provide useful background information about homes and consumers, such as the types of homes and their amenities, people's occupations, or how they travel to work.
- Other useful government publications that you are likely to find in your main library include: *Family Expenditure Surveys*, *Regional Trends*, *Economic Trends* and the *Employment Gazette*.

► A **census** – or an official count of the population – is held every ten years. Every household has to fill in a form that asks questions about the home and the people who live there. The first census in Britain took place in 1801.

Find *Social Trends* in your main reference library and look at the table entitled 'Participation in outdoor sports, games and physical activities: by socio-economic group'. Make notes showing how you would use this information if you were setting up a sports shop.

Unofficial business information

There are many directories that provide useful information, particularly on markets and competitors. Here are some of the main ones:

- *Kompass* provides financial and other information on companies. It is useful for assessing rivals' performance, or benchmarking.
- *Hambro Company Guide* gives detailed information about the balance sheets of companies.
- *Who Owns Whom* lists parent companies and their subsidiaries.
- *Sell's Products and Services Directory* lists companies' names (and addresses) under trade headings.
- *Yellow Pages* gives the names, addresses and telephone numbers of local businesses, classified under trades. (This is an extremely useful reference book for all businesses, particularly the self-employed.)
- *Retail Directory* gives details of department stores, chain stores and mail order retailers. It provides maps of many cities and large towns showing locations of retail outlets.

Other useful printed sources include the trade press, trade association publications and competitors' publications, including their annual report and accounts.

Market information

There are two special sources of invaluable information about markets.

Market reports

These surveys, published by firms such as Key Note and Euromonitor, provide detailed information about dozens of separate markets from cars to carpets. These authoritative reports are based on detailed desk and field research. Some reports cost hundreds of pounds, but they are extremely valuable to the companies that buy them. They could save a person who is starting a business thousands of pounds and months of wasted effort by providing detailed information about a chosen market.

Internal sources of information

Existing businesses have a large store of valuable information in their printed and computer files. Analyses of sales figures can provide information about the market segment, customers and the effectiveness of special promotions and advertising campaigns. Sales department reports may provide information about competitors. This information is available only to the firm itself. It is therefore particularly valuable.

Go to your main reference library and obtain *Kompass*. Select a company at random in Volume 2, 'Company Information'. Write down the name and address of the company. Note the other headings the entry contains – for example, telephone number, type of business – but do not include the actual figures or details. Then find other information about the same company in the relevant directories listed above or in any other business reference books in your library. Make a note of the headings – for example, turnover, profit – but not the actual figures, and state where you found the information. Describe how valuable this information would be to one of the firm's competitors.

1   What is the main purpose of market research?
2   What does 'market share' mean?
3   What is meant by a parent company and a subsidiary company?
4   What is a Census?
5   What book would you consult to find the balance of payments?

Field research

Field research obtains data from customers, suppliers, buyers and users and from a cross-section of consumers. Much field research is based on structured interviews, where the questions have been written in advance. It takes a long time to set up the interviews, design the questionnaire and analyse the results. As a result, field research is expensive and time-consuming; but it does provide up-to-date data and views.

Field research methods

Some firms who carry out a lot of field research have their own market research departments, but most use other firms that specialize in market research.

Data is obtained in a variety of ways:

- **Face-to-face interviews:** Interviewers, using printed questionnaires, interview volunteers in the street, on the doorstep, in their home or at their workplace. This is the oldest form of field research, and it is still widely used.
- **Telephone interviews:** Researchers are increasingly using this method because it is cheaper and quicker than face-to-face interviews.
- **Postal questionnaires:** These are cheap, but the response rate can be low. (Questionnaires are sometimes included in magazines or in the packaging of goods.)
- **Hall tests:** A random group of people are brought from the street into a hall or other building to test a product and provide qualitative data about it.
- **In-depth interviews:** These interviews are conducted in the volunteer's home or workplace. The main purpose is to obtain qualitative data, such as opinions and motivations.
- **Group interviews:** These interviews investigate the reactions of half-a-dozen or so selected people to products, advertisements or packaging. Sometimes a regular panel of people is used for the same purpose.
- **Observation:** Trained observers watch people to assess their reactions to a street advertisement or an in-store display.

Draw up a table with three columns headed *Field research methods*, *Examples* and *Purposes*. Fill in the table, using the text and your own knowledge.

1 What is the main difference between desk research and field research?
2 Why is field research expensive?
3 What is meant by qualitative data?
4 Why are telephone interviews cheaper than face-to-face interviews?
5 What is the main disadvantage of postal questionnaires?
6 State whether you would use desk research or field research to obtain the following information:

(a) the number of people who own a car;
(b) the brand of cereal young children prefer;
(c) the ages of people who go to the cinema;
(d) how many new homes were established in the first quarter of the year;
(e) whether people intend to buy a new car next year.

CONSUMER SURVEYS

Consumer surveys are one of the most common forms of market research. They have a variety of purposes. They can be used to obtain information about an existing product, a new product or competitors' products. The most important objectives are to:

1 assess the market size or the total number of people who would buy a product;
2 identify potential customers who might buy the product;
3 indicate the price at which a product would be bought;
4 find out information about rival products;
5 check whether an advertisement is effective by asking if consumers remember it and how much of its content they can recall;
6 pre-test a product that a firm is considering producing by giving consumers information about it, or by providing a sample.

Some market research has a wider purpose. For example, it might be designed to find out if purchasers of a particular product would be interested in buying a follow-up service. Would people who have bought a second home overseas be interested in letting it during the winter? Would people who use a certain railway station be interested in buying meals from a new adjacent Chinese take-away on their way home?

 Make notes on the main purposes of consumer surveys.

 You are composing a consumer survey questionnaire for a company that makes a washing powder – Brand X. Write one question for each of the items numbered 1 to 4 in the list above. Your aim is to obtain quantitative data. File your answer, but keep it available for further reference.

Selecting samples

It is not possible to interview all consumers everywhere, so market researchers use a representative sample instead. If the sample is carefully selected, there will be only a small percentage margin of error in the results. Usually, a sample of a few thousand people is interviewed. There are two main methods of choosing the sample: random sampling and quota sampling.

Random sampling

A **random sample** is not just picking anyone in an unplanned way. It is a system of choosing people that gives everyone an equal chance of being included. The districts where the interviews are to take place are selected at random, usually by using a computer. The people to be interviewed in these areas are also picked at random in the same way.

The people who are chosen may be scattered all over the country. Because they are the only ones who can be interviewed, it can be expensive and time-consuming to get to them. Therefore, another sampling method is often employed.

▶ The Premium Bond computer – known as Ernie – picks prize winners in the same way, just as the 'random' button on a CD player selects tracks.

Quota sampling

With a **quota sample**, interviewers are told to talk to a specified number of people of a particular sex, age range and social grade. For example, their quota of street interviews might include an equal number of women and men. These two categories are then divided again by age. The interviewers would be told to see a certain number of men and women in the age ranges of 16–24, 25–34, 35–44, 45–64 and over 65. They would then be told to find, within each age range, a specific number of men and women of each of the social grades A, B, C1, C2, D and E.

This may sound a little complicated, but interviewers soon get used to picking out the right kind of person for their quota among the crowds in the street. The interviews take place in a number of cities and towns throughout the country. These **sampling points** may be chosen at random.

▶ There could be other categories such as the number of people in the household, the number of children or the type of dwelling. See **Market segments** in Chapter 9.

 Make brief notes on random and quota samples, bringing out the differences between them.

THE QUESTIONNAIRE

It is not easy to write a good **questionnaire**. It is essential that you have clear objectives and not just a vague idea of what you want to know. For example, you might want to discover the potential market for Brand X washing powder, and consumers' attitudes to Brand X and its biggest competitor.

Clear, unambiguous questions

The questions you ask must be easy to understand, absolutely clear and unambiguous – they must have only one meaning. For example:

'How often do you use your washing machine?' won't do, because the respondent may use a launderette.
'Have you bought a carton of washing powder recently?' won't do either, because there are also liquid products as well as washing powders. Furthermore, 'recently' is too

HOUSEHOLD		

60 Does anyone in your home own or are you considering buying any of the following?

	OWN	CONSIDER		OWN	CONSIDER
Camcorder	(01)☐	(09)☐	Dishwasher	(02)☐	(10)☐
Games Computer	(03)☐	(11)☐	Home Computer	(04)☐	(12)☐
Personal Fax	(05)☐	(13)☐	Hi-fi Separates	(06)☐	(14)☐
Microwave	(07)☐	(15)☐	Mobile Phone	(08)☐	(16)☐

61 a) Has your house been re-roofed in the last 5 years?   Yes   (1)☐

If so what sort of tiles or slates were used?

Concrete Tiles	(2)☐	Natural Slate	(3)☐
Clay Tiles	(4)☐	Manmade Slate	(5)☐
Concrete Plain Tiles	(6)☐	Clay Plain Tiles	(7)☐
Don't know	(8)☐		

b) Would you consider re-roofing your house?
No   (1)☐   Within 1 year(2)☐   Within 5 years (3)☐

c) Which of the following roof tile companies are you aware of?

Redland (1)☐	Marley(2)☐	Russell(3)☐	Anchor (4)☐
Sandtoft(5)☐	Eternit(6)☐	Acme (7)☐	Others (8)☐

62 Approximately how old is your property?
☐☐☐☐ Years

63 Do you live in a mains gas supply area?
Yes(1)☐ No(2)☐

Extract from a questionnaire for the Consumer Choice Survey

vague. Does it mean in the last day, or the last month?
- 'Do you think Brand X washing powder is expensive?' is also too vague. Its price must be compared with something else.

Closed questions

Questionnaires use mainly **closed questions**. These are questions to which the respondent can give a limited number of possible answers. There are three main types of closed questions used in questionnaires:

1 dichotomous questions;
2 scalar questions;
3 multi-response questions.

Dichotomous questions

The simplest type of closed question is the dichotomous question. This is a question that allows you to give only one of two possible answers, which are mutually exclusive or opposite. Usually, the two possible answers are 'Yes' or 'No'. For example:

> 'Do you use Brand X washing powder?'
>
> Yes ☐
> No ☐

Sometimes, it may be necessary to include a third response of 'Don't know', but then the question is no longer strictly dichotomous.

Scalar questions

Another type of closed question is the scalar question. This invites

► These are called **dichotomous questions** from the Greek *dikhotomia*, meaning 'cutting in two'.

the respondent to assess something by choosing one of several answers on a scale. One scale commonly used ranges from 'very good' to 'very poor'. For example:

'How would you rate the cleaning power of Brand X?'

Very good	☐
Good	☐
Neither good nor poor	☐
Poor	☐
Very poor	☐
Don't know	☐

Multi-response questions

Closed questions that are not dichotomous or scalar are known as multi-response questions. The answers need not be mutually exclusive: it may be possible to select more than one answer. For example:

'Which of the following brands of washing powder have you used in the last three months?'

Brand X	☐
Brand Y	☐
Brand Z	☐
Don't know	☐

The main advantage of all types of closed questions is that they provide definite responses. This makes it easy to feed the data into a computer for analysis.

Open-ended questions

An **open-ended question** is one to which there is an unlimited number of possible replies. For example:

'What is your opinion of Brand X?'

It is obvious that this question could produce a great many different responses, some of which might be quite lengthy. As a result, it would be more difficult to classify, or group together, the replies for analysis. For that reason, open-ended questions are rarely used in questionnaires. They are, however, used for in-depth interviews, where the interviewer wants to probe below the surface to discover what people feel and what their hidden motivations are.

 Find the four questions about Brand X that you wrote for the activity on page 124. Revise them if necessary and file them again.

 Make full notes on closed and open-ended questions, giving examples of your own wherever possible.

1 Give the meaning of random sample
2 What is a multi-response question?

3 Write a closed question to discover whether someone owns a bicycle

4 What is the difference between a closed question and an open-ended question?

MARKET RESEARCH RESULTS

When all the interviews have been completed, the data has to be analysed, or put together in such a way that it provides as much information as possible about the objectives of the survey. The findings will then be presented in a report, and often illustrated with charts and graphs.

Let's take a real-life survey to see how this is done. The Realeat survey into meat-eating has been carried out every year since 1984. The surveys are conducted by the independent market research organization Gallup for Realeat, a producer of vegetarian and non-meat foods. In 1993, 4,299 interviews were held at over 200 sampling points. Interviewers were given quotas for sex, age and social group. The results were then analysed and presented in written and graphic form in a report.

The respondents were divided into various groups. Vegetarians and vegans formed one group. People who avoided red meat formed another. The combined groups were described as 'non-meat-eaters'. The survey shows that the number of non-meat-eaters has increased greatly since 1984. Almost half are avoiding meat for health reasons. The most common reason, given by 40 per cent of those eating less or no meat on health grounds, is concern about cholesterol. Other major reasons are fats (28 per cent) and modern farming methods and BSE or mad cow disease (20 per cent).

▶ Vegans do not eat or use anything that derives from animals. Some vegetarians eat eggs and dairy products.

▶ Eating too much animal fat is believed to produce a high level of cholesterol in the blood, which is linked with heart disease.

▶ BSE (bovine spongiform encephalopathy) is a cattle disease that is usually fatal. There is some evidence that it can be transmitted to other mammals, and some reports suggest that it could be transmitted to humans.

ACT IN Study the charts opposite and answer the questions that follow.

1 What proportion of people eat red meat regularly?

2 Which age/sex group has shown the biggest percentage rise in non-meat-eating since 1984?

3 In which age/sex group would you find the most non-meat-eaters? Why do you think this is so?

4 Which social group contains the highest percentage of non-meat-eaters? In your view, what might be the reasons for this?

5 Use the information from the survey to write and design a poster for (a) a butcher's shop and (b) a health food store.

INDUSTRIAL MARKET RESEARCH

Industrial market research and consumer market research are similar, with desk and field research being used in both. The main difference is in the selection of a sample for field research. The

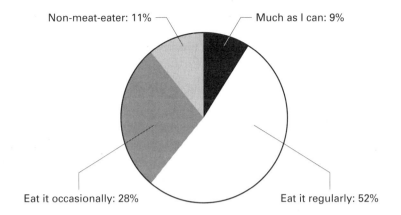

Meat in the diet, 1993

Source: The 1993 Realeat Survey
conducted by Gallup

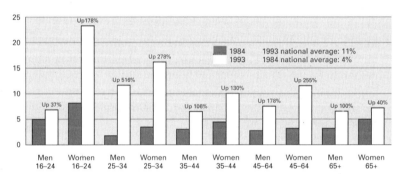

Non meat-eaters by age and
sex, 1984–1993*

*Respondents declared themselves to be
vegetarian, vegan, or avoiding red meat
in their diet.
Source: The 1984 and 1993 Realeat
Surveys conducted by Gallup

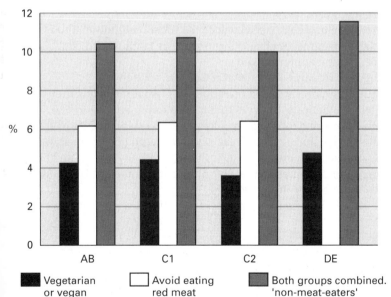

*Non meat-eaters by social
group, 1993*

Source: The 1993 Realeat Survey
conducted by Gallup

quota is generally chosen from business directories. It will usually include both big and small companies in all the sectors that the industrial company supplies. Customers, distributors and suppliers are usually included. If geography has an influence on buying, there will be a geographical element in the quota, too. The interviews are frequently conducted on the telephone.

Hall tests are also used in industrial market research. A random sample is never used. Instead, carefully selected managers and/or workers are invited to attend a demonstration of a new kind of tool or product.

Industrial companies also gain much of their information about their market at trade fairs and exhibitions. Other companies' brochures and pamphlets provide much information about competitors' products and intentions. There is also a chance to talk to customers and suppliers and to gain an overall view of the industry. These fairs and exhibitions are particularly useful for small firms that cannot afford market research.

 Make brief notes about industrial market research

SUMMARY

- Market research is one of the marketing department's main tools. There are two main methods: desk research and field research.
- Desk research, using printed material and information stored in computer files, is quick and cheap, but the information may be out of date.
- There are many methods of field research, including face-to-face interviews, telephone interviews, postal questionnaires, hall tests, in-depth interviews, group interviews and observation.
- The consumer survey is one of the most common methods. Random samples or quota samples are used to find the people to be interviewed.
- Market research interviewers use pre-written questionnaires. Closed questions are usually used as they provide definite answers that can be easily analysed. The questions may allow only a Yes or No answer; a scale of answers, ranging from 'very good' to 'very poor'; or multi-response answers.
- Open-ended questions allow a variety of answers. They are used for in-depth interviews.
- Industrial market research is carried out in a similar way. However, the people to be interviewed are usually selected from relevant trade and business directories.
- Trade fairs and exhibitions provide an extremely useful source of information in industrial markets. They are particularly useful for small firms that cannot afford to carry out market research

(11) *Product*

THE FOUR PS

The next four chapters deal in detail with the four Ps – product, price, place and promotion. Just turn back to Chapter 9 and read the review box on page 111, which gives a brief summary of the four Ps. The review tells that the four Ps are studied separately because it makes them easier to understand. However, while you are studying each of them, you should always try to think of the links they have with the other three Ps.

For example, the product and its price have very strong links. If you are buying a jacket, the price will usually be one of the deciding factors. There may be a jacket that you like most, but you can't really afford it, so you walk away. However, if you have the store's credit card, you may decide to go into debt and buy it anyway. Connections between the four Ps, such as these simple links between product, price and credit, will be explored in greater detail in the next four chapters. You should also try to think of other connections yourself as you read on. The interconnections between the

► An **interface** is a surface that forms a common boundary, such as the shared surface between sea and shore. It is also used to describe the meeting point between people or organizations.

► To refresh your memory on single-use consumer goods, see **Consumer markets** in Chapter 3.

four Ps cannot be stressed too much. They form the marketing mix, which is the essential interface between the firm and its customers.

 Draw up a table with four columns headed *Product*, *Price*, *Place* and *Promotion*, leaving a left-hand margin free. Think of two single-use consumer goods (such as food or drink) that you have bought recently. Write the name of the first single-use consumer good in the left-hand margin. Fill in the four columns, putting in as many factors as possible that influenced your choice. For example, your table might look like this:

	Product	Price	Place	Promotion
Brand A	Rich chocolate	Good value	Easy to find	Coupons for CDs
	Gives me energy	Price reduced		Saw it advertised
	Like its yummy taste			

Then do the same with the other single-use consumer good.

THE IMPORTANCE OF THE PRODUCT

As the activity above shows, buying something is usually influenced by all four Ps. (If it is not, the firm has not done a very good marketing job!) Although all four Ps are important, the product is probably even more important than the others. Without the product, there could be no price, no place, no promotion. The product is the basis of the whole marketing process. In fact, some marketing experts now believe that the quality of the product and its value compared with rival products are the most important aspects of marketing. There is a certain truth in this. Firms sometimes try to sell a new magazine by offering the first issue at a huge discount, by providing a free binder and by advertising the magazine frequently on television. This is certainly great penetration pricing and promotion, but if the magazine does not have a sufficiently wide appeal it will soon close. The same kind of strategy is commonly used with some new food products. They get the same kind of intensive promotion, yet within a year or so they have vanished from supermarket shelves. In marketing, none of the four Ps should ever be ignored, but the product in particular must always receive special attention.

► **Penetration pricing** is setting a low initial price to undercut rivals and gain market share.
► **Promotion**, such as free gifts, is another way to increase sales.

Aspects of the product

Although you may think of a product as a single item, a product has many different aspects. For convenience, these can be divided into three main categories, or classes.

Features of goods

Objective features
These are the physical features of the good which exist for every buyer.

- **Suitability:** It will be suitable for its intended purpose, for example scissors will cut.
- **Quality:** It is of a certain standard and will last for a certain length of time.
- **Design:** This includes the size, weight and shape of the good and materials from which it is made.
- **Colour:** Colours may be 'fast' and not affected by light and water, or they may fade. Sometimes clothes are made to look faded to fit in with a fashion.

Subjective features

These are the features that a particular buyer sees in the good.

- **Value:** The buyer might think that the product provides value for money compared with rival goods.
- **Image:** The good might enhance the buyer's self-image by making him or her feel attractive, fashionable, youthful, etc.
- **Status:** The good might make the buyer feel superior, perhaps by being associated with a social class to which he or she aspires.

Service features

These are the extra features that are obtained as a result of buying the good, for example credit facilities. They are usually more important in consumer durables markets than for single-use consumer goods.

- **Credit:** The seller offers credit so that payments can be spread over a period of weeks, months or years.
- **After-sales services:** These services are provided once the good has been bought. Computer and software manufacturers usually provide a telephone hot-line for answering queries.
- **Manuals:** For products that the consumer has to learn to operate, such as video cassette recorders, washing machines and personal computers, it is important that the instruction booklets or manuals are clear and easy to follow.
- **Guarantees:** Guarantees usually last for a year. Longer guarantees can often be bought as an optional extra.

Some of the objective and service features are guaranteed by law.

▶ See the box on **Consumer protection laws** in Chapter 9, page 115.

ACT IN Draw up a table with three columns headed *Objective features*, *Subjective features* and *Service features*, leaving the left-hand margin clear. Think of a consumer durable you have bought and write its name in the left-hand margin. Fill in the table by describing all the features that influenced your choice.

THE STANDARD PRODUCT LIFE CYCLE

Every kind of good has a product life cycle, stretching in five stages from its introduction to its decline.

Life cycle for a brand-new product

Introduction
The product is put on the market. Because it is new, there might be little competition. Production costs are high because sales are limited. Marketing costs are also high because the product is advertised widely. There have also been research and development (R & D) costs. Therefore, there are usually financial losses at this stage.

Growth
The product is popular and sales rise quickly. Costs fall because a longer production run produces economies of scale. The advertising budget can also be reduced. The product starts to make a profit.

Maturity
Sales are still increasing, but at a slower rate. The profits are greatest at the beginning of this stage, but as other firms put rival products on the market, there is greater competition.

Saturation
The market is now saturated with many products of a similar kind. Sales start to fall, and so do profits.

Decline
Demand starts to shrink and sales fall even further. The point is reached where demand is so low that the product becomes unprofitable. It is then withdrawn from the market.

 Use the text above and the figure on page 135 to make notes on the product life cycle, bringing out the differences between the five stages.

Time scales

The graph that follows shows the standard life cycle for a particular product, such as a wristwatch. The vertical axis of the graph shows sales; the horizontal axis shows time. Some new products are merely copies of goods that are already on the market and may have a very different kind of life cycle (see aborted life cycle on pages 136–7).

The time-scale may range from tens to thousands of years. For example, skateboards were only launched in the United States in the early 1960s, becoming popular in Britain in the 1970s. However, they are already in decline in Britain.

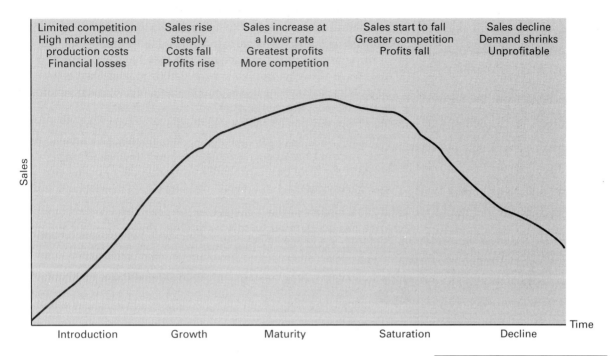

Limited competition High marketing and production costs Financial losses	Sales rise steeply Costs fall Profits rise	Sales increase at a lower rate Greatest profits More competition	Sales start to fall Greater competition Profits fall	Sales decline Demand shrinks Unprofitable
Introduction	Growth	Maturity	Saturation	Decline

Standard product life cycle

Life cycles and technological change

Business history shows the importance of technological change in product life cycles. Some goods have several life cycles because they are updated when technological advances make previous versions obsolete. With pens, for example, there have been six distinct life cycles.

1 Quill pens were made from the hard hollow stem of a bird's feather – swan or goose feathers were commonly used. The life cycle lasted from at least AD 600 to the middle of the nineteenth century when quill pens disappeared from the market.
2 Steel-nibbed pens, with a wooden holder, were put on the market in the 1830s. They had to be continually dipped in a bottle of ink. For general use, the life cycle of this type of pen lasted until the 1930s.
3 Fountain pens were invented in the 1890s. These had metal nibs and a reservoir in the stem that had to be filled periodically with ink from a bottle. The life cycle started in the 1890s and reached its saturation point before and during the Second World War. After the war, the popularity of these pens started to go into decline. In the 1960s, fountain pens that used replaceable ink cartridges appeared, but these too are now in decline.
4 The ball-point pen was first introduced in 1895, but it was not patented until 1937, and its growth stage did not arrive until the 1940s. Conventional ball-point pens have brass writing tips, and the ink is highly viscous and contained in a narrow plastic tube. Ball-point pens are in their maturity stage, but the introduction of a new type of pen with a tungsten carbide

ball, liquid ink in a larger reservoir, and an ink flow similar to a fountain pen, may give the ball-point a bit of a boost.

5 Soft-tip or felt-tip pens were introduced in the 1960s. As writing pens these are in decline, but they have a mature market as drawing implements for children, and may have a growing market for use as highlighters and as markers for white boards, flipcharts, overhead projectors, etc.

6 Fibre-tip and plastic-tip pens arrived a few years after felt-tips, and were better for writing as they produced a finer line. Recent refinements, such as stainless steel cladding around the fibre point, probably mean that they are still in their growth stage.

This brief history of the life cycles of the pen shows how the pace of change has accelerated greatly in modern times. The first life cycle lasted over 1,300 years; while the others last 100 years at most.

 Take any common product and find out about its history. Does it have more than one life cycle? If so, how many life cycles has it had? Which stage of each life cycle has been reached?

1 What is the major P in the marketing mix?
2 What are the objective features that might influence you when buying a pair of jeans?
3 What is meant by a subjective feature in relation to goods?
4 What is a life cycle?
5 What is likely to happen to sales when the market is saturated with a particular kind of good?

OTHER PRODUCT LIFE CYCLES

Some products have a standard life cycle like the one in the figure on page 135; but others have different life cycles. The three main kinds are:

1 aborted life cycle;
2 extended life cycle;
3 brand life cycle.

These will now be examined in turn.

Aborted life cycle

The aborted life cycle is one that marketing people never want to see, yet often do. A product is put on the market, but it fails to achieve adequate sales and it has to be withdrawn within a year or so. There can be various reasons for the failure.

• A competitor might have heard about the idea and rushed out a better product before the other product was launched. (Industrial espionage, or spying, might have been used.)

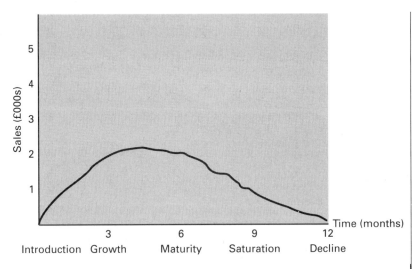

Aborted product life cycle

- The chief executive might have come up with the idea for the product and pushed it through regardless of senior managers' advice. (This does happen with autocratic leaders.)
- The market research and the marketing might not have been thorough enough.
- The idea could have been ahead of its time. (Marketing personnel might have anticipated a want that consumers were not yet ready to accept.)
- It might simply have been a bad idea. Or it might have been a 'me-too' product – a weak copy of a stronger rival product that was already on the market.

 Make notes on the aborted life cycle, giving examples from your own knowledge wherever possible.

Extended life cycle

 Read the following and answer the question at the end.

Ahmad Patel works in the design department of a motor car manufacturer. A low-priced, 1.3 cc hatchback was successfully launched last year. It is now going to be produced in an upgraded version with a 1.6 cc engine. It will have a five-speed gearbox, and a three-speed automatic gearbox will be available as an optional extra.

The 1.3 cc model is a three-door or five-door hatchback with a four-speed manual gearbox. A five-speed gearbox is available as an optional extra. Some of the main features of the basic model are:

- reclining front seats; adjustable front head restraints; one-piece folding rear seat;
- open passenger glove compartment and side pockets in doors; grey plastic fascia; speedometer; petrol and temperature gauges; warning lights;

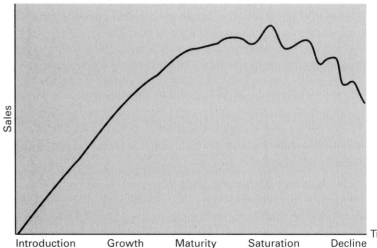

Ford Escorts and Orions: a range of models

- two-speaker stereo radio and cassette with electric aerial; twin door mirrors, manually adjusted; electrically operated sun-roof and windows in front only;
- plastic grey and yellow door trims; grey floor carpets.

This basic model is targeted at the 24 per cent of households that have a second car and at households in the C1 and C2 social grades. The upgraded version will be targeted at BC1 households with young children, for use as a main car.

Ahmad has been asked to suggest new or improved features that should be included in the upgraded model.

1 In your view, what are the four main features that Ahmad should include? Say why they would help in the marketing of the car.

Extended product life cycle

```
Sales
      |
      |                          ___
      |                       __/   \__/\_
      |                   ___/         \  \__
      |                __/              \_   \__
      |              _/
      |            _/
      |          _/
      |        _/
      |      _/
      |    _/
      |  _/
      |_/
      |_____ Time
     Introduction  Growth  Maturity  Saturation  Decline
```

Although all products must finally go into decline, marketing people put up a tremendous fight to keep the product alive. As the graph shows, the product life cycle can often be extended, sometimes for years, by stimulating it and injecting it with new vitality. Firms use a number of techniques to extend a life cycle.

Life cycle extension techniques

Improved models
Producing a new version of a product is one way of extending the life cycle. As the case study has shown, this might involve improvements in some of the main features. This technique is very common with consumer durables, such as cars, cameras and computers. It has a number of advantages. It is very much cheaper, and less risky, to upgrade an existing product than it is to produce a new one. It also helps to fight off competition from other manufacturers who might copy the product. It is mainly for this reason that Japanese manufacturers usually start producing a new version as soon as the original product has been launched.

New uses
Firms can often find new uses for a product that will increase sales or, sometimes, rescue a product from decline. For example, more trainers are now used for general wear than for sport.

More frequent use
This will also result in increased sales. At one time, most people washed their hair only once a week. Now many people have been persuaded by shampoo manufacturers to wash their hair far more frequently, thus increasing sales.

Using other Ps

The other three Ps can also be used to extend the product life cycle.

- **Price:** Price reductions can boost sales; but there is a danger of setting off a price war as other firms cut their prices in retaliation. This can lead to a general fall in profits in that market.
- **Place:** Firms can try to find new outlets for their products. For example, paperbacks are sold in airport lounges and in some supermarkets
- **Promotion:** Sales can be increased by various promotional activities, such as free cosmetics, CDs or garden seeds with magazines.

New packaging can also be used to boost sales. Packaging is a very powerful means of increasing sales because it can be used to enhance the product, to improve distribution, and to announce new promotions. It also has a direct effect on the price.

► Packaging is such an important topic that it will be dealt with in detail later in this chapter.

Find real-life examples of each of the extension techniques described and use them as the basis for your notes on life cycle extension techniques.

BRANDS

Traditional brands

There is such a bewildering variety of products in differing versions that consumers are often lost for choice. To persuade customers to buy their products, manufacturers have to make them different from rival products. Brands are one of the traditional and most successful methods of differentiation. A brand is a trade name that can be used only by the firm that has registered it. Brand names are sometimes the name of the firm, such as Heinz or Black and Decker, but more often they are invented names, such as Surf or Persil. Through massive advertising and other forms of promotion, the brand name may become totally linked with the product. For most people, 'beans' still means 'Heinz'; the brand name says it all. So, when consumers go into a supermarket, they are more likely to reach out for Heinz beans.

► **Differentiation** is the way or ways in which a product differs from similar products.

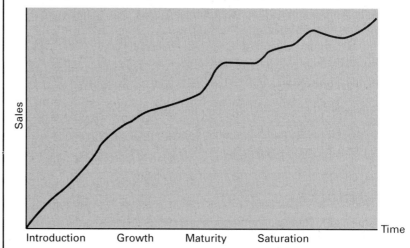

The life cycle of a successful brand

Successful brands have great benefits for manufacturers.

* The constant advertising and promotion make the brand seem so familiar and desirable that it creates a brand loyalty among consumers. They go on buying the same brand week after week and year after year. As a result, sales of the product do not go into decline, but are always rising, as the figure above shows.
* Brand loyalty makes it possible to charge a premium, or a higher price, for the brand.
* Brand loyalty also protects the manufacturer from competition.
* The brand name makes it easier for the product to be sold globally. Is there anyone in the world who has not heard of Coca-Cola?

Not all brands succeed, but many are market leaders with the highest sales in their market. The value of the brand can be written into the balance sheet as a valuable asset. Brands can be sold to other firms for a profit. However, brands have recently had to face a new challenge.

Own-label products

Brands have been so successful that many of the big high-street stores and supermarkets, such as Marks & Spencer, Boots and Sainsbury, decided to get in on the act by selling their own-label products. These brands are made by outside manufacturers (sometimes, manufacturers with a brand of their own). They are sold under the retailer's name, for example Safeway lemon tea, or under a new brand name, like Novon, Sainsbury's own brand of washing powder and liquid. In the last decade, own-label grocery sales in supermarkets have increased from 20 per cent to 30 per cent. About two-thirds of Sainsbury's sales are own-label or own-brand. Retailers can sell own-label goods at a lower price than brands and still make a bigger profit.

▶ Marks & Spencer was founded over a century ago when Michael Marks and Tom Spencer opened a small shop in Leeds selling small, low-priced goods. It now has over 300 stores in Britain and the Republic of Ireland, and others in Europe and the Far East. Marks & Spencer also owns the Brooks Brothers chain in the United States.

Increase in own-label sales

Why have sales of own-label products increased? There are three main reasons.

1 Consumers have become more aware of the choices available to them through articles in newspapers and magazines, radio and television programmes, and publications such as *Which?*.
2 The majority of consumers now believe that there is often little difference between a branded product and an own-label product.
3 Price has become more important for many consumers, who would rather have 'everyday low prices' than brand premium prices. The recession at the beginning of the 1990s has increased this trend.

▶ The Consumers' Association, founded in 1956, did much to educate consumers about products through its monthly publication *Which?*. In 1988, the organization was renamed the Association for Consumer Research; the Consumers' Association is the name of the publishing company within that organization.

1 Give two methods a manufacturer might use to extend the life cycle of a product.
2 What is meant by promotion?
3 What is a brand name?
4 Define brand loyalty.
5 Give three examples of a brand name that has become identified with a particular product.

PACKAGING

Packaging is such a powerful element in the marketing mix that it deserves to be known as the 'fifth P'. It has become an industry in its own right. The packaging industry has a total annual turnover of more than £8 billion, employs over 100,000 people and accounts for 1.5 per cent of the gross national product.

There are three main elements in packaging:

- the materials from which the packaging is made, such as paper, cardboard, plastic or glass;
- the size, shape and weight of the container;
- the label.

Each of these, as you will see, can contribute to the four Ps.

Packaging and product

With many goods, the package is an essential part of the product. For example, liquids and powders could not be sold without containers of some kind, such as bottles for disinfectants and cartons, bags or bottles for washing powders and liquids. Marketing people use the packaging to increase the appeal of the product. For example, CFC-free aerosols and trigger packs are widely used for many products, ranging from furniture polish to shaving foam, because they are easy to use. Ring-pull cans for soft and alcoholic drinks and plastic containers for hamburgers are also easy to use, enabling consumers to snack as they walk.

The materials used, and the size, shape and colour of the container, can also be used to enhance, or increase, the appeal of the product. Take perfume bottles. Different shapes appeal to different kinds of customers. A heart-shaped bottle might appeal to someone buying a romantic gift; a bottle in the shape of an old Roman vase might catch the eye of an AB woman of around 30. The outside container, or box, can also be used for a different purpose: to conceal the actual size of the perfume bottle within!

Packaging and price

The cost of the packaging is often a considerable part of the total price. Plain packaging has been tried for some goods, but it has not been much of a commercial success so far. However, there is a new challenge from warehouse clubs, which are now selling basic goods in bulk in no-frills premises at greatly discounted prices.

Packaging and place

Packaging is an essential element in the distribution of goods. It has to be easy to pack and handle the goods. The packaging must also be strong enough to protect the goods. In addition, it should be suitable for display in shops and stores.

Packaging and promotion

One of the main uses of packaging is to promote the product name, which is always prominently displayed. It can also be used to advertise details of other promotions such as price cuts, size increases, competitions and special offers. The bar code on the packaging makes it easy to keep a check on stock and sales. The label is often used to provide information about the firm or the product, and other information required by law, such as the ingredients of tinned food.

▶ Many countries have now banned, or greatly reduced, the use of **CFCs** (chlorofluorocarbons). They had been used since the 1950s as propellants in aerosols. It is now believed that their release into the atmosphere causes depletion of the ozone layer, which allows harmful radiation to reach the earth, causing environmental damage and skin cancers.

Challenge to packaging

Packaging has come under increasing scrutiny from environmental pressure groups. They criticize packaging as a waste of money and of scarce raw materials. The European Union has recently issued a directive about packaging. Its main aim will be to change all member-countries, including Britain, from throwaway societies to recycle and re-use societies by the year 2000. The packaging industry has had to take these developments into account. Cardboard, paper, tins and bottles are all recycled. Products are increasingly made from recycled materials, for example stationery and toilet rolls.

Take three items that you or members of your household have bought recently. Write notes describing the packaging of each item and explaining how it has contributed to the four Ps.

NEW PRODUCTS

However successful their products may be, all firms have to produce new lines to keep up with changes in the market or to maintain a competitive edge over their rivals. The new product may range from a minor innovation, like a soap containing new ingredients, or a major innovation – a completely new product – such as the personal stereo.

In either case, the risks are high. With a major innovation, the costs of R & D can be very high. To develop a new passenger jet aircraft can cost well over £1 billion with another £1 billion or more for the engine. The lead time would be over ten years. The firm has to try to calculate (or guess) what the world will be like in ten years' time. What will fuel cost? Will there be new laws governing aircraft noise and environmental pollution? What will be the size of the aircraft passenger market? What will the general economic situation be like? Questions like these, and dozens more, are difficult to answer because it is difficult, if not impossible, to predict what the world will be like in ten years' time. However, if the product is put on the market and it does succeed, it can increase the profits of the company enormously. It can also increase the wealth of the country as economic success depends mainly on creating successful new products.

Before any product is launched, it goes through a rigorous screening process. The eight main stages of this process are:

1 product selection;
2 market feasibility;
3 commercial feasibility;
4 production research;
5 product development;
6 test marketing;
7 full marketing;
8 product launch.

► **Lead time** is the time between the product idea and the product launch.

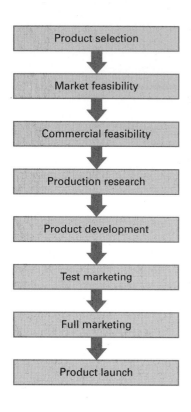

Creating a new product

Product selection

Ideas for new products are produced in various ways. They may come from market research; the R & D or production departments; rival products; trade exhibitions or magazines; customers; the sales force; or 'brainstorming' sessions in which members of various departments come up with as many ideas as possible in a limited time.

Market feasibility

This is the screening stage that asks the question: is there a market for the product? This may be answered by the marketing department staff, using, where appropriate, the services of the regular consumer panel. Alternatively, a market research survey may be carried out. This is one of the most important methods of screening. Many ideas are abandoned at this stage.

Commercial feasibility

At this stage there are several questions that need to be answered. Is it possible for the firm to finance the new product or borrow money to do so? Has it got the necessary staff of all kinds that will be required? How many more workers will it have to employ? Does the new product fit in with the firm's other products – its product mix? What will be the likely profit and the return on capital employed (ROCE)?

Production research

Has the present workforce got sufficient technical ability? Can some components be bought in from other firms? Will new factory buildings be needed?

Product development

Production has to be planned and a production line has to be set up. The product has to be tested against the required standards.

Test marketing

To make sure that the product is feasible, or likely to work, it may be tested out in a particular region of the country or other market segment. As a result of the tests, the product may be modified, or even abandoned.

Full marketing

The marketing department plans the launch in detail, including all aspects of the four Ps.

Product launch

The sales force is briefed. The promotions and the advertising start – while the marketing people wait tensely to see whether the product will succeed.

Many products never reach this final stage. It is estimated that 30 per cent fail in the laboratory while they are being researched. Another 60 per cent fail during development. Of those that remain, only a small proportion succeed. In the grocery industry, for example, 40 per cent of brands are withdrawn from the market in the first five years.

1 What is the 'fifth' P?
2 What are the three main elements of packaging?
3 Why is packaging important in the distribution of goods?
4 Give three examples of the way in which packaging is used to advertise other products.
5 What is meant by recycling?
6 State the advantages and disadvantages of R & D to a firm.
7 How does a firm get ideas for new products?

In your own words, make brief notes of each stage in the development of a new product from product selection to product launch.

Read the following case study and answer the questions at the end.

Mo Osborne has her own small firm which publishes greetings cards. The total market size is £1 billion or 2.5 billion cards a year. It is still growing as some supermarkets have now started to sell cards; other outlets are specialist shops, stationers and CNTs (confectioners, newsagents and tobacconists).

The market is dominated by three large firms who share two-thirds of the market between them. The rest of the market is shared by some 3,000 firms. It is therefore intensely competitive, particularly as cards rarely have a shelf-life of more than a year.

Christmas cards account for about two-thirds of cards sold every year. However, there are cards for many other occasions, including birthdays, anniversaries, engagements, weddings, births, deaths, illnesses, and achievements, such as passing your driving test or examinations. There are also special days, such as Mother's day, Father's day and Valentine's day.

Mo has chosen Valentine's day as her niche market. About 25 million Valentine's day cards are sold each year. Like practically all cards, they are divided into two main types: traditional and humorous.

This year, Mo has decided to change the position of her products in the market. She has drawn a product position chart which shows her present position in the market and her intended new position.

The present product position on the horizontal axis, which indicates card type and ranges from traditional to humorous, shows that her cards are mildly humorous. The

▶ **Shelf-life** is the length of time for which retailers are willing to display and sell goods.

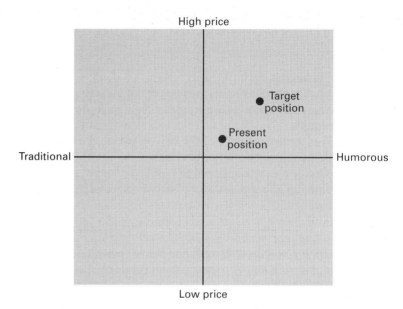

High price

Target position

Present position

Traditional ——————————————————— Humorous

Low price

Product position chart

present product position on the vertical axis, which measures price, shows that the price of her cards is just above industry-average.

Mo thinks that people now want more way-out humour in Valentine's Day cards, so her new product position has been moved to the right along the traditional–humorous axis. She feels that customers will be willing to pay more for these cards, so her new product position mark has been moved up the vertical price scale.

1 How many greetings cards are sold each year?
2 On what occasion are most cards bought?
3 What is the average price of a greetings card?
4 In your view, which other achievements or special days could have their own card? Say why you think they would sell.
5 If you were one of the freelance designers working for Mo, what kind of new card would you design for the new product position? Describe it or draw it.

Collect a number of birthday or Christmas cards given to you, or to a relative or friend. Draw a product position chart like the one above. Number the cards in order, starting with 1. Then assess where the card should be placed on the horizontal axis, ranging from Traditional to Humorous, and on the vertical axis by guessing the price of the card. Put the number of the first card at the appropriate point on the chart. Do the same with all the other cards. When the chart is complete, write a brief analysis of the product positions, stating what it tells you about the taste and expenditure of the people who sent them.

SERVICES AS PRODUCTS

Until the last few years, services were much less heavily marketed than goods. That is changing rapidly. More and more institutions, such as banks and building societies, are marketing their services as products. Take credit cards. There are basic products such as American Express, Visa and Access, but firms try to differentiate their product by offering different versions, such as upmarket gold cards, and different credit limits. Until recently, the price charged for credit – a very high rate – has not varied much from one firm to another. However, in 1993 the Save & Prosper Group cut its Visa card APR interest rate to 14.6 per cent, about 8 per cent lower than most other firms. The places where the cards can be used is another selling point, with firms claiming that their cards can be used in a greater number and type of places than the others. There is massive promotion of the cards on television and in the other media.

Marketing services

It is more difficult to market services than goods. The two main reasons for this are:

1   variations in quality;
2   intangibility.

Variations in quality

With efficient quality control in factories, it is possible to produce goods of a fairly uniform quality. This is much more difficult with services, because personal skills and characteristics are involved. One dentist may be less skilled than another dentist, but any dentist can have an off-day!

These variations create great difficulties in marketing because it is often difficult to promise a certain level of service. One way around the problem is to offer a limited, but highly efficient, service. Fast-food restaurants do this by offering a small range of uniform food that tastes the same in all the outlets. The uniformity is increased by the use of the same livery and brand name. Training in customer relations helps to standardize the staff's personal service.

Intangibility

Goods are tangible, physical objects that can be touched. Services are intangible; they cannot be touched, but only appreciated in the mind. A football, for example, is a good; it can be touched. A football match is a service; it cannot be touched.

Marketing people want to retain and use all the pleasant feelings associated with a service. However, they also want to express them in a physical form to make them more real to the consumer. For that reason, the footballers' strip is changed regularly, and loyal fans will buy the new version. In a similar way, holidays are advertised with lavish photographs of exotic destinations that may have little relation to reality.

Make notes on marketing services.

1 Why are brand names so important in marketing?
2 Give two examples of firms that provide services.
3 Why are services more difficult to market than goods?
4 Explain three methods that banks use to market credit cards.

SUMMARY

- The product is the main ingredient in the marketing mix, because without it the other three Ps could not exist. Goods are not a single entity, but have many different aspects. They can be divided into objective features, subjective features and service features, such as after-sales service.
- Some products have a standard life cycle with five stages: introduction, growth, maturity, saturation and decline.
- Other products have different life cycles. An aborted life cycle is when a product never really takes off and goes into rapid decline before it is withdrawn from the market. An extended life cycle occurs when a firm keeps a product alive by marketing techniques.
- A brand life cycle can show an upwards trend for many years. Intensive advertising of a named brand can create brand loyalty among consumers. However, brands now have to face an increasing challenge from big retailers' own-label goods.
- Packaging is often an essential part of the product. Milk, for example, could not be sold without its container. It has to be strong enough to protect goods in transit and easy to handle, store and display in retail outlets. The packaging can also be used for promotion.
- The cost of packaging is often a considerable part of the price. Critics claim that packaging is a waste of money and scarce resources.
- New products must be created to keep up with changes in the market and to fight off competition. Every new product has to go through a screening process, stretching from product selection to product launch. Nevertheless, most new products fail within a few years.
- The position of a product in a market can be shown on a product position chart. This plots the market position against two axes, which could measure price and type. Quality or status could also be measured.
- Services are being marketed more than they used to be, but they are more difficult to market than goods. Two of the main problems are variations in quality and intangibility.

(12) Price

Chapter objectives

After working through this chapter, you will have the knowledge to:

▌ evaluate the effects of external factors on prices;

▌ understand and apply VAT with or without a discount;

▌ appreciate how other taxes and duties can affect prices;

▌ describe the effect of inflation on prices;

▌ calculate how prices are affected by changes in exchange rates;

▌ describe price elasticity and inelasticity of demand and its effect on business;

▌ distinguish between mark-up and margin and calculate one from the other;

▌ identify the pricing strategies that could be used during the product life cycle

▌ understand retailers' pricing strategies;

▌ state the three main factors that influence the pricing of services;

▌ understand and use the following key terms: price, value added tax (VAT), input tax, output tax, discount, exchange rate, price elasticity of demand, price sensitive, price insensitive, mark-up, margin, overhead, penetration price, skimming price, market leader's price, differential pricing, promotional pricing, destroyer pricing, end-of-life price cut, restrictive practice, manufacturer's recommended price (MRP), price plateau, EDLP (everyday low prices), sales, mark-downs, critical point pricing, loss leader, complementary pricing, variable pricing.

WHAT DETERMINES THE PRICE OF A PRODUCT?

You want to buy a CD that has just won an award. You look in a big chain store in the high street and find it is priced at £14.99. Then you go to a much smaller specialist shop outside the city centre where the CD is being sold for only £13.49. Another shop in the same area has the CD displayed in the window at £11.99, surrounded by other CDs by the same artist, priced at £13.99. Inside the shop, you pick up a music magazine and skim through it. You find that one postal dealer is offering exactly the same CD for £10.99 with no charge for postage, while another is selling it for £9.99 in celebration of the award.

What is the real price of the CD? The short answer is that there isn't a real price for any product. This chapter will show you why the price of the same product varies so much. However, before you come to that topic – pricing strategies – you should first know what proportion of the total price is outside the manufacturer's control.

 To refresh your memory of markets, visit a branch of Our Price, or a similar music store, and find one CD segment, such as classical music. State the niches into which the segment is divided.

Factors affecting prices

Manufacturers have less control over their prices than they do over their products. Unless it is banned by law, they can make any product they like. However, they cannot entirely control the total price of their products. The price is affected by three main factors:

1 government taxes and policies;
2 economic 'laws';
3 business costs.

The first two of these factors can be described as **external forces**; the third is an **internal force**.

▶ See the box on **Consumer protection laws** in Chapter 9, p. 115

GOVERNMENT TAXES AND POLICIES

Value added tax

Value added tax (VAT) is the main indirect tax in all member-countries of the European Union (EU), including Britain. It has to be paid on most goods and services. VAT is paid at every stage of the production of goods and services. For example, the VAT that a furniture manufacturer pays to the Customs and Excise on the wood bought from a supplier is **input tax**. When the manufacturer sells the furniture to a shop, the VAT that is added to the price charged is **output tax**. If the total input tax is larger than the total output tax, the manufacturer can claim back the difference from the Customs and Excise, so he or she is never out of pocket. The only people who cannot claim anything back are the consumers. They buy the furniture for a price that includes the total amount of VAT.

The rate of VAT, and the goods and services on which it is charged, vary from one country to another in the EU. In Britain, the standard rate is 17½ per cent. Some goods are zero-rated, including most food and drink, books and newspapers, and children's clothes and footwear. VAT was imposed on electricity and gas at a rate of 8 per cent in 1994.

▶ Commissioners of Custom were first appointed in 1671 to collect duties on imports. The Excise Department dealt with taxes on goods, such as alcohol, produced for the home market. It was merged with the Customs Department to form HM Customs and Excise in 1909. Its main duties now are collecting value added tax and customs and excise duties, and it works to stop smuggling and the importation of banned goods, such as drugs.

Calculating VAT

Retail prices are calculated by adding 17½ per cent to the basic price of the goods or service. For example:

Basic price	£100.00
Plus VAT at 17½%	£17.50
Total price	£117.50

If there is a discount, that is taken off before VAT is added. For example:

Basic price	£100.00
Less trade discount of 10%	£10.00
	£90.00
Plus VAT at 17½%	£15.75
Total price	£105.75

It is just as easy to calculate the basic price (before VAT is added) from the selling price. The formula is:

$$\text{basic price} = \frac{\text{total selling price}}{(1 + \text{the rate of VAT expressed as a percentage of 1})}.$$

For example, if the rate of VAT was 17½ per cent, you would divide the total selling price by 1.175. If the rate of VAT was 20 per cent, you would divide the total selling price by 1.20.

Take a real-life example. Let's say that the total selling price was £587.50 including VAT at 17½ per cent. What was the basic price?

$$£587.50 \div 1.175 = 500$$

If rate of VAT is increased, businesses have to put up their prices. This could reduce their sales. VAT affects all businesses in the same way, except for very small businesses with a turnover of less than £45,000 (at the time of writing). These small businesses do not have to register for VAT or add it to their sales price.

Calculate the total selling price (including VAT at 17½ per cent) of (a) goods with a basic price of £250 and (b) of goods with a basic price of £1,300 and a discount of 10 per cent. Calculate the basic price when the selling price is £9.40 including VAT at 17½ per cent.

Customs and excise duties

The government also puts customs and excise duties (or taxes) on various goods and transactions, such as duties on alcohol, tobacco and petrol, and stamp duties on buying houses and shares. This means that business has no control over a significant part of the price. This can have a big effect on sales. If the government raises the duty on alcohol, there will be a tendency for consumers to drink less. If it lowers the duty, people may drink more.

▶ No VAT is added to the price of zero-rated goods, but the firms that produce them can claim back any input tax they may have paid. Some services, such as insurance and education, are exempt from VAT. No VAT is charged, but the suppliers cannot claim back any input tax they may have paid.

▶ A **discount** is a reduction in price which is usually expressed as a percentage, for example a 5 per cent discount would reduce the price of a good or service from £100 to £95. Discounts are often given to customers who buy in bulk and sometimes to those who pay in cash.

▶ You can always check that the answer is right by doing the calculation in reverse, for example £500 + £87.50 = £587.50.

▶ Small businesses can sometimes benefit by registering for VAT even if they do not legally need to do so. A designer, for example, would have to charge business customers VAT, but they would be able to claim it back. However, the designer would then be able to claim back VAT on all the supplies he or she bought. (VAT is always charged to a registered person, never to a company, whatever its size.)

▶ Many people who live in the south of England make day trips to France to buy alcohol, because the rate of VAT is lower there.

► Here is an example of the effects of inflation. A woman buys a new car for £10,000 and plans to pay back the loan over two years at a rate of £500 a month. In the second year the rate of inflation is 20 per cent, which means that most goods, services and salaries increase by that percentage. A new model of her car now costs £12,000; and her salary has risen from £30,000 to £36,000. As a result, the repayments on the loan are now a smaller proportion of her income – 0.166 per cent instead of 0.2 per cent.

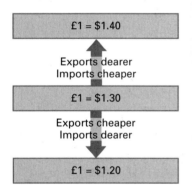

Effects of exchange rates

► 'Guesstimating', or estimating roughly, the rise and fall of currencies is a business in itself. When rates of exchange are changing rapidly, firms and professional dealers in currencies can make millions of pounds if they guess correctly or lose millions if they're wrong. Managers often have to guesstimate in all kinds of business situations when sufficient data is not available.

Economic policy

The government's economic policy also has a great effect on business in general and prices in particular. One of the government's main tasks is to control **inflation**, which is a progressive increase in the general level of prices. If the government keeps inflation low, prices will increase by only a small amount each year, say 1 or 2 per cent. Consumers benefit from low inflation, particularly those on low, fixed incomes, such as pensioners. It is also advantageous for exporters because it means that their prices remain competitive. High rates of inflation make it difficult for manufacturers to sell their goods overseas. High inflation benefits mainly people and companies with large debts. The government with its large national debt and public sector borrowing requirement (PSBR) also benefits, as the interest it has to pay is now worth less.

Exchange rates

An **exchange rate** is the price at which one currency is bought and sold for another. For example, at any one time the pound might buy 1.49 United States dollars, 7.34 French francs, or 2.38 German marks. A year later, the rates might be $1.40, 7.21FF, and 2.29DM.

The government has a great influence on the pound's exchange rate through its control of interest rates and its general economic policy. The exchange rate has a great effect on the prices of exports and imports.

A strong pound will make the prices of imported goods cheaper. For example, if the exchange rate goes up from £1 = $1.30 to £1 = $1.40, then that means that every £1 buys an extra 10 cents worth of United States goods. These price reductions would eventually feed through to the shops. However, British exports would become more expensive because Americans would have to pay 10 cents more for each pound's worth of British goods.

The effects are reversed with a weak pound: imports become more expensive and exports become cheaper.

These price changes can have a devastating effect on businesses. If the pound remains high, firms that export a large proportion of their output may be forced out of overseas markets and may even go out of business. Importers who rely on cheap foreign goods may find their businesses ruined if the pound remains weak.

Business can do nothing to alter the exchange rates, and must learn to adapt when they fluctuate.

1 What would be the effects of an increase in tax on the price of petrol
   (a) on the private motorist?
   (b) on a taxi firm?
2 What does VAT stand for?
3 What is the meaning of zero-rated?
4 Which businesses do not have to pay VAT?
5 What are exchange rates?

6 Who may benefit from inflation?

7 Will a strong pound make imports cheaper or more expensive?

 A British engineering firm is supplying a South African firm with £100,000 worth of equipment. When the contract was made the exchange rate was £1 = 5.20 Rand. The order is now finished and the exchange rate is £1 = 5.45 Rand. How much will the British firm lose or gain by the change in the exchange rate?

ECONOMIC 'LAWS'

Although economic theories do not always hold when put into practice, some provide useful guides for business. One of the most useful is the principle of supply and demand, which was introduced in Chapter 4.

► To refresh your memory, see the marginal note on **Supply and demand**, on page 25 of Chapter 4.

Supply and demand

Although the equilibrium price cannot be found in many markets, changes in supply and demand do have a general impact on prices. For example, if there is a shortage of oil, the prices of heating oil, and petrol and diesel at the pumps, will rise. If consumers are buying fewer clothes in a recession, retailers will reduce prices and hold many sales and sales promotions to try to reduce their stocks.

Price elasticity of demand

Changes in price have a great effect on the quantity demanded, but the effect is not the same with all goods and services. With some goods or services, a moderate change in price (either upwards or downwards) may make very little difference to demand. With other goods and services, it can have a big impact. Economists call this **price elasticity of demand**.

Demand tends to be inelastic, i.e. moderate changes in price make little difference to demand, when the good or service is:

1 a necessity, like basic food and heating or dental treatment for toothache;
2 inexpensive in relation to income, like face flannels or developing and printing films;
3 irreplaceable (without substitutes) such as tea;
4 addictive (habit-forming), such as cigarettes, some hobbies and buying National Lottery tickets.

► **Inelastic** demand is not greatly affected by moderate price changes. The good or service is price insensitive.

Demand tends to be elastic, i.e. even a moderate price change will have an effect on demand, when the good or service is:

a luxury;
expensive in relation to income;
replaceable (one that has substitutes).

► **Elastic** demand is affected by even moderate price changes. The good or service is price sensitive.

Give examples of each of the three kinds of goods and services where demand is elastic.

> ► **Disposable income** is the amount that remains after all compulsory deductions, such as income tax, national insurance and pension payments, have been made from a person's income.

Price elasticity of demand does not provide a complete guide to what happens in real life. Many people now have such a large disposable income that they can afford to go on buying what they want with cash or credit. Nevertheless, firms need to be aware of the theory when they are considering price changes. Business people usually use the terms **price sensitive** (elastic) and **price insensitive** (inelastic).

1 What effect is the shortage of a product likely to have on the price if it is
    (a) a necessity;
    (b) a luxury.
2 What term means the same as price sensitive?
3 Is demand likely to be elastic or inelastic if there is a large increase in the price of:
    (a) a pound of sausages?
    (b) electric fires?
    (c) toothpaste?
    (d) cameras?
    (e) butter?

 Draw up a table with two columns headed *External forces* and *Impact on prices*. Write the first of the external forces in the list below (value added tax) in the first column and then fill in the second column showing how it can affect prices. Do the same with the other items in the list.

value added tax; customs and excise duties; exchange rates; supply and demand; price elasticity of demand.

BUSINESS COSTS

We have seen how various external forces affect the price that a business gives to a particular product. There is also an important internal force involved: the cost of producing the product. One way of calculating a final price is to use **cost-plus pricing**. The direct costs of producing a good and a share of the indirect costs are calculated. Then a **percentage mark-up** is added on to obtain the selling price. For example, a good that cost £10 to produce is marked up by 25 per cent of the cost price, i.e. £2.50. Therefore, the selling price would be £12.50 (£10 + £2.50 = £12.50).

> ► The direct costs of producing a good are composed mainly of raw materials, components and labour; the indirect costs include rent, rates and administration. See Chapter 17.

Note that the mark-up is very different from the **margin**, or gross profit, which is calculated on the selling price. In this case, therefore, the margin would be 20 per cent ((2.50 ÷ 12.50) × 100 = 20).

The margin is always less than the mark-up. The gap between them increases proportionately with the size of the margin, as the note opposite shows.

> ► | Margin (%) | Mark-up (%) |
> | --- | --- |
> | 10 | 11.11 |
> | 30 | 42.86 |
> | 50 | 100 |
> | 60 | 150 |
> | 75 | 300 |

Calculating margin from mark-up

The formula for calculating the margin from the mark-up is:

$$\frac{\text{difference between the selling price and the cost price}}{\text{selling price}} \times 100$$

Take the second example in the margin on p. 154, where the mark-up is 42.86 per cent. It is easy to see how the formula works if the cost price is £100. The selling price is then £142.86 and the difference between the selling price and the cost price is £42.86. Therefore, the margin is calculated as follows:

$(42.86 \div 142.86) \times 100 = 30\%$

The calculation is almost as easy if the cost price is £22. A mark-up of 42.86 per cent results in a selling price of £31.43. To arrive at the selling price, the cost price must be increased by the following amount:

$(22 \times 42.86) \div 100 = £9.43$

The selling price is therefore £31.43 (i.e. £22 + £9.43). So the margin would be:

$(9.43 \div 31.43) \times 100 = 30\%$

Calculating mark-up from margin

The percentage mark-up can be found from the margin by using the following formula:

$$\text{mark-up} = \frac{\text{profit}}{(\text{cost price} - \text{profit})} \times 100$$

In the example above, where the cost price was £22, and the margin was 30 per cent, the percentage mark-up needed can be calculated in the following way. A profit of 30 per cent on a cost price of £22 would be £6.60 ((22 × 30) ÷ 100 = 6.6). The cost price less profit would be £15.40 (22 − 6.6 = 15.4). Therefore, the percentage mark-up required would be 42.86 per cent ((6.6 ÷ 15.4) × 100 = 42.86).

Cost-plus pricing is still used in the building and construction industry and in some branches of retailing. It is less common than it once was because most prices are now determined by the market. However, costs do provide a basic floor price for all businesses. Unless it's for brief periods, as in penetration pricing, businesses can't afford to sell their products below cost price.

 Firm A wants to make a gross profit of 18 per cent on a new product. What would be the mark-up? Firm B has marked up its goods by 37 per cent. What would be the margin?

PRICING STRATEGIES

The price of any product has to include the cost price, VAT and any

The production of digestive biscuits at McVitie's biscuit factory in Harlesden, north London

▶ At the time of writing, there is no VAT on plain digestive biscuits, but there is on chocolate digestives, which are classed as 'non-essential' food!

▶ With other products, the proportion at the manufacturers' and retailers' disposal may be higher or lower.

other taxes or duties. It might seem that business has little room to manœuvre in pricing. However, there is some leeway. Let's take the example of McVitie's biscuits. Every minute of the day and night, nearly 4,000 McVitie's digestive biscuits are baked in Britain's biggest biscuit factory in Harlesden, north London. Over 5 million are produced every day. The retail price is composed of:

- raw materials – 20 per cent;
- manufacturing, packaging and distribution – 30 per cent;
- marketing and manufacturer's profit – 25 per cent;
- retailer's mark-up – 25 per cent.

In this case, the costs of raw materials, manufacturing, packaging and distribution accounts for half of the price. However, the other half is at the disposal of the manufacturer and retailer, which gives them room to manœuvre in pricing (although they have to pay their overheads out of their share).

Manufacturers' pricing strategies

The prices that manufacturers charge is often very closely linked to the position of their product in its life cycle. Let's look at manufacturers' pricing choices at each stage of the product life cycle.

Introduction

Manufacturers have two main choices in the introduction stage. They can use a low **penetration price** to gain as big a market share as possible by undercutting the prices of their rivals. Alternatively, they can use a high **skimming price** to attract wealthier consumers. The high price also helps manufacturers to recoup their R & D and marketing costs as quickly as possible. The skimming price only works well with high-quality products for up-market customers, such as high-

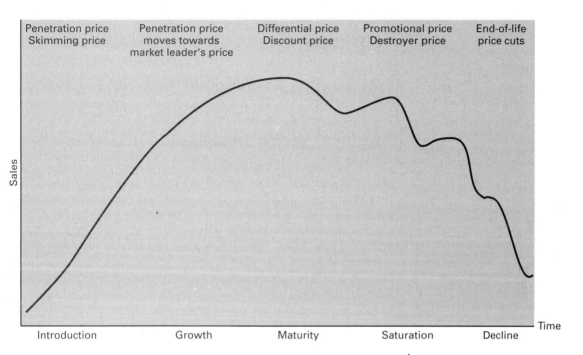

| Penetration price Skimming price | Penetration price moves towards market leader's price | Differential price Discount price | Promotional price Destroyer price | End-of-life price cuts |

Pricing in the product life cycle

precision mechanical watches, or with products that have been intensively marketed in a buoyant market, such as computer games.

Growth

During the growth period, the penetration price will gradually be increased as sales continue to rise, and the skimming price may be lowered so that more customers are able to afford to buy the product. In the end, the penetration price will tend to fall in line with the **market leader's price**, which sets the standard for the whole market segment.

Maturity

In the maturity phase, **differential pricing** is used, i.e. different kinds of customers are charged different prices. It is essential that the customers don't know about the differences in price, or, if they do, that they don't object to them. For example, a farmer might sell his eggs to a packing station at one price, to local shops at a higher price, and to farm shop customers at an even higher price. Manufacturers often give a discount to wholesalers and chain stores that buy in bulk, and charge the standard list price to smaller shops. Both of these strategies might start in the growth stage.

Saturation

During the saturation phase, **promotional pricing** is used to keep the sales rising, i.e. temporary reductions are made in price to help retain old customers and attract new ones. There can also sometimes be dramatic reductions in price – or **destroyer pricing** – to increase market share and to make life difficult for competitors.

► The packing station is charged the lowest price because it has to make a profit itself and allow for the retailers' mark-up. Local shopkeepers are charged a higher price because they have to make a profit only for themselves. Farm shop customers pay the highest price, which is about the same as the retail price in the shops.

Decline

When the product life cycle reaches the decline stage, there may be big, end-of-life price cuts to clear stocks.

 Make notes on manufacturers' pricing strategies, adding real-life examples of your own wherever possible.

Retailers' pricing strategies

At one time, retailers had little choice when they priced their goods. Manufacturers fixed the minimum retail price. They could take shopkeepers to court if the goods were sold below that price. This restrictive practice was ended by the Resale Prices Act of 1964. Most other restrictive practices have now been abolished by British and EU laws. There are a few exceptions. Until 1995, publishers were allowed to fix a minimum price for books so that they could provide a wider distribution of books and small bookshops could survive; but retailers can now cut the price of any book. However the EU has ruled that perfume houses may refuse to sell their goods to stores if they feel that the premises or staff are unsuitable and might affect the perfume's reputation.

Manufacturer's recommended price

Manufacturers can now only suggest a **manufacturer's recommended price** (MRP). This will include a mark-up for the retailer which varies from one kind of shop to another.

For example, confectioners, newsagents and tobacconists (CNTs) usually have a mark-up of about 20 per cent. Chemists have a 40 per cent mark-up for their over-the-counter (OTC) goods. Many boutiques can have a mark-up of 70 per cent or more. Gift shops and perfume shops can have a mark-up of 100 per cent. Some top jewellers and fashion shops in prime London locations may have a mark-up of as much as 300 per cent.

> ### Choosing the mark-up
> Three main factors influence the choice of mark-up:
> - The speed at which stock is turned over, or sold, is a major factor. CNTs with a quick turnover can afford to have a lower mark-up than a boutique.
> - The location of the shop or store is also important. Rents and other overheads are much higher in city centres than they are in the suburbs, or in smaller towns and villages.
> - Consumers' views of prices have a bearing on the mark-up chosen. For each kind of good there is a **price plateau**, or a minimum price level that consumers expect to pay. If the price is below that level, many consumers will think that the product must be of inferior quality. Some wealthy consumers are happy to pay the high prices charged by up-market shops. Perhaps it reassures them to know that they are rich enough to buy exclusive goods that other

► **Restrictive practices** occur when firms try to limit competition, for example by stopping retailers from cutting prices. Other examples are firms sharing out a market between themselves; fixing the price at which a product sells; or stopping competitors from entering a market.

► The fee paid to chemists for dispensing each script (or prescription) is paid from National Health Service funds.

people cannot afford. Although they relish the occasional sale, such consumers might well be deterred from shopping in an up-market shop if it lowered its prices permanently.

Read the following case study and answer the questions at the end.

Malcolm had worked for a chain of menswear shops for ten years. The firm had run into difficulties and had started to make a loss. As a result, it had drawn up new contracts of employment for employees which would reduce their salaries and provide less security of employment. Malcolm had decided not to sign the new contract and to open his own up-market shop instead.

   His shop stocks only the most exclusive, and expensive, designer clothes, including Versace jackets, Armani trousers and Missoni ties. No item costs less than £50, even a tie, and some suits cost over £1,000. The first two years were very difficult and Malcolm nearly went bankrupt. However, business improved as more wealthy businessmen heard about his shop. By the third year, he was doing well, as his (shortened) profit and loss account shows:

Sales	£500,000
Cost of sales	£300,000
Gross profit	£200,000
Overheads	£150,000
Pre-tax profit	£50,000

▶ See **Profit and loss account** in Chapter 19.
▶ Cost of sales includes buying the clothes from manufacturers, and wages.
▶ **Overheads** are the other expenses of running the business.

Malcolm decided that he would like to increase his net profit, out of which he has to pay tax and interest charges. He has been using a mark-up of two-thirds (66.67 per cent). He is working out what his shop prices would be if he raised the mark-up to 100 per cent.

1 Why did Malcolm open his shop?
2 What kinds of clothes does he sell?
3 What was the value of his sales in the third year?
4 What is his gross profit, or margin, as a percentage of sales?
5 What is his net profit, or pre-tax profit, as a percentage of sales?
6 If a suit cost Malcolm £256, what would be the shop price with a mark-up of 66.67 per cent plus VAT at 17½ per cent?
7 What would be the new price in the shop if the mark-up were raised to 100 per cent?
8 In your view, what effects might that have on sales? Describe any ways in which the price rise might be made more acceptable to Malcolm's customers.

Other retail price strategies

As you already know, big retailers no longer accept all manufacturers' recommended prices. They will want big discounts if they place large orders. With their own brand or their own-label products, they set their own prices. Retailers of all sizes now use many of the same pricing techniques as manufacturers.

- **Penetration price:** Retailers may use a penetration price when they open a new store or shop.
- **Differential price:** Some stores sell goods at higher prices in small towns than they do in cities where there is more competition.
- **Discount price:** Stores may give a discount for large orders or cash. Some shops – known as 'swag shops' – sell nothing but discounted goods.
- **Promotional price:** Retailers often use specially low prices for goods that are being promoted in relation to some event or achievement.
- **End-of-life price cuts:** Retailers often cut prices dramatically to sell off slow-moving stock.

Retailers' own strategies

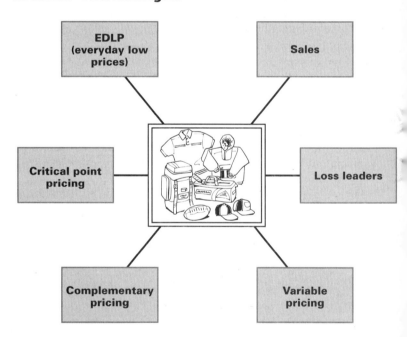

Retail pricing strategies

Retailers also use other pricing strategies of their own:

- **EDLP (everyday low prices):** This strategy is becoming increasingly popular in superstores and DIY stores and affects many fast-selling lines. 'Essential' goods are targeted and their prices are kept low. This keeps consumers happy and helps to fight off competition from other stores that do not have an EDLP policy.

- **Mark-downs:** The use of **sales** – or mark-downs – is one of the main alternatives to EDLP. (Another alternative is a price war.) In a recession, the number of sales increases, with sales at the end of every season, mid-season, and no season at all!
- **Critical point pricing:** Consumers want the best value for money. There is only a penny difference between £10 and £9.99 and a pound difference between £1,000 and £999. Yet most consumers instinctively make a distinction between the two prices, because a critical pricing point has been passed – £10 and £1,000 respectively. That is why you often see prices like £9.99, £19.99, £49.95 and £995.
- **Loss leaders:** Goods in shop windows or in dump bins (wire or plastic containers) at shop and store entrances are sold at cost price to attract customers inside.
- **Complementary pricing:** The retailer may price one good relatively high, while a good that accompanies it may be priced relatively low. For example, men's trousers may be relatively expensive, while trouser belts may be relatively cheap. The relative prices can be reversed. For example a ball-point pen could be relatively cheap and the refill relatively expensive.
- **Variable pricing:** Different prices can be used at different times. A market trader, for example, might sell off vegetables cheap on Saturday afternoons. The same technique can be used for different seasons, for example the price of sunglasses could be reduced in the autumn.

▶ Complementary pricing is the basis of 'pitch marketing' used by market traders. In selling a batch of goods, they will throw in one item for a ridiculously low price; but the customers are paying for it in the price they pay for the other goods.

Make notes on the pricing strategies used by retailers, including real-life examples of your own where possible.

1 Explain the following terms:
   (a) margin;
   (b) mark-up;
   (c) cost-plus pricing;
   (d) differential pricing.
2 What restrictive practice was ended by the Resale Prices Act?
3 What is the difference between a penetration price and a promotional price?
4 Why would it be impossible for a retailer to sell only loss-leaders?

Pricing services

The development of strategies for the pricing of services is still in its infancy. There are three main factors that influence the prices charged for services:

1 **Time:** The main ingredient in fixing the price for a task is often the time taken to perform the task, for example repairs

to machines or equipment, or car servicing. It is often difficult to estimate the time in advance. For example, while a car is being repaired, more than one cause for the breakdown may be revealed.

2 **Direct and indirect costs:** The customer has to pay for the direct costs of any materials or components required and also make a contribution towards the indirect costs of running the business, such as rent, rates, equipment and administration. So the amount you pay for a haircut covers both materials and labour and the hairdresser's overheads.

3 **Skills:** Diplomas and degrees indicate uniform levels of skill, but in practice the levels of skill of service providers vary enormously. A highly skilled and experienced person can regularly charge a higher rate than a novice.

Setting prices for services

Professional people, such as accountants and solicitors, usually make an hourly charge, which includes an allowance for overheads. Business consultants usually make a daily charge. Some businesses have a task-based rate for their services. Electricians often have a fixed charge for a visit, which applies even if they do no more than change a fuse. Many garages have a fixed-price service for different makes of cars. Stockbrokers have a minimum commission for buying and selling shares and a different rate according to the size of the deal, for example £90 on £5,000, £225 on £25,000.

Service-providers use a few of the pricing techniques described on pages 160–1. Differential pricing is sometimes used; electricity companies, for example, charge different prices to domestic and business customers. Variable pricing is also used; British Telecom has two main charge rates – standard and cheap rate – based on the time of the day and the day of the week. The total cost of the call is based also on the length of the call and the distance.

Codes of practice

Some trade associations have drawn up codes of practice to protect consumers. The services covered include car repairs, electrical servicing, funerals, package holidays, electricity, post and telephone. The professions also have their own complaints procedure.

▶ Funeral directors, for example, are not allowed to ask relatives if they can arrange the funeral. If they are asked to do so, they must show the relatives a price list.

 Make notes on how prices are set and controlled in the service sector.

 Refer back to the section about CD prices at the beginning of the chapter, on pages 149–50. Take each of the prices in turn and state what strategies might have been used in choosing the price.

SUMMARY

- All prices are affected by government taxes (such as VAT), economic 'laws' (such as price elasticity of demand) and the general costs of running a business.
- Inflation, or the progressive increase in the general level of prices, is one of the most important external influences on pricing. Change in exchange rates is another.
- Some manufacturers use cost-plus pricing to find a selling price. They calculate the cost of the goods and add a percentage mark-up.
- There are more sophisticated methods of pricing goods. Manufacturers often link their pricing strategy to the position of their product in its life cycle. They use a penetration or skimming price in the introductory stage; the market leader's price in the growth stage; differential pricing and discounts in maturity; promotional pricing and destroyer pricing in the saturation stage; and end-of-life price cuts in decline.
- Retailers use many of the manufacturers' pricing strategies and some of their own. These include EDLP (everyday low prices), mark-downs or sales, critical point pricing, loss leaders, complementary pricing and variable pricing.
- The pricing of services is affected by three main factors: time, direct and indirect costs, and skills.
- Service-providers use far fewer pricing strategies. The main ones are differential and variable pricing.

13 Place

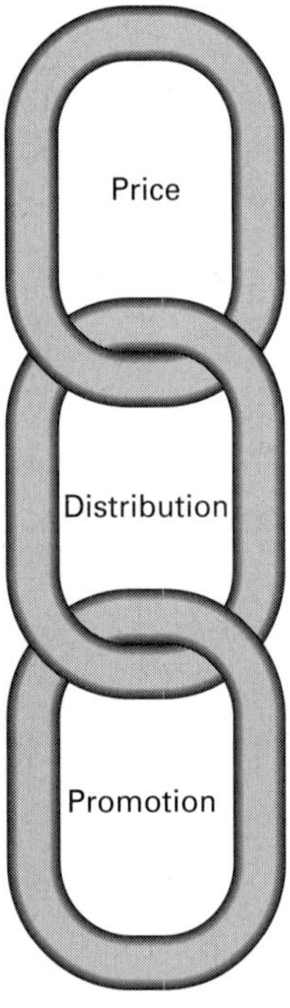

Price

Distribution

Promotion

The distribution link

THE IMPORTANCE OF DISTRIBUTION

'How' and 'where'

The word '**place**' is used in the four Ps because it fits in neatly with the other three Ps: product, price, promotion. '**Distribution**', however, is a more accurate word. There are two aspects to distribution: *how* the product is distributed; and *where*, or the place to which, it is sent. Distribution plays a vital part in the marketing process as it links price and promotion.

Channels of distribution

How the product is distributed is known as its **channel of distribution**. A channel has one or more stages. Literary and musical products commonly have long channels, with six stages, as shown in the char in the margin. An author produces a manuscript – often now on floppy disk as well as paper – and usually sends it to an agent. The agent finds a publisher and negotiates the advance payment and royalties. The publisher uses specialist firms to print and bind the books. If the publishing company is too small to employ its own sales representatives, it uses a bigger publisher's sales force to obtain orders from booksellers. The bookshops then sell the book to customers. The shortest channel of distribution has one stage: for example, a farmer selling eggs to customers at the door.

Effects on price

The length of the channel of distribution affects the price in two main ways. The more stages it has, the greater the number of separate profit margins that need to be built into the final price. In the author's case, the agent, the publisher, the printer, the binder, the bigger publisher and the bookseller all add on their own margins. Therefore, the price of the book is increased.

There is also an increase in **handling charges**, or the costs of loading and unloading goods at the factory, warehouse and shop. This also has to be built into the final price. However, some of these handling charges would occur anyway. If manufacturers did not sell their goods to wholesalers, they would have to do all the wholesaler's work themselves: storing goods, transporting them and finding customers. An efficient wholesaler or a capable agent can sometimes increase sales, and so produce higher profits for the producer.

The physical length of the channel also has an impact on price. The greater the distance goods have to travel, the bigger the cost of transport and the possibility of damage or theft.

Choosing an appropriate place

Where the product is sent – the place – is an equally important aspect of distribution. The place must be appropriate for the market segment or niche. For example, a supermarket would not be a sensible place in which to try to sell real caviar.

Both the place and the length of the channel strongly affect the way in which the product is promoted. High-street retailers, with long channels of distribution, do a lot of in-store promotion. Their shop windows are often their biggest advertisement. Mail order firms, however, spend large amounts of money on advertising and distributing glossy catalogues for free. They can afford to do so because their channels of distribution are shorter – they have no shops.

In some cases, the promotion *is* the place. For example, newspaper and magazine advertisements are often used to sell goods, such as clothes, direct to the consumer. This form of direct marketing combines promotion (advertisements) and place.

A long channel of distribution

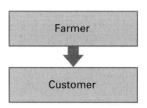

A short channel of distribution

► Agents and brokers are used in many different industries: for example, housing (estate agents); insurance (insurance brokers); stocks and shares (stockbrokers). Manufacturers use overseas agents when it would not be profitable to set up their own distribution system or manufacturing plant. Unlike all the other businesses in the channels, agents never own the product. They usually work on a percentage of the value of the sales.

► See the box on **Direct marketing** in Chapter 14, page 185.

Distribution
Distribution is finding the most effective way of delivering products to customers through the shortest possible channel to the most suitable place at the lowest possible cost.

1 What is meant by a channel of distribution?
2 How does the length of the channel of distribution affect the price of a product?
3 Why can mail order firms spend so much money on their catalogues?
4 Explain the importance of place in the marketing mix.
5 What would happen if one of the stages in a channel of distribution went out of business?

THE DISTRIBUTION INDUSTRY

Distribution is now one of the biggest and most important industries in the country. It employs nearly 3½ million people, about a sixth of the total working population, and accounts for about a sixth of the national income.

There are nearly 120,000 wholesale businesses, which buy goods from manufacturers and sell them to retailers. There are even more road haulage operators, about 130,000, including many small firms and self-employed operators. About 80 per cent of goods are transported by road. Rail accounts for less than 7 per cent. Most rail freight is bulk materials such as iron and steel, building materials, petroleum, coal and coke. The rest of the goods are transported by coastal shipping, inland waterways, air, and pipelines, which are used mainly for oil, gas and petroleum products.

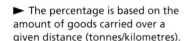

► The percentage is based on the amount of goods carried over a given distance (tonnes/kilometres).

Revolutionary changes

Over the last thirty years, there have been revolutionary changes in the methods of distribution, and these are still continuing to happen. The changes started in the 1960s, when big grocery retailers opened their own **regional distribution centres** (RDCs). The RDCs receive goods from manufacturers by road and distribute them in lorries to the retailer's stores throughout the region. Many RDCs are run by specialist distribution firms, which also provide the lorries and the drivers. The lorries are painted with the retailer's **livery**, i.e. with its company logo and in its distinctive colour. This system of distribution has become increasingly popular with other major retailers and manufacturers of consumer goods.

► **Livery** was the distinctive uniform worn by male servants of the aristocracy. It usually included the aristocrat's coat-of-arms. See Chapter 14, page 174, for an explanation of **logo**.

Many regional distribution centres are now being grouped together in huge **regional distribution parks**, open 24 hours a day. The first planned distribution park in Britain, and the largest in Europe, is Magna Park, near Lutterworth in Leicestershire. It is near the M1 and the M6 motorways. When it is completed, it will cover an area of over 7½ million square feet (about 650,000 square metres). Each of the sites, which are occupied by the warehousing and distribution divisions of retailers and manufacturers and by distribution firms, is a minimum of 100,000 square feet (9,290 square metres). This provides sufficient space for the huge warehouses, and for parking and turning areas.

In the past, wholesalers delivered goods in a variety of vans and lorries to retailers, who stored the goods on their premises until they could be sold. Now goods are more often loaded into bigger

Aerial view of Magna Park, Europe's largest dedicated distribution development, near Lutterworth, Leicestershire

lorries from automated warehouse carousels, and delivered to retailers in just the quantity they require, so that they don't have to hold large stocks on the premises.

Reasons for change in methods of distribution

1   The opportunity cost of holding stock is high, because interest has to be given up if the stock is bought with cash, or paid out if the stock is bought with borrowed money. It saves money, therefore, to have as few goods as possible in the channel between factory and shop.

2   Rents in high-street shops are so high that it is very expensive to use the space for storing stock. It is more cost-effective to use the space for displaying goods for sale.

3   Electronic systems in retailers' stores have made it possible to keep a second-by-second check on stock levels, and to order from the warehouse just before stock runs out. Electronic systems are also commonly used in warehouses to control stock and deliveries.

4   Bigger warehouses benefit from economies of scale.

5   Transport has become relatively cheap and efficient. Bigger lorries are more cost-effective. Over three-quarters of goods transported by road are carried in lorries of over 25 tonnes gross laden weight. Overseas transport has benefited, in both speed and cost, from the use of containers and roll-on, roll-off (ro-ro) ferries. There are also many couriers, or express delivery firms, that deliver goods both within Britain and overseas. Some can deliver goods to virtually anywhere in the world within 48 hours.

6   A reduction in the handling of goods means that there is less damage in transit and less chance of theft.

▶ If the stock is worth £100,000 and the money had been invested instead at a rate of 6 per cent, the interest received after a year would be £6,000. If the money to buy the stock had been borrowed at 10 per cent, the annual interest to be paid would be £10,000.

▶ The recession at the beginning of the 1990s caused the rents of many shops and stores to fall, but at the time of writing, the rents for prime retail sites in London remain high.

▶ See Chapter 23.

▶ Containers – large metal boxes in which goods are transported – are taken on a lorry to a port, and loaded on to the ship mechanically. Roll-on roll-off (ro-ro) ferries enable lorries to cross the Channel without unloading. They face competition from the Channel Tunnel, which creates high-speed rail freight links with many European cities.

Draw up a table with two columns headed *Changes in distribution* and *Reasons*. Fill in the table using the information in the box above.

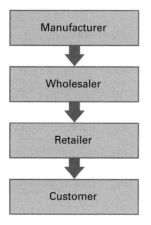

TRADITIONAL CHANNELS OF DISTRIBUTION

The traditional channel of distribution, or the stages through which goods pass before they reach the consumer, is shown in the margin. Many goods are still distributed in this way. The system allows each firm to concentrate on its own business. The manufacturer makes the goods; the wholesaler distributes them; the retailer sells them. Each of them makes their own profit margin.

Wholesalers have important functions in this kind of distribution channel.

- They buy goods in bulk, or large quantities, from manufacturers. The wholesalers then divide the goods into much smaller lots for retailers to buy. (This process is known as **breaking bulk**.)
- Wholesalers store the stock in their warehouses, which means that manufacturers need less storage space in their factories.
- The transport of the goods is simplified. If manufacturers had to deliver their own goods to all their retail customers, the motorways and city streets would be permanently jammed day and night. Instead, manufacturers deliver their goods to warehouses. The warehouses then send out consignments of goods for **multi-drop delivery**, i.e. one vehicle delivers goods to a number of shops.
- Retailers know where they can buy the goods they want in suitable quantities.

 Make notes on the traditional channels of distribution and show what happens to the goods at each stage.

NEW CHANNELS OF DISTRIBUTION

The new channels of distribution are more specialized than the traditional channels, with different lengths for various kinds of goods and services. Most of them are for **fast-moving consumer goods** with a wide market coverage. Some, however, are also used for other goods and services with more limited markets.

The table shows who is normally in control of the four Ps in various channels of distribution.

Channels	A Brands	B Own-label	C Warehouse clubs	D Franchises	E Mail order	F Direct services
Product	Producer	Retailer	Producer	Producer	Producer	Producer
Price	Producer/Retailer	Retailer	Wholesaler Retailer	Producer	Distributor	Producer
Place	Retailer	Retailer	Wholesaler/Retailer	Producer	Distributor	Producer
Promotion	Producer	Retailer	Wholesaler/Retailer	Producer	Distributor	Producer

Most brands (Channel A) are now distributed in this way. Manufacturers have their own warehouse in a distribution park, from which the goods are distributed to retailers throughout the region.

Channel B shows the typical channel of distribution for an own-label retailer, such as Marks & Spencer. Most supermarkets and other multiple chain stores have similar channels of distribution.

Channel C shows a distribution system that could present a threat to supermarkets and other retailers. **Warehouse clubs** have been a big success in the United States. Members pay an annual fee of $20 or so to shop in big warehouse stores. The stores sell foods in bulk packs, and general goods, such as electrical goods and clothing. The bare premises and the shorter channel make it possible to sell goods at a big discount. At the time of writing, warehouse clubs are just beginning to open in Britain. They are similar to **cash-and-carry warehouses**, but are aimed at consumers rather than small retailers. A similar channel exists in the motor trade. Some car dealers are both wholesalers, selling to other garages in their area, and retailers, selling to members of the public.

► See the figure showing the main features of a franchised business, in Chapter 5, page 51.

Franchisers (Channel D) also have a short channel, because they sell their products only through their own retailers, or franchisees. Oil companies with their own filling stations and brewers with their own public houses also have a similar system.

Mail-order firms (Channel E) buy their goods in bulk from manufacturers and distribute them direct to customers through couriers or express delivery services. **Network marketing** operates in a similar way. Some manufacturers of cosmetics, household cleaners, detergents and other goods use a network of distributors who sell the goods to their family and friends. There are about half a million network distributors working full- and part-time in Britain.

Finally, Channel F has the shortest channel of all for the direct marketing of goods – such as fitted kitchens, computers and double glazing – and services – such as hospital and dental treatment. A similar type of direct channel is used by manufacturers who sell industrial goods to other manufacturers and by some small producers, such as specialist craftworkers, who sell their product in their workshops. These both use face-to-face selling.

► See the box on **Direct marketing** in Chapter 14, page 185.

Select the most suitable channels of distribution for the following items and say why you have chosen them:

(a) a well-known brand of camera;
(b) hand-made designer sweaters;
(c) fork-lift trucks;
(d) cooking spices in 1 lb. bags;
(e) pre-packed spices in practical, everyday glass containers.

Make notes on each of the six channels, bringing out the differences between them.

Read the following case study and answer the questions at the end.

▶ Self-governing NHS Trusts were set up from 1991 to run hospitals. They sell their services to the local, and other, health authorities; fund-holding GPs, or family doctors, who have their own budgets for their patients' treatment; and private patients. They are now also selling community care services, mainly for the elderly, to local authority social services departments. It is estimated that 95 per cent of hospitals will be run as trusts by 1995.

▶ 'Obs' is short for obstetrics – the medical care of women before, during and after childbirth; 'paeds' is short for paediatrics – the medical care of children.

A National Health Service (NHS) Trust controls a 1,000-bed district general hospital (DGH) and thirteen smaller community hospitals scattered throughout a large rural area, which has a population of 400,000. There is a main-line railway, but the only station is in the main city. The bus services are poor: some villages have a bus service only twice a week. Most buses do not run after 6 p.m.

The Trust's annual budget of £100 million is financed by:

- the district health authority (79 per cent);
- GP fundholders (12 per cent);
- performing certain kinds of specialist operations for other health authorities (5 per cent);
- other services, including private patients' fees (3 per cent);
- local authority social services department (1 per cent).

The Trust wants to increase its services to the area by 2½ per cent per year over the next three years. It can only do this by changing its channels of distribution. That means centralizing more of its services to make them more cost-effective.

Here are some of its plans for the next three years:

- It plans to close the remaining two general maternity units in the area, with a total loss of thirty-seven beds. All 'obs' and 'paeds' who need hospital treatment will be treated in the DGH, though each community hospital will have midwives and specialist nurses to deal with patients locally.
- It plans to close surgery units in three community hospitals. All surgery will be centralized at the DGH. Most of these fifty-seven former surgical beds will be used as community care beds for the elderly.
- It plans to build a large day surgery unit in the grounds of the DGH where patients will have their operations and leave on the same day. It will be used mainly to treat painful but not life-threatening conditions, such as varicose veins and hernias.
- It will allow a private developer to build a luxury, three-star hotel in the hospital grounds. This will be used to accommodate any patients from the day surgery unit who are not fit to return home, patients from the DGH who no longer require constant nursing attendance, and other patients who are having repeated courses of treatment. The Trust will pay the fee of £70 a night; this is much cheaper than financing a ward bed, which costs between £270 and £330 a day.

The new hospital hotel will let rooms to patients' relatives for £70 per night. The Trust has calculated that as a result of using the hospital hotel it will be able to close at least eighty DGH ward beds.

1 What is the Trust's annual budget?
2 How much does the local health authority pay the Trust each year?
3 If ward beds cost an average of £300 a day to run and eighty DGH beds were closed, what would the Trust's minimum saving be per year by using the new hospital hotel?
4 What effects do you think these changes would have on the people in the area?
5 You work in the Trust's public relations department. Write a brief leaflet, which will be delivered by the Royal Mail's household delivery service to all houses in the area, persuading people that these changes will be of benefit to them.

RETAILERS

Although direct marketing of services and goods has grown considerably in recent years, **retailers** still play an important role in the distribution chain. There are about a quarter of a million retail businesses. Their total turnover is around £125 billion a year, inclusive of VAT. They employ a total of nearly 2½ million people – many of them part-time.

There are many different types of retail outlets, each of which has its own appeal to one or more different market segments:

- The vast majority of retail businesses, about 215,000, are run by sole traders with only one shop. Small shops are still popular with many people, but their market share has been falling through fierce competition from bigger firms, particularly in groceries.
- Co-op retail societies have 4,700 shops with a turnover of well over £7 billion a year.
- Multiple chain stores with more than one branch are found in most high streets. They are common in clothing, footwear, electrical goods and drinks, and there are also mixed retail chains like WH Smith.
- Department stores are less common than they were, but there are still quite a number in the high streets.
- Supermarkets (with a minimum 2,000 square feet of retail area) are now common in even the smallest towns.
- Supermarkets are being superseded by out-of-town hypermarkets (with a minimum 25,000 square feet of retail space) and superstores, which sell a wider variety of goods.
- All cities and many towns have their own shopping centres, where shops are grouped together in covered arcades.
- Out-of-town shopping centres are becoming increasingly common. One of the first was the Metro Centre in Gateshead, Tyne and Wear, which, with 1 million square feet of floor space, is the biggest of its kind in Europe.

Take real-life examples in your own area of the retail outlets itemized above and write a report describing their main advantages and disadvantages from the customer's point of view.

Retailers' services

Retailers provide both **pre-sales** and **after-sales services**, which are important factors in persuading customers to buy and continue to buy from that outlet.

Pre-sales services
These are important in persuading consumers to buy for the first time.

1 Is the shop or store itself appealing, convenient, clean, welcoming and exciting?
2 Are the staff clean, well-dressed, polite, helpful, well-trained and knowledgeable?
3 Are credit facilities available? Credit makes it easier for customers to buy goods when they are short of cash. Many big stores now issue their own credit cards. Others sometimes sell goods, usually consumer durables, on interest-free hire purchase.

After-sales services
These are important in persuading people to buy a second time.

1 Does the firm keep to the dates and times given for delivery? Does it arrange for consumer durables to be installed and the old ones to be taken away? Is there a delivery charge?
2 Is it easy to get advice, service and spare parts if anything goes wrong?
3 Is it easy to return goods, not because they're faulty, but simply because you don't like them? Can you get a refund if you return goods to a different branch of a multiple chain store, or do you have to go back to the original branch?

 1 What is the turnover of the retail trade as a whole?
2 Name four different kinds of retail outlet.
3 Define pre-sales and after-sales service.
4 Use your own or your family's experience to compare the after-sales service of a corner shop and a chain store.

 Take three shops or stores that you or your family use regularly. Rate each one for the three aspects of pre-sales service explained above, using the code: VG = very good (5 points); G = good (4 points); M = neither good nor poor (3 points); P = poor (2 points); VP = very poor (1 point). Add up the total score for each shop or store. Which has the

worst score? Describe any other factors that make you or
your family continue to use it.

SUMMARY

- Place, or distribution, is how the product is distributed and
  where it is sent. Channels of distribution affect price. The
  longer they are, the higher the final price, as more separate
  profit margins must be taken into account. There are also
  higher physical handling charges and higher transport
  costs.
- The place has to be appropriate for the product. It also has a
  great effect on the way the product is promoted.
- There have been revolutionary changes in distribution in
  the last thirty years and they are still continuing to happen.
- Big grocery chains were the first to centralize distribution by
  opening regional distribution centres.
- The latest development is large distribution parks for
  manufacturers, distributors and retailers. Deliveries are
  made on a daily basis by road to retailers, who now hold
  very little stock on their premises.
- The main reasons for the changes are: the high cost of
  stockholding; economies of scale in larger warehouses; and
  more efficient and cheaper transport.
- The wholesaler plays an important part in the traditional
  channel of distribution, which is still used for distributing
  goods to small retailers.
- Wholesalers divide their purchases into smaller lots by
  breaking bulk. They store the goods and deliver them to
  retailers, which saves manufacturers many separate
  journeys.
- New channels of distribution have cut out some stages in
  the distribution channels and have made direct contact
  between manufacturer and customer more common.
  Retailers, however, still play an important part in the
  distribution process.

Promotion

Chapter objectives

After working through this chapter, you will have the knowledge to:

▎ define promotion in its marketing and wider sense;

▎ evaluate the effects of sales promotions on purchases;

▎ understand the work of advertising agencies;

▎ plot the information–influence relationship in advertisements;

▎ identify the four main purposes of advertising;

▎ select the most suitable branches of the media for different advertising campaigns;

▎ assess the effectiveness of direct marketing;

▎ describe the work of the public relations department;

▎ understand and use the following key terms: promotion, logo, merchandising, point-of-sale material, impulse buyer, sales promotion, trade promotion, trade show, advertising, media, advertising agency, media department, creative department, art buying department, information–influence relationship, display advertisement, classified advertisement, quality newspaper, direct marketing, public relations, public relations department.

A TOTAL IMAGE

In a narrow sense, **promotion** means a number of techniques for persuading customers to buy goods and services, but in a broader sense it involves much more than that.

Promotion

Promotion is concerned with the total image that a business presents to the outside world. The products of the company, its advertisements and public relations, the way it treats its employees, its moral attitudes, its relations with the community and the country are obviously all important aspects of its image. But smaller details are of no less significance: its logo, its slogans, its colour schemes, its uniforms, the designs of its offices. Through all of these, it speaks to its customers and the rest of the world.

▶ **Logo** is short for 'logotype', and refers to the emblem, or symbol, that represents a company. A logo can be in the form of the company name, either in full or abbreviated, in a distinctive typeface or combined with some graphical device, or it can be a small drawing. Companies employ designers to produce their logos, and they are generally updated from time to time. The logo is usually included in the company letterhead and on its packaging. An example is the fire and water symbol on the spine of this book, which is the logo for HarperCollins*Publishers*.

Visit one or two branches of two different banks. Note the promotional aspects that distinguish one bank from the other. Describe the image that each bank creates of itself.

The three main aspects of promotion are:

- merchandising
- advertising
- public relations

MERCHANDISING

Merchandising is a means of attracting consumers to a product and persuading them to buy it. One of the most common forms of merchandising is **point-of-sale (POS) material**. Examples include: posters; showcards; display stands and cases; dump bins (wire or plastic containers filled with goods often sited near store entrances); wire racks (like those at checkouts filled with chocolate bars to tempt impulse buyers; and moving and illuminated displays inside stores or in shop-windows.

Sales promotions

Sales promotions are another form of merchandising. Some of the most common are:

- **free gifts:** free air miles with some goods, or gift tokens with petrol;
- **special offers:** discounts ranging from 3p off a bar of chocolate to a £50 trade-in on a new cooker, or three goods for the price of two;
- **discount vouchers:** a few pence off the next jar of jam or packet of biscuits you buy;
- **bonus packs:** larger amounts of a good, such as 10 per cent more cornflakes or shampoo, for the same price as a standard pack;
- **special purchase offers:** a free or reduced-price item when you make a certain number of purchases of a particular product, such as a free mug when you buy three jars of coffee;
- **charity promotions:** donations to charity for each product bought;
- **competitions:** including free scratch cards and bingo cards.

There are many more of these promotional offers. Like point-of-sale material, they usually have only a short-term effect on sales. Some consumers may switch temporarily from one product to another but return to their favourite product in the end.

▶ A market trader who gradually reduces the price of his or her goods, and passes samples around the crowd for inspection, is merchandising. Some merchandisers are highly skilled.

▶ **Impulse buyers** are consumers who suddenly buy something without any previous thought or plan. Most people do this from time to time, but impulse buyers do it regularly.

Free gifts		**Discount vouchers**
Bonus packs		**Competitions**
	Special purchase offer	**Charity promotions**

Sales promotions

 Note down some examples of sales promotions that you see over the course of a few weeks. Draw up a table with three columns headed *Product*, *Promotion* and *Results* (state whether you read it, considered buying it, would have bought it if you had enough money, did buy it or persuaded someone else to buy it for you, etc.). Fill in the table every time you see a sales promotion. When you have enough examples (at least six), describe briefly what effect these sales promotions have had on you as a consumer. Then consider the results from another angle. In view of your actions, how do you rate yourself as a consumer – impulsive, greedy, mean, thoughtful, thoughtless, discriminating, etc.?

Trade promotions

Manufacturers promote sales not only to consumers, but also to retailers to persuade them to increase their stocks. Some of the main methods of **trade promotion** are:

- a percentage discount on cases of goods, or, for example, thirteen cases for the price of twelve;
- a gift with each order, such as a bottle of whisky;
- competitions, with a prize for the retailer selling most in a stated period;
- sale or return for untried goods.

Trade shows

Promotions are often used at **trade shows** and exhibitions for retailers and potential purchasers of industrial goods. Trade shows are held in all parts of the world. They provide a showcase for exporters. At the biggest shows, there is usually a British pavilion showing a range of products. The government provides some financial help to firms taking part in overseas exhibitions.

1 What is a logo?
2 Define merchandising.
3 Give four examples of point-of-sale material.
4 Who do you know who is an impulse buyer? Can you say why they are?
5 What is the difference between point-of-sale material and sales promotions?
6 Give two examples of sales promotions.
7 How do trade promotions differ from sales promotions?
8 What are the main purposes of trade shows?

ADVERTISING

Big spenders

Advertising is the most important and the most expensive way of promoting a business. There are few businesses that do not advertise from time to time, even if it is only a small advertisement in a local newspaper. On the other hand, some big companies that advertise their products regularly spend many millions of pounds each year. As you would expect, manufacturers of brands are the biggest spenders. Unilever, with brands like Flora, Oxo, Persil and many others, is usually at the top, or near the top, of the big advertisers' list. In recent years, its annual expenditure has been around £200 million. Top advertisers use television for most of their advertising. However, television accounts for only about a third of total advertising expenditure.

The total amount spent in various branches of the media in 1991 was £7,577 million. Of this, 64 per cent was spent on advertisements in newspapers and magazines; 30 per cent on television; nearly 4 per cent on posters; and 2 per cent on commercial radio and cinema.

> ► The **media** are the means by which information is communicated to the public and to organizations. For example, television communicates with the general public, trade magazines communicate with a specialized segment and organizations.

1 Why do brand manufacturers spend so much on advertising?
2 Why, in your view, do they use television for most of their advertising?
3 Describe the television advertisement you remember best. What were the main points that made it memorable? (If you can't remember a particular advertisement, watch the television commercials one night and choose the best one.)

Advertising agencies

Advertising has become a specialized and highly skilled industry. Big firms that spend a large amount on advertising employ an advertising agency to run their campaigns.

Market research in advertising

An advertising agency often uses its own market research department to help plan and evaluate the results of the advertising campaign. It does this by:

- analysing the target segment's characteristics and attitudes;
- obtaining consumer reactions to the ideas behind the proposed advertisements and to the draft versions of advertisements;
- evaluating the results by comparing consumer knowledge of the brand before the campaign with knowledge of it afterwards and estimating the number of consumers who now intend to use the product.

Once the agency has worked out a plan for the campaign, it will discuss it with the client firm. When the plan has been approved, the agency's departments start work on the campaign.

- The **media department** buys television time and books space in newspapers and/or magazines.
- The **creative department** is responsible for the Press advertisements. A copywriter writes the text. The artwork is done by a visualizer who plans the general presentation, an artist who does the drawing, and a layout person who does the detailed design.
- The **art-buying department** gets a film production company to make the television commercials or buys in any other specialist creative work needed.

 Choose a brand of consumer goods and make brief notes on each stage of its advertising campaign, using the actual names of television companies, newspapers, magazines or other media throughout. State the reasons why you have identified those particular branches of the media.

Contents of advertisements

Most advertisements try to inform and to influence. A few advertisements are pure information. For example, advertisements that are legally required to be published in newspapers, such as a notice saying that a sole trader has gone bankrupt, contain only information. Advertisements by small businesses in the 'At Your Service' features in local newspapers are also pure information: details of the firm's name, address, telephone number and kind of business.

However, most advertisements attempt to influence consumers. If the name of the firm is A1 Taxis, the owner is trying to persuade people to use his or her firm's services by suggesting that it is the first and the best of its kind. An estate agent's advertisement may seem to be merely informative, but will emphasize the best features

► The name would also have the advantage of appearing at the top of any alphabetical listing. However, it would not be a very effective means of promotion, because the name lacks originality.

of a house in an attempt to influence people to buy it. Most advertisements contain some element of influence. The balance between information and influence can be recorded on a scale, like the one below. The scale has been marked at the point where there is 30 per cent information and 70 per cent influence.

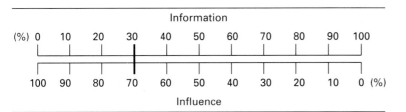

► It could be argued that putting an advertisement in a newspaper or a magazine is in itself an attempt to influence its readers.

The information–influence relationship

 ACT IN Copy the scale above, leaving out the marked example. Take two big display advertisements at random from each of the following: a quality newspaper like *The Times*; a tabloid newspaper like *The Sun*; a local newspaper; a women's magazine; and a hobby magazine. Plot their positions on the scale, using an initial letter to identify them (Q for quality, T for tabloid, L for local newspaper, W for women's magazine and H for hobby magazine). What are your conclusions about the information–influence relationship in different branches of the Press?

► Don't draw any general conclusions from this exercise – the sample is too small.

The purposes of advertisements

Advertisements have many different purposes. Here are some of the main ones.

1 They can provide simple information, such as changes in the times of buses or the closing of a business. The influence element is nil or minimal.
2 They can increase or maintain sales during the course of the product life cycle. The information–influence relationship in the advertisements changes as the life cycle progresses.
3 They can enhance the profile of a business or restore a firm's image if it has been tarnished. In many cases the information content is quite high, but it is carefully selected to reinforce the good image of the company.
4 They can influence people to change their views or attitudes about issues, such as drink-driving. Facts are used dramatically and the influence content is high and often presented for maximum emotional impact.

ACT IN Find examples of each of these four categories of advertisement in newspapers and magazines and describe how well or badly they have succeeded in their objective. (It may be difficult to find an example of number 3. If it is, just take any advertisement that boosts the image of a business in a general way. There are usually quite a few advertisements of this kind in local newspapers.)

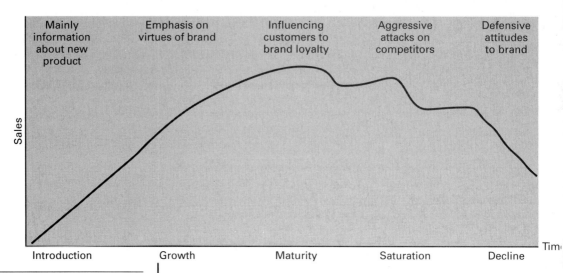

| Mainly information about new product | Emphasis on virtues of brand | Influencing customers to brand loyalty | Aggressive attacks on competitors | Defensive attitudes to brand |

Sales

Introduction   Growth   Maturity   Saturation   Decline

Time

Advertisements and the product life cycle

Planning an advertising campaign

The choice of appropriate branches of the media is of great importance in planning an advertising campaign. Although advertising agencies do this work for big firms, the firm's marketing and advertising departments must possess sufficient knowledge to judge whether the choices are right. Sole traders and small firms need this knowledge even more because they usually plan their own campaign and can't afford to employ an advertising agency.

The choice of media is influenced by a number of factors. Three are particularly important.

1 **The message:** What is the purpose of the campaign? The medium must be suitable for conveying the campaign's main message. It must be appropriate for the information–influence relationship that is needed. If the campaign needs to contain a lot of information, then a newspaper advertisement or a radio commercial would probably be better than a poster on a street hoarding or on the side of a bus. A poster campaign – or a colour advertisement in a glossy magazine or a television commercial – might be ideal where a strong visual impact is called for, which may be the case if the influence content of a campaign needs to be particularly high.

2 **The target audience:** Who do you want to reach? Different market segments will be best reached by different media. The coverage–frequency relationship is always important in choosing the media. Should you aim for a wide coverage of a large audience with just one advertisement or a smaller coverage with a number of advertisements?

3 **The cost:** How much can you afford to spend? Television advertisements cost thousands of pounds even in off-peak periods. If you have a small business, it would be better, and cheaper, to put a number of display advertisements in regional newspapers. Although you might not reach so many people, you would be able to have more

advertisements for the same cost. The opportunity cost of one advertisement on regional television might be three advertisements in regional newspapers.

 Make notes on the factors that influence the choice of media in an advertising campaign.

The media

It is worth studying the branches of the media carefully, as they possess so many different features that it should be possible to select one that is ideal for the purpose required.

Television
Advantages:

- It has movement, colour and sound, which help it to create an immediate and powerful impact.
- It can have great emotional influence.
- It provides high coverage.
- In addition to normal viewing, it can broadcast Teletext (Ceefax from the BBC and Oracle from ITV), which provides information mainly in a text form.

Disadvantages:

- Advertising on television is very expensive. Rates are high, and the production costs of commercials are often higher.
- Its effect is transient – it lasts only a brief time.

Television advertising is charged according to the length of the commercial, the coverage of the channel, and the time at which the commercial is broadcast. Commercials are cheaper outside peak times. The increase in the number of satellite channels has made it more expensive for advertisers to gain wide coverage. Video cassette recorders have also created difficulties for television advertisers, because viewers tend to zap, or speed through, the commercial breaks in recorded programmes. Even with real-time transmissions, many viewers switch channels in commercial breaks or make a cup of tea.

The Press
Advantages:

- Newspapers and magazines are good for conveying information.
- The advertisements are permanent – they can be cut out and saved.
- Different market segments can be targeted easily.

Disadvantages:

- Newspapers and magazines are static and silent, so they cannot achieve the impact that television does.
- Not all publications offer colour.

▶ However, magazines can now give readers a chance to savour perfumes by including a perfume-impregnated sample slip in their advertisements.

- Many advertisements are not read.

The Press offers a great choice – advertisements of different sizes, and many kinds of publications. **Display advertisements**, which are ruled or boxed off from any other text on the page, range from a whole page to a single-column centimetre, with a variety of sizes in between. Their price is determined mainly by the size of the advertisement, the circulation of the publication and the types of readers. It is also affected by where it is situated in the publication (the front page is more expensive) and whether it is a 'solus', or the only advertisement on the page. Smaller, **classified advertisements**, which are printed in columns under headings, are charged per word or per line.

The great variety of publications makes Press advertising particularly good for targeting market segments. These are some of the categories:

- There are twenty-three daily and Sunday **national newspapers**. They are divided into **tabloid** and **quality** newspapers. Tabloids, like *The Sun*, are cheaper, small-format newspapers with mass circulations. Quality newspapers, like the *Guardian*, are more expensive, larger (broadsheet) newspapers with circulations among the higher social grades. National papers provide wide coverage among chosen social grades, but total circulations have been falling.
- There are around 140 daily and Sunday **regional newspapers**. By their nature these are good for geographical targeting, and many have a strong reader loyalty.
- There are over 1,600 free and bought **local newspapers**. Many bought newspapers have become free newspapers, with more advertisements but less editorial content. Local businesses are the biggest advertisers.
- There are well over 2,000 **consumer magazines**. There are magazines covering practically every interest and hobby, including fashion, food and drink, health, sports of all kinds, music of all kinds, motoring, photography and computers. There is a large number of more general magazines aimed specifically at women, and a small but growing number of general magazines aimed at men. Consumer magazines are ideal for targeting specific market segments or niches.
- There are about 4,500 **professional and trade magazines**. These are ideal for industrial advertising.

Posters
Advantages:

- Posters can achieve a high coverage.
- They have a 24- hour impact if illuminated.

Disadvantages:

- For most poster sites, only a simple message can be

conveyed, although posters in public transport can contain much more information.

- It is more difficult to target than with Press advertisements.

Posters are displayed on hoardings at the side of the road or on buildings. They also appear on the sides of buses and taxis, inside underground trains and on special vehicles that function as mobile hoardings, and at railway stations, airports and sports grounds.

Coffee advertisement on a London bus

Commercial radio

Advantages:

- It provides high coverage, especially in rush hours when many drivers are listening to their car radios.
- It is easy to target some market segments, such as young people, mothers of young children and retired people, because radio stations tend to be very segment-orientated.

Disadvantages

- Radio advertisements are easily forgotten, although jingles and catch phrases can remain in the memory for ages.
- They have a low total coverage.

Commercial radio (i.e. not BBC national radio stations 1, 2, 3, 4 or 5, or BBC local stations) includes stations such as Classic FM, Jazz FM, Capital Radio and Virgin.

Cinema
Advantages

- Like television, it has movement, colour and sound, which helps it to create an immediate and powerful impact. However, the big screen gives advertisements an even greater impact than those on television.

- It can have great emotional influence.

Disadvantages

- On the whole, cinema audiences today make up a small segment – mainly 15 to 24 year-olds – though this may now be changing as multi-screen cinemas offer greater choice
- Advertisements may be seen only once.

Most cinemas show advertisements before the main feature film.

There are other forms of advertising, such as in the Yellow Pages and other directories, that are very useful for sole traders and small businesses. We shall next be looking at direct marketing, which is another effective way of advertising products.

 Make brief notes on the different branches of the media.

 Put yourself in the three business situations below.

1 You are responsible for a £10 million advertising budget in a company that makes a long-established brand of paint.
2 You are in charge of the advertising for a new current account aimed at students that is being launched by a top building society. You have a budget of £750,000.
3 You are opening a new hairdressing salon in a city suburb. You have allocated £2,000 for advertising the salon.

State in each case:

(a) the message of your campaign in one, simple sentence;
(b) the percentage spend in the branches of the media you have chosen and your reasons for selecting them;
(c) the information–influence relationship of each advertisement and why you have chosen those percentages.

Evaluating advertising results

It is very difficult to evaluate, or assess, the results of advertising. Sales of a product may rise during an advertising campaign. However, it is impossible to know with total certainty which advertisements were responsible for the increase – the television commercials or the full-page advertisements in tabloid newspapers. Advertising agencies have to rely on market research to evaluate the results.

► See the box on **Market research in advertising**, on page 178 of this chapter.

With direct marketing, however, it is possible to evaluate results with great accuracy. That is why this method of marketing is becoming increasingly popular.

Direct marketing

Direct marketing creates a direct link between the business and potential customers by inviting them to respond personally to advertisements or other means of communication.
There are many kinds of direct marketing:

- **Mail order catalogues** are one of the oldest and most effective methods. They are usually sent in response to Press advertisements. Credit payment facilities make this method of selling even more popular.
- **Press advertisements** can take the form of invitations either to order a particular good, sending payment with the order or paying by credit card, or to request a brochure or catalogue. They can be successful.
- **Magazine inserts** are the booklets or leaflets enclosed in magazines. They enable advertisers to display a wider range of their goods, but the disadvantage is that they are often thrown away unread.
- **Television commercials** are little used for direct marketing, except for mail order of pop discs, holiday offers, etc.
- **Telephone calling** can be used either in response to a request or in the form of 'cold calling' people at random. It is a method favoured by double-glazing firms. Many people resent cold calls.
- **Direct mail** refers to contacting potential customers directly by sending advertising material through the post. Its biggest users are firms offering financial services. Mailing lists are often not accurately targeted. Many people resent 'junk mail' and throw it away unread.
- **Door-to-door delivery** refers to the delivery, by hand, of leaflets and catalogues to private homes by a firm's representatives. Great success can be achieved with catalogues for goods such as houseware.

► As you saw in Chapter 13, direct marketing is also economical in its use of resources as it combines place and promotion.

It is possible to measure the results of direct marketing accurately by calculating:

- the cost per enquiry;
- the cost per order;
- the financial return on the money invested in the direct marketing campaign.

This ability to monitor the results of direct marketing makes it easier to use it cost-effectively.

Draw up a table with the caption 'Direct marketing' and three columns headed *Method*, *Example* and *Effectiveness*. Fill in the table using your own, or your family's actual experiences of all kinds of direct marketing.

PUBLIC RELATIONS

Public relations has two main aims:

- to inform the outside world of the business's achievements by using all branches of the media without paying for advertising space;
- to present a favourable image of the business and its products.

Most big firms have their own **public relations department**. Many people who work in public relations are former journalists. Some firms contract the work out to a specialist firm.

Public relations department

The main tasks of the public relations department are:

- to arrange press conferences and receptions for any company events or achievements that would attract significant media interest, such as the appointment of a woman as the company chairperson;
- to issue press releases to appropriate branches of the media about other achievements or events;
- to make news by creating stories that will be of interest to the media, such as how the chief executive and a factory worker swapped jobs for a day;
- to answer queries from the public about the firm and its products.

In addition, the public relations department tries to improve the company image. Its methods might include the sponsorship of events, particularly sporting events; closer relations with the local community; talks and demonstrations in schools and colleges; and factory visits.

It is difficult to assess the cost-effectiveness of public relations, but there are some useful methods. One way is to count the number of mentions on television and radio and to add up the column centimetres of Press cuttings about the company every month and compare them with previous months.

 Make notes on the work of a public relations department, comparing its effectiveness with that of advertisements.

 Think of a new product, either a good or a service, that you think would sell well. Describe its main features and its target segment. State what the initial price would be, comparing it, if possible, with prices of similar products. Say how you would distribute it, explaining why you have chosen that particular channel. Describe in full how you would promote it.

SUMMARY

- Promotion deals with the total image of a business. Every aspect of the business, big or small, is therefore important.
- Merchandising, or attracting consumers to a product and persuading them to buy it, is an important part of retailing. Point-of-sale material and sales promotions are both used. Other methods are used in trade promotions, which try to persuade retailers to buy more of a firm's products.
- Most businesses use advertisements to promote themselves and their products. The Press is the most popular branch of the media for advertisements, followed by television.
- Advertisements try to inform and to influence. Their main aims are to provide information; to increase or maintain sales; to improve a firm's image; and to influence people to change their views.
- The choice of media in planning a campaign is influenced by the purpose of the campaign, the size and location of the target segment, and the size of the advertising budget.
- As it is often difficult to evaluate the effects of advertising, many firms are now using more direct marketing. This creates a direct link between the firm and its customer by asking them to respond to advertisements or other forms of contact. It is easy to measure results accurately by calculating costs per enquiry, costs per order and return on capital employed.
- Public relations is used to inform the outside world about a firm's achievements and to promote a favourable image of the firm.

(15) Production

Chapter objectives

After working through this chapter, you will have the knowledge to:

∎ describe the changes from labour-intensive to capital-intensive methods of production;

∎ classify job, batch and flow production methods;

∎ analyse how computers have changed design and manufacturing processes;

∎ assess the effects of lean production on the workforce and the organization of work;

∎ compare the functions of a production manager and a purchasing manager;

∎ understand and use the following key terms: automation, capital-intensive, labour-intensive, delivery note, invoice, credit note, statement, job production, batch production, flow production, assembly line, simultaneous engineering, lead time, computer-assisted design (CAD), computer-aided manufacturing (CAM), flexible batch production, lean production, computer-integrated engineering (CIE), just-in-time (JIT), production manager, layout by process, layout by product, benchmarking, purchasing manager, productivity, research and development (R & D), hi-tech industries.

REVOLUTIONARY CHANGES IN PRODUCTION

Manufacturing

In the last few years, there have been revolutionary changes in manufacturing, and they are still continuing. The main changes are:

- a greater use of computers at all stages of production;
- more **automation**, with many tasks being carried out by machines, including robots, instead of by human beings;
- more teamwork on the shop floor in factories;
- companies buying in many more components and parts from outside firms, who deliver them to the factory a few hours before they are required, or 'just in time'.

Secondary sector

As you already know, manufacturing is part of the secondary sector of production. Other businesses in the secondary sector have also become more **capital-intensive**. Production of water, gas and electricity (particularly in nuclear plants) is highly automated and computer-controlled. Computers also play a big part in large-scale construction and building projects, from the design stage to ordering stock.

Primary sector

There have also been changes in the primary sector. Farming has become much more capital-intensive, particularly in arable farming (the growing of crops), with ploughing, sowing, fertilizing and harvesting being carried out mainly by machines. There are even machines to pick the olives used for making olive oil and the hops used in brewing beer.

Tertiary sector

The tertiary sector is still very **labour-intensive**, and some parts of it will probably always be so. Dentists, teachers, nurses and other professionals who provide an essential service, may never be replaced. However, computers are now being used to a much greater extent for office work. In modern offices, individual clerks no longer have to send out delivery notes, invoices, credit notes and statements and fill in complicated forms for other departments in the firm. Instead, one computer operator handles the whole process. As a result, many clerks have been made redundant.

Computer software, such as spreadsheet packages, has made it much easier to handle financial data for forecasts and accounts. Electronic methods of communication, such as fax machines and electronic mail, have speeded up both domestic and overseas communications.

Not all firms have introduced these modern methods of production. However, many of the biggest companies, which face fierce competition in global markets, have modernized their production. Their suppliers then have to use the same advanced methods so that they can work in harmony. Finally, other firms of the same scale as the suppliers also have to update their methods to remain competitive. In that way, modern methods of production spread slowly throughout business.

Make notes on recent changes in methods of production in the primary, secondary and tertiary sectors, in that order, concentrating on the change from labour-intensive to capital-intensive methods.

► To refresh your memory, see **Secondary sector of production** in Chapter 2, pp. 12–13.

► **Capital-intensive** means using a large number of expensive machines in production and fewer workers.

► **Labour-intensive** means using a large number of workers and fewer machines in production.

► Japanese scientists are developing robots that could nurse the sick and infirm by 2020.

► Delivery notes are sent with goods when they are despatched; invoices are itemized lists of goods that have been sent to a buyer with prices and charges; credit notes show a reduction in the amount owing because the customer has returned unwanted or faulty goods; statements show the purchases during the month and the amount of money owing.

► See **Computers in offices** in Chapter 23.

► Cake-making provides good examples of all three methods.

Job: a woman who works at home bakes a designer wedding cake for a local couple.

Batch: a corner-shop baker makes a batch of doughnuts and then a batch of Eccles cakes.

Flow: a computer-controlled factory makes hundreds of fruit cakes in a continuous flow using modern machines and conveyor belts.

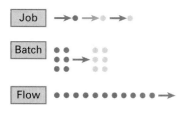

Methods of production

► See the box on **Internal economies of scale** in Chapter 7, page 73.

PRODUCTION METHODS

There are three main ways in which goods and services are produced:

1 **job production**, where different products are produced one after another;
2 **batch production**, where a quantity of one product is produced, followed by a quantity of another;
3 **flow production**, where the same product is produced continuously.

These methods, and how they are applied in the three sectors of production, will now be considered in more detail.

Job production

Job production occurs when different products are made one after another to customers' orders. They are one-off orders which may or may not be repeated at a later date. They can range from a cruise liner to a handmade suit. For example, a wealthy businessman may ask a tailor to make him a suit. The businessman will be measured; the suit will be cut out, stitched and he will try it on to see if it fits; and then there will be a final fitting for any minor adjustments. If the client likes the suit, he may order another one later.

In job production, skilled workers working alone, or in teams, make the product. The emphasis is on quality, not quantity. As there are usually few economies of scale, the price of the finished product can be high.

Examples of job production include: drilling a new borehole for oil; building a new section of a motorway; constructing a luxury home for a pop star; making a film; defending a client in a Crown court.

Batch production

Batch production occurs when a quantity of the same item is produced, followed by a batch of a different item. The production is often split up between different workers. For example, in a clothes factory some workers may cut out the material; others may machine, or stitch, the garments; and another group may finish them. Many of the workers in batch production are skilled. The work is often carried out for another manufacturer. For example, a small firm that makes fish aquaria may drill metal bars for an engineering firm when it has few orders of its own.

With heavier or bigger products, the work is usually organized into sections, with, for example, a group of cutting machines in one part of the factory and a group of drilling machines in another part. Therefore, goods have to be moved from one section to another, and machines have to be reset to do a new kind of job. This takes time. As you will see later in the chapter, modern technology has made flexible batch production possible. This produces a much greater range of versions of a product at greater speed.

Examples of batch production: include making suites of furniture; providing romantic, 'naughty' and cultural weekends in Paris for tourists; growing fields of peas for a processed food manufacturer.

Flow production

Flow production is used for producing large quantities of the same item at high speed. It is used in the electricity industry where highly automated plants produce a continuous supply of energy. Similar methods are used in the gas, oil, chemicals and plastics industries.

Another form of flow production is used to produce consumer goods in large quantities. The products are moved on a conveyor belt or **assembly line** from one worker to another. There is great **division of labour**, so that each worker does only one small job, such as peeling onions for jars of pickled onions or putting a circuit board into a television set. Most of the work is semi-skilled. Machines are used as much as possible.

► See **Division of labour** in Chapter 2.

There are great economies of scale to be made; but the capital cost of buying specialized machinery and setting up the assembly line is huge. Many line workers become bored with their jobs. To give them greater job satisfaction and to improve the quality of the product, many workers now operate in teams, sharing greater control over production.

A production line for Ross Young's frozen pizza

Examples of flow production include: making cars; work at a nuclear power plant; manufacturing soft drinks; a radio station broadcasting around the clock.

1 What is job production? Give two examples of where it might be used.

2 How does batch production differ from job production?
3 State all the places where you would expect to find flow production used.
4 Define flexible batch production.
5 What do some firms do if workers get bored on assembly lines?

  Draw up a table with the caption 'Methods of production' and five columns headed *Method*, *Description*, *Primary sector*, *Secondary sector* and *Tertiary sector*. Use the information in the text to fill in the table for job, batch and flow production methods, giving a brief description of each process and putting examples of each method in the appropriate columns.

NEW MANUFACTURING METHODS

► To refresh your memory, see **New products** in Chapter 11

As you already know, all firms have to introduce new products if they are to survive. In the past, each department did its own work on a new product separately. This often caused delays, conflict between departments and expensive late changes. These problems are avoided with **simultaneous engineering**.

> ### Simultaneous engineering
> In this system, people from the research, design, development, manufacturing, purchasing, supply and marketing departments work in a team, from coming up with the initial product idea to the final launch of the product.

► **Lead time** is the time between the decision to go ahead with a project and its launch on the market.

As a result, **lead time** can be reduced by up to a third, project costs can be halved, and quality improved greatly.

Computers in manufacturing

Most of the manufacturing advances are based on the use of computers. Some of the most common uses are:

Computer-assisted design

Computer-assisted design (CAD) has transformed the first stages of product development. Using special software, products can now be designed on a computer and displayed in colour on its screen. CAD can be used for designing almost anything from a bridge to a dress. The computer can be programmed to show how the product would respond to different conditions or different materials. For example, the dress could be shown with different colours and weights of cloth and in different styles.

Computer-aided manufacturing

Computer-aided manufacturing (CAM) enables the product to be made directly from the display on the computer screen. For example, a chair could be designed on the screen. The instructions to make it could be passed to a numerically controlled machine that cuts out the wooden chair frames, to another machine that cuts out the foam rubber for the cushion, and then to another machine that cuts the material for the cushion cover. The chairs would then only have to be assembled.

Numerically controlled machines are quick and easy to reset. It is therefore very easy to change the design on the computer and to instruct the machines to make a different version of the chair. For example, chairs could easily be produced in different styles, with different wood veneers or with differently coloured cushions. In flexible batch production, smaller quantities of different versions of the same basic product are produced to satisfy customers' demands. This method of production is almost certain to increase greatly in the 1990s. Flexible batch production can also be carried out on assembly lines.

CAM is used in many other industries. For example, computers control the temperature, the mixture and the rate of flow in automated paint-making plants.

1 What is the main advantage of simultaneous engineering?
2 What is lead time?
3 How does computer-assisted design work?
4 In which kinds of factories would you expect to find computer-aided manufacturing?

Make notes about the effect of computers on design and manufacturing.

LEAN PRODUCTION

Computers have provided the basis for the latest form of assembly-line production. Over the years, the line has become more and more automated, with machines or robots replacing human beings. Robots were first used in the 1950s for welding and painting car bodies. Initially, they were not very successful, because workers were not fully trained and motivated to use them. Now, they are used in most car plants. Robots are also used for transporting loads from one conveyor to another.

▶ Robots are also useful for doing work that requires great strength or for work in dangerous conditions such as underwater repairs or in nuclear plants.

Lean production is much more efficient because it reduces the time, money and human resources needed. However, it demands a much higher level of skill in the workforce. Some form of quality management system is therefore essential. As you already know, quality management systems stress the importance of individual performance, teamwork, training, personal flexibility, and quality.

▶ To refresh your memory, see the box on **Quality management systems** in Chapter 8, p. 95.

The Japanese introduced lean production into their car plants in Britain. The system is now spreading into other industries. Lean production has several important features:

► See **Informal groups** in Chapter 8.

- **Computer-integrated engineering** (CIE) controls the whole of the production process. Work is carried out through a series of linked computer databases.
- The work is done by multi-functional teams of eighty or ninety assembly workers with team leaders who are in charge of the work, performance and training. Members of the team continually check the quality of the production and reset machines on the spot, which means that there are fewer faults in the goods. As the workers have more responsibility, they are more motivated in their work. The use of computer databases streamlines management, which makes it possible to get rid of many middle managers.
- Computers also make it possible to use a **just-in-time** (**JIT**) stock control system. In the past, there was always a large stock of components and parts on the premises to make sure there were no delays in feeding the assembly line. Now, components and parts are delivered just in time from the suppliers. They are often delivered automatically to the storage area by the assembly line, which holds a minimal amount of stock. The workforce sometimes has no more than two hours' worth of stock by the line. Holding less stock saves the manufacturer both space and money.
- Car manufacturers now buy in even more components and parts from outside suppliers. They insist on such high quality that the number of suppliers has been greatly reduced.
- This combination of computers, advanced machines, team work and just-in-time stock control has made flexible batch production possible on the assembly line. It is increasingly used in car-assembly plants to produce many different models of the same car.

 Draw up a table with the caption 'Changes in line production' and three columns headed *Technological*, *Organization of workers* and *Organization of work-flow*. Fill in the table using the information you have just read.

Effects on factors of production

► To refresh your memory, see **Factors of production** in Chapter 2, pp. 7–8.

► However, the need for an efficient road transport system has increased the amount of land used for motorways.

Lean production has brought about a great change in the four factors of production. Land is used more economically, as just-in-time stock control means that much less space is needed for storing and warehousing. Labour has been reduced, although the workers who remain must be more skilled. Capital investment in these highly automated plants has increased greatly. Enterprise has also increased, not only on the shop floor where workers have to cope with many more problems themselves, but also among managers who have to set up and run these complex systems.

Effects on manufacturing costs

As a result of the change in the factors of production, the distribution of manufacturing costs has changed greatly. Not so long ago, the costs of labour, overheads and purchased goods and services were all about equal. Now, labour is only about 10 per cent, overheads about 20 per cent, and purchased goods and services about 70 per cent of the total costs in the most modern factories.

Effects on management

Lean production has made the work of both the **production manager** and the **purchasing manager** much more demanding.

Production manager's functions

Under a lean production system, the production manager has responsibility for ensuring the following.

1   An appropriate plant layout must be designed. **Layout by process** is used in batch production where similar machines are grouped together. **Layout by product** is used in line production where machines are installed by the line in a logical order for the assembly of the product. Adequate space has to be left for the storage of components and for any sub-assembly lines.
    - Production must flow freely and machines and workers must be fully employed.
    - Production schedules must be kept to.
    - Products must be of the highest possible quality.
    - Costs must be kept within the production budget.

To help them achieve the highest standards, production managers often use **benchmarking** – comparing their own productivity with that of the leading manufacturers in the field.

Purchasing manager's functions

The great increase in the relative value of purchased goods and services under a lean production system has made the work of the purchasing manager even more important than it used to be. The production manager's main tasks are:

- to buy all the raw materials, components, goods and services that the firm requires, at the highest possible quality and at the most economical price;
- to set rigorous standards for suppliers and to provide training if necessary to ensure that their supplies are suitable;
- to establish a suitable computerized system for ordering stock and controlling its storage and movement;
- to arrange storage space for stock and provide a quick efficient method of locating and retrieving it;
- to make sure that the goods and services are delivered on time, and to ensure that there is adequate buffer stock if a just-in-time system is not being used.

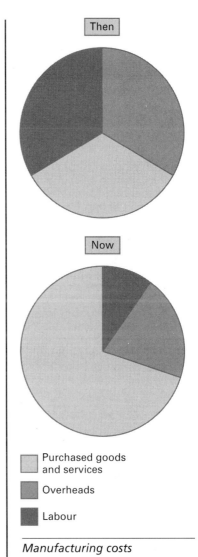

Then

Now

Purchased goods and services

Overheads

Labour

Manufacturing costs

► Benchmarking is now used by firms of all sizes in all three sectors of production. A benchmarking firm measures its own performance in some particular activity, such as distribution, against the performance of other firms. The firms need not necessarily be in the same industry. The benchmarking firm finds out if the other firms are more efficient; and, if they are, how it is done. This benchmark then becomes the standard that the firm tries to achieve.

Make notes on the work of the production manager and the purchasing manager, highlighting any similarities in their work.

Benefits of lean production

Lean production has produced great benefits for firms. There have been dramatic reductions in costs as less stock is held and there is less need to rework and repair products at the end of the manufacturing process. **Productivity** has doubled in some factories. The quality of goods has improved so much that there are hardly any failures on inspection at the end of the line. Many more versions of the same product are produced.

However, the number of British firms that have introduced the new system is small. Lean production needs very high investment. For example, Heinz invested £40 million in its new pasta-making factory with 150 employees at Harlesden in London. Not all firms are able, or willing, to make that kind of investment.

Britain also lags behind many other countries in spending on **research and development (R & D)**. Some British firms started to spend more on R & D in the 1980s, but expenditure fell again in the recession at the beginning of the 1990s. Only two or three British firms are in the world's top R & D league. Yet R & D is vital, particularly in hi-tech industries such as pharmaceuticals, electronics, cars, chemicals and aerospace, if firms are to gain a competitive edge over their rivals. Successful foreign firms are developing products now which will be world leaders in the next millennium.

1 What is just-in-time stock control?
2 Why have modern production methods changed the amount spent on factory labour?
3 What are two of the main functions of:
(a) a production manager?
(b) a purchasing manager?
4 What is R & D? Why is it particularly important in hi-tech industries?

► **Productivity** shows the relationship between output and input. It is measured by dividing the units of output by the units of labour input. For example ten workers using simple tools might produce 100 units of goods in a day (a productivity rate of 10). If large amounts of money were invested in new technology and machinery, two workers might produce 200 units in a day (a productivity rate of 100). Productivity, therefore, has increased ten times. Productivity can be measured for individual workers or plants or whole industries and by the hour, day or year.

► **Research and development** (**R & D**) involves scientific research into new products, materials and production processes, followed by development of the ideas in practice. The main aim of R & D is to use technology to create or improve products and methods of production; to find new uses for by-products, or secondary items, produced in the manufacturing process; to improve quality by using new materials; and to cut costs by creating new processes.

SUMMARY

- There are three main ways of producing goods or services: job, batch and flow production.
- Job production is when products are made one after another to individual customer's orders by skilled workers working alone or in a team.
- Batch production is when a quantity of one item is made followed by a quantity of a similar item. Flexible batch production is when different versions of products are produced at much higher speeds.
- Flow production is when large volumes or quantities of the same item are produced at high speed. This method is used

to produce electricity, gas, paint, chemicals and oil, and consumer goods on assembly lines.

- Production has been revolutionized by the use of computers in computer-assisted design (CAD) and computer-aided manufacturing (CAM). Computer-integrated engineering (CIE) controls the whole production process in lean production.

- Lean production combines computerized systems and automation with quality management systems to provide the most cost-effective method of manufacturing. Multi-function teams are in charge of their own section; stock is delivered only when it is required, or just in time.

- Lean production reduces the use of land and labour; but increases capital investment and enterprise. The work of shop-floor workers and production and purchasing managers is more challenging and demanding.

- Only a few British companies have made the major investment required by lean production. Britain also lags behind other advanced countries in spending on research and development (R & D).

16 Business location

CHOOSING A LOCATION

 Read the following case study and answer the questions at the end.

Rashida has worked as a manager in the textiles industry for nine years, first in factories and then in retail. She has to do a large amount of travelling in her present job. As she is going to have a baby, she has decided to resign and open a shop instead. The shop will sell clothes for young children, and will specialize in Asian fabrics and designs. Rashida is thinking of calling the shop Children's Harvest.

For the last few weeks, she has been looking at premises in various parts of the city. Her notes on the last shop are shown at the top of the opposite page.

1 What is the total weekly bill for rent and rates?
2 What are the main advantages and disadvantages of the location for Rashida's shop?
3 Would you advise her to rent the shop or not? State the reasons for your advice.

PREMISES	Low rent (£4,000 a year) and business rates (£1,200 a year). Long lease. Will need total shopfitting. (Cost: £14,500?). Shop faces north.
TRANSPORT	Main road just round the corner. Many bus services. Near railway station. Easy street parking. No yellow lines planned.
NEARNESS TO MARKET	Passers-by- mainly office workers and older local residents. Three schools nearby, but most of foot and vehicle traffic flows the other way. Nearest high street half a mile away.
LOCAL ENVIRONMENT	Facing park with children's playground. Mainly offices. Few other shops, two of them closed. Several pubs. One or two memos advertising in shop windows for part-time work.

4 If she had been opening a photocopying shop, how would that change your advice? Give your reasons.
5 What other matters would you advise Rashida to investigate before she opened her shop?

MAIN FACTORS IN BUSINESS LOCATION

There is never an ideal location for a business. As the case study has shown, there are always advantages and disadvantages. In this case, the disadvantages seem greater than the advantages. Although the rent and rates are cheap, the shop is a long way from the high street, so if you plan to rely on passing trade you may scarcely ever see a customer. Specialist shops, like Rashida's, hope to pull in customers from a wider area. The local environment then becomes more important. Most mothers of young children wouldn't like shopping in such an out-of-the way place.

A photocopying shop would have a better chance of success, but the likely demand from the nearby offices should be investigated first. For example, if the majority had their own photocopying facilities, there might not be much call for an outside service.

Five separate items feature in Rashida's notes:

1 premises;
2 transport;
3 nearness to market;
4 local environment;
5 labour.

These factors apply to most location decisions. They will now be considered in greater detail.

Premises

To a large extent, you get what you pay for. Retail rents are high in city centres, because that is where most customers are. Rents fall as you move away from the high streets and shopping precincts. The condition of the premises is important, because first impressions affect the success of the business. It can be very expensive to refurbish premises.

Businesses other than retailers are able to consider a location away from city centres in purpose-built premises on industrial estates or greenfield sites.

There is another decision to be made concerning premises. Should you buy the freehold of the premises, or rent the premises on a lease for a number of years? It's not an easy choice. You have to spend, or borrow, a lot of money to buy the freehold, but commercial property usually increases in value over the years. If you buy a lease, it will decline in value as the remaining years of the lease run out; and if you want to renew it at the end of the lease, you will probably have to pay a much higher rent.

▶ An **industrial estate** is a special site in towns and cities that provides new factories and offices and all the necessary infrastructure such as roads, power supplies, water, telecommunications, etc. A **greenfield site** is an industrial, office, or retail development built outside or on the edge of a city.

Transport

Road transport is one of the most important factors in all location decisions. The site should have adequate parking and turning space for the vehicles of customers, staff and suppliers. For manufacturers, access to motorways is of major importance for the supply of goods and components and for the distribution of finished goods. Railway stations are less important now that most goods are transported by road.

In big cities, good public transport is also essential. The government refused to extend the Jubilee line to the huge office development in London's Docklands area when it was being built. This created great problems in attracting staff to work there.

Nearness to market

▶ To refresh your memory, see **New channels of distribution** in Chapter 13.

Better road transport and more sophisticated distribution systems have made closeness to markets less important for manufacturers. The main factor is often the difference in costs between transporting raw materials to the factory and distributing the finished product to the main markets. If the raw materials are heavy and bulky, it is probably more economic to be near their source.

The Single Market, which has increased trade in the European Union (EU), is shifting the focus of many markets. More businesses have to think of trade in European rather than simply British terms. Firms in the south have an advantage over northern and Scottish firms in the time taken to transport goods to the Continent. With the opening of the Channel Tunnel, quicker rail services may reduce this advantage.

Retailers, service industries and some suppliers still need to be near their main markets.

Local environment

A pleasant local environment is important for attracting staff and retail customers. The local environment includes housing; leisure, shopping and entertainment facilities; and education, as colleges can provide training for firms' employees, while polytechnics and universities can provide help in research.

Labour

A suitable supply of skilled labour, or unskilled labour that can be trained, is essential for most businesses. Local wage rates are also an important factor. The differences in wages in various regions of the country are less than they were, but they still exist.

 Choose a particular business, preferably one that you know something about through your family or work experience. Find empty premises that a firm of that kind might use. Through external observation, and any necessary enquiries from estate agents, neighbouring businesses, etc., find out as much as possible about the factors of location described above, and any other factors in location that you think might be important. Write a report about the location of the premises, giving your reasoned verdict on whether it is suitable for that kind of business.

OTHER FACTORS AFFECTING LOCATION

There are three other factors that can influence the choice of location.

External economies of scale

Firms in the same industry have a tendency to set up business near each other. This leads to **external economies of scale**. Organizations providing services to this cluster of firms are able to gain a specialized knowledge of the industry. Colleges, polytechnics and universities, for example, may run training courses and carry out research related to the industry. Banks will understand the particular financial problems of that industry. Firms can also benefit from a concentration of shared resources. Skilled labour, suppliers and sub-contractors will move to the area to provide the essential services that the firms need.

There are many examples of similar firms clustering in the same area:

- retailers in the high street;
- lawyers in the same street, or in the Inns of Court in London;
- restaurants in the same city area;
- electronics firms in the west of London;

► For more on just-in-time, see **Lean production** in Chapter 15.

- suppliers of car parts and components near big car assembly plants – their closeness is essential for just-in-time deliveries.

Other external economies are often provided for a whole industry by trade associations carrying out research and development and organizing training.

 Make brief notes on external economies of scale, adding any examples of your own.

Planning permission

You cannot set up a business anywhere you choose. If you wanted to change the use of premises from, say, a sports shop to a fish and chip shop, you would have to get planning permission from the local planning authority. If you wanted to start a new business, you would have to obtain full planning permission from the local council.

► The council would examine your proposal, and carry out a full investigation if necessary, before it granted or refused permission.

Some kinds of businesses, such as mini-cabs firms, credit and finance companies and many more, also require licences.

It is much easier to get planning permission now than it was in the past, particularly if the firm can show that it is going to create new jobs. Many local councils come to an agreement with developers – giving planning permission for a supermarket, for example, if the council can buy the flats above or if the developers build a new road.

Grants

The government gives **regional aid** to firms in areas with high unemployment. These are called **assisted areas**. Established firms in development areas, where unemployment is highest, get a grant if they create new jobs. Small businesses receive special help. They can obtain a grant of 50 per cent of the costs, up to a maximum of £25,000, for introducing new products or technology. Firms in intermediate areas may get a grant for creating new jobs if they really need financial help.

Much government aid is now directed to inner-city areas, some of which are not in assisted areas.

Enterprise zones
The government has also set up enterprise zones in areas of high unemployment. To attract firms, the government tries to provide a better infrastructure, particularly through new roads and land clearance. The enterprise zones last for ten years. In the first year, firms have a capital allowance of 100 per cent (or tax-free allowance) for building industrial or commercial premises. Firms are also exempted from paying business rates for ten years.

Small businesses
The government provides special financial help for small businesses and the unemployed who want to start their own business.

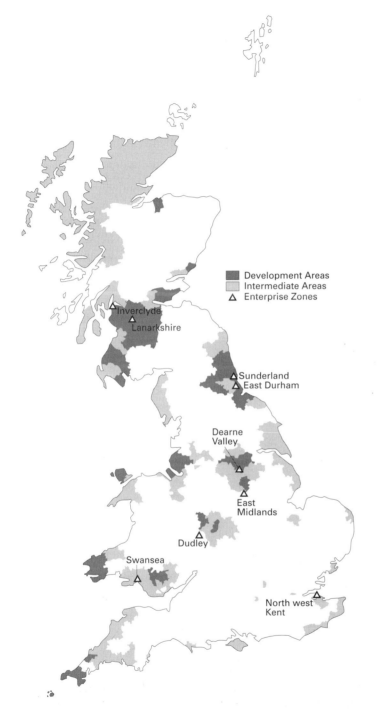

Development Areas
Intermediate Areas
△ Enterprise Zones

Inverclyde
Lanarkshire

△Sunderland
△East Durham

Dearne
Valley

East
Midlands

Dudley

Swansea

North west
Kent

Assisted areas and enterprise zones

Under the **Loan Guarantee Scheme**, the government guarantees 85 per cent of a business loan up to £250,000 for starting or expanding a small business. This encourages banks to lend money to small businesses that otherwise have no security. Government-sponsored Training and Enterprise Councils may give an enterprise allowance to unemployed people who want to set up their own business.

► The Enterprise Allowance Scheme has now been renamed Business Start-Up.

European Union grants

The EU also provides financial aid for both the private and the public sectors. It provides grants and loans for research and development; job creation and training schemes; infrastructure works in coal-mining and depressed industrial and country areas; and for developing energy supplies.

1 What is the difference between an industrial estate and a greenfield site?
2 Explain what the local environment is.
3 Why is skilled and unskilled labour an important factor in the location of business?
4 Give two examples of external economies of scale.
5 When would a shopkeeper need to obtain planning permission and from where would he or she obtain it?
6 How do the government and the EU help businesses in particular locations?

Make notes on planning permission and grants to businesses under the headings: *New firms*, *Established firms* and *Small businesses*.

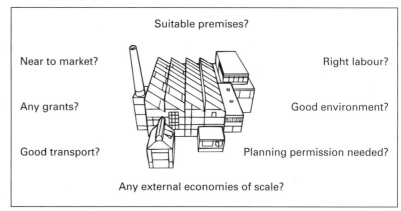

Suitable premises?

Near to market?

Right labour?

Any grants?

Good environment?

Good transport?

Planning permission needed?

Any external economies of scale?

Location questions

> ▶ **Multinationals** are firms that operate in more than one country. They are usually conglomerates with a wide spread of business interests in many countries (see **Conglomerates** in Chapter 7).
>
> ▶ **Subsidiary companies** are smaller companies that are controlled by multinationals or other large companies. The parent company either owns the subsidiary company or has a majority of its voting shares.

LOCATION OF MULTINATIONALS

Multinationals have a wider choice of locations – in fact they could set up business almost anywhere.

The multinational's aim

The main aim of a multinational is to increase its profitability and/or global market share by setting up or taking over subsidiary companies in as many strategically located countries as necessary.

Multinationals may choose a country because it gives them a chance to exploit a new market or to increase their market share. Or the country may provide access to a much larger market which puts high tariffs or quotas on imported goods. Or it may be in an ideal geographical position to sell to neighbouring countries with weaker economies.

There are several other factors that a multinational has to take into account when choosing a country. The main ones are:

- the economic, political and social stability of the country, which is essential to protect the multinationals' investment;
- government and local authority aid and support for business, which will provide a helpful environment for business activities and financial grants;
- an up-to-date infrastructure of roads, railways and airports, and reliable electricity and other power supplies;
- workforce and trade union cooperation, ensuring harmonious industrial relations and high productivity;
- the experience of other foreign firms, which provides a guide to how they will be treated.

 Imagine you were a local council official with the responsibility of trying to attract foreign firms to your area. Describe the advantages of your area for foreign firms and explain any policies you would adopt to make the area more attractive to them.

► One of the reasons for the Japanese opening so many factories in Britain is to gain access to the EU Single Market. They have to use a large percentage of British labour and parts in making their goods; but they are then entitled to export them freely to other member-countries of the EU.

PRIVATE COSTS AND BENEFITS

Multinationals – and other large firms – will only keep a factory open while it is profitable or advantageous to do so. They may have many reasons for closing or selling a subsidiary company. As you already know, large firms can suffer diseconomies of scale which may force them to close some of their less profitable subsidiary companies. A worldwide recession, such as the one at the beginning of the 1990s, can have similar effects. Or the firm may have decided to sell off companies in one of its minority markets, film-making for example, to provide capital for expansion in another market, such as telecommunications.

Firms make these kinds of decisions by looking at the private costs and benefits involved. Some of the private costs might be:

- loss of capital if the company had to be closed or sold off for less than it cost to buy;
- possible damage to future profits (and company image) in that country if the closure produced a very hostile reaction;
- redundancy payments, which have to be paid by law to the workforce.

Some of the private benefits would be:

- reduced costs through closing the company;
- greater profitability for the group as a whole, as it no longer has to support a 'lame duck';
- the probability of improving profits by switching group efforts to an expanding market.

► To refresh your memory, see **Diseconomies of scale** in Chapter 7.

► **Private costs and benefits** are the effects of a firm's decision on its costs and profits.

These costs and benefits can all be calculated in financial terms.

 Make notes on the private costs and benefits for the parent company of closing or selling off a subsidiary company.

SOCIAL COSTS AND BENEFITS

▶ **Social costs and benefits** are the harmful and beneficial consequences for society of a decision by a private firm or a public authority.

A business decision of this kind – closing a company – can have great effects not only on the workforce but also on the local community and the country as a whole. Some of the company's local suppliers might be forced to close; others might have to make some of their workforce redundant. Shops, pubs, restaurants, banks and many other kinds of firms would also suffer through the loss of the company's business and the increase in unemployment. Local educational institutions might lose students and research contracts.

There would also be effects on the whole country. The government (and so, in effect, the whole country) would lose the firm's corporation tax and the income tax and national insurance contributions that the factory's employees once paid. And the government would have to pay the former employees job seekers' allowance and, after six months, social security payments.

The effects described above are the social costs involved. In this case, it is difficult to find many social benefits except, perhaps, a reduction in the volume of traffic and noise pollution.

Many of the social costs of closing the company can be measured in financial terms: the loss of local trade; the effects on local educational institutions; the government's loss of revenue and its increase in social security payments. Yet the big firm contributes nothing towards paying for the social costs of its decision, except for the legal requirement to make redundancy payments to its former employees. The firm might argue that by opening the company it had already provided great social benefits in creating new jobs, trade and prosperity. Critics, however, would probably argue that it should still be forced to make some financial contribution to the social costs of its decision to close the company.

▶ It might also help former employees to find new jobs and/or provide them with counselling services; or make bigger redundancy payments than the legal minimum.

▶ **Bulkheads** are partitions in a ferry's hold that divide it into separate watertight compartments.

It is not always possible to calculate all social costs and benefits in financial terms, particularly where human life is involved. For example, it is generally agreed that roll-on, roll-off ferries could be made safer by installing bulkheads. If the ferry was involved in a collision, the bulkheads would delay the sinking of the ship, giving passengers and crew much more time to escape. Would it be worth spending millions of pounds to install bulkheads in all ferries if they saved human lives? And who should pay: the company out of its profits; the traveller through higher fares; or the government out of general taxation?

ACT IN Imagine that you are the public relations officer in a ferry company. One of your ferries has collided with another vessel in the Channel and sunk with the loss of seventy-eight lives. There have been many letters in the quality newspapers criticizing your company for not having watertight bulkheads in its ferries. Write a letter to *The Times* defending the company's decision not to install bulkheads.

ENVIRONMENTAL RESPONSIBILITIES

Increasing concern

In recent years, there has been increasing public, scientific and governmental concern about the impact of business activities on the **environment** and about the waste of scarce resources. Parents are now much more conscious of the need for a healthy, safe, 'green' environment for their children. Pressure groups, like Greenpeace and Friends of the Earth, have campaigned ceaselessly against industrial pollution and other business activities that harm the environment. Scientists have warned of the dangers of global warming. The pressure has been so great that the government and the EU have been forced to pass laws to protect the environment. The EU has already approved more than 200 directives. Some of the main environmental concerns are listed below.

> ► **Pressure groups** are groups of people who band together to try to bring about a change of policy by firms, public authorities or governments. They may have one specific aim, such as stopping a factory being built in a beauty spot. Or they may have a much broader aim, such as persuading the authorities to bring in an integrated transport system for the whole country.

Environmental problems

- **Global warming** could lead to a rise in temperatures with extensive flooding as ocean levels rise. It is caused mainly by carbon dioxide emissions, produced by burning fossil fuels in power stations and motor vehicles. Forest clearances make it even worse as the removal of trees reduces the absorption of carbon dioxide by the process of photosynthesis. Methane gas is another major cause of global warming. It is produced when rubbish buried in landfill sites decomposes, and in livestock farming. Private individuals are responsible for global warming, but business contributes more than its fair share.
- **Acid rain** is caused by burning fossil fuels. It is the product of chemical reactions between sulphur dioxide, nitrogen oxides and water vapour. Acid rain kills trees, fish in rivers and lakes, and damages the stonework of buildings.
- **Rain forests** are being destroyed in many tropical areas to provide timber products for DIY and furniture stores worldwide. It is likely that many of these ancient forests are now non-renewable. There has also been an adverse effect on the local **ecology**, i.e. the relation between living beings and their environment.
- **Ozone depletion** results from using CFCs and other substances that deplete the ozone layer and thus let in more harmful ultra-violet rays from the sun. It is thought that these can cause skin cancers. The EU plans to end the use of CFCs by 1997.
- **Water pollution** is caused primarily by the discharge of agricultural and industrial effluents, or waste liquids, into

> ► See the marginal note on **CFCs** in Chapter 11, page 142.

rivers and seas. These pollutants include some highly toxic chemical compounds and heavy metals, but many of the most serious pollutants are naturally occurring organic waste products – it is the concentration of the substance that defines it as a pollutant. Untreated sewage, farmyard manure, slurry and organic industrial waste are the commonest water pollutants, as well as chemical fertilizers, particularly nitrates.

- **Air pollution** is the responsibility of many industries. One of the most serious air pollutants in the UK is sulphur dioxide, which is emitted from power stations, factories and oil refineries. The motor vehicle industry plays a major part in air pollution. When nitrogen oxide, released in car exhausts, reacts with oxygen in bright sunlight it produces a cocktail of pollutants known as petrochemical smog. Lead is another pollutant associated with motor vehicles, but lead pollution is declining, as permitted levels in petrol are being reduced and unleaded petrol and diesel-burning cars are becoming more popular. Other air pollutants include those associated with paint-spraying and textile dye factories. Air pollution in the form of solid particles of ash, dust, soot and smoke is associated with some of the older heavy manufacturing industries and mining.
- **Smell pollution** comes from factories and from some retail premises, such as fish and chip shops.
- **Noise pollution** comes from many kinds of factories, businesses and traffic.
- **Waste of scarce materials** is a problem associated with **packaging**. Unnecessary or excessive packaging is not only wasteful, but also helps to create a litter problem. The EU intends to convert all member-countries from throwaway to recycling societies by the year 2000, by recycling paper, cloth, glass, plastics, and aluminium and steel cans.
- **Dangerous wastes**, such as poisonous chemicals and radioactive materials, are produced by some businesses. EU laws now make it obligatory to dispose of dangerous waste safely.

► See **Packaging** in Chapter 11.

 ACT IN Collect news stories and articles from newspapers and magazines about business and the environment. Make a brief summary of the main problems, describing what is being done to solve them.

Calculating costs and benefits

Most of the activities in the box above produce some social benefits as well as social costs. For example, one of the social benefits of packaging is that it provides some 100,000 jobs. Again, it is not always possible to measure all the social costs and benefits in financial terms. Take as an example a proposal to build a superstore in an **environmentally sensitive area** (**ESA**) with its own ecology system, including rare plants and animals. Some of the social costs and benefits of the proposal would be:

Social costs	*Social benefits*
More traffic	New jobs
Effects on small shops	Cheaper goods
Loss of ESA	Greater consumer choice

It is difficult to price greater consumer choice, but it is even more difficult to assess the financial value of an environmentally sensitive area.

However, it is much easier to do a cost-benefit analysis with other environmental issues. Take acid rain. It is easy to calculate the cost of stopping emissions from factories, power stations, vehicle exhausts and other sources. It is just as easy to calculate the likely costs of the destruction of forests, fish stocks, crops and stonework in buildings if no action is taken to end the problem. In this way, it is possible to come to a rational, cost-effective decision.

1 What does infrastructure mean?
2 Describe the social costs of closing a factory.
3 What is a multinational?
4 Why have so many people become concerned about the environment?
5 How would you carry out a cost-benefit analysis?

In each of the following two examples, what would be the social costs and benefits of (a) building another runway at an airport and (b) making it illegal to drink alcohol in any public place other than licensed premises.

Business reactions

In general, business has been slow to end or moderate activities that are environmentally harmful, even though, in some cases, it would be in its own interests to do so. Individual businesses have shown that they are conscious of the need to save resources by recycling water used in industrial processes and by trying to reduce consumption of electricity and gas; this also helps to reduce their costs. Some projects, such as the development of prototype electric and gas-powered cars, are genuine attempts to reduce pollution, but the introduction of **green goods** sometimes has more to do with marketing than with product improvement. Too often, business has been forced into action by impending laws rather than voluntarily leading the way towards a healthier environment.

Most businesses are still reluctant to accept full **social responsibility** for all their actions. However, there is now a much greater public concern about the social responsibilities of business and more pressure for change.

▶ **Cost-benefit analysis** involves calculating a financial value for the social costs and benefits of a planned project, which are then added to the project's costs and forecast revenue respectively. In this way, it is possible to estimate the 'true' value of the project to the firm involved and to the community.

▶ A further problem would arise if it was decided to introduce preventative measures. Acid rain knows no frontiers: emissions can pollute countries miles away. It would, therefore, be necessary to obtain agreement from all European countries to take similar measures.

▶ **Green goods** are goods that are considered to be environmentally friendly, as they are made from recycled materials or are recyclable or biodegradable.

SUMMARY

- The main factors affecting the choice of business locations are: the premises, transport, nearness to market, local environment, labour, external economies of scale, planning permission and grants.
- Multinationals also have to consider other factors, including workforce and trade union cooperation; official aid and support; the infrastructure; and economic, political and social stability.
- Opening a new company can bring great social benefits to the local community and the country; equally, closing it can produce great social costs.
- Social costs and benefits are not always easy to assess in financial terms, but most can be measured.
- In recent years there has been increasing concern about the impact of business on the environment. The government and the EU have passed laws to control environmentally harmful activities
- The main areas of concern are: global warming; acid rain; rain forests; ozone depletion; water, air, noise and smell pollution; packaging; and waste disposal.
- Most businesses are still reluctant to accept full social responsibility for all their actions.

17 Financial planning

Chapter objectives

After working through this chapter, you will have the knowledge to:

▌ make financial forecasts;

▌ distinguish between forecasts and budgets;

▌ identify fixed and variable costs;

▌ construct and interpret breakeven charts;

▌ apply marginal costing methods;

▌ analyse the effects of cutting costs;

▌ evaluate the needs for working capital;

▌ compile, use and interpret cash-flow forecasts;

▌ understand and use the following key terms: forecast, budget, budgetary control, public sector borrowing requirement (PSBR), master budget, business plan, revenue, bad debt, fixed cost, overhead, variable cost, breakeven chart, breakeven point, margin of safety, spare capacity, semi-variable cost, direct cost, indirect cost, absorption – or total – costing, marginal costing, contribution, cash flow, debtor, creditor, liquidity, cash in hand, cash at bank, standing order, direct debit, current asset, current liability, working capital, overdraft, cash-flow forecast, factoring.

INTRODUCTION TO FINANCE

This chapter and Chapters 18 and 19 deal with various aspects of finance, which is the basis of all business activity. Without strong financial foundations, no business can succeed. Finance is involved in practically all decisions made by businesses, whatever their size.

For example, losses through shoplifting in a large CNT (confectioners, newsagents and tobacconists) have recently risen to record levels. The owner has decided to install video cameras in the shops to deter thieves. She finds out how much they cost and decides to lease two cameras, rather than buy them outright. After they have been installed, stock checks show that losses are declining. At the end of the year, her accounts show that she has saved three times as much in reduced shoplifting as she has spent on leasing the cameras. That, in brief, is what finance is about: making a decision and supporting it with money.

▶ The process is: you have a problem – you make a decision – you have to spend money – you decide how to obtain it – you check the results – you see if it was profitable.

▶ See the second figure in Chapter 8, page 92.

Sole traders usually have to look after all aspects of finance themselves, often with the aid and advice of an accountant or bank manager. In bigger firms, a financial director, who is a member of the board of directors, is in overall control of finance. He or she has a number of immediate subordinates who are in charge of various aspects of finance. Their titles and functions may vary from one firm to another; but there are five major aspects of finance that all financial departments have to deal with.

Essentials of finance

1 **Budgeting:** To plan for the future by making budgets, or financial plans. These help the firm to reach its objectives. They also provide a benchmark against which achievement can be measured.
2 **Cost accounting:** To identify costs and to control them so that the firm becomes more efficient and profitable.
3 **Cash flow:** To make sure that the firm has enough money flowing in to pay its wages and salaries and immediate bills.
4 **Raising finance:** To identify the most appropriate sources of finance and to evaluate the profitability of investments.
5 **Financial records:** To keep and interpret records showing the firm's financial transactions and to produce regular accounts, or summaries, for both external and internal use.

Interactive nature of finance

The five essential elements of finance will be dealt with in more detail in these three chapters. However, there are two points you should remember while you are studying them.

Financial essentials

- Like the four Ps in marketing, aspects of finance are studied separately for the sake of easier understanding. However, like the four Ps, they form part of a total process and interact with each other.
- Finance is full of numbers, but these numbers always relate to a real-life business situation.

You must always relate the aspect of finance you are studying to other aspects of finance and to the real business situation that lies behind them. For example, a firm's profits have declined sharply because its major brand has been losing sales. It has decided to repackage it and mount a big advertising campaign at a cost of £2 million. The firm believes that the expenditure will be more than balanced by an increase in profits from the brand. That, again, is what finance is about: making a decision and backing it with money.

 Make notes on the five essential elements of finance.

 In preparation for your study of financial records in Chapter 19, write to the Company Secretary of a large manufacturing company asking for a copy of the latest annual report and accounts. You can find the name and address of a suitable company in reference books in your main library. For example, *Times 1000* gives details of the 1,000 largest British companies. The addresses are in the alphabetical index at the end of the book. Write off immediately, as you will not be able to do some of the exercises in Chapter 19 if you do not have an annual report and accounts.

FORECASTING

Before a business can make any plans, it has to **forecast** what is likely to happen within a given period of time. Forecasting is not just making a wild guess about what might happen in the future. Firms use what has happened in the past to make predictions about the future. Computers have made it easier to make accurate forecasts. Spreadsheets are very useful for asking 'What if?' questions about the future. For example, changes in exchange rates can affect exports and profits. Using a spreadsheet, it takes no more than a few key strokes to find out how foreign sales and profits might be affected if an exchange rate went up or down.

▶ For more on spreadsheets, see **Computers in offices** in Chapter 23.

Internal and external sources

In making forecasts, firms use both internal and external sources of information – as they also do in market research. For example, if they wanted to make forecasts about their own sales and those of their rivals, they would use their own internal records and the published accounts of the other firms to provide data about what has happened in the past. They would use this data to make forecasts about the future.

▶ In fact, market research surveys are frequently used to provide data for making forecasts, for example on likely changes in the market.

 Look at the following sales figures of Brand A, the market leader, and its two nearest rivals, Brand B and Brand C.

	Sales (£ million)		
	1994	1995	1996
Brand A	200	189	174
Brand B	95	101	109
Brand C	77	82	89

The total market for the product, by value, has remained virtually unchanged during the three years.

1 What has happened to the sales of each of the three brands during the three years?
2 What are the sales likely to be (in millions of pounds) of each of the brands in 1997 if the same trend continues?
3 If you had been the marketing manager of Brand A, what actions would you have taken during the three years to retain market share?

► The budget, or the business's main plan, lasts for a year. Short-term plans last for up to three years, long-term plans for up to ten years.

► A similar system is used in the public sector. Every year, each government department makes its own budget showing how much it plans to spend in the coming year and what its income will be (if any). The Treasury, controlled by the Chancellor of the Exchequer, inspects these budgets. It tries to reduce the planned expenditure in the budgets to make sure that it is no greater than the expected income from taxes, duties, etc. If spending exceeds income, there will be a public sector borrowing requirement (PSBR), i.e. the government will have to borrow money to pay for the excess spending. The Chancellor then prepares the Budget. It is explained in detail to the House of Commons each November.

► See the box on **A business plan** in Chapter 6, pp. 66–7.

BUDGETS

Forecasts only state what is likely to happen in the future. Budgets, however, are a detailed financial, or quantitative, statement of what the company hopes to achieve month by month during the following year.

'Our sales will rise next year' is a forecast. 'Our sales will rise by a total of 2 per cent next year' is a budgetary statement.

Budgetary statements have a dual purpose. They provide a target for the business, such as a 2 per cent increase in sales. They also provide a control over performance. Monthly or quarterly targets can be continually checked against actual results.

What happens if there is a large difference between the targets and the results? An investigation can be made; the reasons for the difference can be discovered; and action can be taken to make sure that forecasting is more accurate in the future. This is known as **budgetary control**.

Departmental budgets

Every year, a company's departments prepare budgets showing what they hope to achieve in the next year, and their planned costs. For example, the marketing department will set targets for market share, sales, etc., and state how much it plans to spend on advertising and promotions. The production department will set its manufacturing targets, and state whether any new products will be launched, how many workers it plans to employ, and what its investment programme will be.

Finally, all the budgets have to be collated, or put together, by the finance department to make sure that there is enough money to finance them. After much discussion between the departments, a **master budget** dealing with all aspects of the firm's activities for the next year will be prepared. A budget committee, usually chaired by the chief executive or managing director, has to approve the master budget. This document is for internal circulation only. A **business plan**, which is based upon the master budget, is used externally: for example, when a firm is trying to borrow money from a bank.

The sole trader also needs to make out a master budget upon which a business plan can be based. This should be done before the business is started, and every year after that.

 Read the following case study and answer the questions at the end.

Paul, who is 20 years old, worked as a packer in a meat factory, but he was made redundant in January. He couldn't find another job. It is now March and he has decided to set up his own business, mowing lawns for people who are too frail or too busy to do it themselves.

He has been quite encouraged, as he has already found

two customers. They live near his parents' house, where he still lives. His future customers seem quite willing to pay the £4 per hour he has decided to charge. However, they will only provide four hours work per week. He plans to work 50 hours a week.

Paul has calculated what he will have to spend each year. The road tax and insurance for his van will come to £450; fuel for the mower and for journeys to customers will be £1,500; telephone calls, advertising in local newspapers and shop windows, and incidental costs will come to £550.

He hopes to borrow £2,000 from his bank for a two-year period to buy a second-hand van, a new mower and a telephone answering machine. He has been a customer of the bank for a year and has never been overdrawn.

Out of his earnings, Paul will have to pay income tax and self-employed National Insurance contributions. He will not earn enough to pay VAT.

1 What would be the total amount of Paul's business expenses per year, including £25 per week for repayment of a loan?
2 How much would Paul earn per year if he worked a 50-hour week with two weeks' annual holiday?
3 If you were Paul's bank manager, what would you say to him about his request for a loan?

COSTS AND REVENUE

All businesses, new or old, big or small, need to know what their costs and **revenue** are likely to be, so that they can calculate if they will make a profit. In Paul's case, he had allowed for costs, including the bank loan, of £3,800 a year, and an income of £10,000 a year, producing a profit of £6,200. In fact, the profit would be much lower – he hasn't allowed for the fact that lawns are not mowed for six months of the year!

His business plan was far too vague and badly thought out. Business plans must be based on facts that are as precise and comprehensive as possible. For example, Paul had allowed for road tax, insurance and fuel in relation to the van; but he had not taken into account the costs of new tyres, MOT, repairs and servicing, breakdown service (and possibly the cost of hiring a van if his was off the road).

Revenue

Furthermore, Paul wasn't very realistic about his likely revenue, or receipts over a stated period of time. Paul had decided to work 50 hours a week. Even if he obtained other gardening work as well as mowing, it is unlikely that he would obtain 50 hours work every week. Even if he did, it would not be a realistic target. With breaks for snacks or meals, and journeys to customers, he would have to work a 72-hour week, or a 12-hour day six days a week. It would have been more realistic to aim for 40 hours of paid hours of work per week, which might well be reduced to 30 hours because of bad weather, cancellations and **bad debts**. Bad debts occur when customers who don't pay their bills, which is very common in this type of work.

Before Paul went to his bank manager, he should have made out a proper business plan, including research into the market, which he had totally neglected to investigate. He should also have provided precise calculations of likely costs and revenue, and a breakeven chart showing when his business would break even and start making a profit.

FIXED AND VARIABLE COSTS

Before Paul could draw a breakeven chart, he would have had to divide his costs into two main kinds: fixed and variable.

▶ **Fixed costs** include:
- rent
- business rates
- interest charges
- repairs
- insurance
- administration

▶ **Variable costs** include:
- raw materials
- labour
- fuel
- advertising

- **Fixed costs**, or **overheads**, are those costs that do not change in the short term and have to be paid whether the business is making any money or not.
- **Variable costs** are costs that vary according to the amount of work being done or goods being produced, and are usually in fairly direct relationship to output. For example, if a manufacturer's output increases by 10 per cent, the amount of raw materials used will increase by the same percentage.

 Draw up a table with two columns headed *Fixed costs* and *Variable costs*. Put Paul's costs into the appropriate column.

Estimating costs

▶ See **Insurance** in Chapter 5.

Let's look at Paul's costs again and try to make more reasonable estimates. Paul's annual fixed costs would be his road tax and van insurance, as well as the cost of new tyres, MOT, repairs and servicing, breakdown service and possible van hire. He would also need to take out some other form of insurance, particularly public liability insurance. His fixed costs so far would be about £800. Then there is the repayment of the loan, assuming he obtained one, which would be another £1,300. This makes a total of £2,100.

His annual variable costs would be fuel, which is now reduced because he will be working fewer hours (£950) and telephone calls, advertising and incidental costs (£550). This makes a total of £1,500.

▶ i.e. 30 × 50 = 1,500 hours for a 50-week year.

If Paul obtains 30 paid hours of work every week, his total hours per year will be 1,500. As his variable costs are £1,500 a year his variable costs per hour will be £1.

Breakeven charts

This information is all that is needed to construct a breakeven chart.

> ### Breakeven chart
> A **breakeven chart** is a graph showing the point when costs and revenue are equal. Below this **breakeven point**, the business will be making a loss; above the breakeven point, it will be making a profit.

Once you have worked out the fixed and variable costs and the revenue, creating a breakeven chart is fairly simple.

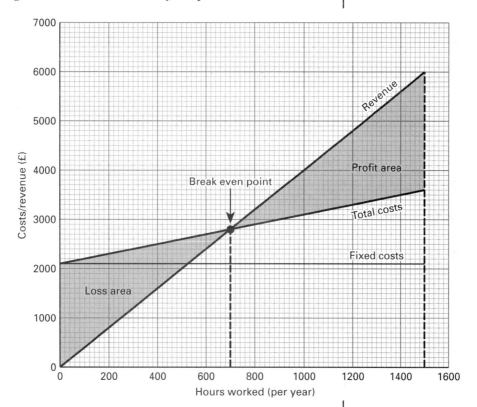

Paul's breakeven chart

Let's look at each feature of the chart in turn.

- The vertical axis shows the annual costs and revenue in pounds.
- The horizontal axis in this case shows the number of hours worked per year. (For both axes, choose a scale that will accommodate the highest number you require.)
- Paul's fixed costs are £2,100 per year. He has to pay these however many hours he works. As the fixed costs never vary, they are shown as a straight line parallel to the horizontal axis at £2,100.
- Paul's variable costs increase in proportion to the number of hours he works. His variable costs are £1 per hour. Therefore, his variable costs for 1,500 hours will be £1,500.

This has to be added to the fixed costs to obtain the total costs. The total costs for 1,500 hours will be £3,600. Therefore a line is drawn from £2,100 on the vertical axis (the fixed costs) to £3,600 (fixed plus variable costs) for 1,500 hours on the horizontal axis.

- The revenue is £4 per hour. Therefore, the revenue for 1,500 hours is £6,000. The revenue line is drawn from 0 to £6,000 for 1,500 hours on the horizontal axis.

Breakeven point

It can be seen that the breakeven point, where the revenue and total cost lines meet, is 700 hours. Below that point, Paul would be losing money, as his total costs would be greater than his revenue. Above that point, he would start to make a profit, which would increase the more hours he worked. It is obvious that Paul's business would not work. Although Paul's costs are low, so is his revenue. There is no way he can reduce his costs. And he cannot increase his revenue by putting up his charges because he would price himself out of the market. Paul will have to think about another business, and make out a proper business plan from the start.

 Copy the breakeven chart on page 217 and explain in your own words how it was constructed.

1 What is the difference between a forecast and a budget?
2 Why is it vital for all businesses to know what their costs and revenue are likely to be?
3 Define fixed and variable costs?
4 What is the breakeven point and where is it found?

Manufacturing firms

It is just as easy to construct a breakeven chart for a manufacturing firm. A small single-product firm makes aluminium loft ladders. The average price to wholesalers is £30. The firm's **turnover** last year was £1.2 million. Therefore, its output was 40,000 ladders a year (1,200,000 ÷ 30 = 40,000). Because of a recession, the factory is only operating at 80 per cent capacity. If it were fully operational, it could produce 50,000 ladders a year ((40,000 × 100) ÷ 80 = 50,000). Its fixed costs are £300,000 a year. Its variable costs are currently £800,000 a year, or £20 per ladder.

The breakeven chart for this manufacturer is constructed in just the same way as Paul's breakeven chart on page 217.

- The costs/revenue are indicated on the vertical axis.
- The scale on the horizontal axis shows the number of ladders or units produced.
- Fixed costs are drawn parallel to the horizontal axis on the £300,000 line.
- The total costs line (including variable costs) is drawn from £300,000 on the vertical axis to £1.1 million for 40,000

► Turnover is the same as sales or revenue.

► £300,000 fixed costs + £800,000 variable costs = £1,100,000

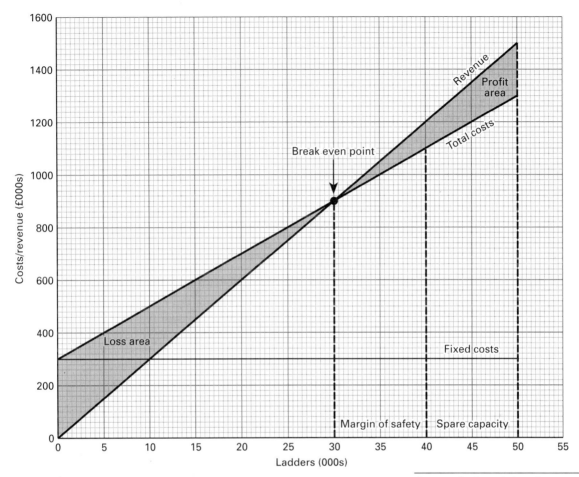

ladders. It is then extended to £1.3 million for 50,000 ladders to show full capacity.

• The revenue line is drawn from 0 to £1.2 million, the firm's present turnover. It is then extended to £1.5 million to show what the turnover would be if the plant was working at full capacity (30 × 50,000 = 1,500,000).

Additional features in the chart

There are two new features in this chart. The **margin of safety** is the difference between the firm's present level of output and the breakeven point. As you can see from the chart, it is making a profit by producing 40,000 ladders, but if its output fell to 30,000 (breakeven point) it would not be making a profit because its total costs and revenue would be equal. If production fell below 30,000 ladders, the firm would be making a loss.

The second feature is **spare capacity**, which is the difference between what the firm is producing and what it could produce if it was working full out. As you can see from the chart, the firm's profit would double from £100,000 to £200,000 if it had a full order

► The factory's total capacity is 50,000 ladders. The variable costs would be £1,000,000 (£20 per ladder × 50,000). The fixed costs are £300,000. Therefore, the total costs would be £1,300,000

book. It is a great financial loss not to use manufacturing capacity to the full. One answer, in this case, might be to diversify into other kinds of ladders.

Other uses of breakeven charts

Breakeven charts are useful for making general forecasts about when a business will start to make a profit and for seeing how profits would grow if a firm was working at full capacity. They can also be used to find the breakeven point for an individual product in a firm that produces a number of products. In addition, breakeven charts can also be used to decide whether it would be more profitable for a firm to make a component itself or buy it from a supplier. If the supplier's total quoted price is lower than the costs at the firm's breakeven point, it would obviously be advantageous to buy in the part. It is quite likely that suppliers may be able to produce parts more cheaply than the firm, as they may be producing the same part for many firms and, therefore, benefit from economies of scale.

► There are more effective ways of making this kind of decision. See **Other costing methods** on page 221.

 Make brief notes on the uses of breakeven charts

 Use the following information to construct a breakeven chart. A firm that makes dressed dolls for gift shops sells them at £15 each to wholesalers. In the run-up to Christmas, it is working at full capacity of 60,000 dolls per year. Its fixed costs are £150,000 and its variable costs are £600,000. What is its breakeven point?

The drawbacks of breakeven charts

Time

Breakeven charts take some time to construct. In fact, the breakeven point can be found much more quickly by using the following formula:

$$\text{breakeven point} = \frac{\text{fixed costs}}{\text{price} - \text{variable costs per unit}}$$

For example, the doll manufacturer has fixed costs of £150,000. The price per doll is £15. The variable costs per doll are £10 (600,000 ÷ 60,000 = 10). Therefore, price – variable costs = 5. The formula can now be used to calculate the breakeven point, which is 30,000 (150,000 ÷ 5 = 30,000).

Although this method is much quicker, it is important that you know how to construct a breakeven chart. Use the formula for checking the result whenever you construct a breakeven chart.

Costs

Identifying costs is another problem. With small businesses, it is possible to define fixed and variable costs with some degree of accuracy. Administration, repairs, maintenance, heating and lighting would normally all be regarded as fixed costs. In bigger firms, however, they could vary as output expanded. For example, machines would be used more constantly so they would probably need more repairs and maintenance. Increased output would mean more paperwork so more office staff might be needed to deal with it. For this reason, administration, repairs, maintenance, heating and lighting are usually treated as **semi-variable costs**. Variable costs may also increase greatly if overtime is worked at full capacity.

Difficulty of forecasting revenue

A final problem is the difficulty of forecasting revenue with any accuracy, as it can be affected by so many outside factors. This applies particularly to new businesses. However, breakeven charts do give a general idea of whether a product or a business is viable. They are probably more useful with small or single-product businesses than with large firms.

 Make notes on the drawbacks of breakeven charts.

OTHER COSTING METHODS

Breakeven charts examine costs in relation to revenue, or sales, mainly to discover when a product or a business will break even and start to make a profit. However, costs can also be looked at in another way, in relation to the product. This way, the real costs of production can be assessed more accurately.

▶ All of the following methods give a truer estimate of costs per unit than variable and fixed costs. However, probably no costing method gives a totally accurate estimate.

Direct and indirect costs

One method is to use direct and indirect costs. **Direct costs** are all costs directly related to the product. They include raw materials, parts, components, labour, and any other services used exclusively in making the product, such as hiring tools or equipment, and using electricity (though this is sometimes difficult to calculate). Then a proportion of all the **indirect costs**, or overheads, is added to provide a total cost for the product.

Absorption costing

As its name shows, **absorption costing**, or **total costing**, attempts to absorb all costs, both variable and fixed, in the cost per unit. It tries to allocate fixed costs (or overheads) to each product that the firm produces. For example it would include a proportion of the rent and business rates for factory floor space in the cost of each product. Variable costs are then added on to give the full cost of a product. However, it is sometimes difficult to share out the fixed costs between each product, for example with clerical work. Furthermore, fixed costs, as noted earlier, may vary as production increases. They are not known exactly until the end of the accounting period. Therefore, the forecasts of fixed costs may be inaccurate.

Make brief notes on direct and indirect costs and absorption costing

MARGINAL COSTING

Marginal costing tries to avoid the difficulty of forecasting fixed costs by concentrating more on the marginal cost per unit. The marginal cost is the cost of producing one extra unit. It is composed of three elements:

- direct labour costs;
- direct material costs;
- variable costs, such as heating, lighting and maintenance, which vary with changes in the volume of production.

Two-stage calculations for marginal costing

Marginal costing separates the calculations of costs and profits into two stages. First of all, it calculates the difference between the sales revenue and the variable, or marginal, costs in order to find the contribution. Then it uses the contribution to calculate how much a product is paying towards the fixed costs or overheads. The final result is the profit.

► contribution = sales revenue – variable costs

► contribution – fixed costs = profit

For example, Joy works at home making novelty masks which she sells for £3 each. The marginal cost is £1.50. She can produce a maximum of 10,000 masks a year, but she is now working at only 80 per cent of capacity. The contribution calculations for 80 per cent capacity and full capacity are:

Production	80%	100%
Sales	£24,000	£30,000
Marginal costs	£12,000	£15,000
Contribution	£12,000	£15,000

That is the first stage of the calculation. Now the fixed costs, which in this case are £3,000 a year, have to be deducted from the contribution. The final figure will then show the profit, if any. The second stage of the calculations is:

Production	80%	100%
Contribution	£12,000	£15,000
Less fixed costs	£3,000	£3,000
Profit	£9,000	£12,000

The profit per unit is £1.13 at 80 per cent capacity (9,000 ÷ 8,000 = 1.125), but £1.20 at 100 per cent capacity (12,000 ÷ 10,000 = 1.2). This is because the fixed costs are shared out among a larger number of goods.

Marginal costing and decision making

This method of calculating costs is very useful for making management decisions. It could be used to calculate if it would be worth while taking an order at a discounted rate when production facilities are not being fully used.

For example, how should Joy react if a special order came in for 1,000 masks at £2 each? Marginal costing shows that she should take it.

	Without order	With order
Sales	£24,000	£26,000
Marginal costs	£12,000	£13,500
Contribution	£12,000	£12,500
Less fixed costs	£3,000	£3,000
Profit	£9,000	£9,500

► Sales with order:
$(8{,}000 \times 3) + (1{,}000 \times 2) = 26{,}000$

► Marginal costs with order:
$9{,}000 \times 1.5 = 13{,}500$

By taking the order, Joy's profit would increase – only slightly, it is true, but in business, every pound of profit counts.

Big firms use marginal costing to calculate the contribution each product is making to fixed costs. If a firm has a wide product mix, management can find the products that are making the least contribution and stop producing them.

 Make notes on marginal costing, showing how contribution and profit are calculated.

► **Product mix** refers to the different kinds of products that a business produces. It may have a wide product mix like a conglomerate, or it may have a deep product mix like a firm that produces many kinds of comb.

 Look back at the information about the loft ladder manufacturer on which the second breakeven chart was based. Assume that the firm is still working at 80 per cent capacity when it receives a special order for 8,000 loft ladders at £25 each. Using the marginal costing method, decide whether it would be profitable for the firm to take the order and, if so, by how much its profit would increase.

CUTTING COSTS

Financial departments are always keen to cut costs because firms can gain a competitive edge over their rivals if they can reduce their costs and their prices. Cutting costs is even more important in a recession, when sales may well be falling.

Reducing costs

Costs can be reduced in a number of ways. Here are some of the possibilities that a firm might consider:

Fixed costs
- **Premises:** A move to cheaper premises will have long-term cost savings, even though the move itself can be expensive.
- **Computers:** Increasing the use of computers can reduce labour costs significantly.
- **Contracting out:** The work of one department can be contracted out to an outside firm: for example, the public relations department can be closed down and a specialist publicity firm used when required.

► See **Computers in offices** in Chapter 23.

► Typical energy costs for lighting, heating, hot water, etc., in offices range from about £8 per square metre per year for open-plan offices (where most people work in one large central room) to about £22 per square metre for luxury air-conditioned offices. (VAT now has to be added to these costs. Tax on fuel was introduced in 1994.)

Semi-variable costs

- **Repairs and maintenance:** This kind of work can be reduced to essential repairs.
- **Heating, lighting and other energy costs:** These can be reduced by improving insulation, replacing old-fashioned plant and making sure that controls are correctly set.
- **Training and R & D:** Provisions for training and R & D can be abolished or reduced.

Variable costs

- **Supplies:** It may be possible to negotiate price cuts with suppliers or switch to suppliers with lower prices.
- **Product design:** In manufacturing, improved product design can reduce the time spent in assembling products, and improve the quality of goods by reducing the chances for error in assembly.
- **Materials:** It may be possible to find ways of reducing waste of materials in the manufacturing process.
- **Advertising:** The advertising expenditure can be reduced – it is, in any case, difficult to quantify results.
- **Business expenses:** Managers' expense accounts can be reduced, for example by putting a limit on the amount spent on restaurant meals.
- **Contract labour:** More workers and staff can be employed on fixed-term contracts so that they can be dismissed in a recession without the expense of redundancy payments. (Temporary staff produce the same advantage.)
- **Short-time working:** If orders are few, workers can be put on a shorter working day or week.
- **Voluntary or compulsory redundancies:** The immediate cost of making workers redundant is high as redundancy payments have to be made; but there will be savings in the long term. If the workers are highly skilled, however, it may be difficult to replace them if they are needed in the future.

 Draw up a table with the caption 'Reducing costs' and three columns headed *Permanent benefit*, *Permanent damage* and *Short-term damage*. Put each of the cost-cutting measures described in the box above in the appropriate column.

CASH FLOW

Forecasting the cash flow each month is one of the most important financial tasks for all businesses, from corner shops to multi-nationals.

Cash-flow forecast

A **cash-flow forecast** is a forecast of the cash, or money, flowing into the business (the receipts) and the cash flowing out of the business (the payments). It is usually made for each month of the year.

As you can see from the example on page 226, a cash-flow forecast covers all kinds of receipts and payments. It covers both revenue transactions that arise in the day-to-day running of the business, and capital transactions for the purchase of assets that will last for longer than a year and for long-term loans or borrowing.

Cash flow is nothing to do with profit. In fact, a firm that is making a large profit by expanding rapidly may have a cash-flow problem. So much of its money may be tied up in unsold stock and debtors that it has no cash to pay its own creditors. Almost any business may have a cash-flow problem at some time of the year when its payments are bigger than its receipts – for example, in the month when it has to pay its corporation tax. This is predictable, and financial managers should allow for it by making sure that cash is available. However, a shortage of cash may be caused by an unexpected event. For example, there may be a sudden drop in sales, or revenue; or a sudden increase in orders may mean that materials have to be purchased before the finished goods are paid for.

1. What are direct and indirect costs?
2. What does 'contribution' mean in marginal costing?
3. Give one example each of how fixed costs, semi-variable costs and variable costs can be reduced.
4. Why is a cash-flow forecast important for all businesses?

What is cash?

Cash is an asset that is liquid or immediately available. Cash can be either in hand or in the bank.

Cash in hand

- This is money in the till or in the cashier's office.
- It can also be **petty cash**, which is kept in the office to pay for immediate needs such as delivery charges, taxis, etc.

Cash at bank

- Funds might be in a current account in a bank, or a cheque account in a building society. Both allow customers to withdraw money on demand or pay for goods or services by cheque, or by standing order or direct debit.
- Funds are also kept in instant-access **deposit accounts** in banks or building societies, from which money can be withdrawn at any time.

▶ For examples of revenue and capital expenditure, see the table in Chapter 18, page 234.

▶ **Debtors** are people or organizations who owe money to a business because they have bought goods, or received services, for which they have not paid. **Creditors** are organizations or people to whom a business owes money. The business may have bought goods on credit or received services, such as legal advice, for which it has not yet paid.

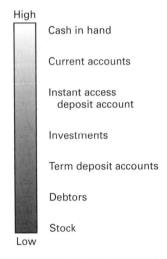

Liquidity scale

▶ A **standing order** is an arrangement for a bank to pay a creditor a fixed amount at regular intervals: for example, monthly. A standing order might be used to pay a hire-purchase debt. A **direct debit** is an arrangement for a creditor to demand a varying payment from a bank account at fixed intervals. A direct debit might be used to pay electricity bills.

Cash-flow forecast from _____ 19 __ to _____ 19 __

Period (e.g. 4 weeks/month/quarter)					TOTAL	
	Budget	Actual	Budget	Actual	Budget	Actual
Orders						
Sales						
Purchases						
Receipts:						
Sales – cash						
– debtors						
Loans/Grants Received						
Capital Injected						
Asset Disposals						
Other Income						
A Total Receipts (CR)						
Payments:						
Purchases – cash						
– creditors						
Wages, salaries, (include PAYE and NIC)						
Rent, rates						
Light, heat, power						
Insurance						
Transport, packaging						
Maintenance						
Advertising						
Telephone						
Postage/stationery						
Professional fees						
VAT (net)						
HP payments/leasing charges						
Bank/finance charges and interest						
Drawings/fees						
Loan repayments						
Tax						
Capital expenditure						
Sundry expenses						
B Total Payments (DR)						
C Net Cash flow (A-B) CR						
DR						
D Opening Bank Balance CR						
Balance Brought Forward DR						
E Closing Bank Balance CR						
(C+/–D) DR						
Agreed Overdraft Facility						

Cash flow forecast form

Source: Midland Bank

These are all totally liquid. There are other assets that are near liquid.

- Investments in subsidiaries or other firms can usually be sold immediately, though payment may not be received for some days.
- Funds in **term deposit accounts** require notice (30 days, 90 days or more) before money can be withdrawn.

There are other assets that are less liquid.

- **Debtors** are people or organizations that have bought goods or services on credit, which usually gives them 30 days to pay. However, some debtors take much longer to pay their bills.
- The value of unsold stock cannot be realized immediately.

WORKING CAPITAL

The items in the list above are a business's **current assets**. They are balanced by its **current liabilities**, the loans and other borrowings, trade creditors and tax, which have to be paid within a year. When liabilities are deducted from current assets, the surplus (if any) is the working capital that is used to pay all short-term financial obligations.

► The current liabilities also include repayments in instalments of medium- and long-term debt.
► Working capital is also known as net current assets. See Chapter 19, page 264.

working capital = current assets – current liabilities

The need for working capital varies from one sector to another.

- Farmers often need a great deal of working capital because of the long interval between payments and receipts. They have to spend a large amount of money raising livestock or sowing seed, but many months will pass before they are paid for their finished product.
- Manufacturers also have large requirements. They usually have no cash sales, only debtors, as well as stocks of raw materials and finished goods. (Stocks can be reduced by using a just-in-time system.)
- Retailers need less working capital. They usually have no debtors, unless they give credit or take orders without deposits; but they have to hold high levels of stock. (They can reduce the cost of holding stock by increasing the rate at which it is sold.)
- Businesses that provide a service, such as cinemas, have least need of working capital, as they usually have no debtors and no stock. (There are exceptions. Professionals are usually paid after they have done the work; and repairers need to hold large amounts of stock.)

ACT IN Draw a scale like the one in the margin, and label it 'Need for working capital'.
     Put the following businesses at the appropriate point on the scale: fisheries; supermarkets; discos; solicitors; car manufacturers; car repairers; house builders.

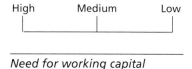

Need for working capital

Overdrafts

From time to time, most businesses have a shortage of working capital, when payments are greater than receipts. To carry them through that period, businesses use a **bank overdraft**. An overdraft allows a customer to withdraw more money from his or her account than it actually contains. The overdraft has a previously

► Many businesses also have a permanent overdraft to cover such items as the purchase of stock.

► A firm has an overdraft facility of £3,000. On Tuesday evening, it has only £100 in its current account. On Wednesday, its receipts total £700 and its payments £1,000. The account has therefore gone into the red by £200, i.e. there is a trading deficit of £300 which is reduced to £200 because there is a balance of £100 in the account. The firm pays interest only on the £200. On Thursday, its receipts total £1,200 and its payments £800. The account goes into the black again by £200. The firm, therefore, pays no interest on Thursday.

agreed limit of a few thousand pounds for a sole trader or millions of pounds for a really big company. This means that the customer can withdraw up to the agreed limit without obtaining permission from the bank every time. The customer, of course, has to pay interest on the amount overdrawn. Furthermore, the bank can call in the overdraft, or ask the customer to repay it, at any time.

An overdraft is a very useful form of short-term finance for a business. It is particularly suitable for cash-flow funding as interest is only charged on the amount overdrawn each day. The rate of interest, however, is usually higher than the rate for long-term loans.

All businesses need adequate working capital and an overdraft facility so that they do not have to sell off their less liquid assets to pay creditors. If investments or stock are sold off quickly to raise cash, they may have to be sold cheaply. There can be an even bigger loss if property is sold quickly to raise cash.

1　Why is cash called a liquid asset?
2　Why do businesses need cash?
3　Give one example of near liquid assets.
4　Distinguish between cash in hand and cash at bank.
5　Which kind of business has the least need of working capital?
6　Why would it be inadvisable to sell property to pay outstanding bills?
7　How can retailers reduce the costs of holding stock?
8　What are the advantages of having an overdraft facility?

Make notes on (a) cash-flow forecasting, (b) cash-flow problems and (c) overdrafts.

FORECASTING RECEIPTS AND PAYMENTS

A cash-flow forecast of receipts and payments is made in the same way as any other business forecast. It must be as precise and comprehensive as possible. If the business is already established, the forecasts can be based on records of what has happened in the past. If the business is new, then reasonable predictions must be made, and will probably be based on the experiences of similar businesses.

In some cases, both the time (and sometimes the exact amount) of payments or receipts are known. Rent, for example, may be paid monthly, quarterly or yearly.

Turn back to the cash flow forecast form on page 226. Draw up a table with the caption 'Fixed receipts and payments' and two columns headed *Receipts* and *Payments*. Put the receipts and payments that occur at a fixed time in the year in the appropriate column. If the actual amount would also be known, add an asterisk.

Compiling the forecast

When all the receipts and payments have been forecast, the totals for each month can be calculated. It is also necessary to know the opening bank balance (the amount in the bank at the beginning of the month). Take a simple example for just four months of the year:

Cash-flow forecast

	January (£)	February (£)	March (£)	April (£)
Receipts	10,000	13,000	11,000	12,000
Payments	9,000	11,000	14,000	14,000
Opening bank balance	1,000	2,000	4,000	1,000
Closing bank balance	2,000	4,000	1,000	(1,000)

To see how the forecast is compiled, take one month at a time. In January, receipts are forecast to be £1,000 more than the payments (£10,000 – £9,000) so there is a surplus of £1,000. This is added to the £1,000 that was already in the bank at the beginning of the month to make a total of £2,000. This is entered as the closing bank balance at the end of January. It will also be the opening balance for the next month, so £2,000 is entered as the opening balance for February.

In February, there is a forecast excess of £2,000 (£13,000 – £11,000), which is added to the opening bank balance of £2,000 to give a closing balance of £4,000.

March starts with an opening bank balance of £4,000. However, there is a forecast deficit of £3,000 (£11,000 – £14,000), so this reduces the closing bank balance to £1,000.

In April, there is a forecast deficit of £2,000 (£12,000 – £14,000), so this reduces the opening bank balance of £1,000 to (£1,000), the brackets indicating that it is a deficit, or loss, or money that is owed.

ACT IN Copy the cash-flow forecast below and fill in the missing numbers.

	July (£)	August (£)	September (£)	October (£)
Receipts	25,500	14,600	22,250	24,380
Payments	20,000	22,000	21,900	19,900
Opening bank balance	1,000			
Closing bank balance	6,500			

ACT IN Read the following case study and answer the questions at the end.

You have been brought in to advise Jane, who has run her own bookshop for many years. This is part of her story:

'As you can see, it's a large double-fronted lock-up shop. The left-hand side has the new books and there are second-hand books over there on the right. It's in a good position, just off the high street. Over the years, quite a few people have offered to buy my lease. Only a month or so ago, a stationer wanted to rent half of the shop for £60 a week. But I don't think I'd like sharing with anyone, even though he was quite nice.

▶ A lock-up shop is one without living accommodation.

'I've never made much profit, because I've always been content to rub along with what I've got. But things have really changed now. Six months ago, the landlord put my rent up to £6,000 a year – that's almost double. And the business rates have shot up, too. I'd thought of packing the shop in, but I don't know what I'd live on. Income support, I suppose! In some ways, I wish I had, really.

'Anyway, I opened a coffee bar in among the second-hand books, serving just tea, coffee and biscuits. It's brought in a little cash, but as I can't afford to employ anyone it's been almost too much for me.

'The students love it. They sit there for hours. I know I shouldn't let them, but I feel sorry for them. They get such small grants, and even the grants they do get have been cut.

'Although I like students, I do wish they wouldn't order books and then not turn up to collect them. It's such a loss for me. But some of my older customers do the same. They at least should know better.

'Times have changed, haven't they? In the old days, I used to have really friendly relations with publishers. It's not like that anymore. Because I was short of cash, I couldn't pay a couple of big publishers on time, so they cut off my credit and said I'd have to pay cash for all orders in future.

'I don't know what I'll do. I'll soon have to order my Christmas stock, but I don't know where I'm going to find the cash. I can't afford not to have the books. I do about half of my trade at Christmas.'

You have been going through her accounts, but as you might have expected, they are in rather a mess. However, you have found out that she has a more or less permanent overdraft facility of £3,000. At the beginning of August, she already has an overdraft of £642. Using the records for the last three years, you have just started to draw up a cash-flow forecast.

Cash-flow forecast

	August (£)	September (£)	October (£)	November (£)
Receipts	1,623	3,360	4,904	7,613
Payments	3,019	3,300	7,562	8,421

1 Complete the cash-flow forecast. When will Jane exceed her overdraft limit?
2 What will her closing bank balance be in November?
3 How would you advise her to deal with her short-term problem?
4 How do you suggest she might solve her long-term problems?

SOLVING CASH-FLOW PROBLEMS

Cash flow is now considered to be such a good indicator of a business's financial health that, since 1991, it has been compulsory for big firms to include a cash-flow statement in their annual published accounts.

Even with the best forecasts, however, any business can run into unexpected cash-flow problems. If this ever happened to you when you were running a business, you should let your bank manager know as soon as possible. You should state the increase you need in your overdraft facility and for how long you will need it. If there are long-term financial problems, you should also state how you intend to solve them and provide plans and forecasts to show how they will be tackled. If you just let your overdraft exceed its limit without contacting the bank, you may be asked to pay off the overdraft immediately, which could mean that the business has to close.

► See **Cash-flow statements** in Chapter 19.

Delaying payments to creditors

There are some other solutions to cash-flow problems. Some big firms increase their own working capital by not paying trade creditors (suppliers), on time. The normal time allowed for paying for goods received on credit is 30 days, although some big companies demand 90 days' credit from their suppliers. On average, big companies take 72 days to settle accounts. As a result, the smaller firms have to increase their overdrafts, which means that they have to pay bigger interest charges. (As the case study of Jane's bookshop has shown, small firms do not have sufficient clout to delay payments to big firms.)

► The Chancellor of the Exchequer announced in the 1993 Budget that the government might bring in a law to make late payers liable for interest on outstanding debt. Small businesses have been campaigning for many years to persuade the government to pass such a law.

Reducing trade debtors

All businesses should try to reduce the number of trade and individual debtors who owe them money. Customers' ability and willingness to pay promptly should be checked by taking up bank and trade references or by asking credit agencies. Credit limits with customers should be agreed and recorded. Invoices and monthly statements should be sent out promptly. If a debtor does not pay on time, a warning should be issued immediately. If there is still no reply, the business should ask a solicitor to send a letter asking the debtor to pay. (About 80 per cent of debtors pay after they receive a solicitor's letter.).

Factoring

There is a much quicker solution to a cash-flow problem for firms that have a large number of debtors. They can ask a **factoring company** to collect the money for them. The factoring company will give them a proportion of the money owed immediately. It will then collect the rest of the debts over a period of weeks or months, deducting its own costs and profit from the total amount received.

Apart from factoring, there are other ways of improving cash flow. For example, more efficient use of stock can help, but it is not a quick solution. Retailers can turn stock round more quickly, dispose of long-standing stock, and concentrate their efforts on core lines that always sell well.

1 Who would you see if you had a cash-flow problem?
2 Describe how a business could reduce trade debtors.
3 What does a factoring company do?
4 Why would increasing the rate of stock turnover help cash flow?

Look at your answers to the bookshop case study above. Revise any of your answers where necessary. (If you do not need to revise them, say why they still hold.)

SUMMARY

- There are five essentials in business finance: budgeting, cost accounting, cash-flow management, raising finance, and maintaining and interpreting financial records.
- Businesses need to forecast the future to make financial plans. They use past experience, computer models and market research to do so.
- The forecasts are used to make an annual budget or master plan. This is a quantitative statement with a dual purpose. It provides targets to aim for, and benchmarks to judge what has been achieved.
- Businesses also need to be able to analyse and forecast their costs and revenue. There are different ways of classifying costs: they can be divided into fixed, semi-variable and variable costs, or into direct and indirect costs.
- This data is used to construct breakeven charts that show when a business will start to make a profit. Other methods of costing include total and marginal costing. It is essential for businesses to identify all costs clearly so that they can make management decisions and reduce unnecessary expenditure.
- Another important financial task is forecasting cash flow. Businesses need to have enough cash available to pay wages and salaries and other immediate bills. This is done by ensuring that the business has sufficient working capital, topped up by a bank overdraft if necessary.
- The amount of working capital required varies from one sector of business to another. Cash-flow forecasts are used to identify the amount of cash that will be needed in various months of the year.
- Some cash-flow problems can be solved by delaying payment to trade creditors, reducing the number of debtors, or using a factor to collect debts.

18 Sources of finance

Chapter objectives

After working through this chapter, you will have the knowledge to:

▌ identify revenue and capital expenditure;

▌ select the most suitable financial method of obtaining a business car;

▌ apply straight-line and reducing-balance methods of depreciation;

▌ classify ways of raising finance according to duration;

▌ explain why it is difficult for the public sector to obtain capital;

▌ distinguish between nominal and annual percentage rates of interest;

▌ describe the main financial institutions and the services they provide for business;

▌ apply P/E ratios and dividend yields in selecting shares to buy;

▌ understand and use the following key terms: revenue expenditure, capital expenditure, drawings, contingency fund, start-up loan, hire purchase, finance lease, contract hire, hiring, retained profits, distributed profits, depreciation, straight-line depreciation, reducing-balance depreciation, venture capital, loan, rights issue, underwritten, reserve, share premium account, debenture, subsidy, nominal interest rate, annual percentage rate of interest (APR), financial institution, retail deposit, wholesale fund, money market, high-street bank, finance house, merchant bank, insurance company, gilt, pension fund, equity, price earning (P/E) ratio, dividend yield, net asset value (NAV), bull market, bear market.

REVENUE AND CAPITAL EXPENDITURE

Businesses have two kinds of expenditure. As you already know, **revenue expenditure** is what is spent on running the business. This includes such items as rent and rates, and raw materials and wages.

The other kind of spending is **capital expenditure**. This is mainly what is spent on setting up a business or on buying long-term assets, such as machinery, vehicles, factories and land, which will

► In other words, revenue expenditure means fixed and variable costs. To refresh your memory, see **Fixed and variable costs** in Chapter 17.

normally last for more than a year. These assets enable the business to operate more efficiently or to expand.

Examples of capital and revenue expenditure

Capital expenditure	Revenue expenditure
Buying machinery	Repairing machinery
Contract hire of lorries and cars	Running costs of vehicles
Buying a factory	Renting a factory
Hiring a postal franking machine	Postage
Purchasing new computers	Insuring computers
Building a new R & D laboratory	Salaries of R & D staff
Installing air conditioning	Maintenance of air conditioning

▶ Capital expenditure appears as 'tangible assets' on the balance sheet. See **Company balance sheets** in Chapter 19.

As you can see from the table above, capital expenditure involves buying, hiring, building or installing permanent acquisitions that will last for a long time. Revenue expenditure involves repairing, renting, insuring, maintaining, paying wages and salaries and any other items that are needed to keep the business going.

 Next time you are in a hairdressing salon or a sports centre or any other public place, look around and note everything involving revenue expenditure and everything involving capital expenditure. Draw up a two-column table like the one above and put your observations in the appropriate column.

INTERNAL AND EXTERNAL SOURCES OF FINANCE

This chapter will deal only with capital expenditure. There are two ways in which this expenditure can be financed. Some is financed internally, i.e. out of the business's profits. However, some items cost so much that they cannot be bought using internal sources alone. Some capital expenditure, therefore, is financed externally, for example by obtaining a bank loan.

▶ It is just the same in personal life. If you cannot afford to buy a television set or a motor car for cash, you may buy it on hire purchase or with a bank loan. Businesses also operate in this way.

There is one big difference between internal and external sources of finance. With internal sources, a business does not have to repay the money or pay any interest charges; with external sources, it usually does.

Different kinds of business have access to various sources of finance. We shall therefore consider sole traders, private limited companies and public limited companies separately, and then look briefly at the public sector.

 1 State whether the following involve revenue expenditure or capital expenditure: car insurance, car purchase, wages, maintenance, buying a site for a new business, purchasing a machine, repairing a machine.
2 When is a business likely to use an external source of finance?
3 What is the major difference between an internal and an external source of finance?

SOLE TRADERS

The sources of finance for sole traders are summarized in the following table.

If Omar wanted to buy the car outright, he would have to take out a bank loan because he has very little cash. He would have to pay interest at a true rate (or APR) of 9 per cent per year which would be fixed for the three-year period. Interest rates are low at the moment, but they are expected to rise in the following year.

▶ Use the formula:

interest payable =

$$\dfrac{\text{loan} \times \text{APR} \times \text{number of years}}{100}$$

i.e. $(£12{,}000 \times 9 \times 3) \div 100 = £3{,}240$

1   How much would each of the options cost over the three-year period?
2   What are the main advantages and disadvantages in each case?
3   Which option would you advise Omar to choose?

 Obtain brochures from different high-street banks about loans for sole traders. If you were starting your own business, explain which one you would choose.

PRIVATE LIMITED COMPANIES

This section deals with both small and medium-sized companies that are not quoted on the Stock Exchange. The sources of finance for these private limited companies are summarized in the following table.

▶ For more on private limited companies, see Chapter 6.

Main sources of finance for private companies

Internal	External
Sale of shares	Going public
Retained profits	Venture capital
Selling assets*	Bank loans*
Depreciation*	Mortgage loans*
	Public authority grants/loans*

*Available for all kinds of business

Internal sources

* **Sale of shares:** Private companies can raise capital internally by selling more shares privately to family, friends or business associates. This, however, may weaken the control of the people who started the company, because the new shareholders may want to change the way the company is run.
* **Retained profits:** These are the profits that a business keeps to pay for new assets or expansion. The rest of the profits – **distributed profits** – are used to pay shareholders a dividend. Retained profits are the most important source of capital for companies, providing over half of their finance.
* **Selling assets:** A company might sell some land it owns to provide finance for expanding its factory. As with investments, only the profit made on the sale of land is a source of finance. The rest is a transfer of one fixed asset into another.

▶ See the marginal note on selling investments above (page 235).

Depreciation

If you buy a new car, its value will start to decrease as soon as you put it on the road, and its value will continue to fall every year after that. For example, a small car that originally cost £8,000 might be worth only £6,500 after one year and only £5,000 after two years. This fall in value of an item over a period of time is known as **depreciation**.

When a private individual sells a car and replaces it with a new one, the cost of replacing it comes out of his or her own pocket. All businesses, however, receive an allowance from the income tax authorities for the depreciation of fixed assets such as vehicles and machinery. This allows the cost of depreciation to be set against, or taken away from, the gross profit of the business.

► See **Profit and loss account** in Chapter 19.

What does this mean in practice? The profits of the business are reduced, therefore it has to pay less corporation tax. No one is giving the business any money, but its cash flow benefits, because the business has allowed for an expense that it doesn't have to pay. Moreover, there is a real financial benefit. The business doesn't gain the full amount of the depreciation, but it does actually save a proportion of it according to the rate of tax it pays. Of course, the business will have to replace the asset in the end, for which it will probably need to take out a loan. Meanwhile, however, it is saving on tax payments and boosting its cash flow. For big businesses, allowances for depreciation amount to savings of millions of pounds every year; even for the sole trader the saving can amount to thousands of pounds.

► Take as an example a small firm with profits of less than £300,000 a year, which therefore pays the lower rate of corporation tax of 25 per cent. Its total depreciation for the year was £50,000. That sum is deducted from the profit it makes. Therefore, its tax bill is reduced by £12,500 ((50,000 × 25) ÷ 100 = 12,500).

Calculating depreciation

There are two main methods of calculating depreciation. The first is **straight-line depreciation**, a widely used method in which the amount of depreciation is the same every year. The firm calculates how long a machine will last and what its residual, or remaining, value will be at the end of its useful life. It then uses the following formula to obtain the annual amount of depreciation:

$$\text{depreciation} = \frac{\text{original cost} - \text{residual value}}{\text{useful life in years}}$$

For example, a horizontal boring machine cost £20,000 new. Its residual value after five years will be £5,000. Therefore the annual straight-line depreciation will be £3,000 ((20,000 − £5,000) ÷ 5 = 3,000).

The other method is **reducing-balance depreciation** where the same percentage is allowed for depreciation each year. Let's say a sole trader bought a new car for £12,000. The annual depreciation allowance was 25 per cent. Therefore the depreciation for the first four years would be:

Depreciation		(£)
	Original price	12,000
1st year	Depreciation (12,000 ÷ 4)	3,000
	Written down value	9,000
2nd year	Depreciation (9,000 ÷ 4)	2,250
	Written down value	6,750
3rd year	Depreciation (6,750 ÷ 4)	1,688
	Written down value	5,062
4th year	Depreciation (5,062 ÷ 4)	1,266
	Written down value	3,796

This method has a high rate of depreciation in the early years, which decreases as the years go by. It is useful for assets such as vehicles and computers which have a relatively short business life. An annual writing-down allowance or percentage rate of depreciation is chosen. The Inland Revenue commonly accepts a rate of 25 per cent. This amount is taken off the original price to give a written-down value. Depreciation is set against this written-down value in the following years.

Make notes on the internal sources of finance for private companies.

Read the following case study and answer the questions at the end.

Keith, who is an arable farmer, has had the same tractor for eight years. Each year, from autumn onwards, he spends thousands of pounds on sowing his winter wheat, fertilizing it and spraying it with chemicals to prevent disease. However, it is not until the following summer that he is paid for the crop. For that reason, he usually has a large overdraft. He doesn't want to take out a bank loan to buy a new tractor because it would increase the interest he has to pay to the bank; and for the last eight years he has never had enough cash to buy a tractor outright.

The last two years have been different. **Set-aside** payments and other factors have boosted Keith's profits considerably. He has decided to buy a new tractor for £50,000, and he hopes that this time it won't be so long before he replaces it. He has calculated that it will have a useful life of five years and a residual value of £10,000.

► There is a surplus of grain in the European Union. The EU pays farmers to **set aside** part of their land, i.e. not to grow food crops on it, to reduce the production of grain. These payments helped to increase the average income of farmers by 60 per cent in 1993–4. Their average income rose 30 per cent the year before that.

1 What would be the total depreciation over five years using (a) the straight-line method and (b) the reducing-balance method?
2 Which method you would advise Keith to choose, and why?

▶ Going public, or becoming a plc, can make the directors of the company millionaires – on paper – as their shares can now be sold to the public. However, they could not take their profit immediately. Other investors watch directors' share dealings closely. If the directors started selling shares, investors might think the company had problems and the price would probably fall.

▶ See **Management buy-outs and buy-ins** in Chapter 7.

▶ See **Grants** in Chapter 16.

External sources

- **Going public:** A successful private company may decide to go public, or become a plc (public limited company), so that the public can buy its shares. The Stock Exchange Council has to approve the company before the price of its shares can be quoted on the Stock Exchange. A broker and often a merchant bank have to sponsor the issue of shares. This costs money, but it is worth it, because the company has access to a much greater source of capital finance from financial institutions and the share-buying public.

- **Venture capital:** Groups of rich people (or 'angels'), who are usually active or recently retired businesspeople, provide venture capital for rapidly growing companies that cannot obtain a big enough bank loan. They also invest in private companies with a bright future that have a temporary cash-flow problem. Venture capital also finances management buy-outs. In return, the investors usually demand shares and/or a seat on the board of directors. Merchant banks also have venture capital departments.

- **Bank loans:** High-street banks provide short-term loans which usually last for up to a year; medium-term loans for one to ten years; and long-term loans for over ten years. A major asset such as a new factory would need a long-term loan, as it might take the company many years to make enough money to pay back the loan. A medium-term loan would be suitable for new machinery. However, banks are now more flexible about the length of loans and also about interest rates, which can be fixed or variable. It is important to choose the right length of loan. If a contractor is building a bridge that will take two years to complete, it would obviously be stupid to take out a year's loan, as the finance would run out before the project is completed. (Yet mistakes of this kind have been made by some big firms!)

- **Mortgage loans:** Banks, insurance companies and pension funds all provide mortgage loans for the purchase of land or buildings.

- **Public authority grants and loans:** The European Union, the government and local authorities provide grants and loans for business.

 Make notes on the external sources of finance for private companies.

PUBLIC LIMITED COMPANIES

Internal sources

The sources of finance for public limited companies are summarized in the following table.

Main sources of finance for public limited companies

Internal	External
Rights issues	Debentures
Selling subsidiaries	Foreign bank loans
Sale and leaseback*	Unsecured bank loans

*Available for all kinds of business

- **Rights issues:** A rights issue of new shares is one of the most common ways for plcs to obtain more capital. The issue gives existing shareholders the right to buy more shares in proportion to their current holding. For example, they might be offered one new share for every five they hold. The issue is normally **underwritten**, i.e. financial institutions guarantee to buy the shares if the shareholders don't want them. This ensures that the company gets its money; but it has pay a fee of about 2½ per cent to the underwriters.
- **Retained profit:** If the retained profit is not spent, it goes into the company's **reserves**. The reserves also include the **share premium account**. When a company goes public, not all the authorized shares are issued at once. Some are issued at a later date when the market price of the shares has risen. For example, the issue price may have been 100p, but when more shares are issued the market price may be 150p. The difference – 50p on each share – goes into the share premium account in the reserves. In a plc, there may be more conflict over profit than in a private company, as directors, managers and shareholders often have differing views about how profits should be used.
- **Selling subsidiaries:** Large plcs sometimes sell subsidiary companies to raise cash if they are in financial difficulties or if they want to concentrate more on their core business.
- **Sale and leaseback:** A plc sells an asset, such as its headquarters building, to a financial institution and then leases it back. It now has to pay rent for the use of the building, but it has gained a large capital sum. (This opportunity is sometimes available to private companies and, occasionally, to sole traders.)

► **Reserves** are accumulated profits and surpluses that may have already been invested in buildings or equipment.

► See the diagram (Conflicts over profit) and the associated text on pp. 65–6 of Chapter 6.

External sources

- **Debentures:** Debentures are long-term loans made to a plc by members of the public for a fixed period of time at a fixed rate of interest.
- **Foreign bank loans:** Plcs, and some medium-sized firms, borrow money from the many foreign banks with offices in London. Multinationals also use the banks in the countries where they operate.
- **Unsecured bank loans:** It is easier for plcs with high credit ratings to obtain unsecured loans because of their large market value of millions of pounds.

Plcs also have access to the other sources described above: investments, hire purchase, finance lease and contract hire in the sole trader section; and selling assets, depreciation, bank loans, mortgage loans and public authority grants and loans in the private companies section.

 Copy the table on page 241 into your notes, adding brief descriptions of each source of finance where necessary.

 Draw up a table with the caption 'Raising finance' and three columns headed *Start-up finance*, *Medium-term finance* and *Long-term finance*. Put all the methods of raising finance for sole traders and private and public limited companies into the appropriate columns.

THE PUBLIC SECTOR

The public sector is far more restricted than the private sector in raising capital. Before 1979, when the Conservative party came to power, it had much greater freedom. The government now holds the purse-strings, however, and has drawn them tighter and tighter.

> ► See **The public sector revolution** in Chapter 4.

As you already know, most of the nationalized industries have been or are being privatized. The government exercises a strict control over the finances of the remaining public corporations and other public bodies. At one time, government provided a great number of subsidies to the public sector. It still provides some – for example, for some rail services – but many have been withdrawn. Most public bodies are now expected to make a surplus, and pay part of it to the government. If the Treasury lends them money for new investment, they are expected to make a 5 per cent rate of return, after allowing for inflation.

> ► **Subsidies** are grants of money that allow a producer to sell goods or services below cost price.

> ► Say a public body borrowed £1 million from the Treasury for capital investment. If the annual rate of inflation was 6 per cent, the public body would have to achieve a minimum surplus or 'profit' of 11 per cent, or £110,000, on the investment during the year (i.e. a 5 per cent rate of return plus 6 per cent inflation).

The government controls local authorities with equal strictness. Their money comes from government grants, business rates decided by the government, and the council tax, which is collected by local authorities. The government not only controls a large proportion of the finance that local authorities receive, but also 'caps' what they can spend by putting an upper limit on expenditure for each council. In addition, they are not allowed to spend some of the money they do have, such as receipts from the sale of privatized council houses, which have been frozen by the government.

 Write brief notes describing sources of finance for public corporations and local councils.

1   What is a rights issue?
2   What is an enterprise allowance?
3   When might security be needed for a bank loan?
4   Who might help a successful private company which has a temporary cash-flow problem?

5 What is the advantage of sale and leaseback?
6 What is the main difference between the straight-line and reducing-balance methods of depreciation?
7 What new capital does a company gain by selling assets?
8 Why is there likely to be less conflict over retained profit in a private limited company than in a plc?

INTEREST RATES

With most external sources of finance, businesses have to pay **interest** on the amount borrowed. This means that the borrower not only has to pay back the loan but is also charged an additional sum for borrowing the money. For example, if you borrowed £1,000 for a year at a nominal interest rate of 8 per cent, you would have to repay £1,080 in total (1,000 + (1,000 × 8 ÷ 100) = 1,080).

However, the nominal, or stated, rate is not the same as the true rate – or the **annual percentage rate** (**APR**). Most loans are paid back in instalments that cover both the repayment of the loan and the interest. If the £1,000 loan was paid back monthly, each instalment would be £90 (1,080 ÷ 12 = 90), which includes the interest charge of £6.66.

This monthly interest charge remains the same as it would be if the loan were still £1,000, but in fact the size of the loan is being reduced each month, because it is gradually being repaid. Therefore, the true rate of interest – or annual percentage rate – is much higher than the nominal rate. It is about twice as much.

By law, lenders now have to quote the APR. They often quote the nominal rate as well, but the only important rate to the borrower is the APR.

Changes in interest rates

The interest rate charged for loans depends on a number of factors: the status and credit rating of the borrower; the security offered; the risk involved; and the duration of the loan.

The general level of interest rates at the time is also an important factor. Banks fix their base (or minimum) rate of interest according to the rate they charge each other. The Bank of England and the government set a general interest rate. If the economy is growing too rapidly, the government will try to raise interest rates to slow down the expansion. If the economy is stagnating, it will lower interest rates to stimulate growth. These changes have a big effect on investment and on consumer spending and saving.

Effects of changes in interest rates

Low interest rates encourage capital investment and consumer spending because the cost of borrowing is low. They also encourage savers to switch their savings from bank or

► Say 1,000 shares were bought at 200 pence each. A year later, the shares might have increased in value to 250 pence with a dividend of 10 pence per share. The value of the dividend would be £100 and the capital gain on the shares would be £500 – a total of £600. In a building society account, paying 4 per cent annual interest, the only gain would be £40. However, with shares, there are dealing charges and possibly a capital gains tax – and the value of shares can go down as well as up. There is little risk in building society deposits.

building society deposit accounts, with comparatively low rates of interest, to shares. The dividends are not much lower than the rate of interest and the price of the shares might rise, which would increase the amount of capital.

High interest rates discourage investment and consumer spending because the cost of borrowing is high. However, high interest rates might encourage savers to switch from equities into deposit accounts paying high rates of interest.

1 If a business borrowed £10,000 from a bank for a year at an interest rate of 11 per cent per year, how much would it have to repay the bank in all?
2 What is the APR?
3 Which is higher – the nominal interest rate or the APR?
4 How do banks fix their interest rates?
5 When might the government increase interest rates?
6 What would be the effects on the economy of a cut in interest rates?

Make notes on all aspects of interest rates.

FINANCIAL INSTITUTIONS AS SOURCES OF FINANCE

So far, you have been considering businesses that want to raise capital; but there are other businesses that exist largely to provide the finance that is needed. **Financial institutions** provide most of the external finance for all kinds of businesses. They are the channels between those who have money, such as people who save, and others who want money, such as expanding companies. The institutions obtain a large part of their funds over the counter from depositors and other customers; these funds are called **retail deposits**. They also obtain **wholesale funds** on the **money markets** from companies and from other financial institutions who temporarily have cash to spare.

For businesses, the most important financial institutions are the following:

► **Money markets** are where the Bank of England, banks, big companies and discount houses, which act as links between the Bank of England and the banks, borrow or lend money in millions, or billions, of pounds in one deal.

► The main banks are the 'Big Four', the high-street banks – Barclays, Lloyds, Midland and National Westminster. There are also smaller English, Irish and Scottish banks, and many foreign banks with offices in London.

- **Banks:** Millions of pounds in cash and cheques flow in and out of the branches of the high-street banks every day. Many of the cheques are just being 'cleared', or transferred from one firm or person to another firm or person; some money is being deposited in savings accounts; some money is being lent to firms or individuals. The banks also provide many other commercial services, including business mortgages, factoring and foreign exchange dealing in various currencies, such as exchanging pounds sterling for US dollars.
- **Finance houses:** Finance houses obtain both retail and wholesale funds to help business finance the leasing of vehicles and equipment.

- **Merchant banks:** Some of the main functions of merchant banks are arranging share issues for companies; negotiating finance for mergers and takeovers; managing investments for pension funds; and providing venture capital. The Big Four banks all have merchant banking departments.
- **Insurance companies:** Insurance companies obtain funds from both business and private insurance premiums, or payments. The insurance companies invest the money in shares through the Stock Exchange. They also invest in **gilts**, which are government stocks paying a fixed rate of interest for a number of years. Gilts are repaid in full at the end of the term. Insurance companies also invest in commercial property.
- **Pension funds:** Every year, billions of pounds are contributed by employees and employers to company pension funds, which provide pensions for employees when they retire. The surplus funds are invested in shares, gilts, commercial property and sometimes in other assets, such as valuable paintings.

 Make brief notes on the financial institutions and bring out the differences between them.

Importance of financial institutions

In many ways, financial institutions are the foundation of the whole business world. Their skill and judgement in investing in the right projects and the right companies at the right time is a critical factor in the future prosperity of business – and of the whole country.

Financial institutions are also businesses in their own right. Like all businesses, they have to make a profit if they are to survive. They do this by charging fees for many of their services. In addition, they make a profit by borrowing money at a low rate of interest and lending it at a higher rate. They invest in **equities**, which provide dividends and an increase in capital if the value of the shares rises. They receive rents from their investments in property and capital appreciation if the value of the properties rises.

Lending money

When financial institutions are asked to lend money, how do they decide whether to say 'Yes' or 'No'? In lending money, there is always a risk that the borrower will not be able to repay the money, or that the assets on which the loan is secured will decline in value. Financial institutions try to cover these risks by obtaining the safest possible securities for loans. If they give unsecured loans, the purpose of the loan and the status and credit-worthiness of the firm are important factors. Financial institutions rely on their own experience and judgement in making small loans. With bigger loans, however, they make thorough financial and technical investigations of the whole project before they say 'Yes'.

Lending policy is also greatly affected by prevailing views about the success, or otherwise, of the country's economy. In the 'boom' years of the 1980s, banks and other financial institutions lent money so freely that they got their fingers burned when the 'boom' ended. They – and their customers – are still paying in the l990s for those errors.

Investing in equities

Fund managers, who invest pension funds or insurance company premiums in equities or shares, have access to much City information (some of it based only on rumours) which is not available to private investors. They are also guided by sophisticated computer analyses of the market. Like other investors, they also use a few simple yardsticks to judge the value of shares in individual companies. Here are three of the main ones:

▶ For example, if the quoted price of a share in a company was 400p and the earnings per share were 20p, then the P/E ratio would be 20 (400 ÷ 20 = 20).

▶ If the same company had a gross dividend per share of 15p, then the dividend yield would be 3.75 per cent (15 × 100 ÷ 400 = 3.75).

▶ For a definition of net current assets, see Chapter 19, page 264.

- **Price–earnings (P/E) ratio:** This is found by dividing the market price of the share by the earnings per share. The ratio shows how long it would take for investors to get their money back if earnings continued at the present rate. The *Financial Times* publishes the average P/E ratios for different sectors of the stock market. If the P/E ratio is above average for its sector, it usually shows that investors expect the company's profits and earnings to grow rapidly.
- **Dividend yield:** The dividend yield is the gross dividend (before tax) expressed as a percentage of the share price. It can be used to make comparisons between different shares and different kinds of investments.
- **Net asset value (NAV):** This is what the ordinary shares in a company would be worth if it went into liquidation. It is calculated by dividing the net current assets by the number of shares issued. The NAV is usually much lower than the market price. However, it doesn't always give a true picture of a business's value, as some companies do not revalue their assets every year, and other companies providing highly profitable services have few tangible assets.

There is a tendency for fund managers to follow the leader in their investment policies. In a **bull market**, when prices are expected to go on rising, most fund managers will continue to buy. In a **bear market**, when prices are expected to fall, they will probably stop buying. Few fund managers foresaw the great Stock Market crash of 1987, when billions of pounds were wiped off the value of shares. It took shares five years or so to regain their previous value.

1 How do financial institutions make a profit?
2 What are the two main risks in lending money?
3 What does a fund manager do?
4 Explain the difference between a bull and a bear market?
5 What kind of market exists at the present time?

Look in the *Financial Times* on any day except Monday and find the water companies section in the London Share Service tables. These tables give details of the current share price in pence; the rise or fall compared with the previous day; the highest and lowest share price for the year; the market value of the company in millions of pounds; the dividend yield and the price–earnings ratio. Study the water companies' performance and choose one that you think will rise in price. Work out how many shares you would receive for £1,000 (excluding dealing charges). Check the price at regular intervals for the next three months and see how much you would have made or lost at the end of the period. Explain why your choice succeeded or failed. (*Note*: In real life, individuals should regard shares as long-term investments of at least three years.)

WATER

	Notes	Price	+or –	1994/5 high	low	Mkt Cap£m	Yld Gr's	P/E
Anglian	♣†N☐	478xd	−8	607	442	1,416	6.1	10.8
Bristol Water	†N	1043	+3	1120	955	73.0	4.1	13.3
Cheam A	†N	503	+5	503	373	25.7	3.7	15.6
B N/V	†N	488	+5	488	358	11.7	3.8	15.6
Chester	†N	195	+2	*208	141	23.4	3.4	19.2
Dee Valley	N	340	......	360	330	33.3	3.5	14.6
East Surrey	†N	434	−2	436	338	55.1	3.7	9.4
Mid Kent	†N	332	+1	365	293	56.8	4.4	11.2
North West	†N☐	515xd	−4	611	454	1,931	5.8	7.4
Northumbrian	♣†N☐	708xd	−5	751	508	484.3	4.5	7.6
Severn Trent	♣†N☐	506xd	−8	645	457	1,826	5.8	8.4
South Staffs	♣†N	1905	+5	1905	1525	110.5	3.6	11.5
South West	†N☐	492xd	−2	675	459	619.9	6.7	7.3
Southern	†N☐	545xd	−2	682	466	922.7	5.5	7.9
Thames	♣†N☐	479	−3	611	434½	1,906	6.1	7.2
Welsh	♣†N☐	598xd	−5	744	546	871.3	5.5	6.6
Wessex	†N☐	275xd	−3	379¾	261	699.6	5.5	7.2
York Works	♣†N	335	+2	351	273	23.1	3.8	13.6
Yorkshire	♣†N☐	504xd	−3	630	458	1,012	5.8	7.4

Extract from Water Companies Share Section, Financial Times

SUMMARY

- Revenue expenditure covers the running costs of a business. Capital expenditure covers the cost of buying fixed assets such as machinery and buildings.
- Capital expenditure can be financed both internally and externally. With external sources, the lender usually charges interest on the loan.
- The main internal sources for sole traders are owner's assets, profits and investments; the main external sources are family loans, bank loans and hire purchase, finance lease and

contract hire. Some of these are available to bigger businesses.

- The main internal sources for private limited companies are private sale of shares, retained profits, selling assets and depreciation; the main external sources are going public, venture capital and bank loans.
- Public limited companies use many of these sources. In addition, they can raise money by rights issues, sale and leaseback, debentures and foreign bank loans.
- The government controls the borrowing of money by public corporations and local councils.
- Interest rates have a big effect on the borrowing of money. If interest rates are high, firms (and people) will tend to borrow less. If interest rates are low, they may borrow more.
- Financial institutions – banks, finance houses, merchant banks, insurance companies and pension funds – provide most of the external finance for business.

(19) *Financial records*

Chapter objectives

After working through this chapter, you will have the knowledge to:

▌ evaluate a chairperson's annual review of the company's affairs;

▌ draw up a trading account for a small retailer;

▌ apply ratios to find gross profit margin, percentage mark-up and stock turnover rate;

▌ understand the profit and loss account for a small trader;

▌ calculate net profit margin;

▌ distinguish between self-employed and company accounts;

▌ interpret a company profit and loss account;

▌ analyse a company balance sheet by using the current ratio, the acid test and the return on capital employed (ROCE);

▌ describe a cash-flow statement;

▌ understand and use the following key terms: accounts, transaction, final account, trading account, ratio, gross profit margin, percentage mark-up, stock turnover, profit and loss account, net profit, overheads, drawings, net profit margin, appropriation account, balance sheet, asset, fixed asset, tangible asset, goodwill, net current asset, current ratio, acid test, return on capital employed (ROCE), cash-flow statement, liquidation.

BUSINESS ACCOUNTS

All businesses have to keep accounts, or financial records, so that they know what is happening to their money from day to day. Every **transaction**, or business deal, has to be recorded, whether it is just buying a postage stamp for a few pence or having a new factory built at a cost of a million pounds. Businesses keep a record of hundreds of different items, such as:

• the value of the goods they have sold each day;
• how much money they owe to other firms;
• how much other firms owe them;
• how much money they have in the bank.

At one time, all these transactions had to be recorded by hand in

► The Inland Revenue, which collects tax from both businesses and individuals, ends it financial year on 4 April. However, businesses are allowed to choose when they end their financial year; 31 December or 31 March are common dates. At present, businesses are assessed for tax on their profits in the previous year. The government is proposing to assess them on profits in the current year.

► If self-employed people have a small turnover (currently less than £15,000 a year) they do not need to show their accounts to their income tax inspector at all. They just have to inform him or her of their total earnings, expenses and profits for the year.

books of accounts (as they still are in some small businesses), but now accounts are more likely to be kept in computer files. At the end of their financial year, businesses use this data to produce their **final accounts**, which are a record of their main financial results during the previous year.

Legally, the self-employed are obliged to show only an income and expenditure account to the Inland Revenue, who assess and collect income tax. If they are liable to pay VAT, they also have to provide the Customs and Excise with a record of their purchases and sales.

Because the public invests its savings in public limited companies, these companies are obliged by law to reveal more details of their financial affairs. They must publish their profit and loss account, which includes their trading account, and their balance sheet in their annual report and accounts.

Annual report and accounts

Annual reports and accounts are of great interest to a variety of people and organizations including:

- shareholders who want to see how their company is performing compared with previous years;
- investors who are thinking of buying shares in the company;
- creditors who want to see that the company is in a healthy financial state and that it is likely to be able to pay its bills;
- other companies in the same line of business who want to make comparisons with their own results;
- successful firms who want to expand by merging with other companies or by making takeover bids;
- financial journalists and City analysts who have to recommend whether shares should be bought;
- business studies students who can gain insight into the business world by studying these reports and accounts.

► Accounts of public limited companies have to be examined and checked by an independent, professional auditor to make sure that they give a true and fair view of the state of the company's affairs. Auditors do not have to check every small detail for accuracy, though they are supposed to be on the lookout for inaccuracies and fraud. However, there have been a number of cases recently where major fraud has occurred even though the accounts had been audited. Critics claim that auditing procedures need to be tightened up.

Even though the final accounts have been audited, they do not necessarily reveal the whole truth about a company's finances. There are many facts that a company does not have to reveal; and clever accountants can present information so that the company appears to be more financially successful than it really is. However, by sifting carefully through the accounts, skilled analysts can find a great deal of information about a company's present financial state and its future prospects.

 Make brief notes on the people and organizations who are interested in companies' annual reports and accounts.

 In Chapter 17, you were asked to send off for a company's annual report and accounts. You will be using this for some activities in this chapter, so find the report and keep it available. For your first activity, read the chairperson's

SUMMARY FINANCIAL STATEMENT

FINANCIAL REVIEW

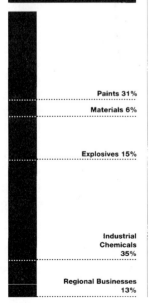

TURNOVER BY BUSINESS SECTOR (CONTINUING OPERATIONS) %

Paints 20%

Materials 17%

Explosives 8%

Industrial Chemicals 39%

Regional Businesses 16%

TRADING PROFIT BEFORE EXCEPTIONAL ITEMS BY BUSINESS SECTOR (CONTINUING OPERATIONS) %

Paints 31%

Materials 6%

Explosives 15%

Industrial Chemicals 35%

Regional Businesses 13%

Summary Directors' Report:
A review of the business during the year and an indication of the likely future developments in the Group are given in the Chairman's Statement, the Chief Executive's Review and the Business Review on pages 2 to 11 which are adopted as part of this Report.

Basis of Presentation
At an Extraordinary General Meeting on 28 May 1993, the shareholders of ICI approved a resolution to demerge Zeneca. The demerger became effective on 1 June 1993 and Zeneca has operated as a separate, publicly listed company since that date.

The results of Zeneca to the date of demerger and those of the European nylon fibres business, comprising the business sold on 1 July 1993 and the remaining fibres subsidiary, Nurel S.A., sold in February this year, are reported as discontinued operations in the Group Profit and Loss Account together with the loss on disposal of the fibres business. The Group Balance Sheet has been prepared on a statutory basis and therefore the comparative figures at 31 December 1992 include the assets and liabilities of those discontinued businesses. The Group Cash Flow Statement includes the cash flows of Zeneca for the periods prior to demerger.

Turnover – Continuing Operations
The ICI Group's performance is tied to the economies of the 24 leading industrialised countries that comprise the Organisation of Economic Co-operation and Development. Growth was weaker here during 1993 than in 1992, although certain countries, such as the UK and the USA, continued to show some recovery. Against this background, the Group benefited from the 9% fall in the trade-weighted sterling exchange rate after its exit from the Exchange Rate Mechanism. A combination of weak demand and excess capacity produced stiffer competition resulting in selling prices in most markets, particularly Japan and Continental Europe, being lower in 1993 than in 1992.

Group turnover from continuing operations in 1993 of £8,430m was 12% higher than in 1992. This was mainly due to favourable exchange rates of 9% with a 1% higher sales volume offset by lower prices. Changes in the

reported population, mainly due to the demerger, accounted for the balance.

All businesses recorded a rise in turnover with good volume increases in Materials and to a lesser extent in Regional: the former business also benefited from the acrylics operations acquired in the third quarter. Lower prices adversely affected Tioxide and Materials but small gains were achieved in Paints.

Just over 40% of the increase in Group turnover arose in the Americas where the improvement was mainly due to exchange rates. Sales in Asia Pacific grew partly due to exchange rates and higher volume. Turnover in Continental Europe rose due to exchange rate benefits. Sales volumes to UK customers were slightly down.

Note 1 on page 19 provides an analysis of turnover and trading profit by business and by geographic area.

Profits – Continuing Operations
The trading profit before exceptional items amounted to £335m, almost double the profit of the previous year. The benefits of lower exchange rates were partly offset by price reductions with increased volumes and fixed cost reductions mainly accounting for the balance.

A particularly good result was produced by Industrial Chemicals which made a profit of £106m compared with a loss of £17m in 1992. Improved results were also achieved in Materials (up £18m) and in Regional Businesses (up £37m) where Australia was the major contributor.

Income from Associated Undertakings was £4m higher than in 1992, partly due to improvements in European Vinyls Corporation (Holdings) BV and AECI Ltd.

Net interest payable of £90m was £39m higher than in 1992. This was primarily due to lower interest income being earned by the Group on its cash and short-term investments and on loans to Zeneca.

Profit before tax for the year at £290m was 78% more than in 1992.

The charge for taxation on continuing operations, excluding exceptional items, of £105m (1992 £124m) represented an effective tax rate of 36% (1992 76%). The higher rate in 1992 reflected unrelieved tax losses together with a number of other items which, following demerger, are not expected to recur.

A page from 'Meeting the challenge', ICI's Annual Review and Summary Financial Statement, 1993

review. State how the review would affect your decision if you were thinking of buying shares in the company

TRADING ACCOUNTS

The **trading account** is the simplest of all the final accounts. Basically, it shows the difference between the cost of the goods and what they were sold for, or the **gross profit**. For example, if a shopkeeper spent £50,000 on buying goods during the year and had total sales of £70,000, the difference would be £20,000. However, this is not all gross profit. The value of the stock of goods at the beginning of the financial year may not be the same as its value at the end of the year. Allowance has to be made for the change in the value of stock before the gross profit can be calculated. An allowance for the difference in stock value is made in the trading account.

▶ Retailers' **stock** is the total amount of goods available for sale. Another name for stock is inventory.

Let's look at the trading account of an imaginary, small garden centre which buys in all its plants and other goods.

Green Lane Garden Centre – Trading Account

Opening stock		£50,000	Sales	£200,000
Purchases	£112,000			
less returns	£2,000	£110,000		
Total stock available		£160,000		
less closing stock		£40,000		
Cost of sales		£120,000		
Gross profit		£80,000		
		£200,000		£200,000

Interpreting the trading account

To help you understand the trading account, let's go through it line by line.

Opening stock	£50,000	Sales	£200,000

▶ Note that the trading account is divided into two sides. Basically, the left-hand, or debit, side shows the money spent. The right-hand, or credit, side shows the amounts received. In double entry book-keeping, the two sides must always balance, i.e. debits and credits must always be equal.

The left-hand side of the account shows the value of the opening stock, or the goods that were available for sale at the beginning of the financial year. This is included so that allowance can be made later in the account for changes in the value of stock during the year. The right-hand side of the account shows the total sales, or turnover, during the year.

Purchases £112,000

This line shows the value of the goods purchased for sale during the year. As a small calculation has to be made to find the true value of purchases, the number is put in the first column on the left-hand side.

less returns	£2,000	£110,000

Some of the goods purchased were faulty and had to be returned. Therefore, the true value of purchases was not £112,000, but £112,000 – £2,000 = £110,000. Now that the calculation has been made, the result, £110,000, is shown in the second column on the left-hand side of the account.

Total stock available   £160,000

If the purchases of £110,000 and the opening stock of £50,000 (shown in the first line of the accounts) are added together, the total stock available for sale during the year was £160,000.

less closing stock   £40,000

To find out the value of the goods that were actually sold during the year, you have to deduct the value of the stock at the end of the financial year. This takes care of the problem, mentioned above, of allowing for changes in the value of stock during the year.

Cost of sales   £120,000

When allowance has been made for the changes of value in stock, the actual cost of sales to the business (i.e. what it has paid for the goods) is £120,000.

Gross profit   £80,000

If the cost of sales (£120,000) is deducted from the sales (£200,000) in the right-hand column, the gross profit is £80,000. Note that the gross, or overall, profit is not the actual profit that the business has made during the year. No allowance has been made for the costs of running the business, or overheads, which are shown in the profit and loss account. After the overheads have been deducted from the gross profit, the net profit, which is the 'real' profit, will be much smaller.

▶ Advertisements offering small businesses for sale often show the gross profit. Although this gives some indication of profitability in relation to other businesses of the same kind, it does not show the true profit of the business since no allowance has been made for overheads or running costs.

              £200,000   £200,000

The final numbers show that the two sides of the account, or debits and credits, are equal.

At first, accounts may look a little complicated, but once you've studied one or two sets you'll find that they are quite simple to 'read' or understand.

 Copy the trading account of Green Lane Garden Centre line by line, making any notes of your own between each line to ensure that you understand the it fully.

Manufacturers' trading accounts

Manufacturers' trading accounts are based upon exactly the same principles as retailers' trading accounts. There are two main differences.

1 Stock includes not only finished goods, but also goods that are being made, and raw materials and components.
2 There is also a difference in purchases. Manufacturers

purchase raw materials and components, but they also employ labour and pay direct production costs in making the goods. Therefore, instead of just one item – purchases – there will be three items in a small manufacturer's trading account: purchase of materials, labour costs, and direct production costs.

Let's say that the Green Lane business had been a small manufacturing firm instead of a garden centre. The trading account of this imaginary firm would look like this:

Green Lane Manufacturing Company – Trading Account

Opening stock		£50,000	Sales	£200,000
Materials purchased	£40,000			
Labour	£60,000			
Production costs	£10,000	£110,000		
Total stock available		£160,000		
less closing stock		£40,000		
Cost of sales		£120,000		
Gross profit		£80,000		
		£200,000		£200,000

Look at the Green Lane Garden Centre trading account on page 252. As you can see, there is very little difference in the two trading accounts. For simplicity, 'returns' have been omitted from the manufacturing account. Apart from that, the only differences are in lines two, three and four. The one item 'Purchases' in the garden centre account has been replaced by three lines:

- 'Materials purchased' includes raw materials, parts and components.
- 'Labour' is the direct cost, or wages, of the employees who make the goods.
- 'Production costs' are the costs that can be directly attributed to making the goods, but not general overheads, such as administration.

Apart from these small differences, the trading accounts – and the year's results – are just the same.

The year's trading figures for an electrical goods retailer are: turnover, £300,000; opening stock, £61,000; purchases, £212,000; returns, £15,000; closing stock £58,000. Using the trading account for Green Lane Garden Centre as a model, draw up the complete trading account for the electrical retailer.

ANALYSING TRADING ACCOUNTS

Final accounts provide a certain amount of information, but, by themselves, they do not tell you very much. The trading account of the Green Lane Garden Centre shows that the business made a gross profit of £80,000. However, you do not know whether that is a high or a low profit unless you compare it with something else, such as sales or turnover. For example, if another garden centre had made a gross profit of £70,000 on sales of £200,000, it would obviously be less profitable than the Green Lane Garden Centre, with its gross profit of £80,000 on the same turnover. You could also compare the Green Lane Garden Centre's gross profit with that of previous years to see whether the business was becoming more or less profitable.

To make it easy to compare results, **ratios** are used. A ratio is simply the relationship between two quantities, such as the gross profit and sales. The result is usually expressed as a percentage, or as numbers, for example 2:1 (two to one).

Gross profit margin

One important ratio that can be calculated from the trading account is the **gross profit margin**. This shows what percentage of sales is gross profit. The formula for calculating the ratio is:

$$\text{gross profit margin} = \frac{\text{gross profit}}{\text{sales}} \times 100$$

Using this formula, the gross profit margin for the garden centre would be 40 per cent ((80,000 ÷ 200,000) × 100 = 40).

A 40 per cent gross profit is reasonable for a business of this kind. However, you cannot reach a final verdict about the 'real', or net, profitability of the business until you have seen the overheads in the profit and loss account. These overheads have to be paid for out of the gross profit. If the overheads were very high, the net profit might be reduced to an unreasonably low figure. If the overheads were low, the net profit would be relatively higher.

It is possible to use the gross profit margin to see how well or badly the business is doing year by year. Say the sales of the garden centre in the preceding year had been £210,000 and the gross profit had been £70,000. The gross percentage profit would have been 33.3 per cent ((70,000 ÷ 210,000) × 100 = 33.3).

Compare the results in the two years. Sales have fallen from £210,000 in the preceding year to £200,000. Yet the gross profit margin has risen to 40 per cent from 33.3 per cent, an increase of 6.7 per cent. Why? The garden centre must have increased its selling prices without losing too many sales.

1 State three kinds of people who would be interested in a company's final accounts.
2 What information can be obtained from a trading account?
3 Why is it necessary to include stock levels in a trading account?
4 Explain why the two sides of an account must balance.

5 State the two main differences between a retailer's and a manufacturer's trading account.

6 Define the word 'ratio'.

7 Give the formula for calculating gross profit margin.

 ACT IN If the garden centre's gross profit in the preceding year had been £90,000 and its turnover had been £190,000, what would the percentage gross profit have been? Suggest possible reasons for the fall in the gross profit margin since then.

Percentage mark-up

▶ For more on mark-up, see **Business costs** in Chapter 12.

The **percentage mark-up** can also be calculated from the trading account by using the following formula:

$$\text{percentage mark-up} = \frac{\text{gross profit}}{\text{cost of sales}} \times 100$$

Using this formula, the percentage mark-up for the garden centre would be 66.7 per cent ($(80,000 \div 120,000) \times 100 = 66.7$).

 ACT IN What would be the selling price in the garden centre of goods that cost the owner £1, £2.60, £30?

Stock turnover

Another useful ratio that can be obtained from the trading account is the rate of **stock turnover**. This involves two simple calculations. First, you have to find the average value of stock held during the year. This is obtained by using the following formula:

$$\text{average stock} = \frac{\text{stock at start of year + stock at end of year}}{2}$$

Using this formula, the garden centre's average stock would be 45,000 ($(50,000 + 40,000) \div 2 = 45,000$).

The rate of stock turnover can then be worked out by using the following formula:

$$\text{rate of stock turnover} = \frac{\text{cost of sales}}{\text{average stock}}$$

Therefore, the stock turnover rate of the garden centre was 2.67 times ($120,000 \div 45,000 = 2.67$).

The stock turnover rate is a guide to the efficiency of the business. The greater the number of times the stock is turned over during the year, the higher the gross profit will be. The stock turnover rate can be compared with rates in preceding years to see whether the business is becoming more or less profitable. It can also be compared with stock turnover rates in similar kinds of business. Note that the rates vary greatly from one type of retail business to another. The stock turnover rate in a CNT (confectioner, newspaper and tobacconist) would be much higher than the rate in an up-market boutique.

As you can see, ratios make it possible to gain a great deal of information from just a few numbers.

 Make notes on the three ratios above, giving the formula for each one and a brief note on the information that the ratio provides.

 Another garden centre, which is for sale, has opening stock of £35,687, closing stock of £49,815 and cost of sales of £86,942. What is its rate of stock turnover? If the Green Lane Garden Centre was also for sale, which one would you choose? State all the reasons for your choice.

PROFIT AND LOSS ACCOUNT

The second final account is the **profit and loss account**, which shows how much **net profit** or loss a business has made during the previous year. The net profit is the profit that a business has actually made after all other expenses, or overheads, have been paid. Net profit is calculated by deducting overheads from gross profits.

▶ Net profit = gross profit – overheads

This is the profit and loss account for the Green Lane Garden Centre:

Green Lane Garden Centre – Profit and Loss Account

Rent, rates, insurance	13,200	Gross profit	80,000
Wages	16,000		
Office expenses	2,250		
Lighting and heating	2,440		
Van expenses	2,750		
Advertising	2,500		
Depreciation	2,000		
Bad debts	600		
Petty cash	260		
Net profit	38,000		
	80,000		80,000

Some of these items need no explanation. Therefore, only those items that you might not understand fully will be explained.

Rent, rates, insurance   13,200   Gross profit   80,000

Note that the gross profit from the trading account is entered on the right-hand side, or credit side, of the account. Any additional income of the business such as rent from owned property and discounts received on purchases would also be entered on the right-hand side

Wages   16,000

Wages can include payments made to members of the owner's family. The owner's earnings, called drawings, are included in the balance sheet.

Depreciation   2,000

Depreciation is fully explained in Chapter 18.

Bad debts   600

Bad debts are amounts of money owing that will never be paid. They are written off as an expense in the profit and loss account.

Petty cash   260

Petty cash is cash paid for small goods or services such as electric light bulbs, taxis and window-cleaning.

Net profit   38,000

The overheads total £42,000. These are deducted from the gross profit of £80,000 to give a net profit of £38,000. Note that net profit does not include the owner's drawings (earnings) or tax. These have to be paid out of net profit.

                  80,000   80,000

The last line of the profit and loss account shows that the left-hand and the right-hand sides of the account balance, or that debits and credits are equal.

 Copy out the profit and loss account for Green Lane Garden Centre, making any necessary notes of your own between the lines, as you did with the trading account, so that you understand the account fully.

 Which of the items in the debit side of the profit and loss account are fixed costs and which are variable costs? (If in doubt, refer back to Chapter 17, page 216.)

Net profit margin

Another ratio that can be calculated from the profit and loss account is the **net profit margin**. The formula is:

$$\text{net profit margin} = \frac{\text{net profit}}{\text{sales}} \times 100$$

For the Green Lane Garden Centre, the net profit margin would be 19 per cent (($38,000 \div 200,000) \times 100 = 19$).

The ratio shows how much of the income from sales is net profit. In this case, for every £1 (or 100p) of goods sold, 19p is net profit. This can be compared with percentage net profit in previous years and with the percentage net profit for other garden centres. In fact, the net profit margin is higher than that of some garden centre chains, so it is a creditable achievement.

 1 What is the main purpose of a profit and loss account?

2 How is net profit found from gross profit?
3 What is petty cash used for?
4 In which account of a sole trader would you find the owner's drawings?
5 What are bad debts?
6 Give the formula for net profit margin.

 Make notes on the net profit margin and how it can be used in interpreting accounts.

COMPANY ACCOUNTS

 Find the profit and loss account in the company report and accounts that you obtained. Describe all the differences in both format and presentation between the company's profit and loss account and the garden centre's profit and loss account on page 257. Keep your notes handy for further use.

Final accounts for public limited companies are based on exactly the same principles as accounts for small businesses, such as garden centres. However, there are some differences in format and presentation.

▶ They are called 'T' accounts because they are shaped like the letter 'T'.

- Most accounts for small businesses are still presented in the traditional 'T' form with a debit and a credit side. Company reports, like those in your annual report and accounts, use a vertical format with both debit and credit items in the same column on the left-hand side.
- The accounts also include results for the previous year.
- Some lines of the accounts contain references to notes following the accounts which provide further information.
- Less information about costs is given in the company profit and loss account than in a 'T' account, even when information in the notes is included.
- The profit and loss account is divided into three parts: an abbreviated trading account; the main profit and loss account; and the **appropriation account**, which shows what the company has done with any profit.

 Look at your answer to the activity on page 257. Alter any answers if necessary and add any points you may have omitted.

Company profit and loss accounts

This is the profit and loss account of an imaginary small manufacturing company, called New Age Engineering plc.

New Age Engineering plc – Profit and loss account

	1996	1995
	(£000)	(£000)
Turnover	1,729	1,603
Cost of sales	(1,246)	(1,162)
Gross profit	483	441
Distribution	(203)	(182)
Administration	(161)	(147)
Operating profit	119	112
Interest receivable (payable)	11	4
Profit before tax	130	116
Tax on profits	(39)	(35)
Profit after tax	91	81
Dividends	58	51
Retained profit	33	30

Analysis of the account

Let's go through the account line by line as we did with the other accounts.

	1996	1995

As you can see, the account covers two years: the previous year, given first, and the preceding year, given second.

	(£000)	(£000)

The next line shows that the numbers are given in thousands of pounds. Therefore, you must add three zeros to every figure in the lines below to obtain the real number.

Turnover	1,729	1,603

Add three zeros to the turnover for the previous year, 1995, and the actual number is £1,729,000. Do the same with the turnover for the preceding year, 1994, and the actual number is £1,603,000. As you already know, turnover is the value of the goods sold during the year.

Cost of sales	(1,246)	(1,162)

These numbers show how much it cost the firm to manufacture the goods it sold. The cost of raw materials, labour, direct production costs and changes in the value of stock have all been allowed for in the cost of sales. As the cost of sales has to be deducted from turnover, the numbers for both years are enclosed in round brackets.

Gross profit	483	441

This line concludes the abbreviated trading account by stating the gross profit for each year.

 Although company trading accounts do not usually provide as much data as a small business account, there is enough data to calculate ratios. Using the company report and accounts you obtained, calculate for both years (a) the gross profit margin, (b) the percentage mark-up and (c) the stock turnover rate. (You will find the value of the stock for the previous year and for the preceding year under the heading *Current assets* in the balance sheet. Use these values for closing and opening stock respectively.) Keep the answers handy as you will need them for another activity at the end of the chapter.

Overheads

Distribution   (203)   (182)

Most companies list the cost of distribution separately in the profit and loss account. As part of the overheads, it has to be deducted from gross profit.

Administration   (161)   (147)

Administration, or managerial costs, is another overhead that has to be deducted from gross profit.

Operating profit   119   112

This shows the profit made on trading before any interest is added or deducted and before tax is paid. If you look in your own company accounts, you will probably find there is a note reference on this line. The note to the accounts usually gives details of deductions for such items as depreciation, hire of plant and machinery, leasing, auditor's remuneration and staff costs. (Sometimes, this information is provided with 'profit before tax' later in the account.) Operating profit is used to calculate the net profit margin.

 ACT IN Calculate the net profit margin for your company for both years. Keep the results with those you calculated in the preceding activity as you will need them for a later activity.

► For the formula, see **Net profit margin** on page 258.

Interest and tax

Interest receivable (payable)   11   4

This line shows the balance between the interest that the company receives from bank and other deposits and the interest it has paid on bank overdrafts, finance leases, etc. If there were a deficit, the number would be bracketed and deducted from the operating profit. In this case, there are surpluses in both years so these are added to the operating profit.

Profit before tax   130   116

This line shows the pre-tax profit.

Tax on profits   (39)   (35)

This line shows how much the company has paid in tax

Appropriation account

Profit after tax   91   81

This line shows the profit that remains after tax has been paid. It opens the appropriation account, which shows what was done with the profit.

Dividends	58	51

This line shows the amounts that were distributed to shareholders as dividends.

Retained profit	33	30

These amounts were retained by the company for investment, expansion, or repayment of debts.

 Make a copy of your company's profit and loss account, writing any necessary explanations between the lines so that you understand it fully.

COMPANY BALANCE SHEETS

A **balance sheet** provides a picture of the financial position of a business at one moment in time – the end of the financial year. It shows what the business owns – its assets – and what the company owes – its liabilities. Most plcs publish balance sheets for both the parent company and the group, which includes its subsidiary companies.

As New Age Engineering plc has no subsidiary companies, there is just one balance sheet. It has been slightly simplified to concentrate on the main items.

▶ If you are analysing company accounts, to see how the company is performing, use the group, not the parent company, balance sheet.

New Age Engineering plc – Balance sheet

	1996 (£000)	1995 (£000)
Fixed assets		
Tangible assets	429	394
Investments	20	40
	449	434
Current assets		
Stocks	238	217
Debtors	434	357
Cash	385	287
	1057	861
Current liabilities		
Creditors: amounts falling due within one year	(686)	(511)
Net current assets	371	350
Total assets less current liabilities	820	784
Creditors: amounts falling due after one year	(105)	(99)
	715	685
Capital and reserves		
Called up share capital	277	275
Share premium account	139	137
Other reserves	1	8
Profit and loss account	298	265
	715	685

Analysis of company balance sheet

The balance sheet will now be examined line by line. (Note that the numbers are given in thousands, as in the profit and loss account, so that three zeros have to be added to obtain the true numbers. Results are, again, given for two years, which makes instant comparison easy.)

Fixed assets

Some of the assets that are owned by the company are physically fixed, like land or buildings. However, the meaning of fixed assets is different in accountancy. The assets are 'fixed' because they are likely to stay in the business for some time, at least a year.

Tangible assets   429   394

Tangible assets include land, buildings, machinery and vehicles that are owned by the company.

Investments   20   40

Investments and other non-tangible assets are included in the fixed assets. One important non-tangible asset is **goodwill**. This is the customer loyalty built up over the years that persuades customers to continue buying from the same firm. Although goodwill has a value, it is difficult to calculate exactly.

                                                449   434

The tangible and non-tangible assets are added together to give the total value of fixed assets.

Current assets

In contrast to fixed assets, current assets change in value from day to day as the business's activities produce alterations in stock and finances.

Stocks   238   217

Stocks change in value every time the company makes or sells a good. Stock is valued at cost price, or at a lower price if it is likely that it will be difficult to sell.

Debtors   434   357

The debtors figure is the amount of money that is owed to the company. Most of it is owed by other firms that have been given credit.

Cash   385   287

This line shows the total of cash in the bank plus petty cash and other cash in hand.

                                               1057   861

This line shows the total of current assets.

► Tangible means 'something you can touch'.

► Some firms now put a value on their brands or patents and include them in their balance sheet as an asset.

► Net current assets are also known as working capital. See Chapter 17, page 227.

Current liabilities

Creditors: amounts falling due within one year	(686)	(511)

This line shows the amount of money the company owes that will have to be paid within a year. It includes trade creditors to whom the company owes money, bank overdrafts, and provisions for tax bills and dividends for shareholders.

Net current assets	371	350

The **net current assets** are calculated by deducting the current liabilities from the total of current assets in the line above, i.e. 1,057 − 686 = 371.

Total assets less current liabilities	820	784

These numbers are found by adding the total fixed assets and the net current assets, i.e. 449 + 371 = 820. (Current liabilities have already been deducted in the line above.)

Creditors: amounts falling due after one year	(105)	(99)

Finally, this line shows the money the company owes that is due to be repaid after more than one year, and this is deducted. It could include bank loans, mortgages and debentures.

	715	685

This line gives the net assets after all debts and loans have been repaid. The rest of the balance sheet shows how the net assets have been financed.

Capital and reserves

Called up share capital	277	275

This shows the nominal, or stated, value of the shares that the company has sold. (They may have been sold at this price when the company was started.)

Share premium account	139	137

Shares have been issued later at a higher, or premium, price, because the company is reasonably successful. This extra money has gone into the share premium account.

Other reserves	1	8

The other reserves of money may have come from changes in exchange rates or from revaluing company property at a higher price.

Profit and loss account	298	265

This line shows the total amount of profits that have been retained from the profit and loss account over the years instead of being distributed to shareholders in the form of dividends.

	715	685

This line shows the total capital, which balances with the net assets above.

Copy out the New Age Engineering balance sheet on page 262 and include any necessary notes between the lines to make sure that you understand the account fully.

Ratios and the balance sheet

A number of important ratios can be calculated from the balance sheet. Two of them deal with a firm's liquidity, or whether it has enough money to pay its debts. These ratios are of particular interest to creditors and investors.

Current ratio

The current ratio shows how many times a company could pay its current liabilities out of its current assets. It is calculated by the following formula:

$$\text{current ratio} = \frac{\text{current assets}}{\text{current liabilities}}$$

In the case of New Age Engineering, the current ratio for 1996 would be 1.54 (1,057,000 ÷ 686,000) and for 1995 it would be 1.68 (861,000 ÷ 511,000).

It is generally accepted that the current ratio should be between 1.5 and 2.0, though the ratio varies greatly from one industry to another.

 Calculate the current ratio for your company for the two years and store the results with those for the previous activities.

Acid test

The acid test provides an even more stringent test of a company's liquidity. Stocks, which cannot necessarily be sold quickly, are omitted from the current assets. This ratio shows whether the company would be able to meet its current liabilities immediately.

The formula is:

$$\text{acid test ratio} = \frac{\text{current assets} - \text{stocks}}{\text{current liabilities}}$$

The acid test ratio for New Age Engineering for 1996 is:

$$\frac{1,057,000 - 238,000}{686,000} = \frac{819,000}{686,000} = 1.19$$

and for 1995 it is:

$$\frac{861,000 - 217,000}{511,000} = \frac{644,000}{511,000} = 1.26$$

Any ratio over 1.0 is satisfactory.

 Calculate the acid test ratio for your company for the two years and keep the results with the others.

Return on capital employed

The **return on capital employed** (**ROCE**) is one of the most important ratios, because it shows how efficiently the company is using its capital to produce profit. Data from the profit and loss account and the balance sheet is used in calculating this ratio. The formula is:

$$\text{ROCE} = \frac{\text{operating profit}}{\text{capital employed}} \times 100$$

(Net assets can be used instead of capital employed as they are equal.)

For New Age Engineering, the ROCE for 1996 is 16.6 per cent ((119,000 ÷ 715,000) × 100 = 16.6) and the ROCE for 1995 is 16.4 per cent ((112,000 ÷ 685,000) × 100 = 16.4).

Although the percentage is low compared with some other sectors of industry, it is not too bad for a manufacturer, because global competition has forced manufacturers to cut their selling prices to survive.

 Calculate the ROCE for your company for each of the two years. Retrieve all the results from your previous calculations, and write a short report on the changes in the company's profitability, liquidity and performance.

CASH-FLOW STATEMENTS

Since 1991, larger companies have been obliged to include a **cash-flow statement** in their annual report and accounts. This account shows how cash has flowed in and out of the business during the year. It gives a much broader picture of cash flow than working capital does as it includes operating activities, investments of all kinds, taxation and financing.

Cash flow is even more important than profit, because if a company does not have enough money to pay its debts, it may be forced into **liquidation** by its creditors. This means that the company will be put into the hands of the Official Receiver who will close it down and sell its assets to pay a proportion of its debts.

> ► Cash also includes cash equivalents, such as short-term investments.

 Find the cash-flow statement in your company report and accounts. Draw up a table with four columns headed *Inflow of cash* and *Outflow of cash* for each of the two years. Put the items in the statement, such as 'interest received' and 'interest paid' (including the numbers) in the appropriate column. Analyse any significant changes in the two years.

 1 What information about a business could be found in its balance sheet?
2 What are tangible assets?
3 What is goodwill?

4 What is called-up share capital?
5 Explain the difference between the current ratio and the acid test ratio.
6 Give the formula for calculating ROCE.
7 State three ways in which a business might use its final accounts.

SUMMARY

- All businesses keep accounts for their own information, but only public limited companies have to publish their final accounts – their combined trading and profit and loss account, a balance sheet and a cash-flow statement.
- A small retailer's trading account shows the difference between the cost of goods and what they were sold for, i.e. the gross profit. It also shows changes in the value of stock. A manufacturer's trading account breaks down stock into work in progress or goods that are being made, raw materials, parts and components. Labour and direct production costs are also included.
- Ratios – the relationship between two quantities – are used to interpret accounts by comparing the latest results with the firm's previous results and with the results of similar firms.
- The gross profit margin, the percentage mark-up and the stock turnover rate can be calculated from the trading account.
- The profit and loss account shows the net profit by deducting overheads from the gross profit. The net profit margin, which is lower than the gross profit margin, can be calculated from this account.
- The accounts of plcs are set out in a different way from those of sole traders. The trading account and the profit and loss account are combined. The account also includes an appropriation account showing how the profit has been used after tax has been paid.
- The balance sheet shows what a business owns – its assets – and what it owes – its liabilities – at the end of the financial year. The current ratio, the acid test ratio and the return on capital employed (ROCE) can be calculated from the balance sheet.
- Cash-flow statements record how cash has been flowing in and out of the business during the year.

20 *Human resources*

Chapter objectives

After working through this chapter, you will have the knowledge to:

▌ analyse what motivates people to work;

▌ describe the work of a personnel department;

▌ select appropriate pay systems for manual workers;

▌ evaluate the benefits of incentive pay systems for employees and employers;

▌ discuss the different kinds of fringe benefits;

▌ explain the advantages and disadvantages of part-time work;

▌ describe the benefits of job improvement systems for employers and employees;

▌ identify laws that provide legal protection for specific groups of workers;

▌ understand and use the following key terms: human resources, personnel department, pay, manual worker, wages, time rate, collective bargaining, overtime pay, shift premium payment, payment by results (PBR), piecework, homeworker, bonus, profit sharing, single status, salary, performance-related pay, commission, profit-related pay, fringe benefit, job satisfaction, absenteeism, flexitime, job improvement, job rotation, job enlargement, job enrichment, teamwork, redundancy payment, voluntary redundancy.

PEOPLE AND BUSINESS

This chapter and Chapters 21 and 22 deal with various aspects of **human resources**, or the contribution that people make to business. In this chapter we shall consider pay, terms of employment and working conditions. Chapter 21 will deal with recruitment, selection and training; and Chapter 22 will examine industrial relations and communication.

In many ways, people are the most important factor in production. Ultimately, business is all about people. Business provides virtually all the goods and services that people need to live a healthy, prosperous and secure life. It does this by using human skills and talents to produce an increasing volume of improved goods and services.

'People are the most important factor in production'

It is true that machines are gradually taking over many of the jobs once done by people. Automation has caused some unemployment, particularly among unskilled workers, but other people are still in great demand to design, make, control and service the machines. No one knows whether more and more jobs will be performed by machines. Machinery has many advantages over human beings. Once a machine has been installed, it will go on working until it needs to be repaired or replaced. Human beings, however, need skilled management that takes account of their individual differences and needs if they are to do their best work. There is often conflict between working people. Moreover, people demand much more from work than machines do.

MOTIVATIONS FOR WORK

Why do people work? At the beginning of the nineteenth century, work provided nothing more than a bare subsistence for many people, whether they were agricultural labourers, or men, women or children working for many hours a day in dangerous and unhealthy factories. Since then, business has provided a much wider choice of work and much greater rewards for the majority of people in the western world. For most people, a job is central to their lives as it can provide so many of the things they want, and fulfil so many of their hopes and expectations. Some of the main motivations for working are:

- **Money:** For most people, money is one of the main reasons for having a job, as it enables them to buy what they consider to be essential goods and services, plus as many luxuries as they can afford.

- **A sense of progress:** Most people want to gain a sense of progress from their work. They are pleased if they are promoted, or if they get a more interesting job with a higher

▶ See **Wants** in Chapter 2.

► Since the end of the Second World War, Japanese salarymen, or business executives as we would call them, could rely on a secure job for life in big companies. However, during the recession in the early years of the 1990s, big companies started to dismiss salarymen. Employees in smaller firms – the majority of the workforce – never had security of employment.

► See the box on **Quality management systems** in Chapter 8, page 95.

salary. Conversely, many people despair if they cannot find a job, and feel a failure if they are made redundant. Many people want security from their job, but the days when a job lasted for life have probably gone for good – in all parts of the world.

- **Status:** Many people gain pleasure from the status, or perceived position in their firm or in society, that their job gives them. People are given important titles, such as Manager of Corporate Development, to indicate their rank. They are also given material symbols, such as larger desks and bigger cars. However, in modern companies, with quality management systems, there is less emphasis on status and more emphasis on teamwork.

- **Togetherness:** The sense of belonging to a group, of being part of a large organization, is important for many people. People can fulfil this need at work both formally and informally. Being a member of a work team provides a formal togetherness. Making friends at work and doing things together provides informal togetherness.

- **Job satisfaction:** Most people want a job that gives them pleasure and seems worth doing. If a job involves endless repetition and has little value, people soon become bored and uninterested. As you will see later in the chapter, modern management tries to relieve the boredom of repetitive work by using new working patterns.

 Draw up a four-column table with the heading *Motivations* in the first column. Write the five motivations listed above on separate lines in the first column. Put the names of three working relatives or three colleagues as headings in columns two, three and four. Then, give each person a score (out of 10) for each of the five motivations. Explain any significant differences in the scores by relating them to either the person's character or their work situation.

THE PERSONNEL DEPARTMENT

In large organizations, a **personnel department**, or a human resources department, manages employees. Generally, it is not cost-effective to have a personnel department in companies with fewer than 100 employees. In small companies, a section of the financial department carries out the work. Sole traders who employ people have to do all the personnel work themselves.

► For example, a manager might try to make people work harder by giving greater opportunities for promotion to the rank of supervisor, but the scheme could cause great resentment among the rest of the workforce if people thought that the new supervisors did not deserve promotion.

One of the main tasks of the personnel department is managing pay and fringe benefits. It also has the difficult task of trying to motivate as many individual employees as possible for the benefit of the business without causing friction among the rest of the workforce. In addition, it has to make sure that the many laws relating to employees are obeyed. It is also in charge of the recruitment, selection and training of employees; industrial relations; and, in many

*The main functions of a
personnel department*

companies, internal communication between departments and
employees.

 Make brief notes on the main functions of a personnel
department.

PAY

There are great differences in rates of pay in Britain. At the bottom
of the pay scale, nearly 5 per cent of all full-time employees earn
less than £130 a week (or £6,760 a year), while at the top, a few
employees, such as professional footballers, earn more than £1 million a year. However, the majority of employees earn neither as
little nor as much.

In the private sector, rates of pay are still decided to a large
extent by the forces of supply and demand. Generally, pay will be
low if the work can be done by almost anyone, such as sweeping
the streets, and pay will be high if the work can be done by very
few people, such as scoring goals in the Premiership. Other factors
that affect rates of pay include:

- the length of time spent in training;
- the level of qualifications required;
- working conditions, and any health or safety risks involved;
- the strength and skills of the trade union or the professional
  body in negotiating pay deals;
- the value of fringe benefits attached to the job.

There is another factor that affects the level of pay. Despite the
Equal Pay Act of 1970, which should have given women and men
equality in pay, women's pay is often less than men's, even for
equivalent work.

► The government has the final
say over pay in the public sector.
Independent review bodies
determine annual pay rises for
many public-sector employees, such
as lecturers and dentists, but the
government can ignore their
recommendations.

► See **Fringe benefits** on page
pp. 276–7.

► For more on the Equal Pay Act,
see page 281.

 1 Describe the most important functions of a personnel
(or human resources) department.

2 What is the main factor that determines the rate of pay in the private sector?

3 Name two other factors that influence the level of pay.

Wages

In most firms, there is a difference in how manual workers and non-manual workers are paid. Most manual workers are paid **wages** every week. Some manual workers are still paid in cash; but the Wages Act of 1986 gave employers the right to pay all new employees by cheque.

Time rates

- **Collective bargaining:** This method of deciding wages is not as common as it was in the past. Wages are based on a time rate, which is negotiated for each industry by the employers' association and the trade unions involved. They agree a basic hourly rate of, say, £6.40 an hour, or £243.20 for a 38-hour week. In some companies, workers may be able to negotiate a higher rate.

- **Overtime:** This is one of the most common forms of additional pay. About half the manual workers of both sexes receive overtime pay – normally time and a half – for about five hours a week on top of their normal 38-hour week. Overtime has advantages for employers as it allows them to produce more goods when order books are full without the expense of recruiting extra workers. It benefits workers too, as they receive higher pay for the extra hours. However, it can cause workers to work more slowly in the hope of going into higher-paid overtime, and can lead to industrial trouble if overtime is stopped when workers have come to rely on it.

- **Shift premium payments:** About 20 per cent of manual workers also receive extra pay for working anti-social shifts late at night or early in the mornings when most other people are not working.

Payment by results

With time rates, workers get the same pay per hour however hard they work. **Payment by results (PBR)** systems try to give workers incentives to work harder by linking what they are paid to what they produce. In all, about one-third of all full-time manual workers receive some form of PBR pay. There are many different systems. Here are three of the main ones.

- **Piecework:** One of the most common PBR systems is piecework. Workers are paid for each item they produce, not for the time they take to make it. Piecework is often used with homeworkers who do repetitive jobs at home, such as making wigs, assembling toys or addressing envelopes, usually for miserably low rates of pay. It is more difficult to use piecework in factories, because much of the work is done by teams not individuals. In some jobs, time

▶ **Manual workers** do mainly physical work, usually with the aid of tools or machines. They are sometimes known as blue-collar workers because of the blue overalls that are still worn by many industrial manual workers. **Non-manual workers**, on the other hand, are known as white-collar workers because the traditional garb of most (male) clerical and professional workers in the first half of this century consisted of a suit, white shirt and tie.

▶ The Wages Act was passed to reduce the large amounts of cash being delivered to factories, which had led to an increase in wage robberies.

▶ Britain is fighting a new EU directive that restricts the hours worked per week to 48. Some British employees work far longer than that. The law is due to come into effect in 1997.

rates and piecework are combined. The normal time rate is paid up to a certain level of output and on a piecework basis after that. With all piecework systems, there is a danger that workers might rush through their work to produce extra items, so an efficient inspection system is essential. However, employers gain from a full piecework system because they have to pay only for items that are produced.

- **Bonuses:** In some factories, workers are paid a bonus at regular intervals or once a year, based on the total output of the whole factory. Bonuses do not provide such a strong incentive as piecework. The bonus is often too small to motivate workers, and it is not strongly linked with their individual effort.
- **Profit-sharing schemes:** Profit sharing provides a stronger incentive than bonuses because there is a direct link between pay and the firm's success, in which all workers are ultimately involved. However, the proportion of profits set aside for workers needs to be sufficiently large to motivate them.

 What pay system would you choose if you wanted:

    (a) to have enough employees to work at night?
    (b) to obtain the highest possible rate of production in decorating plates?
    (c) to persuade enough workers to stay on after their normal day had ended to finish an urgent order?
    (d) to attract highly skilled workers to permanent jobs in your factory?

 Make brief notes on the different methods of payment for manual workers.

Single-status systems

Some progressive firms with quality management systems have introduced **single-status systems**, which abolish many of the distinctions between manual workers and non-manual workers. All employees receive salaries, have the same hours of work and the same holidays, wear the same uniform and eat in the same canteen. However, the majority of firms still keep the distinction between wages and salaries, paying salaries only to non-manual workers such as managers and secretaries.

    1 Who is paid wages?
    2 What is collective bargaining?
    3 Explain what payment by results is and give two examples of it.
    4 What is a single-status system?

 Read the following case study and answer the questions at the end.

▶ A **convenor** is elected by the shop stewards, or part-time trade union officials in a workplace, to represent the workers in negotiations with the management. For more information see Chapter 22.

▶ **State-of-the-art** technology is the most modern form of technology available.

You are a trade union convenor in a factory producing meat pies for supermarket chains. The firm has recently been taken over. The new owners have installed state-of-the-art machinery and made 15 per cent of the workforce redundant. Management has now proposed that the pay system for shop-floor workers should be changed in the following ways:

Present system	Proposed system
Wages paid weekly – some in cash	Salaries to be paid monthly to all workers by cheque
Clocking in and out of work to be abolished	Fixed hours of work with no time cards or overtime
Average wage and other PBR payments of £284 a week, though 2 per cent of workforce earn £364 per week with extra overtime	New basic salary of £14,000 a year with a guaranteed minimum share of profits of £1,000 per worker. The average share per worker over the last three years would have been £2,120 per year.
Promotion by junior managers' qualifications	Promotion by training and recommendations

1 What is the current annual average wage for a 52-week year?
2 How much more per year is earned by the 2 per cent who work extra overtime?
3 What are the advantages and disadvantages of the proposed pay system for the employees and for the employers?
4 If you were the convenor, what recommendations would you make to the workforce about the proposed pay scheme?

SALARIES

Salaries are based on an annual rate of pay, divided into twelve equal parts, paid monthly. For example, a person with an annual salary of £12,000 would receive £1,000 gross pay per month. Salaried employees have their hours of work stated in their contract of employment, but many non-manual workers, such as lecturers and teachers, regularly work late or take work home without receiving any additional payment. Only about one-fifth of salaried persons receive payment for overtime.

▶ Net, or take-home, pay would be much smaller because income tax, national insurance contributions, and often superannuation, or pension, contributions have to be deducted.

Most public sector and some private sector employees have an incremental pay scale with regular annual increases. For example, the pay scale might have a starting salary of £10,000 a year, rising by annual increments of £750 for eight years, to a maximum of £16,000. There are problems with this system for both employers and employees. Employers have to pay the annual increase even if they think the employee does not deserve it. Employees get no further increase in pay after they have had all their incremental pay

▶ There may also be a yearly increase in pay to cover all, or part, of the rise in the cost of living.

rises, so they have less incentive to work hard. To provide more incentive, most employers use schemes that relate pay to the work done.

Performance-related pay

About 70 per cent of employers in the private and the public sector have some form of **performance-related pay (PRP)** system with no automatic pay rises. Increases in pay are given only for better performance, which is assessed by the employee's boss, or line manager.

Although PRP is extremely common, it has attracted great criticism from academics, the Institute of Personnel Management, and even some employers. Critics claim that it is easy to pick out the best and the worst employees, but it is much more difficult to judge the performance of people in the middle. They also claim that PRP often produces a stressful work situation because of hostility between competing employees. Furthermore, they think that some employers have introduced PRP to cut costs by making it more difficult for employees to obtain a pay rise.

Responsible employers now agree that PRP should not be imposed without discussion. Instead it should be introduced in a more considerate way through agreement with employees. One method is to set up a proper appraisal scheme to judge individual performance. The scheme should have clear targets and objectives that have been agreed between each employee and his or her boss.

Profit-related pay

Employees like **profit-related pay** more than performance-related pay. Over a million employees are now members of profit-related pay schemes. These allow firms to pay up to one-fifth of their employees' pay, or £4,000 a year, whichever is less, tax-free. This amount has to be related in some way to the firm's profits.

The scheme has great advantages for both employers and employees, particularly where employees have agreed to give up part of their salary in return for a tax-free payment. For example, employees might take a pay cut of £4,000 a year and be given a £3,500 tax-free payment instead. Their employer would gain because the pay bill would be reduced. The employees would also gain because their take-home pay would be larger. They would have been paying more than £500 tax on the £4,000 that had previously been part of their salary, so £3,500 a year free of tax would be an improvement. It could also be argued that profit-related pay provides an incentive for people to work hard because they have a stake in the firm's profitability. On the other hand, during a recession, employees may be working particularly hard to keep the firm solvent, but profits may fall or there may be a loss. In those cases, profit-related pay will be low or zero, which can have a demotivating effect on employees.

▶ **Commission** is one of the oldest forms of performance related pay. Many sales staff receive a basic salary plus a percentage commission on everything they sell.

(NM) Make notes describing the benefits for employers and employees of incentive pay schemes.

FRINGE BENEFITS

Pay is not the only benefit that people get from working. The majority of employees receive a number of **fringe benefits**, which are goods or services provided by the employer in addition to wages or salaries. There might be just one fringe benefit, such as a discount on goods purchased in the shop where the employee works, or a whole range of them, such as the valuable fringe benefits that some chief executives receive. The advantage for employers is that they can select the fringe benefits that will appeal most to their employee. Employees also gain because they pay no tax at all on the fringe benefit, or only a proportion of the tax they would have paid on an equivalent cash increase. Another advantage for employees is that some fringe benefits – particularly company cars – give them status.

Fringe benefits for manual workers

The public sector and an increasing number of private firms provide pensions for their manual workers. In addition, some employers also provide sick pay schemes and private health insurance. Other fringe benefits include discounts on purchases of the firm's goods or services, free travel to work, subsidized canteen meals, free sports facilities and free uniforms.

Fringe benefits for salaried staff

Big companies provide a whole range of fringe benefits for non-manual staff. The higher the position in the firm, the more fringe benefits the employee will receive. In some cases, fringe benefits can be just as important as the salary. Companies often use a package of pay and fringe benefits to poach top managers from other firms.

Practically all big companies provide managers with pension and sick pay schemes, and private health insurance, usually for all members of the family. In addition, there are many other fringe benefits.

► A State pension is provided for all employees as part of the government's National Insurance scheme. However, the basic State pension is one of the lowest in Europe and provides only a minimal income. It can be topped up with a company pension or a private pension.

The company car

The company car is still one of the most popular fringe benefits, even though the tax charged on its use has risen steadily in recent years. The system was changed in 1994–5, when tax on expensive cars was increased and tax on cheaper cars was reduced. For example, the tax paid on a Jaguar with a list price of £46,000, used only occasionally for business, was £6,440 per year; while the tax on a Metro with a list price of £6,670, used extensively for business, was only £195 per year.

Nevertheless, most of the 2 million business people with company cars wanted to keep them, rather than have an equivalent pay rise, which some employers had suggested. The main reasons they gave were the status that the car provided and the access to trouble-free motoring.

Valuable fringe benefits

Even though a company car may be the most popular fringe benefit, it is by no means the most valuable. Many top managers and directors have the right to buy shares in the company at a bargain price, while others receive many thousands of pounds when they join, or leave, a firm – 'golden hellos' and 'golden handshakes'. Other fringe benefits for executives include: the use of company flats in London and other capital cities; large expense accounts; foreign trips, sometimes accompanied by a partner; cheap loans and mortgages; payment of school fees; and relocation, or moving, expenses.

1 What are the main differences between salaries and wages?
2 Describe the disadvantages of incremental pay.
3 What are the main criticisms of performance-related pay?
4 How does profit-related pay work?
5 Define fringe benefits.
6 What are the advantages of fringe benefits for employees and employers?
7 Give three example of fringe benefits for
 (a) manual workers;
 (b) salaried staff.

JOB SATISFACTION

Although pay and fringe benefits are important, most employees want more from their job. Surveys have shown that workers want an interesting and enjoyable job that gives them personal satisfaction and a sense of security. Top jobs produce great **job satisfaction** as they provide interest, variety and power, though they may also produce great stress. However, if a job is repetitive and boring, it is essential to have pleasant working conditions, suitable hours of work and some form of job improvement to make the work more interesting.

Working conditions

The working environment is an important factor in job satisfaction. Too many workplaces are still badly designed and poorly equipped. Excessive noise levels and inadequate heating, lighting and ventila-

► **Ergonomic** means designed to minimize physical effort and discomfort, and hence maximize efficiency.

► RSI is a condition that certain manual workers (such as chicken pluckers and workers in factories making tennis balls) have been suffering from for years. However, it was only when non-manual workers (particularly journalists) started suffering from it that it became widely recognized and large compensation awards were made.

► **Absenteeism** means staying away from work, with or without an acceptable reason.

► The lack or inadequacy of childcare facilities is still one of the biggest obstacles to true equality between male and female employees, as in most families it is the woman who has primary or sole responsibility for looking after the children. Only a very few big firms provide childcare facilities or adequate subsidies for employing a private childminder.

► There are about 5.8 million part-time workers, of whom 4.7 million are female.

tion can cause stress, carelessness and inefficiency. This applies just as much to office workers as to manual workers. One-third of office workers spend hour after hour keyboarding data into their computer. The lighting is sometimes inadequate or is too glaring. The ventilation may not be adequate. The furniture – desks, computer workstations and chairs – may not be ergonomically suitable for the kind of work being carried out. Continual keyboarding may lead to repetitive strain injury (RSI). Some computer operators suffering from RSI have taken successful legal action against employers and have won substantial awards. In 1993, new regulations were issued, based on a European Union (EU) directive, ordering employers to provide better working conditions for computer operators.

 Observe an outside job, such as installing cables or pipes in roads, and write a brief report on the working conditions, including details of the physical conditions, safety equipment provided, and your suggestions for improvements.

Working hours

The days when nearly everyone had a nine-to-five job are rapidly disappearing. More and more companies allow employees some choice in their hours of work. Flexible hours can also benefit employers as surveys have shown that productivity usually rises and absenteeism falls. Flexible working hours, and part-time work in particular, are useful options for people – mostly women – who have to do at least two jobs: their paid job, and the unpaid work of looking after a home (cooking, cleaning, shopping, etc.), and caring for children or an elderly relative, or both. However, some unscrupulous employers have used flexible hours to cut their costs by employing part-time workers at a lower hourly rate of pay than a full-time employee. Legally, too, part-time workers were not entitled to redundancy money until they had worked for the same firm for five years. In 1994, however, the Law Lords (the highest national court) ruled that British law should be brought into line with European law. Part-time workers now qualify for redundancy payments after two years' work, like full-time employees. Employers can still get round the law by employing people on contracts that run for a fixed term of a year or more. At the end of the fixed term, they can be dismissed without compensation.

 Interview some part-time workers about the benefits and drawbacks of their working hours, pay and conditions. Draw up a table with the main heading 'Part-time work' and with two columns headed *Advantages* and *Disadvantages*. Use your own research and the text above to fill in the table.

Here are some other kinds of flexible working arrangements:

• **Annual hours:** Some firms are now employing people for a set number of hours in a year, for example 1,976 hours a year instead of 38 hours a week. This system has great advantages for employers whose output peaks at certain times of the year. They can arrange for employees to work three or four long shifts in a week followed by a long weekend off. Or if the firm is busier in the summer than the winter, employees can work longer hours in summer and shorter hours in winter. There are advantages for employees, too. They usually have to work fewer hours per year as a reward for agreeing to work annual hours; they know in advance when they will have to work long shifts; they get longer breaks at home and, often, longer holidays.

- **Flexitime:** With flexitime, employees work every day for an agreed number of hours – core time – but can then choose when they work the rest of their hours.
- **Job sharing:** Two people share the same job. One might work in the morning and the other in the afternoon, or they might work alternate weeks. Job sharing is particularly suitable for a couple with children if they can afford to live on one salary. Employers benefit because they can retain experienced staff who are unable to work full time. Job sharing is particularly useful where there is a seven-day week, as in retailing. One disadvantage is that it is often difficult to replace a job sharer who decides to leave.
- **Career breaks:** These breaks are usually unpaid and can last for up to five years. They may be taken in order to look after young children or an elderly relative who has become seriously ill, or to study for a higher qualification. The employer and employee make a formal agreement that the employee will return to his or her former job – or a similar one – at the end of the break.
- **Maternity leave:** Until recently, women had to have worked for the same firm for six months before they qualified for paid maternity leave. In 1994, under a European Union law, all pregnant women became entitled to at least 14 weeks leave at a minimum of £52.50 per week. Some employers provide a longer maternity leave and a higher payment than the legal minimum. Very few firms give paternity leave to the father, though it is given in some other European countries.
- **Holidays:** Annual holidays allowances are becoming longer. Four or five weeks' paid holidays in addition to the eight bank holidays are common. In addition, the Christmas and New Year breaks are now commonly extended to ten days or so.

1 What do employees and employers gain from an annual hours system?
2 Why are many employers putting people on fixed-term contracts?
3 What kind of job might suit a couple who were more interested in bringing up their children than making large amounts of money?

4 Why do women take career breaks?
5 What kinds of employees might favour flexitime working?
6 What recent changes have been made in maternity leave provision?

Job improvement

▶ To refresh your memory, see **Production methods** in Chapter 15.

As you already know, there is a strong link between job satisfaction and the kind of work that is being done. Job satisfaction is at its lowest in flow production and other kinds of routine work. **Job improvement** is used to make this kind of work more interesting.

Job improvement systems

- **Job rotation:** In this system, workers carry out one simple task for a time and are then transferred to another simple task to provide variety. For example, in a supermarket, they might stack the shelves in the drinks section, then pack customers' bags at a check-out, then check the stock in the tinned vegetables section, and so on. Job rotation relieves boredom to a certain extent, but the employer probably benefits most because it creates worker flexibility by enabling workers to do more than one simple task.
- **Job enlargement:** This is a horizontal extension of work which increases the number of tasks at the same level that workers do as part of their normal routine. The aim, again, is to provide variety. For example, a secretary might be allowed to work for more than one manager.
- **Job enrichment:** This involves a vertical extension of work so that workers perform other tasks at a higher level and thus accept greater responsibility. For example, a railway worker might be in overall control of a small station: issuing tickets, loading freight on to trains, seeing that it is safe for the train to leave, and so on.
- **Teamwork:** Teamwork involves all three methods of job improvement, with workers performing any task of which they are capable, and accepting responsibility for their own work. The group of workers, under the control of a team leader, is in charge of a complete process. There is little doubt that teamwork produces better products as the workers regain a sense of achievement and involvement in their work.

▶ At Rover's Land Rover factory, where vehicles are built by teams of sixty people, suggestions for work improvements in 1992 were three times higher than the average in British manufacturing industry. (Rover was taken over by the German manufacturer BMW in 1994.)

 Make notes on job improvement, describing what benefits it provides for employees and employers.

EMPLOYEE PROTECTION

There are many laws to protect the health, safety and rights of employees. Recently, the European Union has passed an increasing number of laws of this kind which Britain, as a member-country, has to obey. Some of the most important laws are:

- **Equal Pay Act 1970:** Employees doing equal work, or, from 1984, work of equal value, must receive the same pay and terms of employment as an employee of the opposite sex.
- **Sex Discrimination Act 1975:** Employees must not be discriminated against in employment, training or recruitment because of their sex. The law, which applies to men as well as women, makes it illegal in most cases to advertise specifically for a male or female employee. For example, a dairy would advertise for a roundsperson, for example, not a roundsman or roundswoman (or milkman or milkwoman). The Equal Opportunities Commission has the task of ensuring that this law and the Equal Pay Act are carried out; but some employers still evade these laws.
- **Race Relations Act 1976:** People must not be discriminated against in employment, training and recruitment on the grounds of colour, race, nationality or ethnic origins. The Commission for Racial Equality tries to promote equality between races; but there are still inequalities, particularly at higher levels of management.
- **Employment Protection Act 1978:** This law gives employees a number of valuable rights, including:
  - (a) the right to receive a written contract of employment, giving the main terms and conditions of employment, and an itemized pay statement;
  - (b) the right to take time off work for public duties (for example as a juror or a magistrate) or to look for other work if made redundant;
  - (c) the right to take time off work for ante-natal care; not to be unfairly dismissed for reasons connected with pregnancy; and to return to work after having the baby;
  - (d) the right to receive a written statement of the causes for dismissal and not to be dismissed unfairly, i.e. without a reasonable cause;
  - (e) the right for employees with at least two years' service to receive **redundancy payments** if their job is being abolished. The payments vary according to age, salary and length of service. Employers often offer more generous terms than the legal minimum to encourage employees to take **voluntary redundancy**.

Health and Safety Regulations, 1993

Six new health and safety regulations came into force in 1993 as a result of an EU directive, or law. They make it obligatory for employers to manage health and safety in the same way as they do any other aspect of their business, such as finance, by assessing risk and taking appropriate action. In particular, employees have to make sure that the risk of both manual and non-manual workers being injured by moving or carrying

▶ Some jobs, particularly in fields such as social work, are treated as exceptional cases, and Section 7 (2) (e) of the Sex Discriminiation Act 1975 and/or Section 5 (2) (d) of the Race Relations Act 1976 would apply. It is possible to advertise, for example, for a black female youth counsellor.

▶ See **Contract of employment** in Chapter 21.

▶ See also **Redundancy** in Chapter 21.

▶ Back trouble is one of the biggest causes of people staying away from work.

heavy loads is reduced to a minimum. Computer operators also have to be provided with suitable working conditions.

The provisions of the Health and Safety at Work Act 1974 have largely been incorporated in the new Health and Safety regulations. Under the 1974 law, employers had a duty to provide safe premises, machinery and working practices as far as possible, and to ensure that the health of employees was not affected by their work. Employees also had an obligation to take care of their own health and that of their fellow workers and to cooperate with the employer in ensuring safe practices. Employees also gained the right to appoint safety representatives who could take paid time off work to carry out investigations into safety. The **Health and Safety Executive** has inspectors who can visit any business premises to see that the regulations and laws are being carried out.

 Describe the legal protection provided specifically for (a) a computer operator; (b) a married woman; (c) a magistrate; (d) a black person; and (e) a person who is made redundant.

SUMMARY

- In some ways, human resources – or personnel – are the most important factor in business, as business exists only to satisfy human wants and needs by providing goods and services through work.
- People work to obtain money, but they are also motivated by a sense of progress, status, togetherness and job satisfaction.
- In big organizations, a separate personnel department looks after all aspects of human resources.
- Pay is still primarily decided by the forces of supply and demand. In most firms, there is a distinction between the pay of manual workers and non-manual workers. Manual workers are paid weekly wages based on a time rate per hour and payment by results systems, such as piecework. Non-manual workers receive annual salaries that are paid monthly. Their pay rises are now often linked to performance.
- Fringe benefits are an important part of the whole remuneration package. At top levels, they can be almost as important as pay. The company car is still one of the most popular fringe benefits.
- Working conditions and working hours play an important role in job satisfaction for all employees. Workers on flow-production lines need to have their interest in work enhanced by some form of job improvement, such as teamwork.
- There are many laws to protect the health, safety and rights of employees, including an increasing number of EU directives.

(21) *Recruitment and training*

Chapter objectives

After working through this chapter, you will have the knowledge to:

■ identify different reasons for recruitment;

■ understand and use the procedures for recruitment including job descriptions, job specifications, job advertisements and application forms;

■ select the most suitable candidate for a post;

■ write a contract of employment;

■ state how laws apply to dismissal procedures and redundancy;

■ produce an induction training programme;

■ evaluate the benefits of training for employers and employees;

■ understand and use the following key terms: recruitment, job description, job specification, career structure, internal and external recruitment, job application form, short-listed, interview, labour turnover rate, contract of employment, disciplinary procedure, dismissal, redundancy, compulsory redundancy, natural wastage, early retirement, redeployment, voluntary redundancy, outplacement, industrial tribunal, sunrise industry, skills shortages, internal training, induction training, on-the-job training, skills analysis training, one-off training, external training, Training and Enterprise Council (TEC), Youth Training (YT).

RECRUITMENT

Recruitment, or taking on employees, is one of the most important tasks in any business, because employing the right people can increase a business's chance of success. New employees may be needed when:

• the business increases its output or expands;
• new skills are needed because of technological advances or changes in the market;
• employees are dismissed, or retire or leave to join other firms.

Stages in recruitment

Employing people is a complex procedure. It involves:

- deciding what kinds of skills and qualifications are needed for the job;
- providing a suitable package of pay and fringe benefits, and a career structure;
- searching for potential employees in appropriate places;
- choosing the right person from all the applicants;
- providing an induction programme when employees join the firm;
- making sure that all the legal obligations relating to employment are carried out.

Sole traders and recruitment

In big organizations, the personnel, or human resources, department is in charge of recruitment. Sole traders, however, have to do all the work themselves, unless they use the local Job Centre or a private employment agency to obtain staff for them. Taking on their first employee can sometimes be a traumatic, or highly stressful, experience for sole traders. When they were working alone, they took responsibility for all the work themselves; they did not have to give orders; they did not have to supervise anyone; they did not have to work out income tax or National Insurance contributions; they did not have all the legal obligations of employing someone else. When they take on an employee, however, they take on all these responsibilities and many more.

 Make notes on all the steps that have to be taken when an employee is recruited.

RECRUITMENT PROCEDURES

Categories of jobs

The way in which employees are recruited varies according to the kind of job involved. In any large organization, there are different categories, or classes, of job. The following eight categories are the main ones.

1 **Unskilled** manual jobs, such as cleaning or delivering messages, can be done by almost anyone.
2 **Semi-skilled** manual jobs, such as packing goods or working on a production line, need only a moderate degree of skill.
3 **Skilled** manual jobs, such as carpentry, need recognized qualifications and skills.
4 **Clerical** jobs, such as secretarial work, need general skills of literacy and numeracy, and some specialized qualifications and skills such as the ability to do book-keeping or use a computer.

▶ **Induction** involves explaining the activities, philosophy and customs of a firm to new employees and introducing them to their fellow workers. (See **Internal training** on page 296 of this chapter.)

▶ See **Employee protection** in Chapter 20.

▶ **Job Centres** are offices controlled by the Department of Education and Employment, which advertise employers' vacancies, try to find suitable employees, and provide other services for job seekers and the unemployed.

▶ **Unskilled labour** is increasingly being replaced by machines (such as coffee and tea dispensers) or the work is contracted out to firms (such as office cleaning and maintenance of plants).

▶ **Literacy** is the ability to read and write; **numeracy** is the ability to understand and use numbers in calculations.

5 **Supervisory** (or **junior management**) jobs, such as supervising shop-floor or clerical workers, demand the ability to supervise employees' work and to motivate them.
6 **Middle management** jobs, such as being in charge of a section within a department, require the ability to plan and control the work of employees in the section.
7 **Technical** or **professional** jobs, such as engineering or accountancy, need higher qualifications and degrees in relevant subjects.
8 **Senior management** jobs call for a range of management and enterprise skills needed to run a whole department in a firm.

Modern firms with quality management systems accept that every employee is of importance to the firm. However, they would make much more effort to recruit a finance director than a semi-skilled worker. This is because a finance director can affect the profitability of the firm and the work of other employees far more than a semi-skilled worker can. The method of recruitment would also differ. Advertisements for a finance director might be placed in top newspapers and/or specialized journals, or the firm might employ an executive employment agency to provide a short list of suitable candidates. Semi-skilled workers, on the other hand, might be recruited through a Job Centre.

► Private employment agencies may be used to **headhunt** suitable people who are working for another firm by offering them the post or asking them to apply for it.

Job descriptions

The first stage in recruiting a new member of staff is to state the exact nature of the job in a **job description**. This is usually drawn up by the department concerned in cooperation with the personnel department.

Job description

A job description is a written statement describing in detail the tasks, roles and responsibilities of a job. It usually contains some or all of the following items:
• the job title;
• the department where the job is located;
• a general description of the job;
• the level of responsibility and/or authority;
• a detailed description of the duties.

A job description for a word processor operator might look like this:

JOB DESCRIPTION

Title:	Word-processor operator
Department:	Marketing department
Function:	To provide word-processing services for the Marketing Director

> ► **Consumables** are items such as paper, envelopes and printer cassettes, all of which are needed for word processing operations and have to be continually replaced.

Responsible to: Personal Assistant to Marketing Director
Responsible for: No one
Duties:
1 Programming the personal computer at the start of day.
2 Word-processing letters and other documents with integrated graphics and other visuals and spreadsheet tables.
3 Maintaining a suitable filing system on disk.
4 Ordering all necessary consumables for the machine and ensuring that there is a sufficient stock of these supplies at all times.
5 General care of the machine.
6 Ensuring that the machine is disconnected at the end of the day.

Job specifications

A **job specification** describes the qualifications, skills, experience and personal qualities that an applicant should have. A job specification to match the job description for a word processor operator above might read:

JOB SPECIFICATION

GCSE English Grade B and at least two other passes at Grade C or above required. Word-processing experience essential. A minimum of two years' full-time experience required, preferably in marketing. Experience of Word for Windows 6.0 preferred. Should be enthusiastic, and able to work well under pressure and with the minimum of supervision.

> ► Word for Windows™ 6.0 is a word-processing software package made by Microsoft®.

1 State three business situations in which it would be necessary to take on new employees.
2 Why is more care taken in recruiting a finance director than a semi-skilled worker?
3 What would you expect to find in a job description?
4 What kind of information does a job specification provide?

Write a job description and a job specification for any job you have had. If you have never had a job, interview a friend or relative who does work, and write a job description and a job specification for his or her job.

METHODS OF RECRUITMENT

There are two methods of recruitment. **Internal recruitment** is recruiting someone who is already working in the organization. **External recruitment** is recruiting someone who works for another organization, or is unemployed, or has never worked before.

Internal recruitment

People can be recruited internally by advertising jobs on staff notice-boards or in house journals (firms' own magazines), or by offering the job to a selected employee. Some firms plan a career structure for each new junior management person they recruit. They hope that the recruit will progress to middle management within a few years. The firm provides the recruit with appropriate experience and training. This kind of in-built career structure is beneficial for the chosen individuals and helps to attract other ambitious recruits. This system, however, may cause resentment among less favoured employees, and the lack of fresh blood may make it more difficult for the organization to produce new ideas.

External recruitment

External recruitment can be carried out in a number of different ways. The following five methods are the main ones.

- **Personal recommendation:** Someone who is working for the firm recommends a friend or a relative for a vacant post. This takes place at all levels from a bricklayer who recommends a friend for a plasterer's job to a finance director who recommends a friend's son to a City firm. Nepotism sometimes provides jobs for unsuitable individuals, but personally recommended candidates can also prove to be excellent recruits, though they can cause resentment among other staff if they have not been through the normal selection procedures.

  ► **Nepotism** means showing favouritism towards a relative or a friend by, for example, obtaining a job for them.

- **Job Centres:** These offices are part of the Department of Education and Employment. They advertise jobs on behalf of employers and try to fill the vacancies with unemployed people who have registered with them. Job Centres deal mainly with manual, clerical and junior management jobs.
- **Private employment agencies:** These organizations provide firms with employees, including temporary staff, for a fee. There are many agencies dealing with office and clerical workers; there are also specialized agencies in such fields as catering, music and childcare. Executive employment agencies headhunt senior managers.
- **Careers offices:** Firms who need recruits can apply to local careers services, to careers offices attached to schools and colleges, and to university appointments boards.
- **Advertising:** This is one of the most common ways of trying to recruit employees. Advertisements range from displaying a card in a shop window for a few pence a week to large display advertisements in quality national newspapers, which can cost thousands of pounds for one advertisement.

 Make notes on methods of internal and external recruitment, assessing the relative benefits.

▶ See **The Press** in Chapter 14.
See also **Employee protection** in Chapter 20.

ADVERTISING JOB VACANCIES

The personnel department usually decides where the job should be advertised, the wording and size of the advertisement, and how often the advertisement should be inserted. The Press offers a great choice of newspapers and magazines for job advertisements. Quality national newspapers are used mainly for advertising managerial, professional and office vacancies in both the private and the public sectors. Business and professional magazines are used mainly for specific technical and professional posts. Local newspapers are used for a variety of local jobs at all levels, ranging from the unskilled to senior management. Advertisers can find out from the publisher the kind of people who read the newspaper or magazine – their social grade, sex, age, etc. This makes it easy to find a suitable publication for the job advertisement.

The advertisement itself is usually a blend of the information contained in the job description and the job specification. Details of the remuneration package and working conditions are also sometimes included.

 Find out how much a word-processor operator would earn in your area by looking in a local newspaper, a Job Centre or a private employment agency. Use this information, and the job description and job specification for a word-processor operator on pages 285–6, to write a job advertisement. It should be no more than seventy-two words in length. State the publication you would use for the advertisement and how many times it would appear. (Find out also whether operators are paid weekly or monthly; what holidays they have; and the length of notice required if they want to leave the job. You will need this information for an activity later in this chapter.)

 How would you try to recruit:

    (a) a marketing director?
    (b) a shop-floor supervisor?
    (c) a clerical worker?
    (d) a temporary word-processor operator?
    (e) a senior engineer?

Application forms

One of the tasks of the personnel department is to design a job application form that will be suitable for as wide a variety of posts as possible. The application form usually asks for the following information:

- **Personal details:** These include the applicant's full name, address and telephone number(s) (home and daytime), date and place of birth, nationality, sex and marital status.
- **Education and training:** Applicants must supply details of

schools, colleges and universities attended, subjects studied, courses taken, examination results, qualifications obtained.

- **Previous employment:** Applicants must list the names and addresses of previous employers, jobs held, wages or salary, reasons for leaving, present position and notice required;
- **Health:** Applicants should state whether they have had any serious illnesses or operations, and whether they are registered as a handicapped person.
- **Reasons for applying for the post**
- **Interests and leisure activities**
- **References:** An employer will require details of previous employers and responsible persons who know the applicant well and who will be prepared to give a written or oral summary of their capabilities.

The application form, and further details about the post and the firm, are sent to everyone who replies to the job advertisement. Sometimes applicants are asked to fill in the application form by hand. Firms in the private sector often ask applicants to send a **curriculum vitae** (c.v.) rather than complete an application form.

Write an application form suitable for the job of word-processor operator that could also be used for a whole range of other jobs.

► *Curriculum vitae* is a Latin phrase meaning 'the course of a life'. A curriculum vitae (c.v.) describes a person's education and career. Applicants write their own c.v.s, or occasionally have them produced by a specialist firm.

► It is estimated that about 5 per cent of companies use the services of **graphologists** in recruiting staff. Graphologists claim that they can gain information about character and aptitudes from people's handwriting. Graphology is more frequently used by German and French firms.

SELECTION METHODS

When all the completed application forms have been received, members of the personnel department and managers of the department concerned study them to find the most suitable candidates. Having all the facts about each candidate listed in the same order makes it easier to compare each candidate. If there are a large number of candidates, the forms may be sorted into three piles – hopeful, doubtful, hopeless. The doubtful candidates will be looked at again: some will be demoted to the hopeless pile and others will be included with the hopefuls. A number of candidates (usually at least three or four) will be short-listed and invited to come to an interview at a stated time on a stated date. A formal letter may be sent to all the other candidates thanking them for applying for the job.

Interviews

Interviews are used for making appointments in virtually all jobs. Sometimes there is just one interviewer, often there are two or three, and with top managerial jobs there is generally a panel of interviewers, usually five to eight or more.

Interviews are useful because the interviewers have a chance to meet the candidates, assess their characteristics, and see how they react to one particular situation – the interview itself.

Read the following case study and answer the questions at the end.

Philippa, from the personnel department, was one of the three interviewers for the candidates for the post of word-processor operator. Using the application forms, she had made the following notes about the three shortlisted candidates, which she took into the interview room.

	Sue	Deva	Clare
Age	22	19	24
Education	Private schools	Comprehensive	Comprehensive FE college
	GCSE English B GCSE Business Studies C GCSE Biology C Pitman's Typing Grade 2	GCSE English A GCSE Business Studies B GCSE Mathematics A GCSE French C GCSE Media Studies B RSA Word Processing Advanced Stage III	GCSE English B GCSE Business Studies C GCSE English Lit B GCSE Sociology D
Previous jobs	Solicitor 3 years Sales 2 years	Temporary work 2 years Magazine 1 year	Local council 5 years
Interests and leisure activities	Swimming Tennis	Rock climbing Travel	Amateur theatre group Reading

During the interview, Philippa made brief notes about the candidates:

	Sue	Deva	Clare
	Self-assured Quick replies	Very intelligent Too confident?	Nice smile A bit dull

1 State two questions that you would always ask applicants at interviews because you think they are vitally important.
2 If you had been the interviewer, which applicant do you think you would have selected? State your reasons.

Other methods of selection

Surveys have shown that interviews do not always give a very reliable indication of whether a person will do well in a job. They do not test all the necessary skills and qualities for the job. They are also too subjective, as the interviewers often let their personal views and prejudices influence their choice. Therefore, it is becoming common for firms to use other methods of selection in addition to interviews. Here are three of the methods:

- **Skills tests:** These assess applicants' skills in performing one of the main tasks they would have to do every day. For example, a word-processor operator could be asked to keyboard a letter within a specified time.
- **Personality tests:** These tests are based on questions that are devised by psychologists and are intended to reveal the applicant's personality and attitudes. Personality tests are used when a job needs people with a particular kind of personality, such as a hotel receptionist, who would need to be friendly and helpful.
- **Group tests:** Groups of applicants are put into in physically and intellectually challenging situations in open-air adventure centres. These tests are often used with a group of applicants for managerial jobs in big companies so that their reactions to demanding situations can be compared.

Outward Bound participants tackle a group challenge

Although these tests probably provide a more reliable assessment of applicants than interviews do, they are still not entirely satisfactory, because most of them are not based on the job itself.

1 Why must application forms be suitable for a range of jobs?

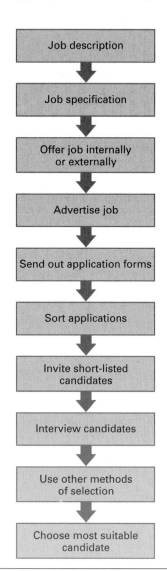

```
┌─────────────────────────────┐
│      Job description        │
└─────────────────────────────┘
              ↓
┌─────────────────────────────┐
│      Job specification      │
└─────────────────────────────┘
              ↓
┌─────────────────────────────┐
│   Offer job internally      │
│      or externally          │
└─────────────────────────────┘
              ↓
┌─────────────────────────────┐
│       Advertise job         │
└─────────────────────────────┘
              ↓
┌─────────────────────────────┐
│  Send out application forms │
└─────────────────────────────┘
              ↓
┌─────────────────────────────┐
│     Sort applications       │
└─────────────────────────────┘
              ↓
┌─────────────────────────────┐
│   Invite short-listed       │
│       candidates            │
└─────────────────────────────┘
              ↓
┌─────────────────────────────┐
│    Interview candidates     │
└─────────────────────────────┘
              ↓
┌─────────────────────────────┐
│    Use other methods        │
│      of selection           │
└─────────────────────────────┘
              ↓
┌─────────────────────────────┐
│  Choose most suitable       │
│       candidate             │
└─────────────────────────────┘
```

The process of recruitment

▶ **Labour turnover rate** means the rate at which employees leave a business during the year. The rate is expressed as a percentage and is calculated by the following formula:

labour turnover rate =

(total employees leaving in a year

average number of employees in a year

× 100

2 What does short-listed mean?

3 What are the main advantages and disadvantages of interviews?

4 Name one kind of test that might be used in addition to an interview and describe the kind of vacancy it might be used for.

 Make notes on methods of selection in recruitment, including the interview.

SOLE TRADERS AND RECRUITMENT

As you can see from the diagram in the margin, recruiting a new employee is a long process. Sole traders need to take just as much care as big firms in recruiting staff, but very few of them do. As a result, they often find they have selected unsuitable, unreliable or dishonest employees. This is less likely to happen if proper recruitment procedures are followed. It is necessary to define the exact nature of the job by writing a job description and a job specification. If this is not done, a grocer, for example, might take on someone who has problems with reading. Most shopkeepers recruit staff locally, but it might be worth while extending the search by advertising in the trade magazine, *The Grocer*. It is possible that the ideal candidate lives 200 miles away, but is about to move to the grocer's area. Although pay is important, opportunities for training and some form of career structure may be just as important to some employees. It is also worth while to be flexible about hours of work, as this might be more important to the employee than higher rates of pay.

It is worth spending a little time and money on recruitment to avoid inconvenience and expense in the future. Some small re-tailers have a very high labour turnover rate. This can often be reduced by providing better working conditions, training, and some form of career structure.

 Imagine that you had set up your own business and it had reached the stage where you needed to take on a full-time employee. Describe how your business reached that point and how you would set about recruiting an employee.

CONTRACT OF EMPLOYMENT

When the successful candidate has been selected, all the legal obligations of employing people come into effect. Within two months, employers must give all employees who work more than eight hours a week a contract of employment. The contract is a written statement of the terms and conditions of their employment.

Contract of employment

The contract must include:

- the title of the employee's job;
- the address of the employer;
- the date when employment began;
- the rate of remuneration, or pay;
- any collective agreements between employers and trade unions affecting the terms and conditions of employment;
- the intervals at which wages or salaries are paid;
- the hours of work;
- the employee's entitlement to holidays (including public holidays) and holiday pay;
- any disciplinary rules or procedures;
- the length of notice that employees should give, or receive, to end their employment.

Details about sickness terms and payments and pension arrangements may be included in separate documents.

 Write a contract of employment for a word-processor operator, using the data from your previous research.

DISCIPLINE AND DISMISSALS

Disciplinary procedures

In addition to recruiting employees, the personnel department is also involved in **disciplinary procedures** and **dismissals**. The contract of employment lays down a set of rules that the firm must follow if it wants to dismiss an employee for unsatisfactory work or misconduct. Usually, a verbal warning is given first, followed by a second warning given at a meeting with a manager, and finally a third warning is issued in writing.

Dismissals

It is only after the full disciplinary procedure has been applied that employees can be dismissed. They must be given the period of notice specified in their contract of employment. Employees may be dismissed without notice only if they are guilty of a gross breach of contract, such as theft. They are then entitled only to the pay they have earned up to the time of their dismissal.

Redundancy

In recent years, far more people have lost their jobs through **redundancy** than misconduct. During the 1990s, redundancy was no longer confined mainly to workers in manufacturing industries as it had been in the 1980s. It affected white-collar workers and man-

► Employees are made redundant because their job no longer exists. For example, their firm may have closed, or their job may have disappeared because of organizational change or new technology. If employees, including part-time workers, have had their job for two years or more, they are usually entitled by law to redundancy payments. These are based on their age, pay and length of service.

► **Compulsory redundancy** is when a firm orders employees to leave their jobs, sometimes with no financial compensation except for the legal minimum.

► See the marginal note on curriculum vitae (c.v.) on page 289.

► The maximum was abolished for women who were forced to resign from the Army, Navy or Air Force because they were pregnant. Two women were awarded around £170,000 and another nearly £300,000 in 1994.

agers in all sectors of production, including banks, which had once provided a safe job for life. In the mid-1980s only about 1½ per cent of managers were made redundant; by the mid-1990s that had increased to over 7 per cent. The main reasons for redundancy were:

- new technology eliminating many jobs;
- intense global competition, particularly from the Far East;
- downsizing, or reducing the scale, of big companies to cut costs and concentrate on the core business.

Firms usually try to avoid compulsory redundancy, by using one of the following means:

- **Natural wastage:** Employees are not replaced when they retire, or leave the company for any other reason.
- **Early retirement:** Employees are allowed to retire before the statutory, or legal, age, often with an enhanced pension.
- **Redeployment:** Employees are given other jobs in the organization, and any necessary retraining.
- **Voluntary redundancy:** Employees are asked to volunteer for redundancy and offered a large payment to persuade them to do so.

When employees are made redundant, many big firms now provide **outplacement** schemes to soften the psychological blow of losing their jobs and to help them to find new ones. The employees may be offered counselling, either individually or in groups. They may be given aid in writing c.v.s, or free facilities for searching for a job, such as the use of personal computers or telephones. The personnel department may also try to find jobs for the redundant employees.

Industrial tribunals

Employers have to be very careful to observe all the employment laws in dealing with their employees. If employees think their employer has treated them unfairly, they can take their case to an industrial tribunal. These tribunals have a legally qualified chairperson. There has recently been a great increase in industrial tribunal cases: between 1991 and 1992 the number of cases jumped from 38,480 to 65,000. As a result, it is sometimes months before a case is heard. The most common cause of complaint – over half of all cases – is unfair dismissal. The maximum amount that a tribunal can award an employee is £21,480, but most awards are much less, with a median, or middle-of-the-range, award of £1,773.

1 What would you expect to find in a contract of employment?
2 What are disciplinary procedures?
3 When can an employee be dismissed without notice?
4 What is compulsory redundancy?
5 Give two alternatives to compulsory redundancy.

6 Describe the work of an industrial tribunal.

 State how laws apply to disciplinary procedures, dismissals and redundancy.

TRAINING

Skills shortages

Although thousands of people are made redundant every year, and although, at the time of writing, there are over 2 million unemployed, there is still a serious **skills shortage**. There are not enough people with the skills required for the new technological age. An extensive survey in 1993 revealed that 16 per cent of employers found it difficult to fill vacancies because they couldn't find the skilled workers they needed. Firms in the **sunrise industries** based on electronics, such as manufacturers of data-processing equipment, had the biggest problems. There were also skills shortages in many other manufacturing and some services industries.

It is not only technical skills that are in short supply. Many adults lack the basic skills of literacy and numeracy, so that they find it difficult to fill in a form or to give change, except from an automated till. According to one comprehensive survey in 1993, one in six adults has difficulties with basic skills. It has been estimated that it costs business billions of pounds every year to correct errors that result from problems with basic skills: for example, sending out incorrect orders to mail-order customers, such as a medium T-shirt instead of a large one.

▶ Problems of illiteracy and innumeracy are even worse in some other countries. It is estimated that 42 per cent of the population of the United States have difficulty with basic skills.

Demographic changes

Demographic changes have made the problem even worse. There is not only a lack of skills but also a decline in the number of people aged 16 to 39 who are usually the most ambitious, knowledgeable and successful section of the working population. It is estimated that the proportion of this age group in the total population will fall from 35.2 per cent in 1991 to 32.6 per cent by 2001 and to 30 per cent by 2011. There has already been a decline in the number of young people coming on to the labour market compared with the 1980s.

This shortfall is partly counteracted by the increase in the number of women who continue to work after they have had a baby, or who return to work when their children start school. The proportion of women in the total workforce is rising all the time. In 1994, there were more working women than men in nine counties in England and Wales.

▶ **Demography** is the study of the size and structure of populations.

Need for training

As a result of all these changes, there has been an enormous growth in training and retraining. Many adults need training in basic skills; redundant and redeployed workers need retraining for new kinds of jobs; young people need training in skills that businesses are seeking; and women who return to work after a career break may need retraining. Working people may also need training to:

- improve product quality and thus reduce the need for supervision;
- increase productivity;
- use new machines;
- adopt new ways of working.

 Make full notes on why there is a need for training.

INTERNAL TRAINING

Internal training is organized by the personnel department and is usually given by members of the firm, though outside specialists may also be used.

Practically all big companies have some kind of formal **induction** programme. This usually involves a talk on the company's history, products and aims, which is sometimes accompanied by a video. There may also be a tour of various departments and sometimes talks by departmental managers.

An induction programme helps to make the employee familiar with the company and the working environment. The employer benefits, too; employees immediately learn how the company operates and what they should and should not do. The induction programme presents the company in a favourable light, which may help to increase employee motivation and reduce the labour turnover rate.

 If you have had a job, describe any induction training you had and suggest ways in which it could have been improved. If you haven't had a job, ask a relative or friend who has, what induction training they had. Describe it and evaluate its effectiveness.

On-the-job training

In addition, firms provide new employees with any necessary training in their job. This may be nothing more than informal on-the-job advice from a more experienced colleague. Although this method costs the firm nothing, it has the disadvantage that sometimes colleagues can pass on bad work practices to new employees. More efficient firms provide proper training programmes led by skilled instructors who ensure that the employees use only the best working practices. In some cases, **skills analysis training** is used. The job is broken down into stages and trainees are shown how to do each stage before doing it themselves under the trainer's supervision. This form of training is very effective, but it is also expensive.

The company benefits from on-the-job training because employees can start doing their job in the shortest possible time. Their efficiency, however, will usually be determined by how much money the employer has invested in the training. Employees also gain as they learn specific skills that will be valuable in their future careers and for which they can be awarded **National Vocational Qualifications** (**NVQs**). These qualifications are awarded on the basis of the work that employees do in their own workplaces.

One-off training schemes

With the increased emphasis on training, many firms now provide **one-off training schemes** to achieve specific objectives that will benefit their business. Such schemes might cover training in better time management for managers, structured selling techniques for sales representatives, or improved customer service for hotel employees. It is essential that the firm has clear objectives, that employees are motivated, and that the results are evaluated to see that the objectives have been achieved. Both the employee and the employer benefit. The employee may obtain any of the benefits described in the margin. The employer gets a more highly skilled workforce and, it is hoped, higher profits.

Some firms prefer internal training because they are in control of it. However, many firms also use some form of external training, particularly for more general training and educational needs.

► Employees could be motivated by being offered an increase in salary or a greater chance of promotion if they are successful on the training course, or by being shown how the training will make their work easier, or more interesting, or safer, or useful to them in their career.

 Make brief notes on the different kinds of internal training.

EXTERNAL TRAINING

External training, or off-the-job training, is provided outside the firm by colleges and other educational institutions. Colleges provide courses that are designed to meet the needs of local businesses, or that lead to recognized qualifications. Schools also provide vocational training for students aged 14 and over, which can lead to nationally recognized qualifications such as GCSE and A level Business Studies, or General National Vocational Qualifications (GNVQs). In addition to these awards, external training in a different environment can provide employees with new ideas and a broader view of their career. Employers are relieved of some of the responsibilities of providing training. Off-the-job training is usually cheaper for them because the training provider has economies of scale.

Government training schemes

The government and government-sponsored bodies provide many kinds of training. The government has set up eighty-two Training and Enterprise Councils (TECs) in England and Wales to give advice on training and to encourage enterprise. TECs provide part-time courses in setting up a business and in expanding and developing it. They also supply open learning courses through

► Many libraries and Job Centres have direct computer links with their local TECs through a touch-screen television monitor, which allow users to investigate training opportunities.

books, audio and video tapes, or computers, and these allow students to learn at their own pace.

Both external and internal training is used on the Youth Training (YT) two-year course for unemployed school leavers, who are paid a small weekly allowance. YT courses combine work experience in a firm with off-the-job training in social and work-related skills at a college. In 1993, the government announced a new apprenticeship scheme under which young people will be able to obtain work-based training leading to technician and supervisor qualifications. The government's Training for Work scheme provides training for the adult unemployed.

Employers gain from government training schemes because the government pays all, or a major part, of the costs. The trainees gain because they are given access to a wide range of training options.

1 Give three reasons for the shortage of skills in Britain.
2 Who is responsible for training in big firms?
3 What are the advantages of an induction programme for employers and employees?
4 Describe the benefits and drawbacks of on-the-job training.
5 Who provides off-the-job training for business?
6 Describe the part the government plays in training.

General benefits of training

Good training programmes provide immense benefits for employers, employees and the whole country. For the employer, training can produce greater productivity and efficiency, better quality products and a reduction in the labour turnover rate. The employee gains through improved skills, better chances of promotion, and increased job satisfaction. The country gains because a better-trained workforce can compete more successfully in the world and provide a greater level of prosperity.

However, compared with most of the other eleven countries in the European Union, the government spends far less on training and job creation for the unemployed. Only Luxembourg and Portugal spend less. Moreover, during the recession at the beginning of the 1990s, many British firms cut their training budgets.

Obtain leaflets and brochures on business training from colleges, libraries, Job Centres and any other sources you can think of. From the information they contain (and the information provided above), write a short report on training, emphasizing the benefits for employers and employees.

Read the following case study and answer the questions at the end.

The personnel department at Savage and Slaney plc is

> ▶ Britain lags behind many other European countries in the number of apprenticeships it offers. At one time, many school leavers joined a manufacturing or construction firm as an apprentice to learn a skilled trade over a long period of time – usually five years. There are still about 250,000 apprentices in Britain, but that is only about a third of the number that there were thirty years ago. Germany has many more apprentices than Britain.

having trouble with its word-processor operators. In the hope of achieving economies of scale, the firm recently set up a secretarial services unit, which carries out word processing for all departments, including departmental heads. To increase productivity, the firm has also introduced the latest word-processing package, which operates at much greater speeds than their old one. The new software allows compound documents, containing text, graphics, charts and spreadsheet tables, to be produced very easily, and it was expected to provide job enrichment for the operators. The software is extremely easy to use, with clear on-screen help and tutorials, but supervisors are being called in to help more often than in the past. The labour turnover rate among operators is also increasing.

Members of the personnel department, the manager of the secretarial services unit, and some supervisors were holding a meeting to see if they could come up with a solution.

Bill, from personnel, said: 'I can't see what the problem is. It can't be the software. I tried it out myself last night, and it couldn't be easier to use.'

Kate, the manager of the secretarial services unit, said: 'Performance-related pay should have solved the problem, but it hasn't. There's a very bad spirit in the unit. I think we ought to go back to uniform payments with profit-related bonuses.'

Tessa, a supervisor, said: 'The software is easy to use, but perhaps they need a two-day course, just to give them confidence.'

Vivien, from personnel, said: 'Perhaps we need to build in more of a career structure. When the operators were working in separate departments, they had more contact with different kinds of staff. They feel isolated now. Perhaps we should introduce a graded pay structure based on word-processing tests and achievements.'

1 How did management know that there was trouble in the new secretarial services unit?
2 What benefits did management expect to gain from setting up the unit?
3 Which suggestion made at the meeting would have improved the operators' performance most? Why have you chosen it?
4 If you had been at the meeting, what suggestions would you have made for solving the problem?

SUMMARY

- Recruitment is one of the most important tasks of the personnel department.
- There are well-established procedures for recruiting staff,

including job descriptions, job specifications, job advertisements and job applications forms. No employer, whether a large plc or a sold trader, should ignore these steps in recruitment.

- Internal recruitment has great advantages because it allows employers to build a career structure for their employees. However, it needs to be balanced by external recruitment to draw in employees with new ideas.
- The interview is not a reliable way of selecting the most suitable candidate, but practically all employers go on using it. Some employers are now using other means of selection as well, such as skills and personality tests.
- The personnel department must obey the many laws relating to employment. Employees must be given a contract of employment within two months. There are other laws regulating disciplinary procedures, dismissals and redundancy, with industrial tribunals to enforce them.
- At the same time as millions of employees are being made redundant, there is also a shortage of labour through lack of skills and the decline in the number of young people. An increase in the number of women returning to work after having children has helped to fill the gap.
- Lack of skills has produced a great need for training. Most firms have some form of induction training, on-the-job training, and one-off training schemes. External training is provided by colleges and by the government.
- The British government spends far less on training and job creation than most other countries in the European Union. Some British firms cut their training budgets to reduce costs in the recession at the beginning of the 1990s.

22) Industrial relations and communication

Chapter objectives

After working through this chapter, you will have the knowledge to:

▮ identify the five kinds of trade union;

▮ describe the organization of a typical trade union;

▮ understand all levels of collective bargaining;

▮ show how different kinds of industrial action have been restricted by law;

▮ evaluate the effects of unemployment on trade union power;

▮ assess the impact of 'new style' trade unions on working practices;

▮ appreciate the importance of hidden meanings in communication;

▮ select the appropriate medium for particular messages;

▮ understand and use the following key terms: industrial relations, trade union, Trades Union Congress (TUC), craft union, industrial union, general union, white-collar union, mega-union, convenor, shop steward, Confederation of British Industry (CBI), trade associations, collective bargaining, work-to-rule, token strike, selective strike, official strike, wildcat strike, sit-in, lock-out, closed shop, Advisory, Conciliation and Arbitration Service (ACAS), picketing, secondary picketing, management of change, 'new style' agreement, pendulum arbitration, human resources management (HRM), communication, feedback, one-way communication, two-way communication.

INDUSTRIAL RELATIONS

The term **industrial relations** covers the whole range of contacts between managers and owners on the one hand and trade unions and workers on the other. Managers represent the interests of the owners of a business in the same way that trade unions represent the interests of the workers.

To a certain extent, there will always be a conflict of interest between the two sides. For example, the owners of a business are usually interested in higher profits, whereas the workers are usually interested in higher wages and better working conditions.

However, the two sides also share some common interests, such as the desire to see that the business does not close, which would benefit neither the owners nor the workers. Progressive management and trade unions now concentrate more on what unites them rather than on what divides them – on their common rather than their different interests.

Industrial relations are closely related to the health of business. If they are bad for a long time, either in particular firms, or more generally throughout the country, business is likely to suffer. Owners and managers will be less willing to invest in firms if industrial relations are bad, so the firm may be downsized, causing redundancies. As a result, the remaining workers will be less inclined to cooperate with management and may take some form of industrial action.

No one works well in an atmosphere of conflict and hostility. It is the task of the personnel department to negotiate with trade unions and the workforce and maintain good industrial relations. The government can also do a great deal to improve, or harm, industrial relations. It can pass laws that will stop managers or trade unions using their powers unfairly. It can also encourage good industrial relations by listening to both sides equally and taking actions that will help to reconcile them. Conversely, it can pass unfair laws and support one side of industry more than the other.

▶ Where the owners of a business are intent on forcing changes in working practices on a reluctant workforce, the personnel department can sometimes do little to prevent a worsening of industrial relations.

 Look in newspapers for reports or articles about any new government laws, regulations or statements concerning trade unions. State the effects they are likely to have on business.

TRADE UNIONS

Trade unions were born out of the general poverty and injustice of working-class life in the nineteenth century. They were formed to obtain better pay and working conditions for their members by negotiating on their behalf with the owners of firms. Trade unions believed that workers would have greater strength and power by acting together. This collective action would prevent workers from being victimized or dismissed, because they would no longer have to speak out individually.

The first trade unions were set up for skilled craftsmen only. Union membership was opened in succession to unskilled workers, women, and white-collar workers and professionals. Over the years, a growth in the number of mergers has greatly reduced the number of trade unions. These mergers proceeded at an even faster pace in the 1990s.

Kinds of trade union

There are fewer than 300 trade unions in Britain today. Most of them are affiliated to the **Trades Union Congress (TUC)**, which was founded in 1868. The TUC decides the policy of the trade union movement and voices its views to the media, government and business. It also deals with any disputes between unions.

There are five kinds of trade union. Some are small **craft unions** formed in the last century for skilled workers in one industry, such as the Society of Shuttlemakers. Many craft unions have been dissolved, or merged with other unions. Most of those that remain have very small memberships of fewer than 500 workers.

Industrial unions serve a single industry, representing both skilled and unskilled workers. For example, the National Union of Mineworkers (NUM) represents coal miners. However, it does not have a monopoly, as there are also other unions like the Union of Democratic Mineworkers (UDM), which represents both skilled and unskilled workers, and other unions that represent the deputies, or supervisors.

Since the end of the Second World War, many industrial unions have merged with bigger unions to form **general unions** representing skilled, semi-skilled and unskilled workers in a whole range of industries. One example is the Transport and General Workers Union (TGWU).

In recent years, there has been a great growth in white-collar unions for office workers, technicians and professionals. For example, teachers have a choice of unions, including the National Union of Teachers (NUT) and the National Association of Schoolmasters and Union of Women Teachers (NAS/UWT). Recently, some white-collar unions have extended their membership to include both professionals and skilled workers. One example is the Manufacturing, Science and Finance Union (MSFU), which has a membership of over 600,000. As there has been a decline in heavy industry, such as coal mining and steel making, white-collar workers have assumed a more dominant role in the union movement. In some areas of the country, there are more white-collar workers than manual workers in trade unions.

In the 1990s, mergers between unions produced a new kind of **mega-union**, with memberships of over a million. In 1992, the Amalgamated Engineering and Electrical Union (AEEU) was formed from a merger of the Amalgamated Engineering Union and the Electrical, Electronics, Telecommunications and Plumbing Union. It has a membership of over 1.4 million. In the following year, the Confederation of Health Service Employees (COHSE), the National and Local Government Officers' Association (NALGO) and the National Union of Public Employees (NUPE) merged to form UNISON with a membership of nearly 1½ million. At the time of writing, talks are going on between the Transport and General Workers' Union (TGWU) and the General, Municipal, Boilermakers' and Allied Trades Union (GMB), which could produce a union with a membership of around 2 million.

► 'Mega' comes from the Greek word meaning 'great'.

ACT IN Look in *Whitaker's Almanack* in your library (or in another reference book containing up-to-date information about trade unions). Find two examples of each of the five kinds of trade union described above, and make a note of their name and the number of members.

Trade union organization

Unions differ in the way they are organized. However, most of them have the same basic structure, which is shown in the diagram in the margin. The union is headed by the president, the general-secretary and members of the national executive committee, who make policy decisions. (These now have to be elected by a secret postal ballot.) They are assisted by a staff of paid officials. In bigger unions, there are district, or regional, committees, also served by paid officials. The district committees are elected by the union branches. The branches cover either one small area of the district or one big workplace. The branch officials, such as the chair, secretary and treasurer, are elected by the members of the branch.

Where there are several unions in a workplace, there is usually a **convenor** from the shop floor who leads the union negotiations with the workplace management. Convenors are recognized by both the management, which gives them time off to carry out their trade union duties, and by their union, which allows them to negotiate with management over shop-floor grievances, payment systems, working conditions, etc. Convenors receive their normal pay, but are not paid by the union. They are elected by **shop stewards**, who are also voluntary, part-time union officials. Shop stewards are elected by the workers who are members of the union.

 Copy of the diagram showing trade union structure on to the middle of a sheet of A4 paper, and add explanatory notes about each item.

► The organizational structure of general and mega-unions is more complex than that of craft and industrial unions, because they serve different grades of workers in many industries. Some, like the TGWU, are organized on an industry-wide basis, while others, like the GMB, are more geographically based.

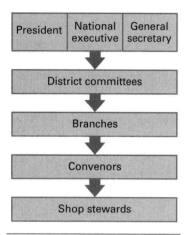

Trade union structure

EMPLOYERS' ASSOCIATIONS

The **Confederation of British Industry (CBI)** is the main voice of British business at home and abroad. All of the 250 large trade associations are members, but the CBI's main strength is the 250,000 private and public companies that belong to it. Trade associations, such as the Engineering Employers' Federation or the British Clothing Industry Association represent employers in separate industries. On the whole, trade associations have usually been much less effective in gaining media publicity about their problems and achievements than trade unions have. Trade associations provide advice and information for member firms, and sometimes carry out research and development for the industry. They also represent the employers in national talks with trade unions over pay and working conditions in their industry. These talks are part of the system of collective bargaining which was common in many industries in the 1970s, but which is now becoming less common.

COLLECTIVE BARGAINING

Collective bargaining deals with such matters as wages, salaries, working hours, overtime, holidays and general working conditions. Instead of employers dealing directly with employees, talks are held by representatives of both management and the workforce. Discussions take place in the industry at all levels from national to the shop floor. General agreements about rates of pay, hours of work and other matters are made at the national level, and are accepted as a basic minimum. Further talks are held at workplace level to take account of local factors. Other company or shop-floor disputes are also discussed by representatives of both sides at the same level. The system of full collective bargaining is used in the public sector and in the private sector where employers still want it, but many companies now negotiate directly with their workforce.

▶ See **Human resources management** on page 310.

Collective bargaining

Level	Union representatives	Employer's representatives	Topics
National	General secretary and officials	Trade association officials	National pay and working conditions
Workplace	Convenors and/or district officials	Middle and senior management	Local pay and major disputes
Shop floor	Shop stewards and/or convenors	Supervisors and/or middle management	Shop-floor disputes, working conditions and grievances

1 Why are industrial relations important?
2 Why were trade unions set up?
3 What is the CBI?
4 Describe the main functions of trade associations.
5 What is collective bargaining?
6 Who is involved in negotiations at a national level and what do they discuss?
7 What topics are likely to be discussed at workplace level?

INDUSTRIAL ACTION

Sometimes the talks between the managers and the union (or unions) fail, at either national or workplace level. Managers might have made an offer that the unions would not accept; or the unions might have made demands that management was not prepared to meet. If the managers refuse to offer anything more, the unions might decide to take industrial action. Over the course of many years, unions developed a whole range of actions to persuade employers to agree to their demands. The following are the main kinds of industrial action.

▶ New laws in the 1980s and 1990s have made most of these industrial actions illegal or extremely difficult to put into effect. See Trade union legislation on page 308.

• **Non-cooperation:** The union may instruct its members not to use a new machine or working practice; or shop stewards or convenors may refuse to attend meetings with managers

- **Work-to-rule:** There are many official rules governing working practices, such as checking parts of a machine before using it. Normally, some of these rules are ignored to speed up production. In a dispute, the union may instruct members to work to rule, i.e. to 'go slow', by observing all the workplace rules. This will bring about a fall in production. Alternatively, shop stewards may take every complaint or grievance to management, where previously they might have settled the matter immediately with the union member concerned.
- **Overtime ban:** Firms rely heavily on overtime to keep to their production schedules, particularly when there is an unexpected demand. An overtime ban hurts firms because cannot fulfil its orders. It also hurts the workers, however, because they lose their higher pay for overtime.
- **Strikes:** A withdrawal of labour is a union's most severe, and usually final, course of action. There are different forms of strikes. **Token strikes** occur when employees refuse to work for part of the day as a warning to employers that they will call an all-out strike if necessary. **Selective strikes** are when only part of the union membership goes on strike, usually in a selected area. This kind of strike can have a big effect on production, but fewer workers are affected. **Official strikes** are those that have the official support of the union. **Wildcat strikes**, or unofficial strikes, are called by convenors or shop stewards in a workplace without the formal support of the union. A **sit-in** is a very different form of strike. Employees refuse to work or to leave a workplace that is under threat of closure. The result is the same as a total strike because production is stopped. Strikes cause firms a great loss; they cannot produce goods or services, and their relationship with their customers may be harmed. Employees also lose as they do not receive their normal pay. The strike pay from their union is too small to compensate for the loss.

Employers' actions

In contrast to trade unions, employers have far fewer forms of industrial action at their disposal. Their main weapon is the **lock-out**. This is when the workplace gates are locked to prevent the employees from entering. However, it hurts the employer more than the workers because the firm still has to pay its overheads and it risks losing valuable orders.

 Make brief notes on the kinds of industrial action trade unions could take up until the 1980s.

Miners' rally, Hyde Park,
October 1992

TRADE UNION POWER

Trade unions reached the peak of their power in the 1960s and 1970s. Union leaders were continually courted and consulted by governments over industrial, economic and social policies – and very often the trade unions had considerable influence over the final outcome. Trade union membership rose to its highest ever figure of 13.3 million in 1979 – over 60 per cent of all employees. To a certain extent, the rise in membership had been brought about by the increase in **closed shops**. You could not work in a closed shop unless you were a union member.

Shop stewards were extremely powerful in many big factories. In some cases they were able to dictate to management how many workers should be employed on a machine or a particular job. This could result in overstaffing and a great escalation of costs. The threat of a wildcat strike was enough to make managers agree to almost any demand.

Not all shop stewards or all workplaces were like this. Many companies had long-established procedures for solving disputes between management and unions which both sides observed. If they could not reach agreement, one side, or sometimes both sides jointly, would call in the services of ACAS to try to settle their dispute. Although strikes caused the loss of a large number of working days in Britain, some other industrial countries lost even more.

The constant threat of industrial action and the uncertainties and hostilities it created began to be a major problem. There was too much concentration on industrial disputes rather than on industrial production. Often, managers were too weak and indecisive to take effective counter-action. As a result, business was crippled by poor quality goods, unreliable deliveries and unnecessarily high costs.

Government intervention

If a union was acting in support of a trade dispute, it could not be

► Closed shops are workplaces where only union members can be employed. Since 1980, a closed shop can be set up only if 80 per cent of union members vote for it in a secret ballot. Even then, workers with strong objections to closed shops cannot be forced to join the union.

► ACAS, the **Advisory, Conciliation and Arbitration Service**, was set up in 1975 as an independent body to help solve problems in industrial relations. It advises both employers and unions. If there is a dispute, ACAS will try to decrease the hostility between the two sides by talking to them and trying to bring them together. If that fails, ACAS will suggest that the dispute goes to an arbitrator, an independent person, whose decision will be accepted by both sides in the dispute.

sued for damages. This immunity covered all their industrial actions. There was a growing feeling that the trade unions were abusing their special legal privilege. Both the Conservative government of Edward (now Sir Edward) Heath and the Labour government of the late Harold (Lord) Wilson tried to reform industrial relations, but without much success. The struggle reached a climax in the winter of 1979, under the premiership of Jim (now Lord) Callaghan, when over 29 million days were lost through strikes, six or seven times as many as the previous average.

The Conservative government of Margaret (now Lady) Thatcher came to power in 1979. Her government, determined to break trade union power, passed a succession of laws during the 1980s that made many industrial actions illegal or more difficult to use. This legislation, and other laws that followed, had several effects.

▶ The winter of 1979 was known as the 'winter of discontent'. Public sector workers, including refuse collectors and gravediggers, went on a prolonged strike in support of higher pay. Piles of rubbish bags lay uncollected in the streets, and large numbers of bodies awaited burial in the morgues.

▶ **Picketing** involves stationing workers at the entrances to a workplace when there is a strike or some other industrial action in order to persuade all visitors (including workers and suppliers) not to enter.

▶ **Secondary picketing** occurs when striking workers picket other firms that have a trading connection with their own firm, for example suppliers or distributors.

Trade union legislation
- Only employees can take industrial action against their employers; it is unlawful for employees working for other firms to join in.
- Picketing must be peaceful, and there should be no more than six pickets at each entrance to the workplace.
- Secondary picketing is illegal.
- Industrial action must not be used to set up or maintain a closed shop.
- Unofficial strikes are illegal.
- Strikes can only be called after there has been a secret postal ballot of union members and the employers have been informed in writing.
- Individual employees can refuse to join in industrial action even if there has been a majority vote in favour of it in the secret ballot.
- Elections for the president, general secretary and governing body of a trade union must be held every five years by a secret postal ballot of members.
- Employees must not be refused employment or dismissed if they refuse to join a trade union.

Some of the laws were so severe that a number of employers refused to put them into effect, fearing that it would do long-lasting harm to relations with their employees. Nevertheless, Conservative governments still continue to pass laws to curb union power. The Trade Union Reform and Employment Rights Act of 1993 makes it more difficult for unions to collect subscriptions directly from their members' pay and gives union members the right to have a secret postal ballot before a merger of unions.

Lock-outs and strikes

The number of strikes rose in the early 1980s as unions fought back against their loss of rights. In succession, postal workers, ambulance workers, miners and nurses all went on strike, and were all defeated. The government cut the social security benefits available to strikers' families. Police were drafted in from other parts of the country when necessary. There were many bloody confrontations, particularly during the long and bitter miners' strike of 1984. The defeat of the miners was the final blow to the trade union dominance of the 1960s and 1970s. Encouraged by the new laws, some employers in the newspaper industry locked out their workers so that they could introduce the new machinery that the unions had refused to operate, and the working practices that they had refused to adopt. There were many violent clashes with police on the picket lines. In the end, the employers won.

 Make notes on the laws restricting trade unions, putting them in order of their effect on trade union power.

THE DECLINE OF TRADE UNION POWER

Trade union power has declined considerably as a result of these laws and other factors. Membership has dropped from its peak of 13.3 million to about 9 million today. In 1992, only 528,000 working days were lost through strikes, the lowest figure since records began over a century ago. There were several other reasons for the change:

- There was a great increase in unemployment in the 1980s and 1990s. When workers are made redundant, they tend to leave their union.
- There was an increase in part-time workers, who are often less keen than full-time employees to join a union.
- Some unions were **derecognized**, i.e. employers refused to recognize the union's right to exist or participate in negotiations.
- There was a change in public attitudes towards unions, brought about in part by the trade unions' own actions but also by anti-union reports and articles in the media.
- The trade union movement as a whole failed to adapt quickly enough to change.

 What do you think might have happened to the trade unions if there had not been such a great increase in unemployment in the 1980s and 1990s?

UNION MODERNIZATION

Many leading companies do not want to see trade unions lose their role as representatives of employees and defenders of their rights. These firms believe that a well-organized trade union can make a big contribution to the **management of change** that is needed to make British business more productive, competitive and efficient.

They have continued to use national collective bargaining. However, even these firms believe that trade unions must modernize, by dropping their old ideas of 'them and us', and by replacing confrontation with cooperation.

'New style' trade unions

Some trade unions have already modernized by introducing **'new style' agreements** with employers, particularly in the car industry. The following features are the main ones.

- The unions agree not to strike. Both sides agree to accept the decision of an arbitrator in any dispute. Pendulum arbitration is often used.
- Only one union is recognized in the workplace. It is easier for management to negotiate if it does not have to make agreements with a number of unions. It also strengthens the union if no other union is allowed to recruit members in that workplace.
- There is single-status employment, with manual workers having the same working week, holidays, canteen facilities, etc., as other employees.
- The union accepts labour flexibility, with workers doing any job of which they are capable.
- There is a greater emphasis on cooperation and team work.

In other words, there is a quality management system to which the union responds favourably.

 How do 'new style' trade unions affect working practices.

HUMAN RESOURCES MANAGEMENT

Some firms have a **human resources management (HRM)** system, based on the philosophy that employees should be managed in the same way, and with the same care, as finance or production. Firms with HRM systems no longer support collective bargaining, but want to make agreements at company or local level only, preferably with individual employees. As a result, the number of employees governed by national pay agreements has almost halved, falling from 60 per cent of the workforce to 34 per cent in 1991.

HRM managers are not always opposed to unions in themselves. They accept the basic role of trade unions as a safeguard against authoritarian and arbitrary management and as representatives and advisors for individual employees who have a grievance. However, they think that trade unions should concentrate more on providing services for their members, such as mortgages, insurance and holiday schemes, as some trade unions already do.

► Under the system of **pendulum arbitration**, both sides submit their case in writing to an arbitrator, who makes a straight choice between them and decides in favour of one without further discussion. This system helps both sides to moderate their demands, because any extreme case is likely to be rejected outright by the arbitrator.

► See the box on **Quality management systems** in Chapter 8, page 95.

► The government also helped to reduce national pay bargaining by abolishing the twenty-six wages councils, which set minimum wage rates for workers in traditionally low-paid industries, such as catering. The councils were abolished under the Trade Union Reform and Employment Rights Act of 1993.

1 State three kinds of industrial action that have been made illegal.

2 What is a lock-out?

3 In your view, why has trade union power declined?

4 Describe the policies of 'new style' trade unions.

5 What is pendulum arbitration?

6 What are the features of human resources management?

COMMUNICATION

There are very real conflicts of interest in business, but these problems can sometimes be made much worse by failures in communication.

> **Communication**
> Communication is the sending, or exchanging, of messages with other people through a selected medium, or means of communication.

The personnel department, which has the main responsibility for the people in an organization, needs to be particularly skilled in communication. Communication may be **one-way**, when no reply is wanted or expected, but most communications are **two-way**, with some **feedback**, or response, required from the receiver. For example, a short notice giving an order, such as 'keep this door shut', may not demand a response. However, if the people who read the notice, the receivers, do not like the message or the sender, they may respond by scribbling rude comments on the notice.

A notice is a form of one-way communication. However, there is no guarantee that the order will be obeyed, because there is no formal means of feedback. If a response was wanted, the sender could change the means of communication. Instead of putting up a notice, he or she could send a memorandum to the heads of all departments stating clearly which door was to be shut. The reason for keeping the door shut might also be included in the message. The sender might ask for the message to be acknowledged. This would then involve an exchange of formal messages, or a two-way communication. This method has obvious advantages. It gives the sender the chance to check if the message has been received. It also involves the receivers in the process of communication by giving them an opportunity to reply.

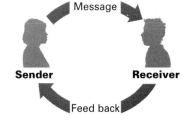

Two-way communication

The message

It is not easy to compose a message that the receiver will immediately understand. To do so, it is necessary to put yourself in the place of the receivers and try to imagine how they will react to your message. One of the main difficulties is that words and phrases do not have the same meaning for different people. They have become loaded with emotions, so that some people on hearing or seeing a particular word will have a stock response, which might be based on fear, love, or hate. Take the phrase 'trade union power'. It can have different meanings for different kinds of people. The phrase might arouse opposite feelings in the sender and the receiver, and therefore any message about the topic might well become distorted.

 In your view, what would the words 'trade union' mean to a Conservative, a keen trade unionist, a Labour party supporter, a part-time worker, a manual worker, a manager, a reader of *The Sun*, a single parent, a corner shopkeeper, a hotel worker, and a college lecturer in history or politics? Then ask all, or some, of these persons their actual view of trade unions. Explain any differences between what they say and what you thought their views would be.

Other barriers to communication

It is not only prejudice or strongly held views that can cause problems in communication. Many senders are unable to construct a clear, concise and precise message. What they write or say may be so badly presented, or boring, or so complicated, that it fails to hold the receiver's attention or confuses them.

The receivers can also contribute to problems in communication. They may be unwilling to take in the message fully for all sorts of reasons, for example because they have too much work to do, or because they have other things on their mind, or because they do not like the sender. There can be even bigger problems if they have to relay the message by verbal means to other persons. Many surveys have shown that the message invariably becomes distorted.

The medium, or the means of communication, is also important. The sender must choose the medium carefully so that the message is most likely to reach the receiver and produce a feedback if required.

► There are also many means of **electronic communications**. Some are verbal, such as recorded messages. Others are written and/or visual, such as faxes and electronic mail. See **Tele-communications** in Chapter 23.

Main methods of communication in business

Verbal	Written*	Visual
Telephone	Memos	Graphs
Informal chats	Letters	Charts
Interviews	Notices	Plans
Meetings	Reports	Posters
Presentations	Company journals	Videos
Annual general meetings	Annual report and accounts	Films

*Some of these also contain visual elements

 Which means of communication would you choose if you wanted to:

(a) make an emotional impact on the receiver?
(b) obtain a quick reply?
(c) explain something in great detail?
(d) give an order to a large number of people?

(e) send a message to your deputy that he or she could not deny receiving?

(f) explain your business plans for the next year to a group of colleagues?

(g) ensure that you received an architectural plan quickly from a foreign country?

You have been asked to design a campaign to encourage employees to stop smoking in your workplace and to lead a healthier lifestyle generally. Write a brief report for your senior manager stating how you will organize the campaign, and the kinds of media you will use and your reasons for choosing them.

SUMMARY

- Good industrial relations are important in business, because no-one works well in an atmosphere of conflict.
- Modern trade unions were set up in the nineteenth century for skilled workers. Over time they have become more open to other kinds of workers, and have grown in size.
- Employers' associations represent employers in a particular industry. They also provide advice and, sometimes, research and development for their members.
- Collective bargaining over pay and working conditions between employers and managers on one side and trade unions on the other takes place at every level from national to the shop floor. Many employers have now abandoned bargaining at national level.
- Workers' industrial action ranges from non-cooperation to official strikes, but recent laws have made most forms of action illegal or very difficult to put into effect. The employers' main form of action is a lock-out.
- Trade union power reached a peak in the 1970s, but since then it has declined, mainly because of trade union laws, unemployment, changes in management and public attitudes and the failure of unions to adapt to change. Some unions have made 'new style' agreements with new human resources managements.
- Communication is an important aspect of management. Two-way communication, with some feedback, is more useful than one-way communication, which may provoke negative responses.
- The sender must select the right medium for the message.

23 New technology

Chapter objectives

After working through this chapter, you will have the knowledge to:

▪ explain how a personal computer is used in factories, offices, shops, warehouses and banks;

▪ distinguish between hardware and software;

▪ select appropriate software for various tasks;

▪ describe recent developments in telecommunications;

▪ evaluate the effects of information technology on business;

▪ understand and use the following key terms: personal computer (PC), floppy disk, disk drive, hard disk, visual display unit (VDU), mainframe computer, workstation, hardware, software, word processor, database, spreadsheet, compound documents, electronic point of sale (EPOS), electronic data interchange (EDI), real time, direct product profitability (DPP), electronic funds transfer system (EFTS), local area network (LAN), wide area network (WAN), modem, telex, electronic mail, fax, video-conferencing, teleshopping, information technology (IT), teleworking.

COMPUTERS

Storing and processing data

The **personal computer** (PC) is at the heart of the new technology that is currently creating a revolution in business. The main function of a PC is to store and process data. It can process data in many different ways, some of which we shall examine later in the chapter. The data can also enter the PC in various ways. Text or figures can be typed in directly using a keyboard. Data can be transferred from a floppy disk containing information that has been keyed in earlier, or using a different computer. It can also be transferred through a communications channel such as a telephone or network connection. Images, such as photographs, can be scanned in using a digitizer or scanner.

Floppy disks are circular metal plates that can rotate rapidly. The disks are coated with a magnetic film containing concentric tracks in which the data is stored. Floppy disks are flexible, but they are usually enclosed in a stiff plastic cover. They are inserted into a **disk drive** where they spin around at high speed to provide access to the tracks containing data. There is another kind of disk – a **hard disk** – which usually stores more data than a floppy disk. A hard disk is normally left in its own disk drive permanently. Disks can store millions of characters (letters and numerals). One floppy disk would typically store the text of three or four books like this one, and a hard disk may store the text of two or three thousand such books! Illustrations and photographs, however, take a lot more computer memory than text.

There are many other ways of storing data. Magnetic tapes, for example, are generally used for regularly backing up the vital information, such as records of financial transactions, that is processed in a large company every day. They are also used for storing large quantities of data in an archive, or library. CD-ROMs are compact disks like the ones used for recording music. However, instead of storing sounds they are used for storing large amounts of data – one disk can contain billions rather than millions of characters. A PC can be fitted with a special CD-ROM drive, similar to an ordinary disk drive.

▶ CD-ROM stands for compact disk read only memory, although it is now possible both to write to and read from CD-ROMs.

Once the data has been entered, it is displayed on the screen of the **visual display unit** (VDU) in written, graphic or photographic form. Every computer has a **central processing unit** (CPU), which is the piece of hardware that actually makes the computer work. In a PC this is called the **microprocessor**. The more powerful the CPU the faster the computer can process data.

▶ The VDU is the computer screen. It is a bit like a television screen, and may display data in monochrome (e.g. white on black, or light green on dark green) or in colour. The microprocessor and the disk drives that make the computer work are usually housed in a separate box, or cabinet.

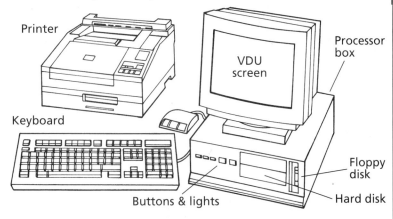

Printer
VDU screen
Processor box
Keyboard
Buttons & lights
Floppy disk
Hard disk

A personal computer

▶ **Hardware** is the actual physical equipment, including the VDU, the microprocessor, the disk drive(s), the printer, the keyboard and the mouse (a mouse-shaped device that is used to give instructions to the computer by pointing an arrow on the screen to the command required).

Today a PC can process data at very high speeds. Thirty years ago, a huge mainframe computer, which was housed in an air-conditioned room in a company's headquarters, would have found it difficult to match the processing speed of a modern PC. Now most new PCs take up little more than a square foot of space on a desk or workstation. Computers can be even smaller than that. Laptop PCs are portable computers that can be folded up to the size of a small briefcase. They provide flexibility for business people who need to work on computers away from their desks – for example, on a long train journey.

Mainframe computers are still used today. They are even more powerful than PCs and capable of storing much more data, but they are very much smaller than they once were. Computers are no

▶ A powerful PC using the latest software can transfer a finely detailed picture from one part of a page to another almost instantaneously and 'wrap' the text around it at the same time.

▶ A **workstation** is a special piece of furniture designed to hold computer hardware.

► Computers are getting smaller all the time. Palmtop computers are now being produced, small enough to be carried in the palm of the hand.

longer installed only in company headquarters. They are found wherever there is business – from the research laboratory, where scientists and technicians are using computers to design a wide range of new products, such as a new composite helicopter rotor, to the small shop where the owner uses a computer for a variety of tasks including keeping accounts, sending invoices and statements, writing letters and keeping a record of customers. Computers have spread out far beyond business to practically every corner of modern life, from primary schools to public libraries.

 Find six places where PCs are used and state what they are used for.

 Make brief notes on how a computer works.

THE USES OF COMPUTERS

Computers in factories

► To refresh your memory, see **New manufacturing methods** in Chapter 15.

As you already know, computers are used extensively in modern factories. They can be used to design goods, by a process called computer-aided design (CAD). Once the design has been finalized, instructions to make different components can be fed into computer-controlled machines, and this is known as computer-aided manufacturing (CAM). Computers can be programmed, or instructed, to give orders to a robot to perform a particular task, such as welding or spray-painting parts of a car on an assembly line. If the design of the car is changed, the robots do not have to be moved. They can be reprogrammed, or given new instructions, to weld new spots on the car which they can easily reach with their long, flexible arms.

► To refresh your memory, see **Lean production** in Chapter 15.

In the most modern factories, computer-integrated engineering is used to control the whole of the production process, with work being checked against instructions displayed on computer screens. Computers are also used for quality control and for just-in-time stock control.

Computers in offices

► **Software** is any program fed into a computer that allows it to perform a particular task, such as word processing. (Note that the American spelling 'program' is used.)

By using different kinds of software, PCs can perform a variety of functions. A **word processor** software package allows a computer, with the aid of a printer, to do everything that a typewriter can do, but also very much more. With a word processor, it is easy to cut and paste, or transpose words or sentences from one part of a document to another part, or from one document to another document. It is just as easy to change the size and shape of the letters that will be used when the document is printed. As a result, it is just as easy to print a notice as a letter. The word processor also contains a mail-merge facility, which allows you to send the same letter, containing individual names and addresses, to a large number of people without having to type each letter separately.

► Some personalized letters are called 'junk mail' because many of them are thrown away unread, but if the letters are properly targeted they can have a high success rate.

A computer being used to check the quality and consistency of McVitie's digestive biscuits

A **database** is another kind of software. This allows a large amount of data to be stored, sorted and retrieved when required. For example, names of customers, their addresses, their age and their sex could all be stored in a database. The data can be sorted very quickly and used to produce a list of, for instance, all female customers between the ages of 24 and 35. This list can be used in conjunction with a mail merge facility to produce personalized letters for these target customers informing them of some new good or service. Databases are a most important tool in marketing and sales as they make it simple to find and contact a target niche.

A **spreadsheet** is used to make 'instant' calculations with financial or other numerical data that can be displayed on the VDU screen. A spreadsheet is particularly useful for financial forecasts, as it will immediately show how other numbers would be affected if one factor, such as the exchange rate, was changed. It could also be used for keeping accounts, though there is special software designed for this purpose alone.

The most basic **accounts programs**, often used by sole traders, will simply record all transactions, keep a constant tally of income and expenditure, and VAT, and provide a record of the bank account. Larger companies use more complex and often customized accounts programs. They generally record sales and purchases separately and then categorize all transactions under various headings. The information stored can be used to prepare reports such as the balance sheet, profit and loss and VAT account. These programs may also deal with stock control, and the employees' payroll.

► Under the Data Protection Act of 1984, businesses that store information about individuals on computers must register with the Data Protection Registrar and state the purposes for which the data is used.

Select the most appropriate software for (a) financial forecasts, (b) making a list of selected customers, (c) keeping accounts, (d) composing a notice and (e) sending out personalized letters.

Latest developments

Most office software now comes as an integrated package. It includes the three applications described above (word processor, database and spreadsheet) plus other facilities such as page layout, graphs, pictures and symbols. This software makes it possible to produce **compound documents** that integrate text, graphs and visuals on the same page. It can also be used to produce brochures and booklets.

Computers have made office work easier and more efficient. For example, at one time different clerks dealt with each process in a business transaction, such as sending out delivery notes, invoices, credit notes and statements. Now, one computer operator can handle the whole process and keep a record of it automatically on disk. As computers in firms are usually linked, it is easy for any other department to obtain information about a transaction if required.

 Get hold of some information about an up-to-date integrated software package and make notes about what it can do. (You could obtain the necessary information from a brochure in a shop, from a computer magazine, or from your college computer suite.)

1 What is a personal computer?
2 Describe a floppy disk and say what it is used for.
3 Give two kinds of software you might find in an office.
4 What is a spreadsheet?

Computers in shops

There has been an equally big revolution in retailing, based on **electronic point of sale** (**EPOS**) equipment at the check-out. Operators scan the bar code with a laser beam. This records all the details of the sale, which are also printed out on customers' receipts. This information is transferred automatically by **electronic data interchange** (**EDI**) to mainframe computers in company headquarters in **real time**. These computers then calculate the **direct product profitability** (**DPP**), i.e. the profitability of each particular line. This information is used to determine the amount of space and the prominence of the display given to individual lines in the store.

▶ A **bar code** is a machine-readable arrangement of numbers and parallel lines of varying widths printed on a package. A familiar part of food packaging, bar codes are now used for other goods, including newspapers and books.

▶ **Real time** is when a computer's input and output are practically simultaneous.

Computers in warehouses

Computers and other electronic equipment are used in warehouses to control orders and deliveries. Bar codes are put on the pallets that contain the goods as soon as they arrive in the warehouse. Hand-held, radio-frequency terminals or long-range scanners are

▶ **Pallets** are portable wooden platforms used for transporting or storing goods.

used to locate them in the warehouse. This means that forklift drivers do not have to leave their vehicles to find and load the required goods.

 Trace the journey of a jacket from supplier to shop, describing all the electronic equipment used during the process.

Computers in banks

Electronic methods for dealing with financial transactions have enabled banks to automate much of their work. This has resulted in many job losses. Plastic cards, with magnetic stripes to identify their owners, are used to withdraw money from bank and building society service tills, and to pay for goods on credit in shops. Other plastic cards use an **electronic funds transfer system (EFTS)** to make payments from a bank account as soon as goods are purchased. Banks also provide businesses with electronic data interchange (EDI) for the direct transfer of funds by electronic means to other business customers. This saves the firms a great deal of paperwork, such as payment orders, remittance and credit advice notes, and acknowledgements.

Financial institutions are themselves linked worldwide by electronic means. For example, stock exchanges all over the world are kept in constant touch by their computers, which can be programmed to buy or sell when share prices reach a certain price.

1 Where would you expect to find EPOS equipment?
2 Who uses EDI?
3 Where would you find EFTS being used?
4 Who uses DPP?

 Draw up a table with the main heading 'Latest electronic developments' and with four columns headed *Offices*, *Shops*, *Warehouses* and *Banks*. Fill in the table using the information above and any knowledge that you may have yourself.

TELECOMMUNICATIONS

PCs can be linked together in a firm's headquarters to form a **local area network (LAN)**. In a LAN, the computers can communicate with each other. They can also share common facilities, such as a printer. The PCs are all linked to the mainframe computer which stores a vast amount of information. For example, the mainframe computer can send relevant parts of the business plan to computers in different departments. A LAN makes it much easier for managers to access information from other departments and to keep a check on work in progress. The LAN can be transformed into a **wide area network (WAN)** which links one organization, such as a weather-forecasting business, with other similar organizations

► A **modem** is a device that allows data from a computer to be sent as signals along a telephone line.

throughout the world. This is done by using a **modem**, which links computers to telephone systems.

Other electronic equipment also uses the telephone systems to send data from one place to another in Britain or abroad. There are several ways to do this.

Electronic communications

- **Telex** is one of the oldest forms of electronic communication, and is still used here and abroad. The sender keyboards a message into a teleprinter and it is printed out automatically by the receiver's teleprinter.
- **Electronic mail**, or 'email', is transmitted directly from one computer to another and stored in an electronic mail box until the receiver wants to view it on the VDU.
- A **fax** machine sends an image of a document, containing words and/or pictorial matter, to another fax machine.
- **Video-conferencing** allows business people to hold meetings even though they are miles apart. The images of the people are reproduced in colour on video screens accompanied by high quality sound.

► Fax is an abbreviation of 'facsimile', which means 'an exact reproduction'.

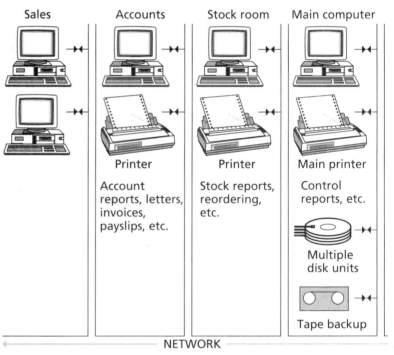

A local area network

A new kind of communications system using different kinds of cables – including glass fibre-optic cables – is being installed in countries all over the world. It allows much more information of all kinds, including video images and graphics as well as voice messages, to be transmitted at much greater speeds. For example, using the new systems, a fax can be sent almost ten times as quickly, and messages between computers even more quickly. When the new communications systems are connected to more homes, people will be able to do **teleshopping** from their armchairs by watching, say, a fashion display on their television screen and ordering what they want by phone. Teleshopping by cable is already happening in a few areas.

The latest telecommunications use wireless instead of fixed telephone lines. Mobile phones can be used anywhere because the messages are transmitted by radio beacons. Messages are already sent through the world telephone network by satellite. There will be an increase in the use of satellites for business communications in the future.

 Make notes on electronic means of sending information.

THE EFFECTS OF THE ELECTRONIC REVOLUTION

It is difficult to state exactly what the final effects of the electronic revolution will be as the process is still going on. It is very easy to make false predictions about the future! When the electronic revolution started some twenty years ago, it was forecast that business would become virtually paperless because all transactions would be made electronically. That prediction has not yet come true. In fact, the amount of paper used has increased, because word processors and laser printers make it very easy to fill reams of paper with words and pictures, even if the contents are of little value. However, some of the effects of the electronic revolution on business are fairly clear.

- If systems are set up correctly, following a careful analysis and according to accurate specifications, then productivity increases, because computer-controlled machines can work more quickly and more accurately than human beings and for longer periods of time.
- There is more competition because the increase in the speed of telecommunications and the greater amount of information available mean that businesses can put in more detailed offers more quickly.
- More capital is invested in information technology (IT) throughout the world. In Britain, business spending on IT increased even during the recession at the beginning of the 1990s.
- There are more redundancies among factory workers, office and shop workers, and middle managers as a result of automation.
- Employees need to be more flexible. All employees must be able to perform more tasks, and technical managers must be able to do other kinds of management.
- More workers have to be trained to do highly skilled jobs, and those made redundant as a result of the introduction of new technology have to be retrained.
- There is an increase in **teleworking**, or working at home by

▶ **Information technology** means any technique or equipment that is used to handle information. It includes computers and telecommunications.

using computers and telecommunications. It is estimated that there are 1.5 million people working at home either full-time or for more than two days a week. Teleworking reduces a firm's costs because it does not have to provide expensive office accommodation for some workers. Surveys have shown that productivity also rises. Employees benefit, too, as they do not have the expense and difficulties of commuting. They can also do the work at their own pace and in their own time. However, the great increase predicted in teleworking has not yet taken place. It may suit mothers with young children and people who like working alone, but not all people want to work in isolation. Moreover, some firms prefer to have personal contact with their employees.

 Describe all the effects that information technology might have on a big firm of architects.

SUMMARY

- The personal computer has created a revolution in business, which is still continuing.
- Modern factories use computers extensively in design and production processes. New expert systems, with 'artificial intelligence', are now being introduced.
- Word processors, accounts systems, databases and spreadsheets have made office work much more productive and efficient
- Big retailers use electronic point of sale equipment at the check-out to control many of their decisions, from giving orders to suppliers to allocating space for goods in their stores.
- Banks and other financial institutions rely increasingly on electronic data interchange.
- Computers can now 'talk' to each other in local, or wide, area networks. Other electronic equipment can send verbal, written, or pictorial information all over the world at high speed.
- The effects of the information technology revolution have already been far-reaching, but even bigger changes may be on the way.

Revision and examination skills

Chapter objectives

After working through this chapter, you will have the knowledge to:

■ understand the assessment objectives for your examination;

■ make a suitable plan for doing coursework assignments;

■ use active methods of revision;

■ make sure that you do your best in your examination.

EXAMINATION BOARDS' REQUIREMENTS

The new syllabuses for GCSE Business Studies are more varied than in the past. One examination board sets only written papers and no coursework assignments. Another board has short answer and data response questions and no open-ended questions in the written examination paper. Some boards have core and optional subjects in the syllabus.

If you have not been told exactly what your syllabus demands, you should read it to find out or ask your lecturer or teacher.

Most boards have separate papers for the foundation, intermediate and higher levels in the final examination. You will be entered for the appropriate level. In the examination, you will be required to meet several assessment objectives.

Assessment objectives

You will be expected to:
- demonstrate knowledge and critical understanding of the specified subject content;
- apply the specified terms, concepts, theories and methods effectively to address problems and issues;
- select, organize, interpret and use information from various sources;
- evaluate evidence, make reasoned judgements and present conclusions accurately and appropriately.

These assessments objectives also apply to coursework assignments. Over the whole examination, the four assessment objectives will each carry 25 per cent of the marks, so they are of equal importance. (A mark of up to 5 per cent of the total may be made for accurate spelling, punctuation and grammar.)

COURSEWORK ASSIGNMENTS

▶ **Coursework assignments** are written pieces of work that allow you to display your skills and abilities when you are free from the stress of the examination room. They usually involve desk and field research; selecting, organizing and evaluating the information you have obtained; and presenting it in a clear and appropriate way.

Coursework is an important part of most of the examinations, providing 25 per cent of the total marks. Again, there is more variety than in the past.

- Some boards set the coursework assignments; others allow you to choose.
- Some boards prescribe two coursework assignments; others only one.
- Some boards state that coursework must be done under supervision.

 If you have not been told already, look in your syllabus and find out exactly what you have to do, or ask your lecturer or teacher.

The syllabus usually contains guidance notes about doing the assignment and an example of an assignment, which is often quite detailed. Study this material carefully and apply the principles to your own assignments. You may also find the following suggestions helpful.

- Make sure that you understand the assignment and what you are required to do before you start work.
- Gather as much information as possible about the topic from desk research in your library and the media.
- This information will provide you with a basic knowledge of the subject. You will now be able to make a list of the further information you must obtain in the outside business world. Make notes of where and how you are likely to obtain it.
- At this stage, it would be a good idea to plan the structure of the assignment – just brief headings will do. This will help you to ask more purposeful questions and provide a framework for the new information that you gather.
- You must now gather information from your selected sources by means of visits, observation and interviews. You will gain much more from these activities, if you make notes about the information you want to obtain before you make your visit.
- When you are interviewing, listen carefully to the replies. Do not be afraid to ask if you do not understand what is said.
- When you have finished your outside activities, you should sort out the information, selecting what is most useful and rejecting the rest.
- You should now be in a position to make out a more

comprehensive plan for writing the assignment. Use a structure for the assignment, similar to the format for a report.

- Think about the topic as you are making out your final plan. Evaluate the material you have gathered. Is it all believable? Is it backed up by other evidence? You should now see your conclusion about the topic beginning to form. Make sure that it is firmly based on all the evidence.
- While you are writing the assignment, continually check that what you have written is easy to read and that it makes sense. You might have to do a draft version first.
- You can make your assignment look more interesting by using pie charts, bar charts and graphs to provide some of the information.
- Make sure that your assignment does not exceed the specified maximum length.

REVISION

In an ideal world you would be reviewing and revising your work from the second day of the course. But we don't live in an ideal world and most people leave revision until the last few weeks before the examination. Nevertheless, if you have taken some of the advice offered earlier, you will have been maintaining good, easily retrievable notes throughout your course and so be off to a flying start when revision time comes.

Work out a revision timetable, with realistic learning objectives at each stage – you will find many of the chapter objectives in this book useful, but you will have to make up some for yourself.

Use past papers, but not to 'question-spot', or try to anticipate questions that will come up. Question-spotting is a bad mistake. Use past papers to identify which broad topics and themes the examiner usually asks about, and revise them carefully. Analyse past papers for their commands. Make sure you know the differences between 'describe' and 'account for', 'list' and 'analyse' and so on.

What you must *not* do is to revise actual questions and prepare model answers. Model questions rarely come up! Ask yourself questions and answer them. Try to think like an examiner. As you approach different topics ask yourself, 'What questions could the examiner ask me about this?'

Revise actively. Make notes and summaries all the time. Make notes of notes and summaries of notes and notes of summaries. Annotate your notes with notes from a textbook and then produce a tidy version. Convert notes in running text to notes in diagram or table format, or vice versa.

As your revision proceeds try to reduce the whole course to a series of trigger words and phrases – just enough to jog your memory.

Practise writing answers under the pressure of time. How much can you get down in the time available? Practise writing answers of that length.

▶ See **Reports and memoranda** in Chapter 1.

▶ Make sure you know how you will be examined. How many exams will there be? How long are they? What will the choice of questions be? Will there be compulsory questions, essay questions, data response questions, short answer questions? All of these require different skills and different ways of revising. Establish, with the help of your tutor, just how much of your syllabus you should revise. Check what are usually called the 'assessment objectives', which are printed in the syllabus document produced by your examination board.

▶ Read the chief examiner's reports for previous years. These are available from the Examination Board, and should be in your college library. Note well what these reports say. Not only does the chief examiner have experience of the mistakes of thousands of students, he or she actually decides what is mistaken and what is correct.

▶ Taking an active approach to revision is essential. Passive revision, i.e. sitting reading through notes and textbooks, is both boring and ineffective. Revise with friends, discussing questions and trying to explain things to each other. Give yourself some time off, especially on the day before the examinations start.

Work in regular sessions, with breaks every hour, but get used to working for three hours at a time before taking a longer break.

THE EXAMINATION

Think of the examination as an opportunity for you to give a performance, with an audience of one – the examiner. You are displaying your knowledge, understanding and skills to someone who wants to applaud you.

Here are some key points to remember about exams:

- Make sure you know when and where the examination will be held. If it is in an unfamiliar place, try to visit it beforehand and check your travel arrangements.
- The evening before, make sure that you have all the pens and pencils and other equipment you will need.
- Arrive in good time, but don't stand around chatting. Go for a walk to loosen up and get the oxygen flowing to the brain.
- When the examination starts, read through the whole paper (or those parts that relate to your options).
- Don't start writing straight away, but settle down, get the feel of the paper, check the instructions and find the questions you feel OK about.
- The marks allocated to each question or parts of each question are a rough guide to how much you should write on each. If two marks are allocated, make two good points and stop. You will get no more than two marks, however many brilliant points you make.
- Draw up a rough timetable for yourself – 'by 10.30 I should have finished the first question', etc.
- Start your first question. Now for the golden rule of all exams:

> **Answer the question set.**
> **Do what the examiner tells you to do.**

- For all but very short answers make a plan.
- Think all the time. Don't just try to remember things, but think about how to use and apply what you know to the question set.
- Don't overrun your time on a particular question. It takes much longer to get a few more marks at the end of one answer than the first few at the beginning of another.
- Take short rests during the exam. Loosen up physically; breathe, stretch and shut your eyes while you are thinking.
- Leave time for checking and polishing your answers. A single additional mark could mean a higher grade.

► Examiners want you to do well. They are instructed to mark your work by giving you credit for everything you do properly, not by penalizing you for your mistakes. Your marks start at zero and go on up whenever you do something right. The examiner is looking for opportunities to reward positive achievements, so supply plenty of these and make it easy for the examiner to find them. Examination answers are vehicles for you to display your achievement.

► If you suffer badly from nerves, learn to relax through the use of deep breathing techniques. Don't take pills, except under medical supervision. Don't drink alcohol before an examination. It relaxes the brain and will stop you thinking clearly.

► The most common reason for candidates failing to get the marks they should is not that they lack the knowledge or the skill, but that they ignore the golden rule. They usually deal with the right topic but they don't 'discuss' or 'compare and contrast' or 'outline' or 'describe', or they don't 'give the reasons for' or 'explain and account for' when this is what the examiner has asked them to do, or they only answer part of a multi-part question.

► Presentation and layout are important, because they should help the examiner to find your good points easily. Use short sentences and paragraphs.

Index